Philosophy, Rights and Natural Law

Philosophy, Rights and Natural Law

Essays in Honour of Knud Haakonssen

Edited by Ian Hunter and
Richard Whatmore

EDINBURGH
University Press

Edinburgh University Press is one of the leading university presses in the UK. We publish academic books and journals in our selected subject areas across the humanities and social sciences, combining cutting-edge scholarship with high editorial and production values to produce academic works of lasting importance. For more information visit our website: edinburghuniversitypress.com

Edinburgh University Press Ltd
The Tun – Holyrood Road
12 (2f) Jackson's Entry
Edinburgh EH8 8PJ

Typeset in 11/13 Goudy Old Style by
IDSUK (DataConnection) Ltd, and
printed and bound in Great Britain.

A CIP record for this book is available from the British Library

ISBN 978 1 4744 4922 9 (hardback)
ISBN 978 1 4744 4924 3 (webready PDF)
ISBN 978 1 4744 4925 0 (epub)

Contents

Part III: Rights and Reform

Introduction

Work on the intellectual history of philosophy, rights and politics is a palimpsest of many underlying inscriptions. Such work is written upon and with (or against) the historical legal, political and religious orders characteristic of national settlements and transnational networks. It is also written on top of unresolved intellectual and ideological conflicts that materially affect the flows of scholarship. Also visible just beneath the surface of such writing are the scholarly networks through which reflection on the history of national and transnational legal and political thought is shaped by academic affiliation, disciplinary training, publication outlets, intellectual and ideological commitments, and friendships. The papers collected in this volume are all to some degree tied to a particular, if loose and expansive scholarly network whose two poles were initially formed by Sussex School intellectual history and Cambridge School history of political thought. The book grew out of a symposium dedicated to honouring the work of Knud Haakonssen in the history of natural law, natural rights, human rights, religion and politics from the sixteenth to the nineteenth centuries. That an expatriate Danish scholar should have played a pivotal role in this network might seem surprising at first sight. Nonetheless, the fact that Haakonssen's orbital career moves through so many mediating points – crossing national, disciplinary, intellectual and ideological borders – holds the key to viewing the present array of chapters, each of which is tethered to the network at a particular point in Haakonssen's scholarly transit. The collection thus offers an unusually wide and variegated overview of the legal and political contexts in which rights and duties have been formulated, bringing together an array of regional, national and transnational cases. Nonetheless, these cases and contexts remain centred on Knud Haakonssen's trademark interests in the role of natural law in formulating doctrines of obligation and rights in accordance with the interests of early modern polities and churches.

In keeping with Haakonssen's remarkable contributions to the field, the editors selected papers providing new insights into the cultural and political role of law and rights in a variety of historical contexts and circumstances, with the resultant variety of forms (and purposes) of natural law being a hallmark of the collection. It is appropriate then that we should begin with a close-up look at Haakonssen's entrance into this network, before pulling back to view his wider intellectual itinerary.

I

Knud Haakonssen was born in rural Denmark in 1947, at Tingsted on the island of Falster. His father was a Swedish refugee from the famines of the second half of the nineteenth century, and worked as a labourer in a sawmill, before setting up a grocery store with his wife. Haakonssen attended the ancient Nykøbing Katedralskole, established in 1498, where he studied humanities and modern languages, and then matriculated at the University of Copenhagen in 1966, reading philosophy. He was the first member of his family to enter higher education. In his final year, Haakonssen's concluding dissertation was entered in a prize essay competition sponsored by universities across Denmark, resulting in him being awarded a gold medal for a 400-page essay on Hobbes's political thought and metaphysics in late 1969. The final element of the assessment was a public lecture, on a subject allowing students seven days to prepare, and for which Haakonssen dealt with Spinoza's political philosophy. He graduated in 1972. Haakonssen was then successful in obtaining a grant towards PhD research in an EEC country, arriving at Edinburgh at the end of 1973.

While at Copenhagen, Haakonssen had been drawn to the faculty with interests in Karl Popper, and one of his first works was a translation, with Niels Christian Stefansen, of Popper's papers, including a chapter from *The Open Society and its Enemies*. This appeared as *Kritisk rationalisme* in 1973. Haakonssen also published a translation of Thomas Kuhn's *The Structure of Scientific Revolutions* (orig. 1962), as *Videnskabens revolutioner*, in the same year, in addition to translations of Brian Magee's *Popper* (1973, also with N. C. Stefansen) and Bertrand Russell's *Problems of Philosophy* (*Filosofiens problemer*) in 1974. Reading such authors had introduced Haakonssen to Hayek. After initially planning to work on Hayek at Edinburgh under the supervision of Harry (H. B.) Acton, Haakonssen changed course, following Acton's death in June 1974, deciding that he wanted to work on Hume and Smith rather than Hayek.[1] For this, he was supervised by another member of the philosophy faculty, George Davie, a leading cultural nationalist, and an expert on eighteenth-century Scottish thought.

During these years Haakonssen faced the question of what sort of philoso-pher he wanted to become. He had been annoyed and puzzled by the fact that modern philosophers had no interest in Hume's *History of England* or indeed in many of Hume's essays, on the grounds that they were not the subject of philosophy, but rather of literary enquiry. Similarly, Smith was seen as a moral philosopher because of his *Theory of Moral Sentiments*, but philosophers did not extend their investigations further to Smith's *Wealth of Nations* because it was seen as an economics text, and therefore of no interest to a philosopher. The resulting impetus to cross the border of philosophy into history was encouraged by Neil MacCormick, the Regius Chair of Public Law and the Law of Nature and Nations at Edinburgh, who was interested in Smith's jurisprudence. Disciplinary boundaries con-tinued, however, especially between philosophy and history. Nevertheless, in terms of reading, Haakonssen had by this time been introduced to the work of Peter Laslett, John Pocock and Quentin Skinner.

Haakonssen's Edinburgh thesis, completed in 1978, was entitled 'Natural Justice: The Development of a Critical Philosophy of Law from David Hume and Adam Smith to John Millar and John Craig'. Before completing his thesis, in 1976, Haakonssen had taken a position in the philosophy department at Monash University in Melbourne, Australia, and had begun to publish work on Hume.[2] He expected to have to return to the United Kingdom for his thesis defence. Haakonssen's external examiner, the prominent Hume scholar Duncan Forbes, decided that this was not necessary and instead encouraged the candidate to seek immediate publication with Cambridge University Press. On receiving the thesis, Cambridge obtained reports from Forbes, and also from the leading Smith scholar Donald Winch. Haakonssen revised the thesis on the basis of an especially detailed report by Winch, who already had access to Smith's 'Lectures on Jurisprudence', which were being edited by Andrew Skinner, D. D. Raphael and Peter Stein, and were published in May 1978. Such was the chain of events that initiated a lifelong friend-ship with Winch, and the appearance of Haakonssen's first monograph, *The Science of a Legislator: The Natural Jurisprudence of David Hume and Adam Smith* (1981).

Haakonssen left Monash in 1979 for a tenured lectureship in the School of Political Science, Victoria University of Wellington, New Zealand. Although it was a congenial environment, where Haakonssen successfully taught political thought and history until 1982, he felt that he would be more at home at the 'History of Ideas Unit' at the Australian National University, where he moved when he was offered a three-year research fel-lowship in the School of Social Sciences, Institute for Advanced Studies.

The move was successful, and Haakonssen ended up staying for thirteen years, becoming Senior Fellow before 1994. The History of Ideas Unit had been created by Eugene Kamenka, formerly a graduate student in the philosophy department at ANU and then a lecturer. In terms of interests, Kamenka was a Marxologist fascinated by the implications of social theory, continental style, both for the history of philosophy and for current political and economic problems. Kamenka had a gift for creating a community of scholars with disparate backgrounds, interests and approaches to the history of ideas. Accordingly, the Unit included Robert Brown, the author of *Explanation in Social Science* (1963) and *Rules and Laws in Sociology* (1973), and Sam Goldberg, a literary scholar and Leavisite who had joined the ANU in 1976, and founded the journal *Australian Cultural History* with the historian F. B. Smith. For Haakonssen, the key to the success of the Unit was the remarkable visiting fellowship programme which brought large numbers of intellectual historians from the UK and North America to Australia, including Donald Winch, in addition to the liberty to undertake research while encumbered only by the teaching of graduate students. The pluralism and liberty that characterised the Unit led Haakonssen to develop his interests in Scottish philosophy, and he published a series of influential essays on Thomas Reid, John Millar, James Mackintosh, James Mill and Dugald Stewart.[3] In addition, he turned to new research fields, inspired by work on Hugo Grotius, natural jurisprudence and moral philosophy across Europe, from the Cambridge Platonists to the Scottish Enlightenment.[4] Despite such wide-ranging work and such productivity, following Kamenka's retirement and the closure of the History of Ideas Unit, Haakonssen chose to move to the United States, having been offered a chair in philosophy at Boston University.

The context of working life at Boston was different again, with the North American emphasis upon teaching geared to the production of professional philosophers with a particular professional persona. This meant that the study of authors such as Pufendorf and Hume sometimes had to be smuggled into acceptable courses focusing on Hobbes. At the same time, the philosophers at Boston were historically minded by contrast with other institutions, with leading scholars such as Charles Griswold and Aaron Garrett, in addition to intellectual historians in the Political Science department, such as James Schmidt. In a decade at Boston, Haakonssen continued to publish prolifically, including *Natural Law and Moral Philosophy: From Grotius to the Scottish Enlightenment* (1996), which underlined his demand for new work on German philosophers, including Christian Wolff and Christian Thomasius. He also launched some of the major publishing projects in intellectual history, ranging from new editions of Thomas Reid and Francis Hutcheson, to the hundred-volume *Natural Law and Enlightenment Classics* series with the Liberty Fund; all this while publishing new editions of Hume and Smith, and editing the two-volume *Cambridge History of Eighteenth-Century Philosophy*.

Haakonssen left Boston in 2004, joining his old friend Donald Winch at the University of Sussex, where he became professor of intellectual history, and founder of the Sussex Centre for Intellectual History. The latter quickly became well known for regular events bringing together scholars young and old under the rubric 'New Work in Intellectual History'. Haakonssen also established a series of lectures in intellectual history, drawing on the wealth of talent to be found in intellectual history across the UK, and from further afield, reflecting Haakonssen's singular range of academic contacts, and the especially large number of graduate students he had supervised in three continents. By now a leading figure in intellectual history, the history of philosophy, and the history of political thought, Haakonssen's passage along and across the border separating philosophy from history had produced the rich and sinuous intellectual itinerary that is traced in this Festschrift.

II

During the 1970s new ways of delineating and crossing this border led to the virtual reinvention of the discipline of intellectual history, particularly in the branches of the history of political and economic thought. In measuring their distance from both Marxian base-superstructure models and Hegelian conceptions of the unfolding of spirit in time, the new intellectual historians sought for alternative models, concepts and practices. Haakonssen's immediate colleagues, Winch and Forbes, were themselves a part of this search for alternatives which put them in touch with the leading Cambridge intellectual historians Quentin Skinner and John Pocock. A characteristic product of this emerging milieu was Winch's exploration of whether 'civic humanism' – the Italian city-state culture that Skinner had excavated as a context for modern political thought – might not also illuminate the work of such Scottish Enlightenment thinkers as Smith and Hume.

Despite Forbes's scepticism in this regard, Winch, reading such works as Pocock's *Machiavellian Moment*, and engaged in intense epistolary and published exchanges, explored such key theses as to whether a non-Marxian genealogy for capitalism might be found in civic humanist discourses on the relation between civic virtue, commerce and corruption. Feeding into the same intellectual milieu was Skinner's consideration of whether Weber's Protestant Ethic – with its account of Calvinist predestination producing an ascetic life-style conducive to the 'spirit' of capitalism – might not also offer a useful model for a non-Marxian intellectual history. Typically it was not the intellectual consequences of economic structures that assumed centre stage, but the unintended economic consequences of theological and ethical cultures. In charting the emergence of political and economic thought from an open-ended variety of discursive and cultural contexts, Skinner's 1978 *Foundations of Modern Political Thought* consolidated the reorientation of the field, while also opening it to further transformations.

One of these transformations would concern what many regarded as a key gap in existing accounts, namely the role of traditions of natural juris-prudence and natural justice. When Donald Winch's book *Adam Smith's Politics* appeared with Cambridge University Press in 1978, Forbes wrote an admiring review in the *Times Higher Educational Supplement*, and wrote separately to Winch about the one critical point made in the review, about the lack of analysis of natural justice: 'I've said in my review that if you had gone into the question of *natural justice* in Hume and Smith more deeply you would have thrown the whole essay out of balance, but that there are one or two places where, as a consequence, a draught blows in, so to speak.' Forbes added that 'the natural justice approach makes a nonsense of Meekery', referring to the work of the Marxist historian Ronald L. Meek, whose *Social Science and the Ignoble Savage* had appeared in 1976; once again, the need to refute Marxist perspectives on the history of ideas was foregrounded. Forbes' final advice to Winch was to look up something he had recently become aware of as a PhD examiner, 'an excellent thesis on "Natural Justice in Hume, Smith, Millar and Craig," for Edinburgh, by Knud Haakonssen'.[5] Haakonssen was, Forbes noted to Winch, 'a philosopher'. Nevertheless, Forbes, a difficult person to please, considered Haakonssen's thesis to have been outstanding, because it provided an account distinct from the current trend towards civic humanist explanations, and focused on the innovations of Hume and Smith with regard to ideas about justice:

> Hume and Smith between them outline a new theory of justice as the foundation for all social and political life. Justice is a mode of assess-ing social and political behaviour, the central point of which is that the motives behind such behaviour must not have an injurious ten-dency which would arouse the resentment of an impartial spectator. This means that they must be in accordance with a general rule which is negative, telling people what not to do and which thus ensures that the behaviour which is allowed as just is as widely compatible as pos-sible with the rest of the values and aims accepted at any given time

by a society. The latter can only be understood as they have developed through the interaction of individual men; and jurisprudence as a critical discipline is therefore dependent upon history as the new 'science of human nature.' Justice is a negative virtue, the rules of which are enforcible for negative utilitarian reasons.[6]

In his reply, Winch acknowledged 'the big hole created by my failure to face up to TMS [Smith's *Theory of Moral Sentiments*] and natural justice more squarely'. In consequence, he wrote, 'my version of Smith's politics lacks an adequate philosophical base'. This was 'partly due to my ignorance concerning antecedents, and partly because, for reasons of earlier deformation, I knew the economistic enemy best'. Winch promised to look up Haakonssen's work as he had 'a vague idea of following up the career of the "science of politics" in the hands of Dugald Stewart and his pupils' and would be visiting Edinburgh, his 'favourite city, the place where I started my teaching career'.[7]

Later in 1978 Donald Winch acted as reader for Cambridge University Press for a manuscript by Haakonssen, which appeared in 1981 as *The Science of a Legislator: The Natural Jurisprudence of David Hume and Adam Smith*. Haakonssen's great achievement, in the view of Forbes and now also of Winch, was to have plugged the gap in scholarship by revealing the importance of the philosophical foundations of Smith's thought in reconstructing his science of the statesman or legislator. For Haakonssen, Smith was strongly indebted to what he termed 'the Continental natural law tradition of Grotius, Pufendorf, and others, and especially to the form which this tradition had been given by his teacher, Francis Hutcheson'. Smith's jurisprudence, however, derived far more 'from Hume's question about the possibility of legal criticism – or of how to avoid a complete relativism – if neither naturally nor divinely given standards were available'. Haakonssen's book gave the most detailed description to date of what Smith had meant in promising 'an account of the general principles of law and government', and in so doing completed the refutation of Marxist accounts, noting that the 'materialist or economic interpretation of Smith's view of history would seem to be inconsistent with the proposal that a normative discipline of natural jurisprudence could have an important influence on the direction of history, if properly applied'.[8] Winch had by this time been converted to the view that it was the history of natural jurisprudence, rather than the history of civic humanism, that was most important to any understanding of eighteenth-century Scottish philosophy.

By 1980–81, all three men, Forbes, Haakonssen and Winch, had been cajoled into being involved, to different extents, with the King's

College Cambridge project 'Society and Political Economy, 1750–1850', which ran for five years from 1978 under the leadership of István Hont and Michael Ignatieff. Hont, a Hungarian exile, played an especially significant role in working out a non-Marxist account of the philosophical foundations of the Scottish Enlightenment in natural jurisprudence. In pursuing this goal, Hont argued that it was vital to write 'philosophical history' but that this could only be achieved by 'conceptually rigorous but nevertheless strictly historical study'. Hont's major claim was that the best guide to this kind of research had to be philosophers and historians who had not been driven to separate empirical research from theory, and indeed who would have rejected any presumption of a separation between such enquiries. Hont stated that it was in the eighteenth century, during the period in Europe termed the Enlightenment, that exactly the kind of philosophy he was interested in could be found. David Hume, Adam Ferguson, Adam Smith, William Robertson and John Millar were in the vanguard of a remarkable series of studies of economic development that were brilliant because they took seriously the historical specificity of any claim about economic action and acknowledged the political limits to economic innovation in addition to the economic limits upon domestic and international politics. Life and history were characterised by the putting into practice of strategies for reform, improvement or survival that always had unintended consequences. A philosophical history focused upon the problems of the present had to acknowledge these facts about the human world.[9]

Hont's approach permeated the 'Society and Political Economy' project, ultimately resulting in the publication of *Wealth and Virtue: The Shaping of Political Economy in the Scottish Enlightenment* by Cambridge University Press in 1983, commencing with the framing essay by Hont and Ignatieff, 'Needs and Justice in the Wealth of Nations'. Hont argued that Hume and Smith were altogether opposed to egalitarian impulses in western thought, which defined justice in distributive terms and held rather that legal and political equality was best sustained by a regime of economic inequality. At the same time, Hont traced Hume's and Smith's acceptance of the justice of overriding property rights in conditions of necessity to John Locke and Samuel Pufendorf, rather than Francis Hutcheson and the so-called Scottish civic moralists. The origins of modern liberalism were to be found in arguments about justice in seventeenth-century Germany, the Dutch Republic and England.

Hont's and Ignatieff's collection *Wealth and Virtue* registered the ongoing debate about what eighteenth-century Scottish philosophers were doing. Indeed, something like a turf war was conducted within the covers. The book contained a number of contributions emphasising the importance of civic humanism, in addition to contributions focused on the tradition of natural jurisprudence, with John Pocock's chapter characteristically charting the resulting tensions, and Winch attacking both sets of tradition-mongers with a piece on 'Adam Smith's "enduring *particular* result"' (emphasis added).[10] One other noteworthy feature of the book was a lack of attention to religion and theology, with John Dunn's chapter describing the movement from David Hume to Adam Smith as being a journey from 'applied theology to social analysis'.[11]

Over the following years, Hont developed his approach to Smith by making a grander argument, holding that the 'system of needs' which Hegel and Marx employed to describe social relationships on the basis of utility was at root called 'socialism', a term employed in the eighteenth century to describe Pufendorf's 'attempt to mitigate Hobbes' theory of Leviathan'. In an unpublished summary of his work, Hont stated that the reason why Rousseau, Hume and Smith all had Pufendorf's work beside them when they wrote was because of his particular modification of Hobbes's rejection of sociability as the foundation of human nature and polity. Pufendorf argued instead that sociability was a product of the utilitarian interactions of humans seeking food, security and friendship:

> Hobbes had rejected the idea that man was a zoonpolitikon and replaced it with a project of pure politics without social foundations. Pufendorf, in answer, substituted a theory of sociability drawn from the idea of utility-led cooperation for the satisfaction of human needs and desires for the Aristotelian moral project of friendship. This genealogy of socialism can be turned into the starting point of an extremely illuminating historical inquiry. First, it is clear that Hegel and Marx's System of Need is a direct progeny of Pufendorf's socialist amendment to Hobbes. Second, by tracking the debate on Pufendorf's theory of utilitarian sociability one can reconstruct the political thought of the century between Hobbes and Hegel. In this mirror, the Enlightenment appears as a grand controversy between market sociability (socialism in this old sense) and its enemies. Third, it might help to solve (or at least explain) the tension between the two current historiographies of the Enlightenment in which the first sees it as an appendix to the seventeenth-century, the other as a precursor of the nineteenth.[12]

If Pufendorf had rejected Aristotelian and Christian scholastic conceptions of man's natural sociability, then Hont was ascribing a different conception to him. Hont's claim was that Hume and Smith were following Pufendorf in arguing that markets could be free but could never be moralised, because they were founded on human beings helping one another for selfish purposes rather than for moral ends. At the same time, market relationships did bring people together, establishing what Kant was later to call 'unsocial sociability'. Like Pocock, Hont regarded the civic humanist tradition as enabling eighteenth-century authors to criticise commercial society by emphasising the loss of public virtue, and the possibility of apocalypse through war, bankruptcy, economic decline, or the rise of demagogic Ceasar figures. For Hont, however, it was vital to tie historical analysis to contemporary problems in politics, and with this in mind he asserted that the reconstruction of the tradition of natural jurisprudence was more relevant to the present. Following Grotius, Hobbes and Pufendorf, Hume and Smith had accepted the imperfections of commercial society while emphasising the benefits, not least that a regime of civil rights and duties best suited the progress of commerce. Natural jurisprudence and the study of natural rights were not initially the medium for attacks on commercial society, which rather developed from civic or humanist claims about lost sociability in modern times, and the need to return to a past characterised by greater social cohesion, morality and public virtue. As the eighteenth century wore on, however, natural jurists, such as Jean-Jacques Rousseau, turned to attacking the advocates of commercial society on their own terms, arguing that however modern societies were evaluated, they failed every test, from happiness to wealth and virtue.

III

Hont's introduction of continental natural law thought into Scottish Enlightenment scholarship marked a significant expansion of the British work in the history of political thought. It is no diminution of Hont's contribution to observe that for him German natural law provided an historical means of solving a modern political-philosophical problem: how to harmonise the polar principles of self-organising society and state 'public authority'. Hont achieved this by treating Pufendorfian sovereignty as grounded in political norms arising from the forms of social exchange and stadial development, rather than in those arising from the commands of a Hobbesian superior. Haakonssen too was interested in relating social and political theories of obligation, but in his *Natural Law and Moral Philosophy* he began to push this relation in directions that would change the itinerary of the discussion. This was in part because Haakonssen cross-cut the society-state relation with an intellectual opposition of a different kind: namely, the relation between rationalist and voluntarist doctrines of moral and political obligation, whose hinterland was as much theological as social and political. But it was also because Haakonssen was interested in a figure like Pufendorf not just with regards to his reception in Scottish social theories of politics, but also in terms of his initial reception in the very different context of German (and Scandinavian) public law and state theory. Finally, without retreating from the intricacies of Smithian moral philosophy and the figure of the impartial spectator, Haakonssen began to explore the very different terrain of Pufendorfian moral and political philosophy. Here obligations were not borne by the person internalising a social judgement but by a persona occupying an office, with office understood in terms of roles and duties constituted for various purposes, including those of maintaining peace through the offices of sovereign and subject. Now rights featured not as the foundation of law and politics but as a by-product of the architecture of offices.

These changes would prove to be dramatic, both in terms of the architectures of political thought, the intellectual materials they deployed, and the historical terrain on which they stood. For Haakonssen, post-scholastic German natural law showed that in large areas of intellectual Europe philosophical anthropologies – whether invested in the rational individual, the virtuous community, or the hidden hand of mutual selfishness – were not foundational for legal and political thought, but rather functioned as a plurality of rival ways of shaping political and religious projects. As capacities for warranting legal and moral action, rights might not be grounded in either the free exercise of individual rationality or in the exercise of virtue that realised human good in a community, and these rival constructions would now be tied to particular cultural and political programmes. On the one hand, this meant that rights and duties would not be derived normatively from a favoured – Lockean, Thomist, Spinozist, Kantian, etc. – anthropology, but historically from an investigation of the circumstances in which and the purposes for which such normative anthropologies had been deployed. Ultimately this would require moving beyond what has been called the 'epistemological paradigm' in the history of philosophy and into an approach that was oriented to the linguistic materials informing normative philosophies and the social and political concerns that shaped their articulation.[13] On the other hand, it meant that the contexts in which such deployments took place would be significantly pluralised, moving beyond heroic accounts in which the thought of Aquinas, Locke, Spinoza, or Kant provided the history of political thought with a unified normative structure, and into an expanding array of intellectual-historical regions where such lesser-known figures as Christian Thomasius (Brandenburg-Prussia),[14]

Ludvig Holberg (Denmark-Norway),[15] or Gershom Carmichael (Scotland) commanded the field of reception in accordance with a variety of local struggles, imperatives and programmes.

In backtracking from its Scottish reception, and following natural law thought back into the very different worlds of European religious conflict, state delineation, diplomacy and public law, Haakonssen opened up new research directions, and the Anglo-centric research network received an influx of European scholars. These scholars were often working on the role of natural law as an intellectual matrix in which a wide variety of moral, political, theological and juridical positions were formulated within early modern European juridical and political orders that were very different from the Scottish and English settings in which natural law had been reconciled with social theories of politics and hidden hand theories of morality. In this expanded field, enlightened thinkers of the Scottish kirk and university, and parliamentary thinkers of the Anglican, common law order, would find themselves alongside absolutist German public jurists seeking rationales for post-Westphalian 'secularised' multi-confessional states. Small wonder that the manner in which law, rights and politics were articulated in these different settings could not be read-off from normative theories of the great thinkers and had to be investigated eclectically and in their own terms.

The sometimes uncomfortable challenges of pluralised contextualisation posed by Haakonssen's European natural law expansion of the history of political thought have been met by the new kinds of research into law, rights and politics reflected in the present array of papers. In Part I, Rights, Religion and Morality, James Moore's historical investigation of the Protestant bases of popular sovereignty and natural rights doctrines sits alongside Maria Rosa Antognazza's more historical-philosophical argument that scholastic natural law need not lead to religious intolerance by enforcing theological truth. Aaron Garrett's following chapter tends to invert the normative thrust of Antognazza's discussion, arguing via the example of Joseph Butler that the meaning and truth of philosophical texts varies with the cultural and political currents informing their current reception. Mads Jensen's discussion of natural law in early modern Copenhagen also focuses on reception, showing that the understanding of natural law in this setting was shaped by a fierce struggle between the advocates of its Pufendorfian-Thomasian form and the defenders of Christian natural law. The expanded and pluri-contextual discussion of natural law rights and duties is thus immediately apparent.

In Part II, Natural Law and the Philosophers, this transnational and pluralised contextualisation of natural law is extended to the history of philosophy. Two of the chapters, by Kari Saastamoinen and Simone Zurbuchen provide close textual accounts of natural law as a grounding for political equality, Saastamoinen arguing that Locke derives equality from the natural right to self-preservation, and Zurbuchen arguing that Pufendorf has a conception of equality grounded in human dignity, interestingly at odds with his related conception of esteem as socially apportioned. In a somewhat similar vein Frank Grunert's chapter explores the role of Wolff's conception of iura connata or innate rights as possible foundations for the modern doctrine of human rights, imbuing natural law with a degree of transhistoricality and engaging with Haakonssen's rather different treatment of Wolff's natural rights as alienable. With Ian Hunter's chapter on Christian Thomasius the pendulum swings back into the contextual register, with Hunter arguing that Thomasius's natural law was not a philosophical theory for his juristic practice, but rather an instrument of the latter, functioning as a means for receiving deconfessionalised post-Westphalian public law in Protestant Germany, and for educating the jurists who would be responsible for this reception. Finally, James Harris's discussion of Hume situates Hume's treatment of justice in the modern natural law tradition in order to bring out what is, in that tradition's terms, both unsurprising and peculiar in the definition of justice that Hume works with. For Hume justice is the essential element of an analysis of the minimal conditions of human sociability. But Hume defines justice exceedingly narrowly, as respect for rights of property. His definition has been severely criticised, both by his contemporaries and in recent Hume scholarship. Harris argues that it was Hume's particular version of the argument against Hutchesonian moral sense theory that led him to define justice as he did.

If one of the goals of sixteenth- and seventeenth-century natural jurisprudence had been to put an end to religious conflict within and between states, the eighteenth century saw a myriad of reform strategies intended to ameliorate the condition of society, and more especially many of the problems associated with commerce. This transition was already underway in Pufendorf's writings. Michael Seidler's chapter reveals Pufendorf's fear of luxury and the possibility of selfishness undermining the practices that maintained communities. Pufendorf's response was a sophisticated engagement with sumptuary legislation, which existed in various forms across Europe, with a view to preventing commerce from acting as a social solvent. Seidler's chapter charts Pufendorf's complicated perspective on the relationship between markets and morals, in addition to showing how the history of economics might be revised, once Pufendorf's singular influence is acknowledged.

The great achievement of the writers who build upon the foundations established by Pufendorf, including Montesquieu, Hume and Smith, was to have created a science of legislation both empirical and historical, the idea being that legislators could be sure that when laws were introduced they would operate in a particular fashion in specified circumstances. Historical research was crucial, because it underlined the uncertain effects of laws due to unintended consequences, but also, once unintended consequences were taken into consideration, why law that was a product of historical reflection might amount to sensible reform. Human beings operated in a second-best world of likely failure, and needed to follow the wisdom of Solon in consequence, always operating on the assumption that what worked in one place would not function in the same way elsewhere. This was why writing histories that revealed the evolution of government and of law were vital, and why Adam Smith had announced the hope of doing precisely this, to complete his science of the legislator. Smith failed, and had his papers burned after his death, leaving modern scholars the difficult task of reconstructing Smith's vision of a law and politics capable of coping with modern problems. Such research has been transformed by the discovery of student notes of Smith's lectures on jurisprudence, and John Cairns's chapter illuminates the consequences of Smith's broad vision for the following generation of his students that ascended to university chairs at Edinburgh in law and history, Alexander Fraser Tytler, Allan Maconochie and Baron David Hume (the philosopher's nephew).

Critics who were sceptical of the particular fusion of law and history in natural jurisprudence launched their assaults in the later eighteenth-century from within established religious denominations, or asserted the view that the anticipated reforms would fail, being insufficiently grounded on an accurate portrayal of human nature. The latter approach has been especially associated with Jeremy Bentham, who for many scholars has become the most prominent opponent of rights-based theories. David Lieberman reconsiders this view, charting Bentham's view of natural rights from his earliest writings to the summary constitutional codes developed for post-Napoleonic Europe. The Bentham who emerges, rather than being a consistent enemy of the kinds of declarations of rights that marked the American and French Revolutions, was instead building upon much of the jurisprudence he condemned in his rhetoric. Lieberman revises the commonplace view of Bentham and his intellectual origins in consequence.

The period of the French Revolution was famous for erecting an entirely new system of government and social mores on the basis of a declaration of the rights of man and the citizen. Everything changed in France, over a remarkably short period of time, leading to an especially intense debate about what a society founded on equal rights for all ought to look like. Richard Whatmore's chapter examines two of the systems expounded, derived from the political philosophies of Thomas Paine and Emmanuel Sièyes. Whatmore examines the shock with which opponents such as Edmund Burke and Edward Gibbon greeted rights-based politics, and what happened when the new worlds of peace and prosperity promised by Paine and Sièyes descended into chaos and poverty. Around the turn of the eighteenth century Whatmore charts a turn away from France and towards Britain as a possible model state for rights compatible with order and with civil liberty; in this turn the history of Scotland, and the existence of brilliant Scottish philosophers, played a prominent role, being proof that Britain was not an empire run for the benefit of a mercantile class based in London, but was rather a cosmopolitan empire whose peripheries benefited as much as the metropole. Still dedicated to the kinds of trans-formative natural jurisprudence promised in the early years of the French Revolution, republican voices shouted from the sidelines that if Britain was now the model state for humanity, then all of the reform projects of the eighteenth century had altogether failed.

In their geopolitical passage from Edinburgh and London to Halle and Copenhagen, and in their intellectual-historical sweep – across Scottish and German enlightenments, scholastic and Protestant natural law, Benthamite reflections on constitutionalism and Burkean reflections on imperialism – the chapters that follow pay testimony and homage to a remarkable intellectual historian: one whose cosmopolitan itinerary has resulted in dazzling illuminations of the regions in which thought has been shaped and put to work.

Notes

1. Haakonssen did later publish on Hayek: preface to Australian edition of *Hayek's 'Serfdom' Revisited* (Sydney: CIS, 1985), vii–ix; critical Note on F. A. Hayek, *The Fatal Conceit*, in *Humane Studies Review*, 6 (1989), 5–6; 'The Philosophy of Law in Hayek's New Constitutionalism', *Rechtstheorie*, 19 (1989), 289–303.
2. Knud Haakonssen, 'Hume's Obligations', *Hume Studies*, 4 (1978), 1–17.
3. Knud Haakonssen, 'From Moral Philosophy to Political Economy: The Contribution of Dugald Stewart', in V. Hope, ed., *Philosophers of the Scottish Enlightenment* (Edinburgh: Edinburgh University Press, 1984), 211–32; 'The Science of a Legislator in James Mackintosh's Moral Philosophy', *History of Political Thought*, 5 (1984), 233–66; 'John Millar and the Science of a

Legislator', *Juridical Review*, 41 (1985), 41–68; 'James Mill and Scottish Moral Philosophy', *Political Studies*, 33 (1985), 628–41; 'Social Contract as Quasi-Contract: Reid versus Hume', *Bulletin of the Australian Society of Legal Philosophy*, 36 (1986), 42–62; 'Thomas Reid's Politics', *Reid Studies*, 1 (1986), 10–27.

4. Knud Haakonssen, 'Hugo Grotius and the History of Political Thought', *Political Theory*, 13 (1985), 239–65; 'Natural Law and the Scottish Enlightenment', in D. H. Jory and C. Stewart-Robertson, eds, *Man and Nature* (Edmonton: Proceedings of the Canadian Society for Eighteenth-Century Studies, Vol. IV, 1985), 47–80; 'Moral Philosophy and Natural Law: From the Cambridge Platonists to the Scottish Enlightenment', *Political Science*, 40 (1988), 97–110; 'Enlightenment Philosophy in Germany and Scotland. Recent German Scholarship', *Aufklärung*, IV (1989), 109–26; 'Natural Law and Moral Realism: The Scottish Synthesis', in *The Philosophy of the Scottish Enlightenment*, ed. M. A. Stewart (Oxford: Oxford University Press, 1990), 61–85; 'From Natural Law to the Rights of Man: A European Perspective on American Debates', in *A Culture of Right*, ed. K. Haakonssen and M. Lacey (Cambridge: Cambridge University Press, 1991), 19–61.

5. Duncan Forbes to Donald Winch, 19 May 1978, Winch papers.

6. Duncan Forbes' notes on Knud Haakonssen's PhD thesis, private papers of Knud Haakonssen.

7. Donald Winch to Duncan Forbes, 25 May 1978, Winch papers.

8. Knud Haakonssen, *The Science of a Legislator: The Natural Jurisprudence of David Hume & Adam Smith* (Cambridge: Cambridge University Press, 1981), 2, 182–3, 188–9.

9. István Hont to David Parry, 29 September 1977, István Hont Papers, University of St Andrews Special Collections.

10. In Michael Ignatieff and Istvan Hont, eds, *Wealth and Virtue: The Shaping of Political Economy in the Scottish Enlightenment* (Cambridge: Cambridge University Press, 1983). On civic humanism see John Robertson, 'The Scottish Enlightenment at the limits of the civic tradition' (137–78) and Nicholas Phillipson, 'Adam Smith as civic moralist' (179–202); on natural jurisprudence see James Moore and Michael Silverthorne, 'Gershom Carmichael and the natural jurisprudence tradition in eighteenth-century Scotland' (73–88). Pocock's chapter was entitled, 'Cambridge paradigms and Scotch philosophers: a study of the relations between the civic humanist and the civil jurisprudential interpretation of eighteenth-century social thought' (235–52). Winch's chapter was at pages 253–70.

11. John Dunn, 'From applied theology to social analysis: the break between John Locke and the Scottish Enlightenment', in *Wealth and Virtue*, 119–36.

12. István Hont, 'Unsociable sociability: the morals and politics of markets in enlightenment thought', Leverhulme Major Research Fellowship Application, 2001–2002, István Hont papers, University of St Andrews Special Collections.

13. Knud Haakonssen, 'The History of Eighteenth-Century Philosophy: History or Philosophy?', in K. Haakonssen, ed., *The Cambridge History of Eighteenth-Century Philosophy* (Cambridge: Cambridge University Press, 2006), 3–25.
14. Knud Haakonssen, 'German Natural Law', in M. Goldie and R. Wokler, eds, *The Cambridge History of Eighteenth-Century Political Thought* (Cambridge: Cambridge University Press, 2006), 251–90, at 261–7.
15. Knud Haakonssen, 'Holberg's *Law of Nature and Nations*', in *Ludvig Holberg (1684–1754): Learning and Literature in the Nordic Enlightenment*, ed. K. Haakonssen and S. Olden-Jørgensen (London: Routledge, 2017), 59–79.

Part I

Rights, Religion and Morality

1

Calvinists, Arminians, Socinians: Popular Sovereignty and Natural Rights in Early Modern Political Thought

James Moore

In closely reasoned and copiously researched books and articles composed over the past thirty years, Knud Haakonssen has identified a tradition of moral and political philosophy that he has called Protestant natural law.[1] One of the merits of understanding early modern natural law theories in this way is that it directs the attention of historians to the theological premises of theories of natural duties and natural rights. The main focus of Haakonssen's studies has been on duties to God, duties to oneself and duties to others. In this essay I propose to focus upon natural rights in the writings of Hugo Grotius, the Levellers and John Locke and the manner in which their understanding of rights was informed by distinctive Protestant theologies: by Arminianism or the theology of the Remonstrant Church and by Socinianism. I will argue that their theological principles and the natural rights theories that followed from those principles were in conflict with the theology of Calvin and the theologians of the Reformed Church. The political theory that marks the distinctive contribution of Calvin and the Reformed to political theory was the idea of popular sovereignty, an idea revived in the eighteenth century, in the political writings of Jean-Jacques Rousseau.

The basic and distinctive characteristics of Calvinism may be summarised very succinctly. The debatable principles had been set down by Calvin himself, in dogmas derived in part from St Augustine:

1. the sinfulness or depravity of our fallen human nature, inherited from the original sin of our first parents;
2. the atonement of our sins by God in the person of Christ, an atonement which made the grace of God available to all who are able to receive it;

3. a sharp distinction between those whom God has predestined to
   receive His grace and those who have not been chosen, who are not
   among the elect;
4. the dogma of double predestination: not only were some chosen or
   saved, others were consigned to eternal punishment for their sins.

It was the duty of the Church and of Christian rulers to enforce these dogmas and punish subjects who persisted in sinful living. And if a ruler failed
in his duty to institute and enforce the Christian religion, as Calvin understood it – if he attempted to impose a false religion and prohibit the true
religion – he might be lawfully resisted and punished by lesser magistrates
upon whom the duty of Christian rulership devolved.[2]

It was from these theological dogmas and the inferences drawn from
them for rulers that Reformed jurists and publicists adduced their doctrine of popular sovereignty. Calvin himself professed no such theory;
but it might be inferred from his theological and political principles that
the institution and enforcement of the Christian religion was the duty of
all who have been elected or chosen to be God's people. This was the
conclusion drawn by the author of the *Vindiciae Contra Tyrannos* (1579),
who appealed directly to the Biblical tradition that God entered into a
covenant with his chosen people to obey God's commandments and to
resist any ruler who would impose idolatry or strange religions upon the
people.[3] This appeal would be reinforced by the observations of classicists
like George Buchanan that the people were the source of *imperium* or
sovereign power and they might withdraw their power from magistrates or
rulers if the power was misused.[4] The political ideas of the *Vindiciae* and *De
Jure Regni Apud Scotos* were integrated with the principles of Calvin's theology in a succession of treatises on Christian politics published in Geneva,
Heidelberg, East Friesland, the Netherlands and Scotland from the late
sixteenth to the end of the seventeenth century.

In this tradition, it was assumed that the natural condition of mankind is a fallen or sinful condition. And government is instituted by God,
through the people, by a formal covenant, or, more informally, by tradition,
for the punishment of sin. For the people understand their sinful human
nature well enough to know that government is indispensable. And they
are also able to distinguish some among them who appear to have been
chosen or elected or accredited somehow by God as persons who have
received the grace of God. And such persons form a natural aristocracy or
ruling class. A Godly people or a people who aspire to receive God's grace
will invest such persons with *imperium* or sovereign power. But if this power
is misused, if the rulers fail in their obligation to punish sin, or, if they

conduct the government in a sinful, which is to say, a heterodox manner, then the people have an obligation to withdraw their sovereignty, and they have a duty, as well, to punish the usurper or tyrant. This was the view of Lambert Daneau (successor of Beza and of Calvin in Geneva), of Zachary Ursinus (author of the Heidelberg Catechism), and of Johannes Althusius (sometimes mistaken for a secular thinker; in fact, he was digesting in a methodical manner this tradition of writing on the sovereignty of the people).[5] The tradition was perpetuated in Great Britain by David Pareus, commenting on Ursinus, by Samuel Rutherford, George Gee, and many others writing on behalf of the Scottish covenanters and their particular initiative in Britain, in the era of the Great Rebellion and subsequent civil war.[6] And it continued in Scotland and the Netherlands to the end of the seventeenth century.[7]

This was the body of literature which Grotius was reacting against in terms of his own distinctive theological ideas. The emergence of the Netherlands, and, more specifically, the province or state of Holland, as a centre of commerce and of toleration of different beliefs, in the early seventeenth century, was a phenomenon justified and legitimated by a movement opposed to orthodox Calvinism. The Remonstrant Church, centred in the great trading cities of Holland, and opposed elsewhere in the Netherlands, was led by the Leiden theologians, Jacob Arminius and Simon Episcopius.[8] They challenged the Calvinist dogmas of original sin, the atonement and double predestination. They contended that the fall of our first parents diminished but did not destroy the capacity of mankind for self-government. The significance of the atonement was that it moved God, the supreme governor of mankind, to remit or dispense with eternal punishment for our sins. God was not a punitive ruler but a provident ruler who had provided mankind with reason, will power and natural affection, sufficient to permit us to live in natural sociability with one another. God had also given us the right to defend ourselves from those who would attempt to deprive us of our lives and our right to share the world given to mankind in general by God.

Hugo Grotius defended this theological position in all his writings. Grotius was not a secular jurist. His famous pronouncement that the laws of nature would oblige mankind even if they were not enforced by God meant only that God should not be understood as a punitive God, but rather as a generous God who has provided us with a world and the faculties and powers to live in it. God has left it to us to defend ourselves and enforce the law of nature, as private persons, in company with others, or by transferring this right of self-defense to a magistrate or ruler to exercise on our behalf. It was an argument designed to liberate individuals and companies (such as the Dutch East India Company, who had originally commissioned his work) to trade freely, taking enemy ships as prizes, if those ships should attempt to appropriate the sea, the God-given natural community of mankind. In this respect, Grotius's great work was as much about the rights of war and the benefits which follow from war as it was about the right to enjoy peace.[9]

Grotius's natural rights' theory justified the rights of individuals, private and corporate, and of rulers. He did not endorse the theory that sovereign power resides in the people. He presented sixteen arguments, in all, in opposition to that theory.[10] His concern was that rulers would be reduced in their ability to secure the rights of individuals if they were confronted by a people which claimed sovereign power for itself. His discussion of this subject was analogous to an argument made ten years earlier, in *On the Sovereignty of the Supreme Power in Sacred Affairs* (1614).[11] There Grotius argued that the ruler must have the power to direct ecclesiastical life. His concern was that the sovereign power claimed by the elders, deacons, consistories and synods of the Reformed Church threatened to destroy liberty of worship and toleration of beliefs different from their own. His apprehensions were well founded. At the Synod of Dort, in 1618, the beliefs of the Remonstrants were denounced as heresies, their ministers were banished and Grotius himself was put in prison. Following his escape, he spent the rest of his life in exile in France.

It was plausible for Grotius, writing in the Netherlands and in France in the early seventeenth century, to suppose that absolute monarchy might defend toleration more effectively than governments in which the people had sovereign power. It was an absolute monarch, Henry IV, who declared, in 1598, in the Edict of Nantes, that French Protestants should be allowed to worship in their own churches. And Huguenots, generally, in seventeenth-century France, were supporters of absolute monarchy.[12] In England, Grotius's views were well received by English royalists who thought that the Church of England might comprehend or embrace dissenters within its ranks by reducing the number of beliefs or articles of faith it was necessary to endorse to be considered a member of the established church. This strategy was pursued by the Latitudinarians; by Edward Stillingfleet,[13] among others, who adopted Grotius's ecclesiology and defended his views on more strictly theological topics. Stillingfleet and other Latitudinarians were also particularly pleased by an early tract of Grotius in which he had been critical of Socinian theology.

The theology of Faustus Socinus and of the small but very thoughtful and influential community he founded in Rakow, on the Polish-Lithuanian border, may be briefly stated. He maintained, contrary to orthodox Christian doctrine subsequent to the Council of Nicea in the fourth century, that the Bible contained no assertions at all concerning the Trinity, the

Incarnation, original sin or the atonement for our sins by Christ. There was one God, the Father; Christ did not claim to be God; he should be considered rather to have been a divinely inspired spokesman of the word of God. The consequence of Adam's transgression was not original and inherited sin but rather human mortality. The lesson to be drawn from the suffering, the death and the resurrection of Christ was that all mankind may anticipate a similar resurrection, so long as they have lived in a manner consistent with the teachings of Christ, which should be understood literally and rationally as the word of God.[14]

Socinus, a native of Siena, had originally hoped to find refuge and a favourable reception for his theology in Geneva, but his ideas were not well received there. Michael Servetus who had held similar views had been burnt at the stake in Geneva, following denunciation of his beliefs by Calvin himself. But Socinus had adopted from Calvin a metaphorical description of the relationship between God and man. Calvin had held that, as sinners, we, all of us, owe a debt to God, and that Christ by his sacrifice had paid that debt; this was the proper understanding of the atonement or the satisfaction made by Christ on behalf of mankind. Socinus took over the metaphor of indebtedness but drew a different inference from it. He considered it inconsistent with the justice, goodness and grace of God that He should be somehow propitiated or satisfied by the suffering and death of His son. It was more reasonable to suppose that if our failings, shortcomings and sins are considered to be debts, then God, as our creditor, might freely forgive us our debts, without any presumption of an expiatory sacrifice.[15]

Grotius, seconded by Stillingfleet, considered that the entire controversy had been conducted on a mistaken foundation; sins should not be understood as debts, nor should God be conceived as a creditor. God is a sovereign ruler; and while it is consistent with God's government of the world that the laws of God should be upheld, the correct inference to be drawn from Christ's sacrifice is that God was moved by that sacrifice to extend clemency and forgiveness to the human race. It may be noted that Grotius's criticism of Socinus applied even more directly to the original Calvinist and Reformed position than to the spirit of Socinus's reading. This was remarked to Grotius in an extended response by Johannes Crell, perhaps the most acute of the Socinian writers, who commented that 'if Grotius contends for no more than that Christ did avert that wrath of God which men had deserved for their sins, [we] would willingly yield him all that he pleads for . . .'.[16] Grotius, in exile in Paris, became friendly with members of the Socinian community who perceived him and the Remonstrants to be their allies in theological controversy. There remained significant differences, however, in their respective views on social and political subjects.

Socinus and his followers found refuge in a region inhabited by other anti-trinitarians, Anabaptists, Mennonites, Hutterites and Moravians. These communities were for the most part pacifist. Socinus himself believed that war was always wrong; one must never take the life of another, in a private or in a public capacity. Many Socinians were also attracted to the Anabaptist ideal of communal ownership.[17] But the social and political opinions of the Socinian community changed during the course of the seventeenth century. This debate among themselves is reflected in the writings of the Polish brethren, the *Bibliotheca Fratrum Polonarum*, published in eight volumes in Amsterdam, in 1656. Johannes Crell proposed that the spirit of Christian community could be better expressed by distributing whatever one owns beyond the necessities of life to the needy, or at least to share with others one's tools, servants and oxen.[18] The pacifist disposition of the early Socinians was also transformed in the course of the seventeenth century, following the destruction of their city, Rakow, in 1658 and the dispersal of the Socinian community to Berlin and particularly to Amsterdam, where they were admitted to the churches of the Remonstrants. The writings of the most determined critic of Socinian pacifism, Samuel Przypkowski, were communicated to Phillipp van Limborch in 1682. Those writings on Christian magistracy were published, with an introduction by Limborch, in 1692.[19]

In a recent very thoughtful, thorough and judicious account of John Locke's position with respect to Socinianism, John Marshall has observed that Locke's notebooks and journals reveal an extensive preoccupation with Socinian literature.[20] His interest in Socinianism may have begun as early as the 1660s, but the frequency of annotations increased in the late 1670s, and continued to the end of his life. Limborch seems to have assumed Locke's familiarity with the writings of Przypkowski when he reported to Locke in 1692 that Przypkowski's writings were now in print. But there is also a revealing comment on how Locke perceived Grotius. It is recorded, from Stephen Nye's *History of Unitarianism* (1687) in Locke's handwriting, on an interleaved page of his copy of Thomas Hope Blount's *Censura celebriorum authorum*. It reads:

Hugo Grotius Is Socinian all over. This great man in his younger years attacked ye Socinians in a principal article of their Doctrine. But being answered by J. Crellius, he not only never replied but thanked Crellius for his answer. And afterwards writing annotations on the whole scriptures, he interspersed everywhere according to the sentiments of the Socinians.[21]

I owe this reference to the generosity of Marshall, who brought it to my attention many years ago. Marshall himself is more reluctant than I am to identify the corpus of Locke's writings (after 1667) with Socinian ideas. And it must be acknowledged that Locke would have found natural rights theories supported by similar theological convictions in England earlier in the century.

Grotius's ideas were taken up by English radicals of the 1640s: by Henry Parker, Richard Overton and the Levellers. On the authority of Grotius, they held in particular that there were certain fundamental rights: the right to life, to defend oneself, to liberty of conscience or judgement, to property, which no rational man would relinquish or transfer to another. Indeed, they considered it consistent with one's duty not only to oneself and to others to defend these rights, but also to defend them as an obligation derived directly from God. Richard Tuck has argued, in *Natural Rights Theories: Their Origin and Development* (1979), that the Leveller position may be explained as a development of an assumption in Grotius's work, which he calls 'interpretive charity'. It might be logical to suppose (as Hobbes did) that men must surrender their rights to a sovereign, but it was also more charitable to assume that subjects had retained certain rights for themselves.[22] I would suggest that it was not 'interpretive charity' which led the Levellers and others in the seventeenth century to take this important step in natural rights theory. It was rather that they had adopted the theological position to which Grotius himself was inclined in the later years of his life. Their theology was consistent with Socinianism.

In one of the first of his known publications, *Man's Mortalitie*, published in 1643, Richard Overton elaborated his basic theological premises.[23] He argued that there is no good reason to believe, on grounds of perception or testimony or even analogy, that the soul is immortal and survives the death of the body. It is more reasonable to believe, he thought, that soul and body die together. And the message delivered by Christ was that persons who live their lives in accordance with the laws of God and nature might look forward to an entire resurrection of soul and body on the day of judgement. This was the heresy of 'mortalism', held by Anabaptists and Moravians and given a systematic exposition in the theological writings of Socinus and his followers. It had the effect of diverting Christians from belief in a fallen or sinful human nature to the view that each of us is made or created directly by God and is expected to live in a manner consistent with our God-given faculties or powers. It was a view which could be accommodated, with some modification, by the Remonstrants. The significance of Christ was not his death and supposed atonement for our sins, but his life, his moral teachings.

It was a role consistent with the character sometimes given him by Overton and others, when they described Jesus Christ as the first Leveller. Christ was a divinely inspired teacher; he was not himself God. There was one God, the father. And God's relationship with each man was a direct relationship, a relation of proprietorship or *dominium*.

This was also John Locke's understanding of the relationship between man and God, set out in *The Reasonableness of Christianity*, in his *Letters Concerning Toleration* and in *Two Treatises of Government*.[24] In the second *Treatise of Government*, Locke brought together several sources; foremost among them, no doubt, Pufendorf's shorter work *On the Duty of Man and Citizen*. Any comparison of the structure of the two works will exhibit a conspicuous resemblance between them: in the order of the presentation, and in the correspondence of chapters and subject matter (Chapter 4 on slavery, Chapter 16 on conquest). There were good reasons for eighteenth-century commentators on Pufendorf's work to regard Locke's second *Treatise* as another commentary on Pufendorf. Pufendorf was not a Socinian; he perceived himself to be a Lutheran – a Pietist, not a scholastic Lutheran. This was a theological position which has relevance for the orientations of Pufendorf's natural law theories (or so I have argued in another context).[25] But Pufendorf's determination to separate the divine forum from the human forum (itself a Lutheran motif) made it possible for jurists who held theological positions different from his own to impart their distinctive convictions to it. And such appears to have been the case with Locke: on the law of nature (the obligation to preserve ourselves and others as a consequence of God's proprietorship); on the right to punish (confined to reparation and restraint, as distinct from retribution); on property (and the obligation to ensure that the needs of others are attended to). Here I should like to focus particularly upon the implications of Locke's theological convictions for his ideas concerning sovereignty and popular government.

It is sometimes said by scholars that the Levellers and Locke both maintained theories of popular sovereignty. So far as I am aware, neither Locke nor any of the Levellers ever employed the term sovereignty when referring to the political power of the people. Whenever editors of Locke's writings or of the Leveller manifestoes refer (in their indices) to the sovereignty of the people, you will not find the term in the originals.[26] Locke's extensive discussion of the concept of sovereignty, in his first *Treatise of Government*, is entirely critical. He was criticising the claims of Filmer and of Church of England men who held that God's sovereignty is communicated in various ways (by donation, by inheritance, etc.) from God to the king. Locke rejected all these claims. And we have seen that an argument similar to the Church of England theory is found in Calvinist or Presbyterian political writers when they argued that God's sovereignty is communicated from God to his chosen people to elected officials of their choice, who were also God's choice, i.e., persons chosen or elected to rule and so signified by God to the people. In all Trinitarian political theories, sovereignty is communicated from God to rulers: in Catholic political thought, this communication is mediated by the Church; in Church of England political theory (in the divine right of kings theory) it is communicated directly to the king (through Christ the King); in Presbyterian political theory it is communicated by signification to a chosen people. These theories all have their analogues in theories of divine communion or the Eucharist. In anti-trinitarian theories, such as those of the Levellers and of Locke, there is no such communication of attributes; because Christ is not God: he is a man, a teacher; as Locke put it simply, he is the messiah.[27]

Locke, the Levellers and their many followers in the eighteenth century refer not to the sovereignty of the people but to the *supremacy* of the people. And they are equally clear about the respect in which the people are thought to be supreme: they are the residual or ultimate or supreme judges of whether the government is being conducted in a just or legitimate manner. The people (however exclusively or inclusively this term is used) understand that governments are established to secure the rights of persons who live under them. The relation of subjects to government is not a relation of *covenant* to establish the right religion or the right code of morals: it is rather a relation of *consent*. Subjects consent to be governed, as long as the government is conducted in a just or legitimate manner, not in an absolute or arbitrary manner. Governments are not granted sovereign power by the people or by God or by any other agency; governments enjoy their right to govern on the basis of *trust*. And when they violate that trust, they lose the confidence of the people. The difficulty with the Calvinist idea of popular sovereignty in the view of its Remonstrant and Socinian critics was, above all, that it threatened the capacity and the right of individuals to make judgements (about their religious beliefs, their personal morals, their economic and social relations) and the capacities and rights of peoples to reach agreements of judgements. This is a concern of some importance for the logic of popular government. It is a concern that has implications for the theology and the political thinking of Jean-Jacques Rousseau, whose political ideas were shaped by Calvinism and the changing fortunes of Geneva.

The political institutions of Geneva had undergone a transformation in the eighteenth century. Whereas in the sixteenth and seventeenth centuries Geneva was ruled by a Grand Council, in which every citizen was entitled to a vote, by the 1730s effective political power in Geneva was exercised by a Small Council of twenty-five citizens. The economy of the city was characterised by ever increasing inequalities of wealth, as French expatriate financiers continued to profit from banking and investments in France and its colonies.[28] These were the circumstances that prompted Rousseau to protest against the loss of simplicity, equality and civic virtue in his native city in the *Discourses* written in the 1750s. His remedy for these conditions, outlined in *The Social Contract*, was to propose, in effect, a return to the politics of the Reformed.

> Those who know Calvin only as a theologian much underestimate the extent of his genius. The codification of our wise edicts, in which he played a large part, does him no less honour than his *Institutes*. Whatever revolution time may bring in our religion, so long as the spirit of patriotism and liberty still live among us, the memory of this great man will be forever blessed.[29]

Like the author of the *Vindiciae*, Althusius and Rutherford, Rousseau argued that in any properly constituted state, sovereign power must be exercised by the people. He did not mean, of course, that God communicates sovereign power to the people by covenant; he argued, rather, that a people, if it wishes to be free, must impose sovereign power on itself. 'Each of us puts his person and all his power in common under the supreme direction of the general will, and in our corporate capacity, we receive each member as an indivisible part of the whole.'[30] This was not an agreement of the people as the Levellers had described it, nor was it a judgement of the people as Locke understood it. It was an act of will on the part of every individual, which would bring about a union of wills. One people, one will, to be determined by referenda or popular vote, as in ancient Rome, but without debate. 'Let us judge of what can be done by what has been done . . . It is very singular that in Rome . . . some of the citizens had to cast their votes from the roofs of buildings.'[31] But in Rome there was also a forum for public debate, in the Senate. There is no senate in Rousseau's republic. In place of debate it was expected that citizens would divine the will of the people intuitively.

> A state so governed needs very few laws; and, as it becomes necessary to issue new ones, the necessity is universally seen. The first man to propose them merely says what all have already felt, and there is no question of faction or intrigues or eloquence in order to secure the passage into law of what everyone has decided to do, as soon as he is sure that the rest will act with him.[32]

There would be tribunes, but they are not expected to propose new laws; they would speak to preserve laws that have already been enacted. There would be censors to enforce morality and, above all, there would be a civil religion. That religion could not be any version of the Christian religion; it would be a contradiction in terms to speak of a Christian republic; the terms are mutually exclusive. Christianity preaches only servitude and dependence. 'True Christians are made to be slaves; they know it and do not much mind.'[33]

Rousseau's friends in the Socinian community of Geneva were aghast. Jacob Vernet denounced Rousseau in *Le Christianisme de Jean-Jacques Rousseau*, and Rousseau complained in *The Confessions of Jean-Jacques Rousseau* that Vernet 'turned his back on me, like everyone else, after I had given him proofs of affection and confidence which should have touched him if a theologian is capable of being touched by anything'.[34] Rousseau's books *The Social Contract* and *Emile* were burned by order of the Small Council of Geneva, who also reserved the right to defend Geneva from Rousseau, if he should ever return to the city. He never did. He renounced his citizenship in April 1763. In his reply to his Genevan critics, in *Lettres écrits de la montagne*, he wrote:

> I am not the only person who, in treating abstractly of political questions, has treated them with boldness and freedom [but] I am the only person who has been punished for it. Locke, Montesquieu, the Abbe St. Pierre have all treated the same subjects, and often with the same freedom. Locke, in particular, has treated them on the same principles as I have done. All three were born under kings, have lived in peace, and died honored in their countries. You know how I have been treated in mine.[35]

Rousseau neglected to mention, of course, that Locke never acknowledged his authorship of *Two Treatises of Government* or his *Letters on Toleration* or *The Reasonableness of Christianity* in his lifetime; they were acknowledged to be his writings in a codicil to his will. Nor was Rousseau a theorist of natural rights in any sense comparable to Grotius, the Levellers and Locke. In 'The Geneva Manuscript', prefaced to his *Discourse on the Origin of Inequality*, he disavowed any law of nature that might have served as a foundation for rights.[36] In *Emile*, he proposed that the best foundation for rights is compassion.[37] But the limits of compassion would seem to have extended, in Rousseau's mind, no further than the boundaries of the canton, or at best the nation. In *Considerations on the Government of Poland*, he lamented that 'Today there are no longer Frenchmen, Germans, Spaniards, or even Englishmen; there are only Europeans . . . They are at home wherever there is money to steal or women to seduce.'[38]

Rousseau's thinking stands at the threshold of modern nationalism: the theory that in any properly constituted state, nations must impose sovereign power on themselves. The relevance of the distinction between the sovereignty of a people and the judgement of a people is that it may remind us that a people may be constituted by qualities other than the sameness of the religion practised, the morals observed and the language spoken. A people may be composed of citizens who respect one another for, among other things, their differences, and such a people will govern democratically not by asserting an assumed sovereign power but by respecting the judgements of citizens and by seeking agreements of judgements in order to reconcile citizens on matters of fundamental importance. In early modern theories of government there is, in short, an alternative to the theory of the sovereign power of peoples. This was the contribution of the theological politics of the Arminians and the Socinians, the defenders of the judgement of the people.

Notes

1. Knud Haakonssen, 'Protestant Natural Law Theory: A General Interpretation', in *New Essays on the History of Autonomy: A Collection Honoring J. B. Schneewind*, ed. Natalie Brender and Larry Krasnoff (Cambridge: Cambridge University Press, 2004), 92–109; *Enlightenments and Religions* (Athens: Institute for Neohellenic Research, 2010); 'Natural Jurisprudence and the Identity of the Scottish Enlightenment', in *Philosophy and Religion in Enlightenment Britain*, ed. Ruth Savage (Oxford: Oxford University Press, 2012), 258–77.
2. Richard Stauffer, 'Calvin', in *International Calvinism 1541–1715*, ed. Menna Prestwich (Oxford: Clarendon Press, 1985); William J. Bouwsma, *John Calvin: A Sixteenth-Century Portrait* (Oxford: Oxford University Press, 1988); Harro Hopfl, *The Christian Polity of John Calvin* (Cambridge: Cambridge University Press, 1982).
3. The identity of the author of *Vindiciae Contra Tyrannos* has been in dispute ever since publication of this important work in 1579. In a scrupulous scholarly examination of this question, it has been proposed that 'the most likely scenario is some form of close collaboration between [Hubert] Languet and [Philippe du Plessis-] Morrnay'. George Garnett, editor's introduction to his translation of *Vindiciae Contra Tyrranos: or, concerning the legitimate power of a prince over the people, and of the people over a prince* (Cambridge: Cambridge University Press, 1994), lxxvi.
4. George Buchanan, *De Jure Regni Apud Scotos* (1579) (London, 1721).
5. Lambert(us) Daneau (Danaeus), *Politices Christianae libri septem* (Geneva, 1596); Zacharias Ursinus, *Exercitationes theologicae* (Heidelberg, 1612); Johannes Althusius, *Politica Methodice Digesta* (1614), trans. and abridged by Frederick S. Carney as *The Politics of Johannes Althusius* (London: Eyre and Spottiswoode, 1965).

6. Samuel Rutherford, *Lex, Rex . . . with a Scriptural Confutation of the Ruinous Grounds of W. Barclay, H. Grotius, H. Arnisaeus, etc.* (London, 1644); Edward Gee, *The Divine Right and Originall of the Civill Magistrate from God* (London, 1698).

7. Ulric Huber, *De Jure Civitate libri tres* (Franeker, 1694 [1st edition 1672]). An English translation of Huber's *The Jurisprudence of my Time*, by Percival Gane, was published in Durban, South Africa (Butterworth and Co., 1939). Huber's work has been considered by E. H. Kossman to be the culmination of seventeenth-century Dutch constitutional thought (cited by G. O. Van de Klashorst, Hans Blom and E. O. G. Haitsma Mulier, *Bibliography of Dutch Seventeenth-Century Political Thought, an Annotated Inventory, 1581–1710* [Amsterdam: APA-Holland University Press, 1986], x). Huber's work is profoundly Calvinist in its theological orientation; see James Moore and Michael Silverthorne, 'Protestant theologies, limited sovereignties: natural law and conditions of union in the German Empire, the Netherlands and Great Britain', in *A Union for Empire: Political Thought and the Union of 1707*, ed. John Robertson (Cambridge: Cambridge University Press, 1995).

8. J. A. Dorner, *A History of Protestant Theology . . .*, translated by the Rev. George Robson and Sophie Taylor (Edinburgh, 1871), provides a *summary* of the more notable features of Arminian theology in Volume I, 415ff. On the history of the period, see Pieter Geyl, *The Netherlands in the Seventeenth Century, 1609–1648* (London: Cassell, 1961), 42ff. See also Th. Marius van Leeuwen, Keith D. Stanglin and Marijeke Tolsma, eds, *Arminius, Arminianism and Europe* (Leiden: Brill, 2009).

9. Hugo Grotius, *Mare Liberum* (1608), *The Freedom of the Seas, or the Right of the Dutch to take part in the East Indian Trade* (New York: Oxford University Press, 1916); *De Jure Praedae* (1868), *Commentary on the Law of Prize and Booty* (New York: Oceana Publications, 1964); *De Jure Belli ac Pacis* (1625), *The Rights of War and Peace* (London, 1738).

10. Hugo Grotius, *The Rights of War and Peace*, ed. Richard Tuck (Indianapolis: Liberty Fund, 2005), Book I, chapter III, section VIII, 260–76.

11. Hugo Grotius, *De Imperium summarum potestatum apud sacra* (1614), *Of the Authority of the Highest Powers about Sacred Things* (London, 1651).

12. Elisabeth Labrousse, *'Une foi, une loi, un roi?' La Revocation de l'Édit de Nantes* (Genève: Labor et Fides, 1985).

13. Edward Stillingfleet, *The Irenicum, A Weapon Salve for the Church's Wounds* (1661) (Philadelphia, 1842).

14. See G. H. Williams, ed., *The Polish Brethren* (Harvard Theological Studies XXX) (Missoula: Scholars Press, 1980), Documents III (Faustus Socinus et al.) and XII (John Krell, 'Two Books Touching One God the Father').

15. Edward Stillingfleet, *Sermons Preached on Several Occasions. To which a Discourse is Annexed Concerning the True Reason of the Sufferings of Christ Wherein Crellius his Answer to Grotius Is Considered* (London, 1673).

16. Ibid., 375.

17. Françoise Le Moal, 'Les idées politiques des frères polonais', *Politique*, X (1967), 7–43.

18. Stanislaw Kot, *Socinianism in Poland* (Boston: Starr King Press, 1957), 156.

19. Ibid., 196–204. See also Luisa Simonutti, 'Resistance, Obedience and Toleration: Przypkowski and Limborch', in *Socinianism and Arminianism: Antitrinitarians, Calvinists and Cultural Exchange in Seventeenth-Century Europe*, ed. Martin Mulsow and Ian Rohls (Leiden: Brill, 2005), 196–204.

20. John Marshall, 'Locke, Socinianism, "Socinianism" and Unitarianism', in *English Philosophy in the Age of Locke*, ed. M. A. Stewart (Oxford: Clarendon Press, 2000).

21. Sir Thomas Pope Blount, *Censura Celebriorum Authorum* (London: 1690), Item #358 in *The Library of John Locke*, ed. John Harrison and Peter Laslett (Oxford: Clarendon Press, 1971). The leaf appears at 663 of Locke's copy of Blount.

22. Richard Tuck, *Natural Rights Theories: Their Origin and Development* (Cambridge: Cambridge University Press, 1979), Chapter 7.

23. Richard Overton, *Mans Mortalitie* (1643), ed. Harold Fisch (Liverpool: Liverpool University Press, 1968).

24. James Moore, 'Theological Politics: A Study of the Reception of Locke's *Two Treatises of Government* in England and Scotland in the Early Eighteenth Century', in *John Locke and Immanuel Kant: Historical Reception, Contemporary Relevance*, ed. Martyn Thompson (Berlin: Duncker and Humblot, 1991).

25. James Moore and Michael Silverthorne, 'Protestant Theologies, Limited Sovereignties: Natural Law and Conditions of Union in the German empire, the Netherlands and Great Britain', in Roberston, ed., *A Union for Empire*.

26. John Locke, *Two Treatises of Government*, ed. Peter Laslett (Cambridge: Cambridge University Press, 1960); *The Leveller Tracts, 1647–1653*, ed. William Haller and Godfrey Davies (New York: Columbia University Press, 1944); *Leveller Manifestoes of the Puritan Revolution*, ed. Don M. Wolfe (1944) (New York: Humanities Press, 1967). Wolfe does not refer to the sovereignty of the people; he refers, more appropriately, to the 'People, the source of authority, a Leveller tenet'.

27. John Locke, *The Reasonableness of Christianity* (1695), ed. I. T. Ramsey (London: Adam and Charles Black, 1958).

28. Herbert Luthy, *From Calvin to Rousseau* (New York: Basic Books, 1970).

29. Jean-Jacques Rousseau, *The Social Contract and Discourses*, translated with an introduction by G. D. H. Cole (London: J. M. Dent and Sons, 1913), Book II, Ch. 7, 33.

30. Ibid., Book I, ch. 6, 13.

31. Ibid., Book III, ch. 11, 34, 78–9.

32. Ibid., Book IV, ch. 1, 85.

33. Ibid., Book IV, ch. 8, 113.

34. Jean-Jacques Rousseau, *Les Confessions: Edition Integrale ... par Ad. Van Bever* (Paris: Les Editions G. Cres it Cie, 1928), Vol. 2, 226: 'le Professeur Vernet, qui me tourna le dos, comme tous le monde, après que je lui eus donné des preuves d'attachement et de confiance qui l'auroient de toucher, si un théologien puvoit être touché de quelque chose'.

35. *Lettres écrites de la montagne par J. J. Rousseau* (Amsterdam, 1764), 247–8: 'Je ne suis pas le seul qui, discutant par abstraction des questions de politique, ait pu les traité avec quelque hardiesse; . . . je suis le seul qu'on punisse . . . Locke, Montesquieu, l'Abbé de Saint-Pierre, ont traité les mêmes matieres, & souvent avec la même liberté tout ou moins. Locke, en particulier, les a traité exactement dans les mêmes principes que moi. Tous trois sont nés sous des Rois, ont vécu tranquilles, & sont heroes dans leurs Pays. Vous savez comment j'ai été traité dans le mien.'

36. 'The Geneva Manuscript', in *On the Social Contract with Geneva Manuscript and Political Economy*, ed. Roger D. Masters, trans. Judith R. Masters (New York: St Martin's Press, 1978), 159.

37. Jean-Jacques Rousseau, *Emile or On Education*, Introduction, Translation and Notes by Allan Bloom (New York: Basic Books, 1979), 17–20 and 221ff.

38. 'Considerations Sur le Gouvernement de Pologne', in *The Political Writings of Jean-Jacques Rousseau*, ed. C. E. Vaughan (Oxford: Basil Blackwell, 1962), Vol. II, 432: 'Il n'y a plus aujourd'hui de Francais, d'Allemands, d'Espagnols, d'Anglais même, quoi qu'on dise, il n'y a que des Européens . . . Pourvu qu'ils trouvent de l'argent à voler et des femmes à corrompre, ils sont partout dans leur pays.'

2

Truth and Toleration in Early Modern Thought

Maria Rosa Antognazza

The issue discussed in this chapter is as topical today as it was in the early modern period.[1] The Reformation presented with heightened urgency the question of how to relate the system of beliefs and values regarded as fundamental by an established political community to alternative beliefs and values introduced by new groups and individuals. Through a discussion of the views on toleration advanced by some key early modern thinkers, this chapter will revisit different ways of addressing this problem, focusing on the relationship between truth and toleration. The comparison between different proposals in their historical and political contexts will reveal a variety of understandings of toleration and of models for its promotion. These understandings will be shown to be grounded in different conceptions of religious belief, of its relation to truth, and of human reason's ability to reach it. They will provide a map of possible models for addressing conflict in a pluralist world from which lessons of enduring relevance can be learnt.

The upshot of the chapter is that, from a theoretical point of view, the culprit in intolerance is not in itself belief in some objective truth. Some of the common assumptions about the denial of religious truth or the reduction of religious truth to a minimal creed as the best paths to universal toleration will be challenged. Likewise, the narrative centred on England and France which has led to the celebration of the heroes of a supposedly 'universal' toleration that still manages to exclude millions of people will be shown to be in need of significant revision. After discussing approaches based on the rights of the individual conscience and on the unknowability of religious truths above human reason, the chapter will finally investigate whether grounds for a general and principled theory of toleration can be found in religious truth itself and, following the tradition of natural law, in some universal truth discoverable by natural reason.

The Denial of Religious Truth as a Path to Toleration

With the outbreak of the Protestant reformation in the early sixteenth century, the clash between diverse religious communities and their systems of beliefs and values intensified. If the horror of early modern wars and persecutions ultimately resulted from disagreement about the objective truth of some fine points of theology, it is tempting to conclude that one straightforward way to avoid such disasters in the future would be the elimination of the very notion of religious truth. Such an elimination could be pursued in a number of ways. For instance, one could argue that there is some sort or another of objective truth, just not a *religious* one. Voltaire's witty depiction of religious sects in the *Lettres philosophiques* (1734) went a long way towards suggesting that the best basis for toleration was a thoroughgoing scepticism towards any claim to truth of alleged divine revelations. If there is any religious truth, Voltaire claimed in the article 'Foi' (Faith) of his *Dictionnaire philosophique* (1764), this is discovered by reason not by faith:

> It is evident to me that there is a necessary, eternal, supreme, intelligent being. This is not a matter of faith, but of reason. I have no merit in thinking that this eternal, infinite being, who is virtue, goodness itself, wants me to be good and virtuous. Faith consists in believing, not what appears to be true, but what appears to our understanding to be false.[2]

A more radical, and philosophically more original, denial of any pretence of faith to truth had already been proposed by Baruch Spinoza.[3] Spinoza had himself suffered religious persecution. Born in Amsterdam on 24 November 1632, he belonged to the Portuguese-Jewish community of so-called 'Marranos', that is, Jews forced to convert to Catholicism who had fled their country to be able to worship in accordance with Judaism. On 27 July 1656, the twenty-three-year-old Spinoza was 'excommunicated and expelled from the people of Israel' by the Sephardic community of Amsterdam. The *Cherem* (or ban) read in the synagogue 'cursed and damned' him in the harshest terms for his 'evil ways', 'abominable heresies' and 'monstrous deeds'. As a result, no one was to 'communicate with him, neither in writing, nor accord him any favour nor stay with him under the same roof nor come within four cubits in his vicinity; nor . . . read any treatise composed or written by him'.[4]

In the event, plenty of people did read the treatise published anonymously by Spinoza in 1670 in Amsterdam under the title of *Tractatus Theologico-Politicus*. Against the backdrop of the developing metaphysical theses of his *Ethica*,[5] Spinoza advocated the most radical separation between faith and reason, theology and philosophy. Truth, he argued, belongs only to philosophy; faith and theology are concerned instead only with obedience and piety:

> between faith and theology on the one side and philosophy on the other there is no relation and no affinity, a point which must now be apparent to everyone who knows the aims and bases of these two faculties, which are as far apart as can be. The aim of philosophy is, quite simply, truth, while the aim of faith, as we have abundantly shown, is nothing other than obedience and piety. Again, philosophy rests on the basis of universally valid axioms, and must be constructed by studying Nature alone, whereas faith is based on history and language, and must be derived only from Scripture and revelation.[6]

Thus, each person's faith 'is to be regarded as pious or impious not in respect of its truth or falsity, but as it is conducive to obedience or obstinacy'.[7] Faith was defined 'as the holding of certain beliefs about God such that, without these beliefs, there cannot be obedience to God'.[8] From this separation it followed, for Spinoza, that

> faith allows to every man the utmost freedom to philosophise, and he may hold whatever opinions he pleases on any subjects whatsoever without imputation of evil. It condemns as heretics and schismatics only those who teach such beliefs as promote obstinacy, hatred, strife and anger, while it regards as faithful only those who promote justice and charity to the best of their intellectual powers and capacity.[9]

In brief, provided that religious beliefs led to obedience and piety, it did not matter what one believed since, in any case, such beliefs did not have to do with truth. Nonetheless, Spinoza went on to identify the only dogmas which 'a catholic or universal faith' should contain, namely 'those dogmas which obedience to God *absolutely demands*, and without which such obedience is *absolutely impossible*'.[10] These dogmas

> must all be directed (as evidently follows from what we have demonstrated. . .) to this one end: that there is a Supreme Being who loves justice and charity, whom all must obey in order to be saved, and must worship by practising justice and charity to their neighbour. From this, all the tenets of faith can readily be determined, and they are simply as follows: 1. God, that is, a Supreme Being, exists, supremely just and merciful . . . 2. God is one alone. No one can doubt that this belief is

essential for complete devotion . . . 3. God is omnipresent . . . 4. God has supreme right and dominion over all things . . . All are required to obey him absolutely . . . 5. Worship of God and obedience to him consists solely in justice and charity, or love towards one's neighbour. 6. All who obey God by following this way of life, and only those, are saved . . . 7. God forgives repentant sinners . . .'[11]

Consistently with the divorce between faith and truth, the chief criterion for the identification of these dogmas was not their truth but their being conducive to obedience. Spinoza's philosophical investigation culminating in the *Ethica* made abundantly clear that God is not really a personal being with moral attributes such as justice and mercy. *Belief* in such a being, however, was to be commended since it led those incapable of reaching truth to charity and love of the neighbour, motivated by obedience to a God imagined as just and merciful.

One may wonder, however, to what extent such a divorce is in itself conducive to a general and principled theory of toleration. Spinoza clearly thought that there are plenty of truths which reason and philosophy can reach. They include, for instance, the claim that without such dogmas as the unicity of God 'obedience is absolutely impossible'. It seems, therefore, that polytheist religious beliefs are not acceptable even if it is not their *truth* which is at issue. In other words, whether there is, or there is not, such a thing as religious *truth* is in itself neutral as regards toleration since the matter at hand is not whether some position is, or is not, objectively true, but whether what one *believes* to be true can be tolerated.

In fact, if one turns to Spinoza's actual recommendations for the way in which a government should deal with religion, one finds that they are far from an inclusive policy of toleration of a plurality of religious beliefs and their expressions. According to Spinoza, 'it is established both by reason and experience that the divine law is entirely dependent on the decrees of rulers'. Therefore, 'sovereigns are the interpreters of religion and piety'.[12] It is 'the duty of the sovereign alone to decide what form piety towards one's neighbour should take, that is, in what way every man is required to obey God. . . . Therefore no one can practice piety aright nor obey God unless he obeys the decrees of the sovereign in all things.'[13] Thus, 'whether a man be a citizen or an alien, a person in private station or one holding command over others, if the sovereign condemns him to death or declares him an enemy, no subject is permitted to come to his assistance'.[14] As for the view that the sphere of competence of religious and civic authorities should be distinguished, Spinoza refused even to discuss the matter.[15]

Moreover, he claimed, 'devotion to one's country is the highest form of devotion'.[16] Before adopting Spinoza as the standard-bearer of modernity one should carefully consider the danger of transforming this 'devotion' into an authoritarian form of secular religion, attested only too often in the past and by no means absent from the present.

To be sure, Spinoza was clear that freedom of thought is inalienable. Hobbes had already drawn attention to the difference between inner faith (*fides*), which cannot be compelled, and external profession, which can (and, for Hobbes, should) be enforced as a merely external act of obedience to the worship prescribed by the sovereign.[17] In a similar way, Spinoza distinguished between 'inward worship of God' and 'outward forms of religion':

> I speak expressly of acts of piety and the outward forms of religion, not of piety itself and the inward worship of God, or of the means whereby the mind is inwardly led to worship God in sincerity of heart; for inward worship of God and piety itself belong to the sphere of individual right ... which cannot be transferred to another.[18]

However, as he would have known from his own Jewish upbringing (and, more specifically, from the Marranos experience), the public and socially shared worship of one's religious beliefs may well be integral to those very religious beliefs. It would not do, therefore, to say that anyone is completely free to believe whatever they wish and *inwardly* worship whichever way they want, if their religious beliefs include the need to worship publicly,[19] or if their beliefs require them to refrain from the public worship of false gods, even if prescribed by the sovereign. Likewise, one may believe that 'worship of God and obedience to him' *does not* consist 'solely in justice and charity, or love towards one's neighbour'[20] but also and *essentially* in praying five times per day facing Mecca. Spinoza could reply that 'as for other dogmas, every man should embrace those that he, being the best judge of himself, feels will do most to strengthen him in love of justice';[21] but this does not quite capture the point of view of such believers. For the crux of their disagreement is precisely with the status of *adiaphora* bestowed upon what they believe to be, on the contrary, a practice essential to God's worship – a disagreement entailing the rejection of one of the dogmas of the (allegedly) universal faith according to which 'worship of God and obedience to him consists *solely* in justice and charity'.

Once again, whether such belief belongs, or does not belong, in the realm of applicability of the notion of truth seems neutral to the question of whether such belief should be tolerated. Thus, should a sovereign allow, *in principle*, public worship which does not align with the religion of the land? It seems not, according to Spinoza. As for Hobbes, freedom of belief does not entail freedom of worship in which belief finds its expression. The enlightened philosopher who reads the *Ethica* will *know* that it does not matter in the least to engage in external acts of divine worship. The (seemingly largely fictional) followers of the 'universal' faith will *believe* it. The others will either be lucky enough to belong to the official state worship, or will be left with the (at least practical) intolerance of their beliefs. The view that 'truth' is an inapplicable category for any religious belief may even help account for Spinoza's willingness to allow government a free hand in curbing and shaping acceptable worship. The fact that the government in question should be, ideally, a democracy does not seem to help either. That is, the fact that the rules of official worship are dictated not by a monarch but by a government supported by a majority does not in itself advance the principled toleration of those who, precisely due to their status as minorities, are most in need of it.[22]

Historically, Spinoza's appeal to a drastically pared-down dogmatic content aimed not at truth but at a practical attitude was undoubtedly meant to promote the pacification of religious conflicts. His claim that 'religious law' is dependent on the decision of 'those who hold the sovereign power' as the sole 'interpreters of the divine law'[23] was historically aimed at thwarting, through the intervention of political authority, opposing religious factions which were threatening peace. As a universalisable rule, however, it was all too easily convertible into state-led religious repression and persecution.[24] In the Netherlands, the Remostrants (or Arminians) found at their own expense that Arminius and Grotius's political theories, entrusting the *summa potestas* to the magistrate also in religious matters, did not result in the religious tolerance they were hoping for.[25] In England, the religious intolerance which followed the restoration of the Stuarts eventually convinced Locke to abandon his early view that the *jus circa sacra* falls on the sovereign as *Conservator Pacis* and *Defensor Ecclesiae*.[26] In France, the same kind of absolutistic power of the sovereign advocated by Hobbes and Spinoza was used by Louis XIV to withdraw toleration from the Huguenots in the most notorious act of religious cleansing of the seventeenth century.

For someone prizing state security above all, the view that, in any case, religion does not have anything to do with truth may even provide a comforting thought in a state-led programme of religious homogenisation for the greater aim of stability.[27] At any rate, the denial of religious truth does not appear to provide, per se, a general and principled justification of toleration.

A possible way forward would be to argue that Spinoza did not go nearly far enough. One could maintain that, to lay the foundation of a truly tolerant society, he should have denied not only the existence of religious truth but the existence of any *objective* truth. A radically relativist position could take the view that 'truth' is a subjective notion or, at best, a merely social construct.

The denial of *any* objective truth, however, is hard to sustain. Is it, for instance, an objective truth that there is no objective truth? An easier path is to claim, more modestly, that we are unable to know whether there is any objective truth and that we have to settle, therefore, on some socially or politically agreed 'truths'. The sceptical tradition rejuvenated in the sixteenth and seventeenth centuries by authors such as Michel de Montaigne, Pierre Charron and François de la Mothe Le Vayer could be regarded as a more comprehensive basis for a dismantling of intolerant claims to objective truths.

But how does the status of being 'agreed truths' (as opposed to 'objective truths') advance toleration? Their status as 'agreed' seems in itself neutral in relation to toleration. How would it advance the cause of toleration to hold the socially agreed view (as opposed to its being objectively true) that atheists are incapable of morality and, therefore, cannot be tolerated? In fact, scepticism about rationally discoverable objective truths was not uncommonly paired with fideistic appeals to exclusive trust in revelation – and unmitigated fideism rarely proved to be a natural road to toleration.

The Appeal to the Individual Conscience as a Path to Toleration

A more promising option seems to stress that, whether or not there is some objective truth (and, in particular, some objective *religious* truth), what matters is the sincerity with which one holds what one believes to be the truth. As long as there is sincerity of conscience, there is no culpability, and therefore no ground for punishment, even if the belief which is held is objectively false. Moreover and most importantly, salvation requires sincerity of conscience. Conversely, hypocrisy is a sin. A forced conversion, far from compelling the converted to enter the gates of heaven, could jeopardise her eternal life even if the religion she embraced were the true one. As Locke crisply stated in his *Letter Concerning Toleration* published in 1689:

> No way whatsoever that I shall walk in, against the Dictates of my Conscience, will ever bring me to the Mansions of the Blessed . . . Faith only, and inward Sincerity, are the things that procure acceptance with God . . . In vain therefore do Princes compel their Subjects to come

into their Church-communion, under pretence of saving their Souls. If they believe, they will come of their own accord; if they believe not, their coming will nothing avail them ... And therefore, when all is done, they must be left to their own Consciences.[28]

This was a position particularly consonant with the Protestant's stress on the direct relationship of the individual with God, based on the reading of Scripture without the mediation of a church and its doctrinal authority. In Locke's immediate environment, the rights of the individual conscience were forcefully defended by the architects of Anglican Latitudinarianism. William Chillingworth's *Religion of Protestants* (1638) provided a clear and influential statement of the claim of an individual to direct access to the source of religious truth, the Bible,[29] while Benjamin Whichcote (whose sermons at St Lawrence Jewry in London were attended by Locke) preached the '*judicium discretionis*' as 'the foundation of Protestancy'.[30] During his exile in Holland in 1683–88, Locke encountered a similar emphasis on the individual conscience in the Remonstrant circles to which his new friend, the theologian Philipp van Limborch, belonged. Simon Episcopius had already stated in the Remostrants's *Confessio* that the only obligation of 'the conscience of the faithful' is to the 'divine word'.[31] Limborch's *Theologia Christiana* (1686) reiterated the freedom of believers in their reading of Scripture and denounced as 'a crime' the attempt to subject the individual conscience to anyone else but Jesus Christ.[32] Against the backdrop of the traditional doctrine of the distinction between the spiritual kingdom and the temporal kingdom,[33] these considerations played a key role in the development of Locke's conception of the church as a 'free and voluntary Society', which no one should be forced to enter, or in which no one should be forced to remain.[34] 'Liberty remains to Men in reference to their eternal salvation', Locke maintained in the *Letter Concerning Toleration*, 'and that is, that every one should do what he in his Conscience is perswaded to be acceptable to the Almighty'.[35]

From a different point of view, the focus on conscience converged with the traditional Roman Catholic distinction between material and formal heretics. According to this distinction (pressed especially by the Jesuits), those who believe objectively false doctrines in good conscience are merely material heretics and are not excluded from salvation. Only formal heretics, that is, those who consciously reject what they know to be the doctrine of the universal church, are worthy of damnation. As Leibniz pointed out to Roman Catholics, however, the latter appears to be a very rare case – if there is such a case at all. Those who reject the doctrines of the Roman Church do not in fact believe it to be the truly catholic or universal church. Roman Catholics ought therefore to extend also to them the category of material heretics.[36] Indeed, Leibniz noted with approbation, '[t]he Jesuits have maintained that invincible ignorance excuses, and that therefore the sincere conscience of anyone is always the last judge down here, *in conscientiae foro*'.[37] 'If someone were to embrace truth in bad conscience,' he went on to claim, 'he could be said a formal, and not a material heretic; and would be worthy of punishment although he did not err.' A bad conscience (*malum animum*), as opposed to a false belief, is what 'constitutes the formal nature of heresy'.[38]

Arguably, the strongest epistemological underpinning of the non-culpability of an erroneous conscience was the doctrine (embraced by both Locke and Leibniz) of the non-voluntariness of belief. '*Articles of Faith . . .* which are required only to be believed', Locke wrote in the *Letter Concerning Toleration*, 'cannot be imposed on any Church by the Law of the Land. For it is absurd that things should be enjoyed by Laws, which are not in men's power to perform. And to believe this or that to be true, does not depend upon our Will.'[39] In the *Essay Concerning Human Understanding*, which appeared the same year in which the *Letter Concerning Toleration* was published,[40] Locke provided the full epistemological grounding of this claim. 'As Knowledge, is no more arbitrary than Perception,' he explained, so 'Assent is no more in our Power than Knowledge. . . . And what upon full Examination I find most probable, I cannot deny my Assent to.'[41] The will can influence belief only obliquely, that is, we can stop our enquiry, or fail to attend to supporting evidence,[42] or turn 'our attention away from a disagreeable object so as to apply ourselves to something else which we find pleasing; so that by thinking further about the reasons for the side which we favour, we end up by believing it to be most likely'.[43] Culpability may lie in our refusal to attend to reasons and to employ fully our faculties of knowledge and judgement in the search of truth, but not in our believing what seems to us true on the basis of an attentive and honest consideration of the issue at hand.[44] Belief, therefore, cannot be coerced. As Leibniz wrote in 1693, giving as an example the still controversial case of the Copernican system:

> to believe or not to believe is not a voluntary thing. If I believe I see a manifest error, all the authority of the world could not change my view if this [authority] is not accompanied by some reasons capable of satisfying my difficulties or of overcoming them. And if the whole Church were to condemn the doctrine of the movement of the Earth, the able astronomers of this opinion [*ce sentiment*] could certainly dissimulate, but it would not be in their power to give up [their view].[45]

Amongst those embracing instead a Cartesian epistemology, according to which assent is given voluntarily, and error is squarely attributable to the will assenting to what is not clear and distinct,[46] it was easier to come to the view that 'all Errors are Acts of the Will, and consequently morally evil'.[47] As Pierre Bayle lucidly explained in his *Philosophical Commentary*, published in three parts and a supplement in 1686–88:

> The new Philosophers teach with a great deal of Reason, that what was formerly call'd the second Operation of the Understanding, is truly an Operation of the Will; that's to say, all the Judgements we make upon Objects, whether by affirming concerning 'em that they are such and such, or by denying, are Acts proceeding from the Soul, not as capable of perceiving and knowing, but as capable of willing. Whence it follows, that since Error consists in our affirming concerning Objects what does not belong to 'em, or in our denying what does, therefore every Error is an Act of the Will, and consequently voluntary.[48]

Bayle pointed out, however, that to conclude, from these epistemological premises, that 'all Error proceeds from a Source of Corruption, and consequently deserves Hell-Punishment' is absurd. Also within a Cartesian epistemological framework one could and should distinguish between culpable and non-culpable error. According to Bayle, 'there are Errors which are innocent tho voluntary'.[49] The difference between sinful and non-sinful error rested, for him, on the *motives* which have led the will to an erroneous judgement, not on the object presented by the understanding to the will for its judgement:

> All Error is sinful, when the Party is led into or entertain'd in it by any Principle of which one knows the Disorder, as a Love of Ease, a Spirit of Contradiction, Jealousy, Envy, Vanity. . . . But I dare not make the same Judgment on a Man, who without any secret Reserve, or hidden Motive whose Obliquity he perceives or knows . . . quits the best Sect of Christianity, to embrace one with a thousand Errors in it. . . . all the Morality which enters into the Acts of our Soul, proceeds from the Motives which determine it, with the Knowledge of the Cause, to direct these Acts towards certain Objects; . . . the Nature of the Objects makes no alteration, consider'd as it is in it self, but only as envisaged in the Understanding.[50]

Bayle recognised, however, that neither the affirmation of the non-culpability of an erroneous conscience, nor the non-voluntariness of belief supported by Locke and Leibniz, provided on their own a sufficient basis for a general theory of toleration. To start with, one had still to contend with the Augustinian view that, even if belief is not voluntary, some amount of coercion in religious matters is still justified. Measures ranging from compulsory attendance of Sunday classes to forced removal of children from their heretical parents to be raised in the true religion, so the argument went, may well result in sincere belief. As for the non-culpability of an erroneous conscience, this doctrine would oblige one to defend the non-culpability of the conscientious persecutor who sincerely believed he had a duty to spread his religion with all means, including burning heretics and engaging in holy war against the infidel.[51]

Toleration of All but the Intolerant as a Path to Toleration

One way to address the conscientious-persecutor objection would be to endorse toleration of all but the intolerant. Both Bayle and Locke proposed versions of this view. Bayle, who courageously affirmed in the *Philosophical Commentary* that 'Toleration is the thing in the world best fitted for retrieving the Golden Age, and producing a Harmonious Consort of different Voices',[52] went on in the same chapter to clarify:

> I extremely approve, and think it the indispensable Duty of Princes, if new Sects arise, who offer to insult the Ministers of the establish'd Religion, or offer the least Violence to those who persevere in the old way, to punish these Sectarys by all due and requisite methods, and even with Death if occasion be; because in this case they betray a persecuting Spirit, they break the Peace, and aim at the Subversion of political Laws.[53]

Locke, on his part, wrote in the *Essay Concerning Toleration* of 1667:

> Papists are not to enjoy the benefit of toleration because where they have power they thinke them selves bound to deny it to others. For it is unreasonable that any should have a free liberty of their religion, who doe not acknowledg it as a principle of theirs that noe body ought to persecute or molest an other because he dissents from him in religion. . . . It being impossible either by indulgence or severity to make Papists whilst Papists freinds to your government being enemys to it both in their principles &; interest, & therefor considering them as irreconcileable enemys of whose fidelity you can never be securd, whilst they owe a blinde obedience to an infalible pope, who has the keys of their consciences tied to his girdle, & can upon occasion dispense with all their oaths promises & the obligations they have to their prince espetially being an heritick.[54]

In the later *Letter Concerning Toleration*, Locke adopted a more nuanced stance towards Roman Catholics. On the one hand, he maintained that all speculative opinions should be tolerated if they have 'no manner of relation to the Civil Rights of Subjects', explicitly giving as an example the Roman Catholic belief in Eucharistic transubstantiation.[55] On the other hand, he reaffirmed that

> That Church can have no right to be tolerated by the Magistrate, which is constituted upon such a bottom, that all those who enter into it, do thereby, *ipso facto*, deliver themselves to the Protection and Service of another Prince. . . . Nor does the frivolous and fallacious distinction between the Court and the Church afford any remedy to this Inconvenience; especially when both the one and the other are equally subject to the absolute Authority of the same person.[56]

No one could miss the reference to Roman Catholics, especially when coupled with the mention, a few paragraphs earlier, of those 'who teach that *Faith is not to be kept with Heriticks*'[57] – a view widely denounced by Protestants as the underpinning of the revocation of the Edict of Nantes in 1685.[58]

Although adopting the rule of excluding from toleration only the intolerant may seem straightforward, it proved far from easy to determine in practice who counted as intolerant and therefore intolerable.[59] Bayle presumably did not intend to number Protestants amongst his 'new Sects', or Roman Catholics amongst 'those who persevere in the old way', but it is not difficult to imagine Pope Leo X thinking that Martin Luther was indeed 'insulting the Ministers of the establish'd Religion' by identifying the Roman Pontiff with the Anti-Christ, thereby 'breaking the Peace' and deserving punishment 'by all due and requisite methods'. Similarly, a peaceful atheist in Locke's England may well have been excused for thinking that the intolerant one was Locke in denying toleration to atheists on the ground of their alleged unfitness for moral life.[60] Spinoza's advice that it was only 'seditious opinions [opiniones seditiosae]' which should not be tolerated does not seem to help either, given that his own opinions were regarded as seditious (not least by his own Jewish community) and were, therefore, not tolerated.[61]

The exclusion of Roman Catholics from toleration, supported by both Bayle and Locke, is a particularly interesting example of the difficulty of disentangling contingent political reasons for regarding a certain religion as intolerable from a principled appraisal of any religion's claim to toleration.[62] This exclusion is not uncommonly mentioned en passant as an unremarkable matter of course. One may think that it went without saying that toleration could not be granted to masters of intolerance such as Louis XIV. This approach, however, arises less from a careful scrutiny of early modern Catholicism than from the deep-seated English tendency to conflate continental Europe with France. Half of continental Europe was Roman Catholic, and most of it regarded Louis XIV as their worst enemy. Indeed, the principal opponent of the Sun-King was another Roman Catholic, namely the Holy Roman Emperor, Leopold of Habsburg. Far from trying to use his power to deny toleration to Protestants (as Locke claimed Roman Catholic authorities always do), the Emperor sponsored talks for the reunification of Catholics and Protestants. Locke's claim that Roman Catholics could not in principle be trusted because of their oath of allegiance to a foreign power would have seemed wishful thinking to Pope Clement VII, cowering in the Castel St'Angelo as the armies of the Catholic Charles V sacked Rome in 1527. In Locke's days, his doctrine must have elicited a wry smile from the Popes of Louis XIV's reign, struggling as they were to maintain theological authority (let alone political power) over France against the push of Gallicanism, spearheaded by the preceptor to the Dauphin and Bishop of Meaux, Jacques-Bénigne Bossuet.

Locke, Bayle and other authors' perception of Roman Catholics, and of Jesuits in particular, as intolerable[63] was equally at odds with the experience of a subject of the Holy Roman Empire such as Leibniz. A Lutheran for all his life, Leibniz's intellectually most open patrons and friends included Roman Catholics, amongst them not a few Jesuits, whose efforts at the *propagatio fidei per scientiam* he greatly admired.[64] In the Empire, Roman Catholics such as the Archbishop of Mainz, Johann Philipp von Schönborn or Duke Johann Friedrich of Hanover, ran tolerant courts and organised ecumenical colloquia. Protestant Princes received Papal envoys with pomp and ceremony. Catholic and Protestant Electors sat together in the Imperial Diet in Regensburg, and the three main Christian confessions which they represented (Catholic, Lutheran and Calvinist) were not merely tolerated but legally guaranteed the right to practise their religion with the full protection of the law – a remarkable feat achieved through the adoption of a legal framework which suspended judgement on the truth claims of rival confessions as a means to ensure the cohabitation of competing doctrinal systems.[65]

In brief, viewed from the pluralistic perspective of the Holy Roman Empire rather than the fiercely anti-papal England after the Glorious Revolution, the exclusion from toleration of millions of Roman Catholics was not a minor omission.[66] Rather, it reflected a theory of toleration still heavily influenced by contingent political reasons which were universalised as grounds for a principled denial of toleration to Europe's largest and oldest religious denomination. Although it softened over the years, it is remarkable that Locke maintained a strong anti-Catholicism despite the fact that calls for the toleration of Catholics were spreading in his own circle, not least voiced by the very translator of his *Letter Concerning Toleration*, William Popple.[67] English Catholics such as John Gother did point out that it was a misrepresentation of Catholics to regard them as embracing the principle 'to keep no faith with any that are reputed heretics'.[68] Locke, on his part, in the *Letter Concerning Toleration*, still regarded Catholics as, strictly speaking, not even qualifying as heretics. To be a heretic, he reasoned, one has to belong to the same religion. Due to the reliance on authority and tradition as the rule of their faith, as opposed to *sola Scriptura*, Catholics were of another religion altogether than Protestants.[69] This view seems to suggest that Locke's resistance to granting toleration to Catholics was not based purely on political grounds (as it is commonly assumed) but also on theological reasons. The principle of Papal authority appears to have been regarded by both Locke and Bayle as an intrinsically intolerant 'forcing of conscience' which disqualified *ipso facto* Roman Catholicism from toleration. As Bayle wrote in the *Philosophical Commentary*:

> That Party which, if uppermost, wou'd tolerate no other, and wou'd force Conscience, ought not to be tolerated. Now such is the Church of *Rome*. Therefore it ought not to be tolerated. . . . there is this material difference between her [the Church of Rome] and us, that Non-Toleration on our part is depriv'd of that fearful Sting, that most odious and most criminal Quality which it has from Popery, to wit, the forcing of Conscience.[70]

Whether such judgement could be squared with the view that any belief (including, one may think, belief in a principle of authority in speculative doctrinal matters) had a right to be tolerated as long as it did not result in unlawful actions is at best doubtful. Moreover, as anyone familiar with Shi'a Imams and Sharia Law would know, and as Spinoza had experienced in Amsterdam in his own Jewish community, a principle of authority in religious matters which could be construed as a 'forcing of conscience' is far from unique to Roman Catholicism. Bayle had, of course, abundant reasons to denounce the appalling treatment to which he, his brother, and his co-religionists had been subjected at the hands of French Catholics. As a universalised approach, however, in different times and historical contexts, the line taken by Bayle and Locke against Roman Catholicism could well be used (for instance) for an exclusion of Islam from toleration in traditionally Christian countries. The early modern view that some individual Catholics might have been tolerable although their religion as a whole was not is no more helpful for a principled theory of toleration than the qualification by a present-day politician that 'some [Mexicans], I assume, are good people'.[71]

In any case, Locke concluded, the epithet of heretics ought instead to be reserved for those Protestants who made a 'Separation . . . in their Christian Communion, for Opinions not contained in the express words of Scripture', such as (it turned out) *Lutherans, Calvinists, Remonstrants, Anabatists*, and other Sects'.[72]

Religious Truth Minimalism as a Path to Toleration

This quite extraordinary claim, for a champion of toleration, that not only were Roman Catholics not of the same religion as Protestants, but most Protestant churches may as well qualify as heretical, should be read in the context of the doctrine of fundamental and non-fundamental articles of faith. This doctrine was well established in Protestant circles, and constituted the backbone of one of the most influential approaches to religious toleration in the early modern period – an approach built upon the reduction to a minimum of the religious truths required for qualifying as Christians.

The key claim – deeply grounded in the Protestant appeal to Scripture and its direct reading by the individual as the sole rule of faith – was that all articles of faith necessary to salvation must be contained *in terminis* in Scripture. Only these articles are fundamental, and only these articles need to be embraced to be part of the Christian community. Toleration should be extended to all Christians who hold them as true, leaving all the rest to the liberty of individual opinion and indifferent matters.

In the early modern period, versions of this doctrine went back at least as far as the humanist approach of Erasmus, who proposed a distinction between the 'childish trifles', or *adiaphora*, which divide the Church, and the essential core of Christianity, for the discovery of which it is necessary to go back to the sources of the Christian faith, the Gospels.[73] In Remonstrant circles, all main authors embraced versions of the distinction between fundamental and non-fundamental articles as a way to overcome ecclesiastical divisions, including Arminius, Grotius and Limborch.

Likewise, in the Anglican Church, the focus on the core truths of Christianity, leaving the rest to the freedom of opinion, shaped Latitudinarian theology. Influenced especially by the thought of Grotius, Chillingworth and the Cambridge Platonists, prominent Anglican divines such as Bishop Gilbert Burnet advocated this approach as the only solution to controversies which were tearing apart not only Catholics and Protestants but also Protestants amongst themselves.[74]

Although a promising way forward in principle, finding agreement on what counted as fundamental articles proved far from straightforward. To start with, the point which was controversial in the doctrine of fundamental and non-fundamental articles of faith was not that there are some articles which are more fundamental than others, but that *all* the articles which are fundamental are contained clearly and explicitly in Scripture. Catholic champions of controversies with Protestants such as the Bishops of Cologne, the brothers Adrian and Peter van Walenburch, were quick to note that Protestants could not agree even amongst themselves about which articles were fundamental: 'the Protestants read the Holy Scriptures diligently: nevertheless, they did not find a catalogue of necessary articles, which are proved sufficiently as such by Scripture alone. In establishing the necessary articles, Lutherans do not agree with Lutherans, nor Reformed with Reformed.'[75]

Grotius himself had a taste of the bitterness of the intra-Protestant disagreement denounced by the van Walenburchs. In his widely read *De Veritate Religionis Christianae* (1627), he defended the truth of the Christian religion on the basis of its conformity with natural reason as regards the existence of God and his attributes; its morally superior teaching; and the authenticity and lack of corruption of Scripture.[76] The treatise sailed virtually undisturbed through the Spanish and Venetian Inquisitions, and was applauded by eminent Roman Catholic clergymen, such as Cardinal Francesco Barberini. In this case it was hard-line Calvinists who loudly castigated Grotius as a crypto-Socinian for the absence in *De Veritate* of the doctrine of Trinity.[77] Grotius, for his part, had deemed it sufficient to show with historical and philological arguments the reliability of biblical texts, as befitting his view that Christians should turn directly to the reading of Scripture where all the necessary articles of faith were clearly and explicitly contained.

The acute frustration with divisions amongst Protestants on doctrinal issues was apparent in Locke's closing paragraphs of the *Letter Concerning Toleration* in which, as we have seen, he went so far as to regard Protestant churches as heretical if they insisted on requiring as necessary articles of faith which were not directly contained in Scripture. Locke himself turned to Scripture, rigorously applying his criterion. The result was *The Reasonableness of Christianity* of 1695. After a full immersion into the New Testament, Locke emerged with the view that the only article of faith expressly required to become a Christian was to recognise Jesus of Nazareth as the Messiah. Such minimalism proved too much even for otherwise fairly Latitudinarian theologians. It was soon Locke's turn to be accused of anti-trinitarianism by Anglican divines, including not only Calvinists and High Churchmen like John Edwards, but also Latitudinarians like Edward Stillingfleet.[78]

In fact, precisely the doctrine of the Trinity, which had already caused trouble for Grotius, was also at the centre of the dispute in England. Although strongly endorsed by Lutherans and Calvinists alike, was it really contained *in terminis* in Scripture? And if not, were traditionally defining doctrines of Christianity at risk, including the divinity of Jesus Christ? The predictable answer by the likes of Adrian and Peter van Walenburch was to fall back into the view of the Roman Church: '*Without the tradition of the unwritten Word of God, and the witness of the Church, it is not possible to know what the necessary articles are*. . . . Without tradition, and the witness of the Church, no one can know the true meaning of the necessary articles.'[79]

Be that as it may, *mutando mutandis*, Spinoza and Hobbes also suggested a minimalist approach to religious belief through the identification of the only dogmas which 'a catholic or universal faith' should contain.[80] 'The (*Unum Necessarium*) Onely Article of Faith, which the Scripture maketh simply Necessary to salvation,' Hobbes wrote in the *Leviathan*, 'is this, that *Jesus is the Christ*.'[81] Everything else, including which consequences follow or do not follow from this single article, was for the sovereign to regulate.[82]

Other authors of various stripes drew up their own lists of what was necessary and sufficient for salvation, increasingly basing the short-listing process on the reduction of religion to natural religion.[83] As early as 1633, Herbert of Cherbury's *De Veritate* identified five *notitiae communes* (common notions) in which was distilled the fundamental content of true religion. These common notions (namely, that there is a supreme Deity, that worship is due to this supreme Deity, that the most important aspect of this worship is a life of virtue and piety, that vices and wicked actions must be expiated by repentance, and that there is reward or punishment after this life), defined, in his view, the true catholic or universal church.[84] Since 'God, at all Times, has given Mankind sufficient Means, of knowing whatever he requires of them', Matthew Tindal argued in 1730, there was no need for churches and their worship. 'The Religion of Nature is an absolutely perfect Religion; and . . . external Revelation can neither add to, nor take from its Perfection.' On the contrary, any deviation from natural religion could only be detrimental to true religion.[85] Last but not least, Jean-Jacques Rousseau's idea of a minimalist 'civil religion' as a necessary basis for maintaining sovereignty stretched into the eighteenth century Hobbes's inheritance of a state entrusted with religion and morality.[86]

The question still to be answered, however, is whether the drastic reduction of the doctrinal content of religion is in itself always a remedy to intolerance. Requiring everyone to hold that only a certain minimal set of beliefs is sufficient is not *per se* tolerant of what (rightly or wrongly) religious believers actually believe to be essential to their relationship with

God, eternal life and so on. Their disagreement is precisely on whether their beliefs over and above the proposed minimal core of religious truth are dispensable. To answer that these beliefs can be tolerated as long as they are declared non-fundamental is tantamount to the non-toleration of these belief systems. If Moses's special mission, or the divinity of Christ, or the divine inspiration of the Qur'an, are essential tenets of true religion for their religious communities, it would not help to say that Moses, Christ and Mahoumet may well be three impostors since all acceptable religion is to be reduced to some minimal truths of natural reason.[87] In other words, the danger of intolerance is far from over even if it comes from an enlightened, minimalist religion which rules out as heretical, or unacceptable or dispensable, supposedly less enlightened religious beliefs and their manifestations. Paradoxically, by labelling all members of all mainstream confessions – Catholics and Protestants – heretics from the perspective of his minimalistic creed, Locke was being intolerant of the beliefs of a far larger share of the European population than the confessional churches were.

The Unknowability of Religious Truth as a Path to Toleration

A different approach which fully acknowledged revealed truths while opening a path to toleration was based on the traditional distinction between 'contrary to reason' and 'above reason'.[88] Both Locke and Leibniz defended an epistemic space for truths which are 'above reason', while adamantly rejecting the claim that there can be truths 'against reason'. Their religious epistemologies sharply distinguished between the sphere of knowledge and the sphere of belief and faith.[89] The proper epistemic sphere of faith was, for them, the sphere of truths 'above reason' which are not *known* but *believed*. Such beliefs, however, ought to be rationally justified. In other words, according to their conceptions of knowledge, truths 'above reason' are unknowable but not irrational.

This was not, however, a sceptical position, since the objective truth of revelation was fully endorsed.[90] In fact, according to Locke and Leibniz, there are also religious truths which are demonstrable (e.g. the existence of God) and which are, therefore, knowable. On the other hand, most religious truths cannot, in the strict sense of the term, be known, leading to a religious epistemology which is tolerant towards religious diversity.

Locke embedded these distinctions into the innovative conception of knowledge and its limits explored in the *Essay Concerning Human Understanding*. 'Knowledge', he wrote, 'seems to me to be nothing but *the perception of the connexion and agreement, or disagreement and repugnancy of any of our Ideas. In this alone it consists.*' It extends, therefore, only as far as we can perceive the agreement or disagreement between our ideas: 'Where this Perception is, there is Knowledge, and where it is not, there, though we may fancy, guess, or believe, yet we always come short of Knowledge.'[91]

When we cannot *perceive* (by intuition or demonstration) the agreement or disagreement amongst our ideas, we leave the sphere of knowledge and enter the sphere of judgement,[92] that is to say, we *judge* (as opposed to perceive) whether two or more ideas agree or disagree on the basis of testimony from others and external evidence. The sphere of judgement is the sphere of *belief*, defined by Locke as 'admitting, or receiving any Proposition for true, upon Arguments or Proofs that are found to perswade us to receive it as true, without certain Knowledge that it is so'. Such belief or assent has degrees that range 'from full *Assurance* and Confidence, quite down to *Conjecture, Doubt*, and *Distrust*'.[93]

When testimony is from God himself, Locke continued, that is, when we are confronted with divine Revelation, our assurance of the truth of what is revealed is as strong as any certainty we reach through knowledge:

> Besides those we have hitherto mentioned, there is one sort of Propositions that challenge the highest Degree of our Assent, upon bare Testimony, whether the thing proposed, agree or disagree with common Experience, and the ordinary course of Things, or no. The Reason whereof is, because the Testimony is of such an one, as cannot deceive, nor be deceived, and that is of God himself. This carries with it Assurance beyond Doubt, Evidence beyond Exception. This is called by a peculiar Name, *Revelation*, and our Assent to it, *Faith*: which as absolutely determines our Minds, and as perfectly excludes all wavering as our Knowledge it self; and we may as well doubt of our own Being, as we can, whether any Revelation from GOD be true. So that Faith is a setled and sure Principle of Assent and Assurance, and leaves no manner of room for Doubt or Hesitation.[94]

However, to avoid the risk of falling into religious fanaticism or 'enthusiasm', we must be sure that what we are believing is a genuine divine revelation, and not something absurd or irrational. Locke distinguished therefore between propositions which are 'according to reason', propositions which are 'against reason', and propositions which are 'above reason' – the latter constituting, as we have seen, the proper sphere of faith.[95]

Leibniz proposed a similar religious epistemology.[96] 'A truth will never be against reason,' we read in the *Theodicy*, 'and very far from a dogma fought and refuted by reason being incomprehensible, one can say that nothing is easier to comprehend nor more manifest than its absurdity.'[97] Truths, however, can be 'above reason':

what is against reason is against the absolutely certain and indispens-able truths; and what is above reason, is only against what one com-monly experiences or comprehends. . . . This distinction is certainly well founded. A truth is above reason, when our spirit (or even every created spirit) cannot comprehend it: and such is, in my opinion, the Holy Trinity; such are the miracles reserved to God alone, as, for exam-ple, the Creation; such is the choice of the order of the Universe, which depends on the Universal Harmony, and on the distinct knowledge of an infinite number of things at once.[98]

But how can we be assured that a proposition which we 'cannot compre-hend' is not merely 'above reason' but 'contrary to reason'? In other words, how can we test the non-contradictoriness of what is 'above reason'? Leibniz tackled the problem head-on, devising a sophisticated religious epistemol-ogy based on the notion of 'presumption'. For doctrines 'above reason', the non-contradictoriness of which cannot be positively demonstrated, one can appeal to a 'presumption' of possibility which remains valid until there is proof to the contrary, that is, until someone is able to demonstrate impossi-bility. In other words, putative revealed doctrines are 'innocent' until proved 'guilty'. A religious believer is rationally justified in holding them as true, on the basis of motives of credibility such as a long ecclesiastical tradition, until a proof of contradictoriness is forthcoming.[99]

Moreover, Leibniz noted, presumption 'has the power to shift the *onus probandi in adversarium*, or of charging the opponent with the burden of proof'.[100] The task of the believer is merely to respond to objections against the possibility of doctrines held as true, not to present positive arguments in their favour. The believer's bet is that there will be no proof of contra-dictoriness since an authentic revelation can never be against reason.[101] In principle, however, it cannot be excluded that what was believed to be true could in fact be demonstrated to be false, and hence not at all a divine revelation. 'Faith is to believe', Leibniz thought, and 'to believe is to hold as true [verum putare]' as opposed to *knowing* that something is true.[102] As in the case of *any* belief, the possibility of error could not be excluded.

In this way, belief in objective revealed truth was wedded by both Locke and Leibniz to a more humble epistemic attitude that does not claim knowl-edge of truths above reason, and 'does not imagine that reason is always on its side'.[103] After all, as Locke noted in the *Letter Concerning Toleration*, 'every Church is Orthodox to it self; to others, Erroneous or Heretical'.[104]

A more radical affirmation of the unknowability of religious truth was found in the author most directly targeted by the 'Preliminary Discourse' of Leibniz's *Theodicy*, namely, Pierre Bayle. In his enormously influential *Dictionaire historique et critique*, Bayle claimed that reason was 'a way which leads astray', 'a principle of destruction, and not of edification', due to its relentless doubting.[105] Most importantly, reason could not reconcile the presence of evil in the world with the Christian conception of an omnibenevolent, omniscient and omnipotent God.[106] This failure, however, was a consequence of human reason's weakness and should not result in a rejection of revelation. Rather, in matters of faith, reason should be silenced, fully acknowledging its incapacity to attain what is superior to it.[107] Religious truths handed down by revelation were not denied. But, as regards religion, no one could claim to *know* to be in possession of absolute truth.[108] Thus, in the *Philosophical Commentary*, Bayle argued:

> If you demand any thing further [than searching for the Truth], it's plain you demand that a Man shou'd fix his Love and Zeal on nothing but absolute Truth, known certainly and acknowled'g for such. Now it is impossible, in our present state, to know certainly that the Truth which to us appears such (I speak here of the Truths of Religion in particular, and not of the Propertys of Numbers, or the first Principles of Metaphysics, or Geometrical Demonstrations) is absolutely and really the Truth . . . It's plain then, we can't by any infallible Mark or Character distinguish what is really Truth when we believe it.[109]

This epistemic status of religious truth constituted one of the pillars of Bayle's doctrine of toleration.[110] Once acknowledged, Catholics and Protestants alike could no longer maintain that their use of coercion was justified by their knowledge of possessing truth. Given human epistemic weakness, the only thing one could do was to follow what sincerely *appeared* true to his/her individual conscience, abandoning any pretence of *knowledge* of absolute religious truths to be forced upon others.

Religious Truth as a Path to Toleration

Revealed truth embraced by faith could, in turn, help ground an inclusive theory of toleration. The aim of Bayle's massive *Philosophical Commentary* on the words of Luke 14:23, 'Compel them to come in, that my house may be full', was to reject a literal interpretation justifying religious coercion. Such an interpretation, Bayle argued, was contrary to the spirit of the Gospel:[111]

> The more any Religion requires the Heart, the Good-will, a Persuasion thorowly enlighten'd, and a reasonable Service, as the Gospel does, the farther it shou'd be from any kind of Constraint. I observe in the

second place, that the principal Character of Jesus Christ, and, if I may say it, the reigning Qualitys of His Soul, were Humility, Meekness, and Patience.[112]

Similar considerations contributed to reorienting Locke's views on toleration from their initial focus on juridical issues[113] to a more capacious theory appealing to the teaching of the New Testament itself. Especially in the context of the Protestant's emphasis on the direct reading of Scripture, this line of argument provided a path followed by a number of authors.

Toleration, Leibniz wrote, is 'necessary on account of the principle of Christian charity';[114] 'it is clear that the spirit of Christianity should lead to mildness'.[115] In his *Institutiones Theologicae* (1650–51), Episcopius had already proclaimed the opposition between coercion and 'the law of charity, clemency and grace' promulgated by Jesus Christ.[116] Revisiting the history of the Inquisition, Limborch denounced the contrariety of persecution to the original teaching of the Gospel and of the primitive Church. 'The precepts of the Gospel themselves', he noted, 'exude only charity and love; the Saviour calls charity his new precept, from which he wishes his disciples to be recognized. But nothing is more opposed to charity than the punishment of the errant.'[117] Locke's *Letter Concerning Toleration*, addressed to Limborch himself, took as its point of departure precisely this sort of theological consideration:

> I esteem that Toleration to be the chief Characteristical Mark of the True Church. For whatsoever some People boast of the Antiquity of Places and Names, or of the Pomp of their Outward Worship; Others, of the Reformation of their Discipline; All, of the Orthodoxy of their Faith; (for everyone is Orthodox to himself:) These things, and all others of this nature, are much rather Marks of Men striving for Power and Empire over one another, than of the Church of Christ. Let any one have never so true a Claim to all these things, yet if he be destitute of Charity, Meekness, and Good-will in general toward all Mankind, even to those that are not Christians, he is certainly yet short of being a true Christian himself.[118]

Universal Truth, Natural Law and Natural Rights as a Path to Toleration

On the other hand, a line of argument drawing on the teaching of the Gospel could not claim the universality needed for a theory of toleration fully sharable also by non-Christians. Many of the authors appealing to

Scripture to ground toleration, however, took the view that the relevant teaching of the Gospel agreed with natural reason. Thinkers like Leibniz would argue that since both reason and revelation come from God, there could be no opposition between them.[119] It was, therefore, far from surprising that universal moral truths discoverable by natural reason, and inscribed in human nature by its creator, were in conformity with the Gospel. Most importantly for the matter at hand, the Gospel's golden rule 'do to others what you would have them do to you',[120] in both its positive and negative formulations, endorsed a universal rule of reciprocity to which 'the light of nature, or the first principles of reason universally receiv'd' already led.[121]

'Universality' was precisely the missing element of other approaches to toleration. Only a theory grounded in universal truths, presented by the natural light of reason common to all human beings, could provide a truly general approach. This stress on universality was in itself nothing new to the early modern period. In fact, it constituted the backbone of medieval theories of natural law of which Thomas Aquinas had given the most influential formulation. In one of his writings, Aquinas stated that the natural law 'is nothing other than the light of intellect infused within us by God. Thanks to this, we know what must be done and what must be avoided. This light or this law has been given by God to creation.'[122]

As the 'participation in the rational creature of the eternal law' governing all creatures, the natural law was conceived by Aquinas as proper to human nature and as universally shared by humankind due to its being a manifestation of natural reason. 'The light of natural reason,' he concluded, 'whereby we discern what is good and what is evil, which is the sphere of pertinence of natural law, is nothing else than an imprint on us of the Divine light.'[123]

In the sixteenth and seventeenth centuries, the grounding of natural law in eternal reason was seized upon by Jesuit thought to stress the independence of natural law from any will, including the will of God.[124] Francisco Suarez distinguished between the 'content' and 'form' of natural law. Grotius went further, attempting to show that not only the 'content' of natural law would be valid independently of God's will; there could be an 'obligation' to follow the natural law even without God because the honouring of rights was good and obligatory in itself.[125] In this way, Grotius prepared the ground for a notion of the moral autonomy of human beings on which a general and principled theory of toleration could be founded. Independently of particular religious views, or even of any reference to God, human beings could appeal to a universal rule of reciprocity presented by the natural light of reason.[126]

It was this light, Bayle strongly argued, that unequivocally rejected a literal interpretation of Luke's *Compelle intrare*.[127] According to Bayle, although natural reason was unable to attain religious truths, it did know moral principles, notably 'the natural Idea of Equity' which regulated all other moral laws:

> We can never be assur'd of the truth of any thing farther than as agreeable to that primitive and universal Light, which God diffuses in the Souls of Men, and which infallibly and irresistibly draws on their Assent the moment they lend their Attention. . . . my meaning is, that all moral Laws, without exception, ought to be regulated by that natural Idea of Equity, which, as well as metaphysical Light, *enlightens every Man coming into the World*.[128]

Leibniz, on his part, appealed to the 'natural right [*droit naturelle*] to express what one believes to be the truth', to cast doubts on the 'right to proceed . . . to the ultimate punishment' even in the case of atheists. It is not opinions but actions which are punishable and, most importantly, it is 'natural right' which provides the criteria for identifying intolerable actions:

> it is against natural right to punish someone because he is of some opinion, no matter which, as opposed to punishing someone for some actions; *for the penalty for one who is mistaken is to be taught*. And again, I do not believe that we have the right to punish someone with corporal pains for actions which he undertakes in accordance with his opinion, and which he believes his conscience obligates him to perform, unless these actions are evil in themselves, manifestly contrary to natural right. As if someone wanted to trouble the State and use violence and poison for a religious principle.[129]

Conclusion

In theory and in practice, the paths to toleration are, and have been, many. The question of which one is most appropriate or most effective is inextricably interwoven with the historical contexts in which they were developed. Historically, each path has shown its merits but also its shortcomings. The chief aim of this paper has been to evaluate the relationship between truth and toleration. Its main conclusion is that, from a theoretical point of view, the culprit in intolerance is not in itself belief in some objective truth. On the contrary, the acknowledgement of some universal truth discoverable by natural reason and endorsed by many religious traditions, such as the 'golden rule' of reciprocity, can provide the underpinning of a general and principled theory of toleration.[130]

Moreover, it is not belief in some religious truth and in its objectivity which is per se intolerant. For instance, one may regard as a religious truth that religious coercion is against the spirit of the Gospel or that Jihad should be interpreted as an internal struggle to become good, not as a call to holy war against all infidels. Nor is the denial of religious truth in itself a path to toleration. Historically, it has also been a route to intolerance, as communist totalitarianisms of the twentieth century have shown. Vigilance seems also to be needed towards the rise of a 'liberal' or 'progressive' intolerance of those who do not align with every article of the latest liberal or progressive orthodoxy, such as (once upon a time) the minimalist civil religion of the Enlightenment. A liberal, tolerant society must retain the capacity to tolerate dissent towards its own liberal views, provided such dissent is expressed within the limits of what is 'lawful in the ordinary course of life'.[131] In sum, belief in truth or in some objective values is not in itself intolerant, but a tolerant society can never assume that possessing a 'very clear creed' gives it the right 'to enforce [its] values right across the spectrum'.[132]

Notes

1. This paper benefited from participation in a Liberty Fund conference on 'Liberty and Toleration in the Writing of Spinoza and Bayle' organised by Chandran Kukathas in June 2015. My thanks to conference participants, and especially to Chandran Kukathas and Rainer Forst, for thought-provoking exchanges. I am very grateful to Howard Hotson and Ian Hunter for their insightful feedback on a mature draft.

2. Voltaire, *Philosophical Dictionary*, trans. and ed. T. Besterman (Harmondsworth: Penguin, 1971), 208.

3. In an interesting article comparing Spinoza and Lodewijk Meyer on the issue of toleration, Jacqueline Lagrée argues that Spinoza, qua philosopher, is not especially tolerant since he thinks to know what is true. As a 'theologian', however, he can be tolerant precisely because he firmly separates theology (or faith) and truth. See Jacqueline Lagrée, 'Théologie et Tolérance: Louis Meyer et Spinoza', *Revue de théologie et de philosophie*, 134:1 (2002), 15–28.

4. Quoted from Steven Nadler, *Spinoza: A Life* (Cambridge: Cambridge University Press, 1999), 120–1.

5. The *Ethica* appeared posthumously in 1677 in Amsterdam, shortly after the death of Spinoza. Spinoza had been working on it since the early 1660s and the manuscript circulated amongst his friends.

6. Baruch Spinoza, *Tractatus Theologico-Politicus*, ch. 14 (hereafter TTP; quotations from Samuel Shirley's translation in Spinoza, *Complete Works* [Indianapolis: Hackett, 2002], 385–585, here 519).

7. TTP, ch. 14 (517).
8. TTP, ch. 14 (516).
9. TTP, ch. 14 (519).
10. TTP, ch. 14 (517). My emphasis.
11. TTP, ch. 14 (517–18).
12. TTP, ch. 19 (560). A similar position is supported by Thomas Hobbes, whose work had a seminal influence on Spinoza. According to Hobbes, the sovereign embodies the unity of church and state. The power and authority to withdraw or grant religious toleration rests solely on him. Toleration is not a good in itself but a means to an end, namely, it may be granted when needed for the preservation of peace. Moreover, the sovereign dictates the form of public worship, and has the right to shape the opinions of the citizens through whatever means are deemed necessary. Cf. Rainer Forst, *Toleration in Conflict: Past and Present*, trans. Ciaran Cronin (Cambridge: Cambridge University Press, 2013), 188–96.
13. TTP, ch. 19 (561).
14. TTP, ch. 19 (561).
15. TTP, ch. 19 (562): 'As for the arguments by which my opponents seek to separate religious right from civic right, maintaining that only the latter is vested in the sovereign while the former is vested in the universal church, these are of no account, being so trivial as not even to merit refutation.'
16. TTP, ch. 19 (560).
17. Thomas Hobbes, *Leviathan*, ed. Noel Malcolm (Oxford: Clarendon Press, 2012), Vol. 3, ch. 42, 782–7.
18. TTP, ch. 19 (558).
19. Cf. John Locke, *A Letter Concerning Toleration* (London: Awnsham Churchill, 1689), 9: 'A Church then I take to be a voluntary Society of Men, joining themselves together of their own accord, in order to the publick worshipping of God, in such manner as they judge acceptable to him, and effectual to the Salvation of their Souls'; 12: 'The End of a Religious Society . . . is the Publick Worship of God.' Cf. also 27–30.
20. TTP, ch. 14 (518).
21. TTP, ch. 14 (517).
22. Cf. Forst, *Toleration in Conflict*, 205–6.
23. TTP, ch. 19 (557–8).
24. Cf. the critical appraisal of Spinoza's position by Forst, *Toleration in Conflict*, 206: 'the price which Spinoza is ultimately willing to pay for the freedom to philosophise is a high one, specifically an absolute sovereign, a reduction of religious faith to ethical, and ultimately political, obedience, and restrictions on freedom of worship and action in general at the sole discretion of the sovereign'.
25. Cf. J. Arminius, *Articuli nonnulli*, 'De Magistratu', in *Opera theologica* (Leyden, 1629), 965, and H. Grotius's posthumous *De imperio Summarum Potestatum circa Sacra* (Paris, 1647).

26. Cf. Locke's *Treatises on Government* of 1660 and 1662.
27. Cf. Leibniz to Ernst von Hessen-Rheinfels, 4/14 August 1683 (in G. W. Leibniz, *Sämtliche Schriften und Briefe*, ed. the Academy of Sciences of Berlin, Series I–VIII (Darmstadt, Leipzig, Berlin, 1923ff.), Series I, Vol. 3, 534 (hereafter A, followed by series, volume and page).
28. Locke, *Letter Concerning Toleration*, 26–7. This was a translation by William Popple of the original Latin version which had appeared earlier that year in Holland. Cf. Leibniz's letter of March 1685 to Landgraf Ernst von Hessen-Rheinfels (a Catholic convert from Calvinism) (A I, 4, 352): 'One should not create hypocrites, since a true Huguenot is incomparably more worthy than a false Catholic and will sooner be saved without any doubt.' Unless otherwise stated, translations are my own.
29. William Chillingworth, *Religion of Protestants* (Oxford, 1638), 375–6.
30. Cf. Benjamin Whichcote, *Second Letter*, in Samuel Salter, ed., *Moral and Religious Aphorisms collected from the Manuscript Papers of . . . Whichcote* (London, 1753), 56.
31. See 'Praefatio' in *Confessio sive Declaratio, Sententiae Pastorum, qui in Foederato Belgio Remonstrantes vocantur*, 1622.
32. Cf. Philipp van Limborch, *Theologia Christiana* (Amsterdam, 1686), Book V, ch. 63, §25.
33. For the appropriation of the two-kingdoms doctrine in Luther, see Forst, *Toleration in Conflict*, esp. 118–21.
34. Locke, *Letter Concerning Toleration*, 9–10. Cf. Mario Sina, 'Tolleranza religiosa e scetticismo in Locke', *Vita e Pensiero*, 72:12 (1989), 839–50, and Mario Sina, 'Il cammino di Locke verso la dottrina della tolleranza religiosa', in Mario Sina, ed., *La tolleranza religiosa: indagini storiche e reflessioni filosofiche* (Milan: Vita e Pensiero, 1991), 199–222 (republished in Mario Sina, *Studi su John Locke* [Milan: Vita e Pensiero, 2015], 123–34 and 135–54).
35. Locke, *Letter Concerning Toleration*, 43. In the *Letter Concerning Toleration*, Locke limited the sphere of competence of the Magistrate to 'civil' or temporal interests, sharply excluding any extension to the care and salvation of souls (see especially 6–9).
36. A I, 6, 164–5: 'Mr Pellisson . . . admits amongst material heretics only those who do not know, or do not believe, that the dogmas in matter of faith which they reject are the doctrine of the Catholic Church. If we apply this restriction to the Protestants we will find that they are of this number. . . . So it is not easy to prove to the Protestants that they deny what they know to be decided by the Catholic Church.' Cf. also A I, 6, 165–8.
37. A I, 6, 94.
38. *De Haeresi Formali et Materiali*, c. 1695 (A IV, 6, 337). See also A I, 6, 141: 'One can be of bad faith and obstinate even if he asserts the truth, that is to say, when this is maintained without foundation on the basis of a bad principle.' Cf. Locke, *Letter Concerning Toleration*, 26–7.
39. Locke, *Letter Concerning Toleration*, 39. See also 7–9.

40. The first edition of Locke's *Essay* appeared at the end of 1689, although the title page bore 1690 as the year of publication.

41. John Locke, *An Essay Concerning Human Understanding*, ed. P. H. Nidditch [The Clarendon Edition of the Works of John Locke] (Oxford: Clarendon Press, 1975), 717 (Book IV, ch. 20, §16). Commenting on this paragraph, Leibniz noted in the *Nouveaux Essais* (trans. Peter Remnant and Jonathan Bennett [Cambridge: Cambridge University Press, 1981], 517): 'what we believe is never just what we want to believe but rather what we see as most likely'.

42. Locke, *Essay*, Book IV, ch. 20, §16 (Nidditch ed., 717): 'But though we cannot hinder our Knowledge, where the Agreement [of any two ideas] is once perceived; nor our Assent, where the Probability manifestly appears upon due Consideration of all the Measures of it: Yet *we can hinder both Knowledge and Assent, by stopping our Enquiry*, and not employing our Faculties in the search of any Truth.'

43. Leibniz, *Nouveaux Essais*, Book IV, ch. 20, §16 (Remnant and Bennett trans., 517).

44. Cf. Locke, *Essay*, Book IV, ch. 20. Leibniz wrote in 1684 (A I, 4, 320): 'opinion is not something which depends on the Empire of the will and which can be changed as one pleases'. In 1711, he reiterated: 'one does not have a belief at will, but acts as one wills; it is not the lack of belief which deserves properly to be punished' (G. W. Leibniz, *Die Philosophischen Schriften*, ed. C. I. Gerhardt, 7 vols [Berlin: Weidmannsche Buchhandlung, 1875–90], Vol. III, 415; hereafter GP, followed by volume and page).

45. G. W. Leibniz, *Textes inédits d'après les manuscrits de la Bibliothèque Provinciale de Hanovre*, ed. G. Grua, 2 vols (Paris: PUF, 1948), Vol. 1, 216.

46. Cf. Descartes, *Fourth Meditation*: 'the scope of the will is wider than that of the intellect; but instead of restricting it within the same limits, I extend its use to matters which I do not understand. Since the will is indifferent in such cases, it easily turns aside from what is true and good, and this is the source of my error and sin.' (René Descartes, *Oeuvres de Descartes*, ed. C. Adam and P. Tannery, 12 vols [Paris: Léopold Cerf, 1897–1910], Vol. VII, 58; trans. John Cottingham, Robert Stoothoff and Dugald Murdoch in *The Philosophical Writings of Descartes*, 3 vols [Cambridge: Cambridge University Press, 1984–1991], Vol. 2, 40–1.)

47. Pierre Bayle, *A Philosophical Commentary on These Words of the Gospel, Luke 14:23, 'Compel Them to Come In, That My House May Be Full'*, ed. John Kilcullen and Chandran Kukathas, general ed. Knud Haakonssen (Indianapolis: Liberty Fund, 2005), ch. xvii, 485.

48. Ibid., 486.

49. Ibid., 485–7.

50. Ibid., 488–91. See also 494.

51. Cf. ibid., 242, 333–4, 356–9, 360, 375–81, 512–14.

52. Ibid., 200.

53. Ibid., 202.
54. John Locke, *An Essay Concerning Toleration*, ed. Philip Milton and J. R. Milton [The Clarendon Edition of the Works of John Locke] (Oxford: Clarendon Press, 2006), 290–1. Cf. Bayle, *Philosophical Commentary*, 193–4.
55. Locke, *Letter Concerning Toleration*, 40: 'If a *Roman Catholick* believe that to be really the Body of Christ, which another man calls Bread, he does no injury thereby to his Neighbour.' Later in the *Letter*, 53–4, Locke maintained that public worship should be permitted to all 'those whose doctrine is peaceable'.
56. Ibid., 47.
57. Ibid., 46.
58. See John Marshall, *John Locke, Toleration and Early Enlightenment Culture* (Cambridge: Cambridge University Press, 2006), 691.
59. Marshall's monumental study documents in great detail that the justification of intolerance, with the attendant intolerant practices, was as widespread amongst Protestants as amongst Catholics. Not only followers of Luther and Calvin joined Catholics in defending their right to coerce and stop with whatever means the spread of 'heresy'; religious intolerance was theorised and practised also amongst Anglicans, Huguenots, the Dutch Reformed Church and even Polish Socinians, as shown by the imprisonment of Ferenc David for his Christological views.
60. See Locke, *Letter Concerning Toleration*, 48.
61. See TTP, ch. 20. Cf. Forst, *Toleration in Conflict*, 205: 'it is important to recognise how difficult it is to draw the boundary between the harmful, "seditious" opinions, which Spinoza wants to exclude on the grounds that they constitute actions, and the unorthodox opinions that the citizens are permitted to express.'
62. On the exclusion of Catholics from toleration, with particular reference to Bayle and Locke, cf. Marshall, *John Locke*, 681–94. It should be noted that in Locke as in Bayle there are also signs of a more nuanced attitude towards Catholics. In the *Philosophical Commentary*, while listing 'particular reasons against tolerating Papists', and advising that states with 'Papists still in their Bosom, shou'd keep 'em chain'd up like so many Lions ... by the severest Penal Laws', Bayle also supported the 'private Exercise of their Religion', including their right to raise children 'in their own Faith' (185, 191).
63. Cf. Marshall, *John Locke*, 689, 691.
64. They included Baron Johann Christian von Boineburg, Archbishop Johann Philipp von Schönborn, Duke Johann Friedrich of Hannover, Ernst von Hessen-Rheinfels, Bishop Rojas y Spinola, Joachim Bouvet and Bartholomew Des Bosses.
65. The suspension of religious truth claims as a condition of religious pluralism was also discussed among eighteenth-century German constitutional jurists. Such 'suspension' seems to constitute a form of legal agnosticism regarding religious truth which needs to be distinguished from the denial,

minimalisation or homogenisation of religious truth on the part of the state and its juridical system. I am grateful to Ian Hunter for drawing my attention to this issue.

66. Interestingly, the Holy Roman Empire is not included in the extensive study by Marshall on *John Locke, Toleration and Early Enlightenment Culture*, and Leibniz is barely mentioned in Forst's insightful volume *Toleration in Conflict*.

67. Cf. William Popple, *A Letter to Mr Penn* (London, 1688), and *Three Letters Tending to Demonstrate How the Security of This Nation Against All Future Persecution for Religion, Lys in the Abolishment of the Present Penal Laws . . . and the Establishment of a New Law for Universal Liberty of Conscience* (London, 1688). See Marshall, *John Locke*, 692.

68. See Gother's influential *A Papist Represented and Misrepresented* (London, 1685). Gother argued (41): 'Why therefore should the Character of the *Church* of *Rome* and her *Doctrine* be taken only from the loose Behaviour and wicked Crimes of such, who, tho' in Communion with her, yet live not according to her Direction? She teaches Holiness of life, Mercy to the Poor, Loyalty and Obedience to Princes, and the necessity of keeping the *Commandments*, (witness the many Books of Devotion and Direction, made *English* for Publick benefit, written originally by *Papists*,) and great numbers there are (God be prais'd) who practise this in their Lives.' Marshall, *Locke*, 691, notes that Gother's work reached its third edition by 1687.

69. See Locke, *Letter Concerning Toleration*, 57–8.

70. Bayle, *Philosophical Commentary*, 193–4. See also 214: '*a Religion which forces Conscience, does not deserve to be tolerated*'. Cf. Locke, *An Essay Concerning Toleration*, 291: Roman Catholics cannot be tolerated because 'they owe a blinde obedience to an infalible pope, who has the keys of their consciences tied to his girdle'. Another Protestant, Leibniz, who lived side-by-side with Catholics in the different political context of the Holy Roman Empire, and had stayed for an extended period in Rome, came instead to a different view: 'The authority of the pope which frightens off many people above all, in fact deters me least of all, since I believe that nothing can be understood as more useful to the Church than its correct use' (A VI, 4, 2286–7).

71. Donald Trump, speech announcing his candidacy for the Republican presidential nomination, New York (Manhattan), 16 June 2015.

72. See Locke, *Letter Concerning Toleration*, 58–60.

73. Cf. Forst, *Toleration in Conflict*, esp. 103–5, quoting Erasmus of Rotterdam, *The Manual of the Christian Knight* [Enchiridion militis christiani] (London: Methuen, 1905), 208–10.

74. See, for instance, a letter of 27 February 1699 by Gilbert Burnet to Leibniz (A I, 16, 595).

75. Adrian and Peter van Walenburch, *Tractatus Generales de Controversiis Fidei* (Cologne: I. W. Friess Jr., 1670), treatise III, section III, 23. The third treatise is devoted specifically to the problems raised by the distinction between

fundamental and non-fundamental articles of faith (*De Articulis Necessariis, Fundamentalibus, seu Essentialibus: Eorundemque Oppositis Erroribus*).

76. Cf. Maria Rosa Antognazza, 'Introduction', in Hugo Grotius, *The Truth of the Christian Religion. With Jean Le Clerc's Notes and Additions*, trans. John Clarke (1743), ed. Maria Rosa Antognazza, general ed. Knud Haakonssen (Indianapolis: Liberty Fund, 2012).

77. A notorious example of Calvinist intolerance towards anti-trinitarianism was the execution of Miguel Servetus in Geneva in 1553, supported by Calvin himself, who went on to justify persecution for the suppression of heresy.

78. Cf. John Edwards, *Some Thoughts concerning the several causes and occasions of Atheism* (London: J. Robinson and J. Wyat, 1695); John Edwards, *Socinianism Unmask'd* (London: J. Robinson, 1696); Edward Stillingfleet, *A Discourse in Vindication of the Doctrine of the Trinity* (London: Henry Mortlock, 1697).

79. Van Walenburch, *Tractatus Generales de Controversiis Fidei*, treatise III, section XVI, 30.

80. TTP, ch. 14 (517–18). As discussed above, the category of 'truth' does not really apply to these dogmas.

81. Hobbes, *Leviathan*, Vol. 3, 938.

82. Cf. ibid., Vol. 3, esp. 952. Cf. also Samuel Pufendorf's advocacy of the state's right to establish a uniform, official worship and creed (*De habitu religionis christianae ad vitam civilem*, 1687; English translation: *Of the Nature and Qualification of Religion in Reference to Civil Society*, trans. Jodocus Crull, ed. Simone Zurbuchen, general ed. Knud Haakonssen [Indianapolis: Liberty Fund, 2002], sec. 49: 'it is to be wished, and ought to be endeavoured, to procure but one Faith and Religion in a State . . . But where there is not any Publick Form of Religion established in a Commonwealth, it is the Sovereign's care, that one may be composed by the assistance of such as are well versed in the Holy Scripture, which being approved by the general consent of his Subjects, ought to be professed by all'; see also sec. 7).

83. Cf. for instance *A Summary Account of the Deists Religion*, in Charles Blount, *The Oracles of Reason* (London, 1693) and Matthew Tindal, *Christianity as old as the Creation: or, The Gospel, a republication of the Religion of Nature* (London, 1730).

84. Herbert of Cherbury, *De Veritate* (London, 1633), 208–21.

85. Tindal, *Christianity as old as the Creation*, v–vii.

86. See Forst, *Toleration in Conflict*, 196. Forst notes the shortcomings for toleration of a conception based on a minimalist approach which purchases 'the possibility of toleration at the price of declaring religious differences, which give rise to the most acrimonious conflicts, to be merely "incidental matters", and in addition at the risk of according primacy to the contents of one's own religion in a supposedly higher-order, neutral core religion. This is shown not least by where the limits of toleration are drawn, namely with those who do not agree with this core religion, and this concerns not just atheists' (262).

87. Cf. the famous *Traité des trois imposteurs* which circulated in manuscript form under various titles until it was published in Amsterdam in 1719.

88. A version of this distinction is found, for instance, in Thomas Aquinas (see *Summa contra Gentiles*, Book 1, ch. 7: 'The truth of reason is not contrary to the truth of the Christian faith. Although the truth of the Christian faith which we have discussed surpasses the capacity of human reason, nevertheless what reason is naturally endowed with cannot be contrary to that truth'). An extensive study tracking this distinction in early modern British thought is offered by Mario Sina, *L'avvento della ragione: 'Reason' and 'above Reason' dal razionalismo teologico inglese al deismo* (Milan: Vita e Pensiero, 1976).

89. It should be noted also that this distinction was not new. For instance, it is explicitly proposed by Thomas Aquinas in *Summa Theologiae* IIa IIae, q. 1, art. 4 and 5.

90. The claim that the roots of Locke's doctrine of toleration are to be found in theological scepticism is strongly rejected by Sina in 'Tolleranza religiosa e scetticismo in Locke'.

91. Locke, *Essay*, Book IV, ch. i, §2.

92. Locke, *Essay*, Book IV, ch. xiv, §4 (Nidditch ed., 653): 'Thus the Mind has two Faculties, conversant about Truth and Falshood. *First, Knowledge*, whereby it certainly perceives, and is undoubtedly satisfied of the Agreement or Disagreement of any *Ideas*. *Secondly, Judgment*, which is the putting *Ideas* together, or separating them from one another in the Mind, when their certain Agreement or Disagreement is not perceived, but *presumed* to be so; which is, as the Word imports, taken to be so before it certainly appears. And if it so unites, or separates them, as in Reality Things are, it is *right Judgment*.' Cf. also Locke, *Essay*, Book IV, ch. xv, §1.

93. Locke, *Essay*, Book IV, ch. xv, §2 and 3.

94. Locke, *Essay*, Book IV, ch. xvi, §14.

95. Cf. Locke, *Essay*, Book IV, ch. xvii, §23 and ch. xviii, §6.

96. For a full discussion see Maria Rosa Antognazza, 'Faith and Reason', in Maria Rosa Antognazza, ed., *The Oxford Handbook of Leibniz* (Oxford: Oxford University Press, 2018), and 'The Conformity of Faith with Reason in the "Discours Préliminaire" of the *Theodicy*', in Paul Rateau, ed., *Lectures et interprétations des Essais de théodicée de G. W. Leibniz* [*Studia Leibnitiana* Sonderhefte 40] (Stuttgart: Steiner, 2011), 231–45.

97. Leibniz, *Theodicy*, 'Preliminary Discourse', §23; GP VI, 64.

98. Ibid.

99. See, for instance, Leibniz's early *Defensio Trinitatis*: 'Until the contrary has been more adequately proved, we will continue to maintain this statement: that the Son and the Holy Spirit are he who is the one God' (A VI, 1, 520); 'Anything is presumed [to be] possible until the contrary is proved' (A VI, 1, 522). Later on, in 1702, Leibniz repeated (GP III, 444): 'possibility is always presumed and must be held as true until impossibility is proved.'

100. GP III, 444.
101. Cf. Thomas Aquinas, *Summa Theologiae* I, q. I, a. 8: 'since faith is based on infallible truth, and it is impossible to demonstrate the contrary of truth, it is evident that arguments brought against faith are not demonstrations but arguments that can be answered'.
102. *Commentatiuncula de judice controversiarum*, c. 1669–1670 (A VI, 1, 550).
103. Leibniz's remark on a letter by Paul Pellisson-Fontanier of 4 September 1690 (A I, 6, 87). Cf. Maria Rosa Antognazza, 'Leibniz and Religious Toleration: The Correspondence with Paul Pellisson-Fontanier', *American Catholic Philosophical Quarterly*, 76:4 (2002), 601–22, and 'Leibniz's doctrine of toleration: philosophical, theological and pragmatic reasons', in J. Parkin and T. Stanton, eds, *Natural Law and Toleration in the Early Enlightenment* (Oxford: Oxford University Press – The British Academy, 2013), 139–64.
104. Locke, *Letter Concerning Toleration*, 16.
105. Pierre Bayle, *Dictionaire historique et critique*, 2nd edition (Rotterdam, 1702), 2432 and 2026.
106. Cf. Bayle, *Dictionaire*, article 'Manichéens', D.
107. Cf. for instance Bayle, *Dictionaire*, articles 'Bunel', E; 'Pyrrhon', G.
108. Forst, *Toleration in Conflict*, argues against a sceptical interpretation of Bayle's position, tentatively suggesting the neologism of 'rational fideism' (257, footnote 183). His conclusion is that 'Bayle was the first thinker to develop this notion of "reasonable faith" in such a consistent way' (257). It seems to me, however, that Locke and Leibniz developed robustly consistent notions of 'reasonable faith' without sliding, like Bayle (at least as interpreted by Forst), into fideism and its possible 'enthusiastic' excesses (to use Locke's phrase). A different interpretation of Bayle that emphasises his rationalism is proposed by Antony McKenna, *Études sur Pierre Bayle* (Paris: Honoré Champion, 2015). According to McKenna, Bayle was a staunch rationalist in the field of ethics who sought to demonstrate that Christian faith is irremediably irrational. See especially 'Pierre Bayle historien de la philosophie', *Lexicon philosophicum*, 5 (2017), 21–59; cf. also Michael W. Hickson, 'Bayle on Évidence as a Criterion of Truth', and Kristen Irwin, 'Les implications du scepticisme modéré académique de Bayle pour la connaissance morale', in Antony McKenna and Pierre-François Moreau, eds, *Libertinage et philosophie à l'époque classique*, n. 14, *La pensée de Pierre Bayle* (Paris: Classiques Garnier, 2017), 105–25 and 127–46.
109. Bayle, *Philosophical Commentary*, 261–2. See also 263, 272.
110. Cf. Forst, *Toleration in Conflict*, 238–65.
111. See in particular Bayle, *Philosophical Commentary*, part I, ch. 3.
112. Bayle, *Philosophical Commentary*, 83. See also 84.
113. Cf. the two early *Treatises on Government*.
114. A I, 14, 691.
115. A I, 4, 341. Cf. also *Oeuvres de Leibniz*, ed. A. Foucher de Careil, 2nd edition (Paris, 1869), Vol. 2, 173: 'Charity (which is the highest of virtues), the

love of peace, so recommended by Jesus-Christ, and the proofs of Christian moderation given for such a long time by this side [i.e. the Lutherans], demand that we omit nothing now which is in our power and which could serve to remove or diminish the unfortunate schism which is so harmful to souls and which has rent the West for over a century and a half.'

116. Cf. Episcopius, *Institutiones Theologicae*, Book III, ch. 9, 2, in Episcopius, *Opera Theologica*, I/I, 2nd edition (London, 1678), 104.

117. Philipp van Limborch, *Historia Inquisitionis* (Amsterdam, 1692), 2.

118. Locke, *Letter Concerning Toleration*, 1. The examples of Locke and Limborch show with particular clarity how religious truth minimalism of a doctrinal sort could be combined with appeals to the model of Christ as the bearer of a morally edifying religious truth which supports toleration.

119. *Theodicy*, 'Preliminary Discourse', §§39, 61. This thesis, of course, was not novel. See for instance Aquinas, *Summa Contra Gentiles*, Book 1, chs 3–8.

120. See Matthew 7:12 and Luke 6:31. The negative form 'do not do to others what you would not like done to yourselves' is attested in Tob. 4:15 and in second-century Christian documents. The 'golden rule' is found also in various forms in Jewish, Ancient Greek and Roman writings, and in Confucius.

121. Cf. Bayle, *Philosophical Commentary*, 65 and part I, ch. 3. Forst, *Toleration in Conflict*, identifies this rule of reciprocity, independent of particular religious assumptions, as one of the two complementary elements of a novel normative-epistemological foundation by Bayle of a general theory of toleration (see esp. 246–50, 255, 264). In their introduction to Bayle's *Philosophical Commentary*, John Kilcullen and Chandran Kukatas stress that 'the mark of Bayle's intellectual style is his energetic effort to argue from "common principles"' (xxi) and that, for him, 'natural law must guide the interpretation of religious doctrine' (xvi).

122. Thomas Aquinas, *In Duo Praecepta Caritatis et in Decem Legis Praecepta Expositio*, c. I, in *Opuscola Theologica*, Vol. II: *De re spirituali* (Turin and Rome: Marietti, 1954), 245.

123. Thomas Aquinas, *Summa Theologiae* Ia-IIae, q. 91, a. 2. The key texts for the formulation of Aquinas's theory of natural law are questions 90–7 in *Summa Theologiae* Ia-IIae. See especially question 94.

124. See Knud Haakonssen, 'Natural law', in Lawrence C. Becker and Charlotte B. Becker, eds, *Encyclopedia of Ethics* (New York: Routledge, 2001), Vol. II, and Knud Haakonssen, *Natural Law and Moral Philosophy: From Grotius to the Scottish Enlightenment* (Cambridge: Cambridge University Press, 1996), ch. 1.

125. See Haakonssen, *Natural Law and Moral Philosophy*, 26–9. For an illuminating account of the journey from natural law to natural rights as underived fundamental moral features of human beings, see ibid., ch. 10. For Grotius's definition of right/rights (*jus/jura*) see Hugo Grotius, *De jure belli ac pacis* [*The law of war and peace*], I.1.iii–iv and ix.

126. On the importance of the notions of moral autonomy and reciprocity see Forst, *Toleration in Conflict*, esp. 246–7, 427–8.
127. See Bayle, *Philosophical Commentary*, ch. 1. Cf. also 84.
128. Ibid., 69.
129. Leibniz to Ernst von Hessen-Rheinfels, 4/14 August 1683 (A I, 3, 535).
130. This is not to deny that appeal to universal truths and natural law could also be used to support intolerance.
131. Locke, *Letter Concerning Toleration*, 33.
132. David Cameron, 20 July 2015, speaking in Birmingham as British Prime Minister.

3

The History of the History of Ethics and Emblematic Passages

Aaron Garrett

The History of the History of Ethics

Knud Haakonssen has suggested in the opening chapter of the *Cambridge History of Eighteenth-Century Philosophy* that the history of the history of philosophy should be far more central to the history of philosophy than it currently is.[1] Investigating and understanding how texts have been organised, edited, made available (or not), advocated for by their boosters, denigrated by their opponents with terms like 'Hobbist' or 'Schoolman', and above all offered as curricula for the education of philosophers and historians of philosophy allows us to get some purchase on what past philosophy means for us (as well as why other philosophy is ignored or even ceases to be philosophy). Beyond tracing influence and reception, the history of the history of philosophy involves reflecting on what roads are taken or not taken, why, and what is at stake. And through the practice of the history of the history of philosophy we discover why we have the history we have and what (in part) this history is.

More concretely I mean that Locke, when invoked by contemporary philosophers and historians of philosophy, is a grouping of passages and texts, a bundle of philosophical issues and literature on these philosophical issues by other philosophers and historians. At the core of 'John Locke' for philosophers is perhaps empiricism, personal identity, clusters of positions in the theory of perception and knowledge, the primary quality/secondary quality distinction, the nominal and real essences, etc., as well as particular problems and examples (e.g., Molyneux's problem), and other philosophers such as Hume, Berkeley, Mackie, et al. (understood again as bundles of texts and problems), etc. And, depending on who is invoking Locke, contractualism, classical liberalism, and property, Malebranche, Catherine Cockburn Trotter, Thomas Reid, may be more or less peripheral. Further out are toleration, positions in religion, the philosophy of education, and issues and positions even more remote. Even when applied to passages, texts and problems outside of these restricted contexts by very skilled and knowledgeable historians, they often guide how 'Locke' is taken up and understood. This will vary in different national and academic contexts, but that it happens is beyond dispute. With a wide-ranging figure like Locke who is canonical in many areas, what is viewed as centre and what as periphery reflects the priorities of the discipline as a whole.

In this chapter I will first reflect quite generally on the genealogy connected with this process. I will then consider more particularly some of the special features of how this process occurs in ethics or moral philosophy. In the second part of the essay I will turn to a particular case – a passage from Joseph Butler. I'm interested in this particular case because one worry about our practices as historians of philosophy is that due to our tacit reliance on these heuristic maps, and other issues I will discuss in what follows, it becomes very difficult to recognise when philosophers are failing to see issues that we find compelling for both philosophical and non-philosophical reasons. In other words, a particular reading of a passage can, indeed often does, fuel the historical importance of a particular passage which in turn reinforces not only that this is the passage to read in order to understand the importance of the philosopher, but also a restricted range of readings.

I

It may seem that I am targeting historians of philosophy who focus on the rational reconstruction of arguments. I am not. What I will describe is, to my mind, ubiquitous, generally irresistible (although locally resistable), and holds of all sorts of historians of philosophy in philosophy departments – myself included. Indeed, I think that many historians of philosophy who are oriented towards casting arguments as clearly as possible in contemporary philosophical terms and then evaluating them tend to avoid two problems that many more 'contextual' historians sometimes do not. They are open to the fact that problems and arguments might be more interesting than figures and schools and thus they avoid advocating for a particular historical figure (I will discuss this further below). Relatedly, they often accept that arguments need not be defended at all costs, that they are often bad or false or even not philosophical by contemporary standards. This doesn't mean that I'm advocating for this approach either. Rather, I want to underscore that what follows is not directed at one particular approach.

Most historians of philosophy are acutely and personally aware that the way they present history, and the history they are given to present, is indebted to the process of organisation and selection I began to describe above. We produce syllabi and anthologies that require us to make choices of inclusion and exclusion. And we are critically aware of the process, to a degree. For example, many or even most of the historians of philosophy I know who teach the standard 'British Empiricism', 'Continental Rationalism' and 'History of Modern Philosophy' courses offered in many philosophy departments try to modify the structure of their course to include figures other than Descartes, Hume, Locke and Leibniz as well as a broader range of topics and problems – some non-white male authors, some moral or political philosophy, a few issues connected with theodicy, etc.

But the basic framework is relatively set, by curricular requirements imposed by the institutions we teach in and work in, or self-imposed by our sense of what is the core knowledge that needs to be acquired. In his discussions of the histories of philosophy produced by Reid and Kant (and by Kantian and Reidian historians), Haakonssen suggests that these frameworks are the result of presenting the history of philosophy as wholly or pivotally concerned with a restricted set of problems and subject areas – for example problems in the theory of knowledge as understood by some Scottish and German philosophers in the second half of the eighteenth century – that place the interests and achievements of a few philosophers – Reid and Kant – as *leitfaden* and *telos* of Philosophy writ large. As Reidean and Kantian identified philosophers became powerful, trained pedagogues, and began to structure curricula, the writing of the history of philosophy began to reflect this in the problems discussed and in the philosophical ancestors and antecedents offered.[2] This process also determined and determines how canonical passages, sentences, phrases and bits of text are understood in relation to these histories and figures, and how the emblematic importance of these passages – as bearers of weighty problems or decisive arguments – provides warrant for the reader not reflecting on their history. I will discuss this at greater length in a moment.

First though, I am describing the way in which contemporary trends in the disciplines clearly have and have had a great effect on what historians choose to write about and how they choose to present what they choose to write about. The reasons for this are not mysterious. Most historians of philosophy are educated in contemporary philosophy in addition to their specialties, and this informs – sometimes decisively – how they think about their discipline. For example, what draws historians of philosophy to study their discipline is often closely connected with their interests in contemporary philosophy.[3] If they are trained in history within a philosophy department it is often tailored to and in service of these philosophical interests. Generally, they find the subject matter interesting *qua* philosophers, and what they find interesting is often a consequence of their orientations *towards* contemporary philosophy or contemporary presentations of figures and problems in the history of philosophy.

For example, if my interest in the history of ethics is in tandem with an interest in contemporary virtue ethics I will be motivated to investigate and present the past on the basis of a contemporary philosophical position that I use to orient myself towards, restrict, cull, organise and make sense of past texts. I may believe that the philosophical position I hold, or more precisely the cluster of beliefs I have about virtues and happiness and so forth, was held by Aristotle, although more likely I am wholly aware that Aristotle's natural slave argument or his discussions of women and so forth are not positions I maintain. But it is still likely that I hold 1) that there is a core view called Aristotelian virtue ethics that is compatible with my beliefs despite some notable differences, 2) this is the 'philosophical' core of the position held by Aristotle, and 3) how I exclude elements from the core or even the passages that jump out at me as important are likely a consequence of my beliefs qua contemporary philosopher.[4]

I do not wish to deny that moral philosophers have been influenced by Aristotle's actual views or by reading Aristotle. Rather, there is a culling of acceptable views or interesting contents in connection to preferred elements of contemporary positions – in this case 'virtue ethics', as a response by some mid-twentieth-century (and later) moral philosophers to what they saw as limitations and defects in the range of contemporary positions in moral philosophy – which often goes hand in hand with advocacy for the position. And I wish to suggest that this is happening in tandem with an accretive process whereby the choices that come to mind – emblematic passages, authors and problems – are further restricted by the repeated iteration of this process: the accretion of the stock of the history of philosophy according to the needs and interests of historians of philosophy are often organised – knowingly or not – around the views and interests of well-recognised and/or powerful philosophers. Because historians of philosophy tend, and have tended, to be interested in philosophy as understood by their contemporaries, because of the esteem they and others have for their most brilliant philosophical contemporaries, and because of the importance these contemporaries have in orienting philosophical interests, the ways in which philosophers who have great stature in the profession have represented their history has a far more pervasive and long-lasting influence on this process than how historians who are not well-known or powerful philosophers have presented it. We just take the end result of this process as 'what's philosophically interesting'.

There is also, in parallel, an advocacy for the positions – either for the importance of the philosophers and problems, or for these positions as true and philosophical. Consider how rare it is to meet a historian of philosophy who does not believe that they hold a variant of the views expressed by the philosophers they work on. Again it is obvious why this is the case. Historians of philosophy are drawn to certain views minimally because they think they are philosophically interesting, but also often because they hold them to be true. Furthermore they need to demonstrate to their colleagues who have no historical interests, or sideline historical interests, as well as to other historians who work on different areas, that what they have invested so much time and effort in is worthwhile. I'm not suggesting bad faith, far from it. Rather, I am suggesting that there is a tendency to defend one's historical choices philosophically, that this leads to advocacy for an author or a corpus *as* history, and that the most successful language of advocacy is the language that one's fellow philosophers recognise.

What I am describing is often not so active. There is a stock of choices, the stock is very interesting, and there's often little motivation to go beyond the stock and ask about the content and structures of one's own biases (what's interesting) and motivation (why). The literature on canonical topics – Hume on causation for example – is often sophisticated and deep, and deeply historically intertwined with issues of contemporary interest. I would say that topics like this have been selected for reasons of their intrinsic philosophical interest, but in many cases it is difficult to separate that interest from the history that has followed from them, and difficult to separate all of this from what philosophy is (they are central to what philosophy is) and how it changes as such. Indeed it is a kind of history of philosophy as contemporary philosophy. One does have to narrow one's interests, obviously, but it seems how and why one narrows one's interests, and how much of this involves extra-disciplinary and arbitrary factors, are worth some reflection. The history of the history of philosophy provides one axis for reflecting on this process.

There are other influencing factors that reinforce what I am describing, of which I will only mention a few. The avenues of publication taken seriously by philosophers in general, and the comparative respect afforded publications in top-tier non-historically oriented journals versus historically oriented journals, both militate against certain types of historical work. Top-tier generalist journals tend to be tipped, understandably, towards history of philosophy that may be of interest to their more

general (and thus non-historical specialist) readership and so is focused
on the sorts of problems and topoi I have mentioned. A related effect
is the consequence of the comparative esteem afforded different areas
of contemporary philosophy: aesthetics versus metaphysics for example.
Furthermore, there are factors like professional esteem which has a direct
effect on jobs and appointments, the aforementioned esteem in the eyes
of one's non-historian colleagues which has an effect on salary and quality of life, and concern for doctoral students' future prospects if they do
not work within a recognisably philosophical area and exhibit some of
their skills in terms of contemporary philosophy. The result is a kind of
self-selection and also self-censorship. This is not to suggest that views
do not change; they obviously do. But the changes are often driven by
contemporary philosophical views.

Some of these are endemic to academia as a profession and some are
special problems in philosophy. But there are two special problems in the
history of ethics that I would point to. First, moral philosophers often have a
different attitude towards the positions they adopt and their arguments than
philosophers in other areas. If I write a paper on a view in metaphysics – for
example arguing that anything can form a composite with any other thing
and this composite gives rise to a new thing – there may be a great deal at
stake intellectually, but less personally. If you criticise my view I may be thin-
skinned and I may feel you've attacked my abilities as a philosopher. But the
views of moral philosophers are often more intimately connected with how
they understand themselves not as philosophers but as persons. They reflect
what they understand to be a worthwhile moral agent, character or action.
To undermine moral views is sometimes to suggest that the holder of the
view is morally questionable or a less than decent person – as for example in
repugnance objections.

Why I think this is the case is connected with a further restriction.
Contemporary moral philosophy is often subject to a restriction on worthwhile philosophical positions by the intuitions and beliefs of a very narrow
group – academics (mostly white, developed-world, male) – about morals
and moral subjects worth pursuing independently of philosophical reflection. This is not a recent phenomenon, but I would like to suggest that one
of the consequences is that what is considered to be an ethical position or
a figure worth investigating in the history of moral philosophy may be both
more restricted and more contingent than what is considered to be a position worth investigating in metaphysics or philosophy of mind.

I suggest that as a consequence this makes what is tendered as plausibly
'moral philosophy' even more restricted in a given era than in other 'core'

areas of philosophy. Think for example of times when moral philosophy was thought of as the same as natural religion, or as a part of political philosophy. It also often makes past examples of non-canonical 'moral philosophy' seem much stranger to readers from a different era than discussions of metaphysics or mind. When settled intuitions about moral practices and the kinds of moral philosophy that take up and analyse these moral practices change they just seem like what they are describing is not moral philosophy at all, and when philosophical fashions change whole areas are just sent off the pitch. Think, for example, about the comparative neglect of seventeenth-century moral philosophy over Hume, Kant and Bentham.

When taken together, these special restrictions in the history of moral philosophy – the proximity of what we identify as our moral beliefs to what we are and the force of contingent intuitions in guiding the philosophical analysis – tend to make the history of the history of philosophy even less wanted here than elsewhere. Since the history of philosophy is mixed with contemporary philosophy, for the reasons I have suggested, it is somewhat desirable by philosophers and historians of philosophy. But the history of the history of philosophy is a kind of meta-endeavour that is not clearly philosophical and so less desirable.[5]

That said, a few authors and a few passages do persist, some for a very long time and some less so. The passages are what I have referred to as emblematic passages and essential ingredients in the construction of figures (like 'Locke'), problems and even movements. Because of shifts in what counts as philosophy and what is philosophically interesting, those that persist have a very special role in unifying the discipline and its self-understanding. One can think of a number of famous and coarse-grained examples – Aristotle's natural slave argument and Plato's 'noble lie' have been emblematic for aeons, but what they are emblematic of and how they are emblematic has changed in response to contingently connected historical changes, as for example with the use of Aristotle's argument in the antebellum South and the comparisons made in the twentieth century between totalitarianism and Plato's ideal city. These are extremely famous emblematic passages that have had an effect beyond philosophical schools. Some less famous passages have only local interest to fragments of academia. The roles of passages change, often very subtly, as contemporary philosophical concerns change and the problems the philosophers are discussing change accordingly. And as the range of what is philosophy changes – i.e. natural religion or natural philosophy are no longer philosophy so they are more rarely consulted by historians of philosophy in understanding emblematic passages – the role of these passages changes.

I've painted this picture in broad strokes, but the main point is that for us intellectual choices happen in a world of institutions and biases much as they did for our predecessors, and the choices we make both reflect our honest intellectual interests and a wide range of biases and restrictions. Indeed, although these are conceptually distinct they are not separable in practice; they are mutually interconnected and reinforcing. The history of the history of philosophy makes this apparent in ways that the history of philosophy does not. Our own views about the history of philosophy are formed very much like those of past philosophers and historians of philosophy at points during periods of the dominance of academic philosophy, within institutions and responding to a wide variety of causal factors. One way to respond to this problem is by focusing narrowly on the history of the role of particular emblematic passages in the history of moral philosophy and thinking about how they've come to have the functions they have and why we read them the way we do. I will discuss a brief example of this in the next section. Be warned this is not a presentation of a smoking gun. To paraphrase Sterne, it is a too quick account of how an emblematic passage has swum down the gutter of time.

II

The appendix to this chapter reproduces the final objection (hence 'the fifth objection') from Joseph Butler's 'Of the Nature of Virtue' (ONV) (commonly known as the 'Dissertation on Virtue'), and the discussion that follows it. 'Of the Nature of Virtue' was one of two dissertations appended to the *Analogy of Religion*; the other dissertation, 'Of Personal Identity' (OPI), was also emblematic. They are today normally discussed and taught in distinct philosophical contexts – criticism of Locke and (as we shall see) deontic criticisms of utilitarianism – but it is notable that they were both originally part of a work arguing for the probable evidence of natural and revealed religion based on inductive arguments drawn from analogies with natural processes. When I say 'part of' I mean it literally. Although appended in the printed editions, the dissertations were originally parts of the chapters 'Of a Future Life' (OPI) and 'Of the Moral Government of God' (ONV) respectively. Butler removed them because they detracted from the main subject of the *Analogy of Religion* in so far as they are not really support for analogical arguments.[6]

ONV (and within it the fifth objection) is brief (brevity is important for emblematicity) and one of a number of emblematic quotes, stretches or passages in Butler's work.[7] It has led, in conjunction with a few passages on foregiveness in the first few of Butler's *Sermons*, to Butler being taken as a kind of British proto-Kant,[8] a Kant without the full-fledged rational machinery but with an inkling of the internal ought. The first quotation in Sidgwick's *Methods of Ethics* is from Butler's reflection on this passage,[9] and Sidgwick viewed Butler as both a central inspiration to his way of thinking about moral philosophy *in regard to* the 'dualism of practical reason',[10] and as having offered powerful criticisms of utilitarianism that he felt had to be responded to.[11] In addition Sidgwick's methodology in ethics has a strongly Butlerian flavor. It is noteworthy that when Anscombe attacked the Sidgwickian tradition in ethics in 'Modern Moral Philosophy' the first philosopher she tossed into the flames was 'stupid' Butler.[12]

For my purposes, a notable example of the fifth objection being taken as emblematic is John Rawls's mention of the passage in his *Lectures on the History of Ethics*. The *Lectures* were posthumously published and edited by one of Rawls's most influential students, Barbara Hermann. This is a long-standing pattern in the history of philosophy, that lectures on the history of philosophy by philosophers viewed as great, as central to the canon or as making a claim to being central to the canon – whether the sayings, lectures or essays of a number of ancient philosophers, Benjamin Whichcote's *Sermons*, or Hegel's *Lectures on the History of Philosophy* – are posthumously edited and preserved by the students and disciples who were influenced by them and believe that others ought to have access to them. In Rawls' *Lectures*, Butler is briefly discussed twice in the context of Hume. Here's the more extensive of his discussions:

> To his *Analogy of Religion* (1736), Butler attached a short appendix titled 'On the Nature of Virtue.' In this he argued, among other things, that many of our conscientious moral judgments do not seem to be guided by the principle of the greatest balance of happiness. Rather, our conscience, which Butler views as authoritative and regulative of our nature, is such as to 'condemn falsehood, unprovoked violence, and to approve of benevolence to some preferably to others, abstracted from all consideration, which conduct is likeliest to produce an on overbalance of happiness or misery' (section 8).
>
> In such a manner Butler believes God has framed our conscience and we are to act accordingly. Butler entertains the purely hypothetical possibility that God might follow the principle of greatest happiness; but even if so, that does not change the fact that our conscience as framed by God is to be our guide. We are to follow conscience.[13]

Section 8 is the concluding passage of the fifth objection. Rawls likely read the passage in either of the widely read anthologies of British moral philosophy edited by D. D. Raphael[14] or by L. A. Selby-Bigge.[15] Raphael followed Selby-Bigge in his selections from Butler. Schneewind also seemed to follow them in his anthology, but with the exception of the inclusion of the entirety of ONV as opposed to just the passage in the Appendix.[16]

Selby-Bigge, today best known as the editor of a standard edition of Hume, studied at Oxford and gained 'firsts in classical moderations (1881) and in *literae humaniores* (1883)'.[17] Butler's *Analogy* and *Sermons* were both central in (respectively) the theology and moral philosophy curricula at Oxford in the later eighteenth century and throughout the nineteenth. Indeed, Butler's *Sermons* was the sole modern moral philosophy text in the Greats curriculum after the reform of 1853.[18] It appears that at Oxford the long-standing role of Butler's moral philosophy was as a Christian moral counterpart to classical authors, and Selby-Bigge's selection reflects this in so far as it presents Butler as a teleological moral philosopher making room for Christian virtues.

Selby-Bigge grouped Butler with Shaftesbury and Hutcheson as the 'three principal texts of the Sentimental school'.[19] The selections from the sermons 'Upon Compassion' and 'Love of One's Neighbour' justify presenting Butler as a sentimentalist, as does placing Samuel Clarke, whom Butler greatly admired, in volume II. It is motivated by the fact that Selby-Bigge was a great admirer of Hume and structured his anthology to reflect Hume's view of his predecessors. Butler does discuss moral sentiments at great length.

Selby-Bigge's anthology set a pattern for how the British Moralists are read in general, and Butler in particular, in so far as non-specialist philosophers, if they know Butler, likely know him via that anthology, or others patterned on it. But the Butler texts selected by Selby-Bigge reflected a prior selection by William Whewell, today primarily known as Mill's opponent on the question of induction in science but also a dominant figure in nineteenth-century moral philosophy.[20] This takes us to Cambridge.

In the mid-nineteenth century, Whewell was one of the most influential figures at Cambridge, which was with Oxford the most influential academic institution in the Anglophone world. Whewell was deeply disturbed by the fact that William Paley's *Principles of Moral Philosophy* had become the sole text of moral philosophy required in the Cambridge curriculum. Cambridge was dominated by Newtonians, and centered on what we would call mathematics and natural science in distinction from philosophy. As Sidgwick notes, this *was* philosophy in late eighteenth-century Cambridge. In 1772 Jebb listed the four branches of philosophy as 'Mechanics, Hydrostatics,

Apparent Astronomy and Optics'.[21] It offered only one Tripos (the honours bachelor's degree with set subjects, readings and exams) up to the establishment of the Moral Science Tripos in the mid-nineteenth century.[22] Paley's scientistic, teleological, theological utilitarianism was an ideal moral philosophical text to accompany those in a curriculum structured by the likes of Jebb.

But Whewell was wholly opposed to Paley, and as he ascended at Cambridge he sought to dislodge Paley's dominance with his own moral philosophy. Butler, the untouchably credentialed Anglican Bishop, was already very much central to the Oxford curriculum. He provided the ideal vehicle for Whewell. In 1837 Whewell gave four lectures, the express purpose of which was to substitute Butler for Paley.[23] The lectures were extremely successful. Whewell succeeded in getting Butler's moral philosophy into the Cambridge curriculum and in upending the dominance of Paley at Cambridge. What was the general view that Whewell wanted to substitute for Paley? In his *Lectures on the History of Moral Philosophy* Whewell distinguished moral philosophy into two antithetical positions – Dependent and Independent Morality. Dependent Moralists 'assert it to be the law of human action to aim at some external object', while Independent Moralists 'would regulate human action by an internal principle or relation, as Conscience, or Duty'.[24] Whewell proceeded to describe the two sides in a historical moral conflict, with the Epicureans, Hobbes, Bentham and Paley on the one side and Plato, Butler and himself on the other.

This is a questionable precursor of the internalism/externalism distinction combined with normative anti-utilitarian commitments,[25] but Whewell used the distinction as an editorial principle to determine what in Butler it was essential to read. He suggested an arrangement of the *Sermons* – deciding which were the most important and their order – which forms the basis for the various anthologies described above. He also published his own redacted Butler that presented him as primarily an independent theorist of conscience coupled with ONV.[26] Butler's work was taught at Cambridge before Whewell, but Whewell managed to replace Paley with Butler in the curriculum both prior to and then with the establishment of the Moral Sciences Tripos.

Sidgwick followed Whewell as a dominant figure in moral philosophy at Cambridge and of course in ethics to the present day. He was not an admirer of Whewell, and sought further reforms and changes in the system. Butler became emblematic of a utilitarian/anti-utilitarian conflict, and this passage brought the issues to focus. Sidgwick was also a great exponent of Butler as previously mentioned – Butler was ubiquitous in this curriculum – so he was trying to both appropriate him as a paradigm formal philosopher and as someone who deepened utilitarianism. Sidgwick argued that Butler was preferable to contemporary intuitionists, while at the same time attacking what he shared with Whewell.[27] This further cemented his central influence at Cambridge, as well as the central normative (utilitarianism vs. deontic intuitionism) and metaethical (externalism vs. internalism) issues that dominated through Moore and onward.

It also set how we philosophers read Butler to the present day, in so far as the passages that became emblematic in these controversies and advocacies remain emblematic – cf. from Whewell to Sidgwick to Rawls. So, to get a take on the ONV passage, who is Butler attacking? He is attacking those theorists who take benevolence to be the whole of virtue. The obvious candidate would be Francis Hutcheson,[28] since he indeed took benevolence to be the whole of virtue, and his major philosophical works where he argued for this had appeared long before 1736.[29] A second and I think even more likely candidate would be John Gay, whose 'Preliminary Dissertation' appeared attached to Edmund Law's translation of William King's *De Origine Mali* in 1731. Butler would very likely have been aware of this work before 1736. In the 'Preliminary Dissertation' Gay argues for a theological utilitarianism according to which happiness is the sole moral value to be promoted.

But the ONV passage has Samuel Clarke in the background as well. Clarke was of course a major moral philosopher and theologian, and a major inspiration to Butler. Butler had corresponded with Clarke when he was still at grammar school,[30] and although he was highly methodologically critical of Clarke he shared many of his substantive insights. The *Sermons* opens with a famous discussion of two methods in ethics that are complimentary, the former proceeding from abstract relations of reason, i.e. Clarke, and the latter from empirically discoverable aspects of our moral frames or matters of fact, i.e. Butler. As the *Analogy of Religion* is a work of philosophical theology it would be surprising if Clarke is not a relevant context. Indeed the fifth objection refers the reader back to *Analogy of Religion* I.vi, which in turn refers the reader to ONV.[31]

Furthermore, the Selby-Bigge grouping suggests that Hutcheson and Butler follow one school – the sentimentalists – and that Clarke is the source of another opposed and parallel school – the rationalists. Gay is in the Appendix. A post-Selby-Bigge reader might find it hard to see Butler responding to these authors in the manner that (I think) he does. As suggested above, one of the things the history of the history of emblematic passages hopefully makes us aware of is how anthologies and school group-ings offer up certain obvious interpretations and restrict others.

How does Butler's criticism go? Roughly:

1. Benevolence (and the lack of benevolence) cannot be the whole of virtue.
2. If benevolence were the whole of virtue then we would only approve and disapprove of degrees of benevolence.
3. Imagine two competitors – Peter and Paul [AG – my names] – for something of equal advantage to both of them.
4. If a stranger aided Paul, that would on this account be virtue in so far as the stranger would be benevolent in making Paul more happy (considered independent of distant consequences).
5. Now suppose a stranger robs Peter to benefit Paul, 'who he thought' would benefit sufficiently more than Peter would have such that it overmatches Peter's pains.
6. Furthermore suppose there are no further bad consequences.
7. The action would still be vicious in so far as we are constituted in such a way as to condemn these actions as vicious as well as to be partial in our benevolence independent of 'which conduct is likeli-est to produce an overbalance of happiness or misery'.
8. 'And therefore, were the author of nature to propose nothing to himself as an end but the production of happiness, were his moral character merely that of benevolence; yet ours is not so' (ONV §8).
9. 'Upon that supposition, indeed, the only reason of his giving us the above-mentioned approbation of benevolence to some persons rather than others, and disapprobation of falsehood, unprovoked violence, injustice, must be vice in us, and benevolence to some preferably to others, virtue, from all consideration of the overbalance of evil or good which they may appear likely to produce' (ONV §8).

In their intepretations of Butler, Whewell and Sidgwick focused on the conflict between 'intuitive' and utilitarian views.[32] The fifth objection is almost always read as highlighting this conflict as a problem for utilitari-anism as a normative view. This is reflected in the most important recent secondary literature.[33] Whewell and Sidgwick differed in their assessment of the respective merits of these normative theories and the harm of the fifth objection to utilitarianism. But for all, the fifth objection highlighted the conflict between two normative theories. I would like to suggest there is a different way of reading it. Butler is not focusing on intutionism as superior to utilitarianism, but rather on the idea that *nothing* derived solely from theoretical reason is exclusively the whole of virtue.

Now let's return to Rawls's description. It is mainly accurate if – as might be expected from lecture notes – not particularly edifying.[34] But there is a subtle point of interpretation nonetheless which falls in line with the others described above. Rawls's phrase 'Butler entertains the purely hypothetical possibility that God might follow the principle of greatest happiness' implies that God does not follow the principle of greatest happiness. This would suggest that the conflict Butler is interested in is between the greatest happiness principle and what our ordinary moral faculties tell us, i.e. a normative conflict.

Butler does not use the phrase 'greatest happiness', which from Hutcheson on has become associated with utilitarianism as a normative theory (and thus signals that the conflict is one between normative theories). The stress in Butler's passage, though, is on 'nothing to himself as an end' *other* than happiness – i.e. the *exclusive* nature of the explanation. In other words it is not on *greatest* happiness – it is on *solely* happiness.[35] Consequently, what Butler seems to be suggesting is that were God only interested in happiness, this would make what we commonly take to be virtue – being specially benevolent to one's children – to be vice. But this is of course reversible. If God were only interested in righteous punishment, then the desire for happiness might be vice. Butler is less interested in a conflict between normative theories than in the inevitability of self-refuting conflict between exclusive moral justifications.

That Butler stresses our epistemic limits is evident from what follows the fifth objection. I would suggest that there is an obvious reason why Butler is not interested in the conflict between utilitarian and deontic theories. That there are a few exclusive normative theories, or that normative accounts were independent of metaethics or moral epistemology, was not yet in currency because exclusive normative views were the exception not the rule. Even Hutcheson's view was mixed in a number of ways. The default position was a pluralism that invoked virtue in many contexts;[36] consequently it makes more sense to view the passage as attacking exclusive theories, the main examples of which were Hutcheson (very inconsistently) and John Gay (very consistently). But before John Gay it is very hard to give an example of a consistent, exclusive normative theory.[37] And, as Whewell makes clear, afterwards as well!

This gets to the aforementioned Clarke. There is a second point being made here, that one ought not to imitate God in deciding what is one's best conduct. Clarke allowed different guides to human moral conduct including equity and benevolence.[38] It was unproblematic to Clarke that there are non-exclusive guides to conduct for a similar reason that it probably was to Butler, assumptions that love of God trumped and providence worked out the details. For Clarke the existence of God was deducible and the providentialism that followed from this certain. So Butler shared Clarke's belief in plural duties or values anchored by divine governance.

But, as noted, Butler and Clarke differed on the best method in ethics, and we can see in this passage the difference coming to a head in a way that it didn't in the *Sermons*.[39] Clarke stresses that we ought to maximise the benevolence in our action because God is maximally benevolent and so maximising benevolence provides a guide to our conduct.[40] But, as Butler is noting in the fifth objection, what we know about our frames conflicts with taking a general standard that applies to God as a guide to our conduct, even if in a finite measure. Clarke is alluded to[41] in a passage in *Analogy* I.vi.12 very close (i.e. two paragraphs before) the paragraph that Butler references in the fifth objection.

In the main body of the text Butler notes:

> For the Conclusion, that God will finally reward the righteous and punish the wicked, is not here drawn, from it appearing to us fit, that He should; but from it appearing, that He has told us, *He will*. And this he hath certainly told us, in the Promise, and Threatning, which it hath observed the Notion of a Command implies, and the Sense of Good and ill Desert which he has given us, more distinctly expresses. And this Reasoning from Fact is confirmed, and in some degree verified, by other facts.[42]

When we ignore reasoning from fact this allows self-deceit in, a point that holds independent of particular normative accounts. It seems likely that the purpose of the passage is to convince readers to avoid philosophies that promote 'benevolent' actions like those sketched in a sentence two paragraphs later in ONV – 'such supposed endeavours to promote happiness for many others proceed, almost always, from ambition, the spirit of party, or some indirect principle, concealed perhaps in great measure from persons themselves'. In other words, the fifth objection condemns philosophies that promote self-deceit by arguing that we ought to pay attention to general metaphysical reasons (or fitnesses) for conduct over and above the reasoning from fact.

That this is what Butler has in mind is reinforced by the passages from the *Analogy* to which he refers in the fifth objection. The main focus of *Analogy* I.vi – 'Of the Opinion of Necessity considered influencing Practice' – concerns how general necessitarian metaphysical doctrines offer poor and self-refuting guides to conduct; 'with regard to Practice, it is as if it were false, so far as Experience reaches'.[43] This is a general point concerning exclusive theories that are self-refuting in practice and prone to self-deception, not a point about combating normative theories.[44]

In further support of this reading of the fifth objection, Butler remarks 'For to pretend to act upon Reason, in Opposition to practical Principles, which the Author of our nature gave us to act upon; and to pretend to apply our Reason to Subjects, with regard to which, our own short Views, and even our Experience, will shew us, it cannot be depended upon.'[45] The paragraph that Butler explicitly references stresses that there is nothing wrong with speculative reason in and of itself but rather our capacity for self-deceit ought to make us continually wary of how its application allows in 'Prejudice and Perversion'. Butler is furthermore worrying, like Berkeley and many others did, about how speculation of this sort can provide a warrant to immoral actions and self-deception by reformers and others who are not philosophers.

So, to conclude this discussion, it seems from the evidence of who and what Butler is likely criticising, and from the context of the passage in Butler's no longer philosophical works (i.e. the *Analogy*), that the purpose of the discussion is not to highlight a conflict between normative theories but instead to highlight two problems of methodological exclusivity. This is the methodological analogue of Butler's stress on balance, moderation and the importance of a multiplicity of principles[46] as well as his commitment to the plurality of values throughout.[47] Exclusive reliance on one moral justification results in ignoring or conflicting with another. Exclusive reliance on speculative reason results in allowing self-deceit in via ignoring matters of fact and allowing them to be self-deceitfully modified.

This is not to say that the standard themes might not be there, but rather to argue that the themes I have just discussed are much harder to see. Emblematic passages are often like this: they can be taken as insightful for a cluster of different views, and what they are emblematic of is a function of how the insights are prioritised. And it is to underscore, in keeping with the first part of the chapter, that due to the background history of the text (the anthologies, editing, curricular place, etc.), the special force of ethics for us, its place in arguments by influential philosophers, and present concerns, there will much less interest in reading texts in ways that are less 'philosophically' pressing however plausible an interpretation.[48] Indeed, it seems as if the self-deceit and practical components barely constitute a *philosophical* explanation, and yet they are the focus of the passage. But, again, the purpose of this discussion is not to say one ought only to read it, but rather to exhibit an emblematic passage and show how it is read, and – too sketchily – why.

Appendix: The Fifth Objection

Fifthly, without inquiring how far, and in what sense, virtue is resolvable into benevolence, and vice into want of it; it may be proper to observe, that benevolence, and the want of it, singly considered, are in no sort the whole of virtue and vice. For if this were the case, in the review of one's character, or that of others, our moral understanding and moral sense would be indifferent to every thing, but the degrees in which benevolence prevailed, and the degrees in which it was wanting. That is, we should never approve of benevolence to some persons rather than others, nor disapprove injustice and falsehood upon any other account, than merely as an overbalance of happiness was foreseen to be likely produced by the first, and of misery by the second. But now, on the contrary, suppose two men competitors for any thing whatever, which would be of equal advantage to each of them; though nothing indeed would be more impediment, than for a stranger to busy himself to get one of them preferred to the other; yet such endeavour would be virtue, in behalf of a friend or a benefactor, abstracted from all consideration of distant consequences: as that example of gratitude, and cultivation of friendship, would be of general good to the world. Again, suppose one man should, by fraud or violence take from another the fruit of his labor with intent to give it to a third, who, he thought, would have such pleasure from it as would balance the pleasure which the first possessor would have had in the enjoyment, and his vexation in the loss of it: suppose also, that no bad consequences would follow; yet such an action would surely be vicious. Nay, farther, were treachery, violence, injustice, no otherwise vicious, than as foreseen likely to produce an overbalance of misery to society; then, if in any case a man would procure to himself as great advantage by any act of injustice, as the whole foreseen inconvenience, likely to be brought upon others by it, would amount to, such a piece of injustice would not be faulty or vicious at all; because it would be no more than, in any other case, for a man to prefer his own satisfaction to another's in equal degrees. The fact then appears to be, that we are constituted so as to condemn falsehood, unprovoked violence, injustice, and to approve of benevolence to some preferably to others, abstracted from all consideration which conduct is likeliest to produce an overbalance of happiness or misery.

And therefore, were the author of nature to propose nothing to himself as an end but the production of happiness, were his moral character merely that of benevolence; yet ours is not so. Upon that supposition, indeed, the only reason of his giving us the above-mentioned approbation of benevolence to some persons rather than others, and disapprobation of falsehood, unprovoked violence, injustice, must be vice in us, and benevolence to some preferably to others, virtue, from all consideration of the overbalance of evil or good which they may appear likely to produce. (ONV §8)

[The passage is followed by Butler's reflection on the fifth objection, which includes the passage from Sidgwick mentioned above. – AG]

Now if human creatures are endued with such a moral nature as we have been explaining, or with a moral faculty, the natural object of which is actions: moral government must consist, in rendering them happy and unhappy, in rewarding and punishing them, as they follow, neglect, or depart from, the moral rule of action interwoven in their nature, or suggested and enforced by this moral faculty (A I.vi.14); in rewarding and punishing them upon account of their so doing.

I am not sensible, that I have, in this fifth observation, contradicted what any author designed to assert. But some of great and distinguished merit, have, I think, expressed themselves in a manner, which may occasion some danger, to careless readers, of imagining the whole of virtue to consist in singly aiming, according to the best of their judgement, at promoting the happiness of mankind in the present state; and the whole of vice, in doing what they foresee, or might foresee, is likely to produce an overbalance of unhappiness in it: than which mistakes, none can be conceived more terrible. For it is certain, that some of the most shocking instances of injustice, adultery, murder, perjury, and even of persecution, may, in many supposable cases, not have the appearance of being likely to produce an overbalance of misery in the present state; perhaps sometimes may have the contrary appearance. For this reflection might easily be carried on, but I forbear – the happiness of the world is the concern of him, who is the Lord and the Proprietor of it: nor do we know what we are about, when we endeavour to promote the good of mankind in any ways, but those which he has directed; that is indeed in all ways, not contrary to veracity and justice. I speak thus upon supposition of persons really endeavouring, in some sort, to do good without regard to these. But the truth seems to be, that such supposed endeavours proceed, almost always, from ambition, the spirit of party, or some indirect principle, concealed perhaps in great measure from persons themselves. And though it is our business and our duty to endeavour, within the bounds of veracity and justice, to contribute to the ease, convenience, and even cheerfulness and diversion of our fellow-creatures: yet from our short views, it is greatly uncertain, whether this endeavour will in particular instances, produce an overbalance of happiness upon the whole; since so many and distant things must come into the account. And that which makes it our duty, is, that there is some appearance that it will, and no positive appearance sufficient to balance this, on the contrary side; and also, that such benevolent endeavour is a cultivation of that most excellent of all virtuous principles, the active principle of benevolence.

However, though veracity, as well as justice, is to be our rule of life; it must be added, otherwise a snare will be laid in the way of some plain men, that the use of common forms of speech generally understood, cannot be falsehood; and, in general, that there can be no designed falsehood without designing to deceive. It must likewise be observed, that in numberless cases, a man may be under the strictest obligations to what he foresees will deceive, without his intending it. For it is impossible not to foresee, that the words and actions of men in different ranks and employments, and of different educations, will perpetually be mistaken by each other: and it cannot but be so, whilst they will judge with the utmost carelessness, as they daily do, of what they are not, perhaps, enough informed to be competent judges of, even though they considered it with great attention. (ONV §§9–11).

Notes

1. K. Haakonssen, ed., *Cambridge History of Eighteenth-Century Philosophy* (Cambridge: Cambridge University Press, 2006). Why the history of the history of philosophy is not central to the history of philosophy will be made clear.
2. That this is what is going on can be seen by comparing a Kantian history of philosophy to the work of an 'Eclectic' historian of philosophy such as Brucker writing a century before. One note of caution: what am I describing holds just as much of 'Eclectic' histories as of Kantian histories.
3. I am using contemporary philosophy in a very vague sense here to include many kinds of current philosophy, issues that seem currently important or pressing, etc.
4. As to 3) many historians of philosophy have had the experience of reading a very familiar passage and noticing a sentence or passage for the first time, despite having read (and perhaps taught) the passage many, many times.

This experience points to both the steady operation of 3) and the fact that all of the phenomena I am describing are common, but not without exception. I'm not suggesting anything like absolute closure.

5. A fair response might be: this all sounds Nietzschean/Foucaultian, which sounds pretty philosophical! The methodological considerations may be in line with the arguments of some philosophers, but actually engaging in the practice of the history of the history of philosophy seems quite something else.

6. J. Butler, *The Analogy of Religion, Natural and Revealed, to the Constitution and Course of Nature*, second edition (London: J. Knapton, 1736), 438.

7. The most emblematic quote in Butler is no doubt 'everything is what it is and not another thing' (*Fifteen Sermons Preached at Rolls Chapel*, second edition (London: J. Knapton, 1729), §39), although it has lost any connection to its context since being used by Moore as the epigraph to *Principia Ethica*. That Moore choose this epigraph says a lot about Butler's foundational place in the British moral philosophical tradition.

8. J. Schneewind, *The Invention of Autonomy: A History of Modern Moral Philosophy* (Cambridge: Cambridge University Press, 1998), 522.

9. 'The happiness of the world is the concern of him, who is the Lord and the Proprietor of it: nor do we know what we are about, when we endeavour to promote the good of mankind in any ways, but those which he has directed; that is indeed in all ways, not contrary to veracity and justice.' H. Sidgwick, *Methods of Ethics* (6th edition, London: Macmillan, 1901), quoting ONV §9.

10. That practical reason both justifies egoism and utilitarianism, and cannot adjudicate between them. For a sense of the expansive literature on the topic, see B. Schultz, 'Henry Sidgwick', *The Stanford Encyclopedia of Philosophy* (Summer 2015 edition), ed. Edward N. Zalta, at http://plato.stanford.edu/archives/sum2015/entries/sidgwick.

11. R. Crisp, *The Cosmos of Duty: Henry Sidgwick's Methods and Ethics* (Oxford: Oxford University Press, 2015), 2.

12. G. E. M. Anscombe, 'Modern Moral Philosophy', *Philosophy*, 53 (1958), 2.

13. J. Rawls, *Lectures on the History of Moral Philosophy* (Cambridge, MA: Harvard University Press, 2000), 65–6.

14. D. D. Raphael, ed., *British Moralists 1650–1800*, 2 vols (Oxford: Clarendon Press, 1969).

15. L. A. Selby-Bigge, ed., *British Moralists, Being Selections from Writers Principally of the Eighteenth Century*, 2 vols (Oxford: Clarendon Press, 1897). Rawls's quote from Butler is cited in the printed text of the *Lectures* from Jerome Schneewind's collection *Moral Philosophy, From Montaigne to Kant* (Cambridge: Cambridge University Press, 1990), which presents the last of the five objections as an extract from ONV along with the 'Preface', the first three of Butler's *Sermons* ('Upon Human Nature') and selections from the sermons 'Upon Compassion' and 'Love of One's Neighbour'. It is likely that Rawls was not citing the passage from Schneewind but rather that Hermann

had located the citation in Schneewind in order to provide a readily available text for readers of Rawls's *Lectures*, since Schneewind's anthology first appeared in 1990.

16. ONV was long commonly read appended to an edition of the *Sermons* and far less likely to be read in its original context appended to the *Analogy of Religion*. The *Analogy of Religion* was scarcer in philosophy departments in the mid-twentieth century US than it had been in the previous century. E. C. Mossner's edition of the *Analogy* even left the ONV and OPI out. Presumably this was because ONV had migrated over the course of the nineteenth century to the *Sermons* (although an egregious editorial lapse all the same, given that ONV was initially part of the *Analogy*, and Butler stated this in the *Analogy* itself).

17. N. D. Daglish, 'Bigge, Sir Lewis Amherst Selby-, first baronet (1860–1951)', *Oxford Dictionary of National Biography* (Oxford: Oxford University Press, 2004); online edition, January 2008, at http://www.oxforddnb.com/view/article/63835.

18. W. Walsh, 'The Zenith of Greats', in M. G. Brock and M. C. Curthoys, eds, *The History of the University of Oxford, Volume VII: Nineteenth-Century Oxford, Part 2* (Oxford: Oxford University Press, 2000), 313.

19. Selby-Bigge, *British Moralists*, I:vi. These kinds of typologies are highly flexible. Notably, Adam Smith (who follows Butler in the Selby-Bigge anthology) placed Shaftesbury with Clarke and Wollaston as a rationalist in his own survey of moral philosophy in *The Theory of Moral Sentiments* (Oxford: Oxford University Press, 1976), VII.ii.1.

20. Beyond the choice of Butler selections, Selby-Bigge – the promoter of Hume – had wholly different philosophical commitments from Whewell.

21. H. Sidgwick, 'Philosophy at Cambridge', *Mind*, I:2 (1876), 235–46.

22. For a detailed discussion see J. R. Gibbens, 'Constructing Knowledge in Mid-Victorian Cambridge: The Moral Science Tripos 1850–70', in Jonathan Smith and Christopher Stray, eds, *Teaching and Learning in Nineteenth-Century Cambridge* (Woodbridge: Boydell Press, 2001), 61–88.

23. W. Whewell, ed., *Butler's Three Sermons on Human Nature and Dissertation on Virtue* (London: Deighton, Bell, and Co., 1865), iv.

24. W. Whewell, *Lectures on the History of Moral Philosophy* (Cambridge: Deighton, Bell, and Co., 1862), 1–2.

25. In referring to it this way I am talking the language of post-Sidgwickian moral philosophy (and far later). Attacking confusions in Whewell was of course a central motivation in Sidgwick's epochal and epochally careful work.

26. Whewell, ed., *Butler's Three Sermons*.

27. On the conflict in general see J. Schneewind, *Sidgwick's Ethics and Victorian Moral Philosophy* (Oxford: Oxford University Press, 1977); L. Snyder, *Reforming Philosophy: A Victorian Debate on Science and Society* (Chicago: University of Chicago Press, 2006); S. Cremaschi, '"Nothing to invite or to reward a separate examination": Sidgwick and Whewell', *Etica & Politica*, X:2 (2008), 137–84.

28. Schneewind, *The Invention of Autonomy*, 351–2.

29. Irwin also suggests Cumberland as a background. T. H. Irwin, *The Development of Ethics: Volume II: From Suarez to Rousseau* (Oxford: Oxford University Press, 2008), 521.

30. See A. Garrett, 'Reasoning about morals from Butler to Hume', in Ruth Savage, ed., *Philosophy and Religion in Enlightenment Britain* (Oxford: Oxford University Press, 2012), 169–86.

31. The passages from the *Analogy* are not in the Selby-Bigge anthology since when the latter was created the *Analogy* was no longer obviously a work of philosophy or relevant to philosophy.

32. Sidgwick's *Methods of Ethics*, 86.

33. For example, Penelhum refers to ONV as 'Butler's anti-utilitarian arguments' (T. Penelhum, *Butler* [Boston: Routledge and Kegan Paul, 1986], 82–5) as does Irwin (*The Development of Ethics*, 525). Both of these authors are (obviously) immensely learned, deeply immersed in all of Butler's works, and offer sophisticated, sensitive readings that allow for the ambiguous context. They are not reading from Selby-Bigge! My point is just that the back story makes it desirable to cast what Butler is doing as an 'anti-utilitarian argument'.

34. Rawls goes on to make the very edifying (and I think correct) point that there is continuity between Butler and Hume here despite Hume's hostility to philosophical theology.

35. W. D. Ross, the most Butler-inspired of major twentieth-century metaethicists, and in his capacity as an Aristotle scholar a *very* careful reader of texts, quotes the fifth objection nearly in its entirety in *Foundations of Ethics*. He introduces the passage by describing Butler as the most sagacious of the British Moralists and adds: 'In his ripest work on ethics, the *Dissertation on the Nature of Virtue*, Butler indicates more clearly than in the *Sermons* his distrust of the view which treats zeal for the general good as the only virtue'. W. D. Ross, *Foundations of Ethics* (Oxford: Clarendon Press, 1939), 78. If 'zeal' is understood as a sole and unreflective concern for happiness this is consistent with part of my interpretation. Ross then goes on to identify the 'zeal' with utilitarianism, but criticises utilitarianism for not providing an account of morality that reflects the complexity of our duties and of our moral life (79).

36. See M. B. Gill, *Humean Moral Pluralism* (Oxford: Oxford University Press, 2014).

37. I have much more to say about this but cannot within the restricted context of this essay. In short, I hold that Gay effected the distinction between normative explanation and moral epistemological (moral sense) and metaethical considerations, and before Gay these distinctions were unclear.

38. S. Clarke, *A Discourse Concerning the Unchangeable Obligations of Natural Religion, and the Truth and Certainty of the Christian Revelation* (London: J. Knapton, 1706), 82ff.

39. Sidgwick (*Methods of Ethics*, 86n) noted a shift in Butler from the *Sermons* to ONV to recognising the conflict between utilitarianism and ordinary intuitionist notions of virtue. This is why ONV is so crucial for Sidgwick.

40. Clarke, A *Discourse Concerning the Unchangeable Obligations of Natural Religion*, 92–7.
41. That Butler has in mind the *Sermons* distinction between Clarkean reasoning about fitnesses and his own reasoning from fact is underscored by a more technical footnote that makes stronger use of Clarke's language (*Analogy*, 169 n1). Butler does love technical footnotes!
42. Ibid., 169–70.
43. Ibid., 162.
44. Butler adds: 'such is in Fact our Condition and the natural Course of things, that whatever we apply it to Life and Practice, this Application of it, always, misleads us, and cannot but mislead us, in a most dreadful Manner' (ibid.). Self-deception is stressed by Penelhum in his interpretation (*Butler*, 82–5).
45. Butler, *Analogy*, 164.
46. Schneewind, *The Invention of Autonomy*, 342–5.
47. See Gill, *Humean Moral Pluralism*.
48. Maybe they are now easier to see because of Ross and the rise of the post-Wolf and post-Williams interest in non-exclusive normative theories.

4

Natural Law and Natural Rights in Early Enlightenment Copenhagen

Mads Langballe Jensen

The official political ideology in the Danish-Norwegian dual kingdom until the early eighteenth century is generally considered to have been a strongly theological divine right theory. It would, therefore, seem of great interest to know the circumstances and content of the first teaching of natural law in Copenhagen. This occurred during the years following a violent polemic between Christian Thomasius, the Leipzig jurisconsult and natural lawyer, and Hector Gottfried Masius, the court preacher to the Danish king Christian V, which culminated in Thomasius's writings being burned on the public square in Copenhagen by the executioner and contributed to his banishment from Leipzig to Halle.[1] Nevertheless, the natural law theories of the first Danish teachers of the subject, Henrik Weghorst and Christian Reitzer, have not been the subject of detailed historical analysis. By offering such a study, this chapter aims to contribute to the intellectual and political history of early enlightenment Denmark-Norway as well as the scholarship on the history of post-Grotian natural law theorising. In particular, by discussing Weghorst's and Reitzer's theories of natural law, this chapter aims to ascertain to what extent the innovations in theories of natural law and natural right ascribed in particular to Hugo Grotius and Samuel Pufendorf were carried forward by the two Danish writers.

The chapter is structured as follows. The following section will give an overview of the existing scholarship on Henrik Weghorst and Christian Reitzer. Section three will then outline the institutional context of natural law teaching in Copenhagen. The following two sections turn to analyses of Christian Reitzer's and Henrik Weghorst's theories of natural law, arguing that their substantial differences reflected the different academic contexts in which they had studied natural law: Thomasius's rendition of Pufendorfian natural law in Halle in the case of Reitzer, and a tradition of Christian natural law in Kiel in the case of Weghorst. The final section then turns to a discussion of whether these differences were reflected in the way they construed the relationship between natural law and natural right.

Henrik Weghorst and Christian Reitzer in the Historiography

Natural law as a prominent political discourse in the centuries following the publication of Hugo Grotius's *De iure belli ac pacis* in 1625 has received increasing scholarly attention in recent decades. The significance of natural law for the history of a wide range of disciplines, including moral and political philosophy, law, economics and theology, and a range of issues, including the development of the absolutist state, the relationship between church and state, theories of rights, secularisation and toleration in various forms of enlightenment, and in particular the distinctive contributions of Thomas Hobbes, Samuel Pufendorf and Christian Thomasius to so-called 'voluntarist' natural law have been investigated in detail.[2]

Furthermore, in line with the general trend towards localised and contextualised studies of the history of political thought, scholars have emphasised the need for studies of how the writings and teachings of the 'innovators', such as Grotius and Pufendorf, in the discipline of natural law was received, adapted, used and transformed in different places by their students.[3] Thus it has been highlighted that so-called minor or second generation teachers of natural law often were even more influential than the canonical thinkers in shaping how natural law was taught and implemented in political reforms.[4] This raises the further question of the existence of local 'dialects' of the discourse of natural law, and how such local 'dialects' were adapted to local concerns.

While there have been detailed studies of the reception and influence of post-Grotian natural law in Sweden, there are no comparable studies of its reception in the other Scandinavian state, the double monarchy of Denmark-Norway.[5] Despite the fact that central figures in early enlightenment Denmark-Norway, including Christian Reitzer, Ludvig Holberg and Andreas Hojer, are conventionally characterised as being influenced by Pufendorf and Thomasius, neither the reception of the Pufendorfian-Thomasian natural law in Denmark-Norway nor its place in early enlightenment thought has been the subject of detailed historical enquiry.[6]

Henrik Weghorst and Christian Reitzer are usually discussed together in the scholarship as the two responsible for introducing modern, that is, post-Grotian, natural law. Like many other authors from the time, however, they are primarily set as background to the pre-eminent figure in the Danish-Norwegian enlightenment, Ludvig Holberg. Accordingly, the content of their natural law works is rarely discussed, with scholars contenting themselves with characterising them as following one or other of the 'great thinkers'. Edvard Holm, in what is still considered his classical study of Ludvig Holberg's political views, characterises both thinkers as following Pufendorf.[7] Kåre Foss's study of Ludvig Holberg's theory of natural law against, as the title says, 'its intellectual background' likewise characterises all Danish natural law before Holberg, that is Weghorst and Reitzer, as 'diluted Pufendorf'.[8] The most recent account of the history of law at Copenhagen University introduces a slight variation, characterising Reitzer as following Grotius and Pufendorf while claiming that Weghorst's work on natural law was 'entirely orientated towards Grotius'.[9]

From surveying the scholarship, then, one gets the sense that both Weghorst and Reitzer offered more or less the same thing: the first brief – and Latin – introductions to natural law on the basis of Grotius and Pufendorf, soon to be superseded by Ludvig Holberg's great Danish introduction to natural law on the basis of Grotius, Pufendorf and Thomasius. However, Grotius's and Pufendorf's theories of natural law were by no means identical or indeed necessarily compatible, and so, how the two were combined would prove a decisive difference. Moreover, 'following' or 'being orientated towards' Grotius or Pufendorf, or a combination of the two, would always involve an act of interpretation, adaptation and use, which would influence the 'Grotian' and 'Pufendorfian' natural law thus developed. It will be shown that Weghorst and Reitzer in fact developed two fundamentally different positions on natural law reflecting the different local academic contexts and discourses in which they were educated, Kiel and Halle.

The Institutional Context of Natural Law in Denmark-Norway

Although the absolutist constitution of Denmark-Norway, the Lex Regia of 1665, was significantly influenced by the contractual framework of Grotian natural law, the constitution was kept secret and only published in 1709. The official ideology was one of divine right absolutism, as represented for instance by the bishop Hans Wandal and the court preacher Hector Gottfried Masius.[10] While Masius's intentions with Interesse principum circa religionem Evangelicam (The Advantage of the Evangelical Religion to the Princes), the work which sparked off the polemics with Thomasius, were primarily confessional, it included arguments critical of 'secular' natural law. Worried by the prospect of increased Calvinist immigration following the revocation of the Edict of Nantes, Masius warned against the subversive nature of Calvinist religious doctrine, advising the king that his best interest lay in maintaining the purity of Lutheran doctrine among his subjects.[11] As part of his argument that political order could only be maintained on the grounds of the true Lutheran doctrine, Masius had explicitly denied the validity of a natural law on the basis of reason. Divorced from revealed religion, natural law was a 'maimed and mutilated doctrine'. The duties towards God were taught exclusively by religion, while those towards oneself and others were determined partly by right reason and partly by religion. As such revealed religion should take 'first place' in any doctrine of natural law.[12]

Despite Masius's highly critical remarks concerning the discipline of natural law in a work that received official support, steps were being taken to introduce precisely this academic subject in the University of Copenhagen, seemingly as part of a general endeavour to raise the quality of education in the capital. A draft of new university statutes from 1691 stipulated that the professor of law 'should explain the law of nature and of nations'.[13] Although teaching of natural law was first codified in the new statutes for the University of Copenhagen in 1732, with a chair in 'the law of nature and of nations as well as public law [Jus Publicum]' and moral philosophy,[14] natural law was taught in the 1690s at the modern (albeit short-lived) Knights' Academy in Copenhagen and probably at the University as well.

The Knights' Academy in Copenhagen was founded in 1691, on the model of the knights' academies in the German lands.[15] It seems Christian Reitzer had been first choice as professor of law, but (probably because of his appointment at the University) Weghorst was appointed in the spring of 1692 instead.[16] In a report of his teaching from October 1693 Weghorst declares his intention to turn to the law of nature and nations.[17] The following year Weghorst had completed a manuscript textbook on natural law, the Compendium Juris naturæ (Compendium on natural law), which likely formed the basis of his lectures on the subject.[18] The first three parts of the Compendium provided the material for a dissertation presided over by Weghorst on 19 March 1696, the Compendii juris naturæ, Dissertatio prima (Compendium on natural law, first dissertation).[19] In 1693 Weghorst had been appointed professor designatus in the faculty of philosophy at the University, where he became ordinary professor sometime between 1698 and 1700. In 1704, a personal chair in 'Juris & moralis scientiae' was created for Weghorst, a post which he held to his death in 1722.[20]

Having been *professor designatus* in both philosophy and law since 1689, and having studied in Halle in 1690–92, Christian Reitzer returned to take up the chair as professor of law at Copenhagen University in 1692 (the only chair in law until 1732), a post he held until 1723.[21] According to the official catalogue of public lectures at the University, Reitzer taught natural law in 1700–1.[22] Although there is a gap in the catalogue for the years between 1686 and 1698, there is some evidence that Reitzer taught natural law earlier in the 1690s as well. In 1694 Reitzer published the short (and incomplete) *Positiones ex jure divino, sive universali, sub præsidio Christiani Reitzer defendent nobilissimi alquot & lectissimi juvenes* (Subjects from divine or universal law, which some most noble and learned youths will defend, presided over by Christian Reitzer), which, considering the title, is likely to have grown out of his teaching.[23] The topic of universal divine law proved a continuing topic in Reitzer's teaching, and in 1702 he published a revised and much longer version of the work, (although also incomplete) *Positionum ex jure divino universali partis primæ caput primum, seu de iis, quæ universo in iure præcognita esse debent* (Subjects from divine universal law, part one chapter one, or the fundamentals of universal law), which was explicitly conceived as an aid to students studying natural law.[24] In addition, Reitzer had published the dissertation *De obligatione sontium ad subeundam poenam dissertatio* (On the obligation of the guilty to submit to punishment) in 1693, in part a criticism of Hobbes's position on the subject on the basis of Pufendorfian natural law.[25]

Weghorst's and Reitzer's careers, then, were parallel: they were both appointed professors of law in the early 1690s and both devoted significant parts of their academic endeavours to teaching the new post-Grotian natural law, Weghorst at the Academy and the University in the faculty of philosophy, and Reitzer in the faculty of law. It is therefore not surprising that they have been mentioned together in the existing historiography touching on natural law in Denmark-Norway, and perhaps this parallel in their academic careers has led scholars to see parallels also in the substance of their teaching. However, as we shall see in the following, Weghorst and Reitzer developed decidedly different theories of natural law.

Pufendorfian Natural Law: Christian Reitzer's *Positionum ex jure divino universali*

Christian Reitzer's works on natural law reflect the fact that he had studied in Halle in 1690–92 under Christian Thomasius. In 1688, Thomasius had published his *Institutes of Divine Jurisprudence*, which was largely a defence and elaboration of Pufendorf's theory of natural law.[26] Thomasius lectured on his *Institutes* in 1691 (in private *collegium*) and it is likely that Reitzer attended at least some of these, and perhaps even discussed issues of natural law with Thomasius himself.[27] In the invitation to this *collegium*, which was published as an introduction to later editions of the *Institutes*, Thomasius gave a brief account of the history and present state of the discipline of natural law, highlighting the contributions in particular of Grotius and Pufendorf and explaining how his own *Institutes* were intended as a defence of Pufendorf against the Leipzig theologian Valentin Alberti. The introduction to the *collegium* is interesting for our purposes as it provides a succinct summary of the perspective on natural law which Reitzer would take with him from Halle to Copenhagen as well as the issues at stake between him and Weghorst.

Thomasius presented the recent advances in the discipline of natural law as part of a general progress of learning in the Protestant universities during the second half of the seventeenth century, abolishing the 'servitude' that had characterised previous centuries. Although the 'scholastics among the papists' had written numerous works on natural law they had completely confused Scripture, nature and human laws in a way more likely to confuse 'a reasonable human being' than anything else. What was more, this form of scholastic natural law had been appropriated by the Protestants, as evidenced by the works of the Tübingen theologian Johann Adam Osiander.[28]

According to Thomasius, it was Hugo Grotius who had first begun to rescue the 'noble discipline' of natural law and clean the 'dust of the schools' from it, and had thus given the discipline a high standing.[29] His books had been very well received in the universities (though obscured by commentaries), but this, Thomasius argued, was only because Grotius was the first to 'break the ground', for, being first, his breach with tradition was insufficient. Although Grotius sought the law of nature in human nature, he retained many scholastic errors in his 'definition of the law of nature'. These included the doctrines that things prohibited by the law of nature 'were morally bad in themselves and prior to divine will' and the doctrine that natural law would obligate even if God did not exist.[30]

That Thomasius was right about the reasons for the good reception of Grotius was brought out by the violent abuse and polemics that met Pufendorf when he had attacked these scholastic remnants in his 1672 *De iure naturae et gentium libri octo* (On the Law of Nature and Nations).[31] According to Thomasius, it was thus a common characteristic of all the anti-Pufendorfian works that they criticised sociality as the 'principium

cognoscendi of the law of nature' and sought to reassert the existence
of a 'lex aeterna' and that certain things were good or bad in themselves
prior to the divine will. In his *Institutes*, Thomasius had criticised these
doctrines, defended Pufendorf's magnum opus and asserted sociality as
the principle of natural law, in particular against the attacks by the Leipzig
theologian Valentin Alberti.[32]

Reitzer's *Positionum* is structured as introductory discussions of key concepts falling under the category 'Right in general' (*Ius in genere*). These
include the meaning of the concepts 'law', 'right' and 'obligation', and
accordingly also the moral nature of man, moral status and other relevant
issues. The work is clearly incomplete as Reitzer in several places referred
to a second chapter which would discuss the principles of natural and universal positive divine law.[33] Nevertheless the often detailed discussions
mean that Reitzer touched upon a wide range of issues to substantiate
his definitions and their implications, drawing predominantly on the early
chapters of Pufendorf's *De iure* and *De officio hominis et civis iuxtam legem
naturalem* (On the Duty of Man and Citizen According to Natural Law),[34]
Thomasius's *Institutes* and Grotius's *De iure belli ac pacis*. The work thus
provides ample material to show that Reitzer, like Thomasius, followed the
fundamentals of Pufendorf's position, and precisely those that were considered most controversial at the time: his moral voluntarism, the doctrine
of *entia physica* and *moralia* and imposed statuses, and the injunction of
sociality as the foundational precept of natural law.[35]

Reitzer signals his commitment to Pufendorf's and Thomasius's
advances in the theory of natural law by prefacing the *Positionum* with a
brief account of the importance and development of the discipline similar
to the one given by Thomasius.[36] Among the greatest advances of the
modern age was that the 'discipline of universal divine law' had been put
on a firm foundation. Grotius was the first properly to distinguish natural and positive law. On this basis, the 'clouds' with which the scholastic
moralists had obscured Scripture were dispersed, the boundaries between
(divine) natural law and divine positive law were defined and each thus
put on a secure basis.[37] However, this did not mean that Reitzer was primarily a 'Grotian', and in fact he criticised Grotius along lines suggested
by Pufendorf.

The first criticism of Grotius came early in the work, where Reitzer
adopted Pufendorf's voluntarist and anti-scholastic definition of law as a
command issuing from a superior. In a note to *positio* 5, Reitzer explained
that this definition was in contrast to 'what Grotius seems to establish
with the scholastics, when in the *Prolegomena* to *De iure belli ac pacis*

§11 he says that "the law of nature would obligate even if God did not exist".[38] In elaborating on this definition in the following *positio*, Reitzer further argued that since a law is the command of a superior, and since God has no superior, God cannot be subject to law. On this basis he criticised a doctrine held not only by Catholic scholastics, but also, as Reitzer undoubtedly knew, by many Protestant natural lawyers (including, as we shall see, Henrik Weghorst): 'And from this follows that the "eternal law" according to which the scholastics say God acts is a pure figment of the imagination.'[39] Despite his praise of Grotius in the preface, then, Reitzer, like Pufendorf and Thomasius, saw his break with scholasticism as incomplete in crucial respects. Indeed, Reitzer also followed the implications of Pufendorf's voluntarism for his understanding of man's moral nature and the character and principles of natural law. Of these two central topics, the first received the most thorough discussion, as the discussion of the second belonged to a later (unfinished) part of the work.

Reitzer's discussion of moral status, in which he followed Pufendorf's distinction between physical and moral entities, came in *positio* 23 on how man can hold rights.[40] 'Rights belong to a person', Reitzer explained, 'not as a physical but as a moral person, and indeed as a man considered as existing in a certain status.' A status, then, was a given man's 'place and condition in communal life', according to which a person holds certain rights and obligations granted to him by a superior.[41] Reitzer emphasised two aspects of this definition of person and status. First, the complete separation between man's physical nature and moral personhood. Thus, a single natural person could 'enjoy several statuses', such as 'father in the house, advisor in the court, senator in the senate, captain in the army, etc.', along with the different rights and obligations of each as long as they were compatible. Moreover, several natural persons could be considered as one 'complex person' if united in moral status, such as states, churches and universities. Second, although status was a moral quality superimposed on man, man was never in fact without a particular moral status of one sort or the other. For at the very least man was in a natural state or state of humanity, in which he enjoyed certain rights and obligations, itself a status imposed on man as a moral person – by God.[42]

Natural law, then, was the law God had imposed on man to govern his behaviour in the 'natural state'.[43] As mentioned, Reitzer did not discuss natural law as an independent subject of a *positio*, but his position is evident from places where natural law is touched upon in discussing other issues. Thus, in *positio* 32 Reitzer made it clear that sociality, by which the temporal happiness of mankind is maintained, was the foundation of natural law.[44] From the fact that human nature was such that it could not be maintained without this law, one should conclude that God in fact obligated men to obey it: 'By the very act by which God the Creator of all things imposed on us a certain nature, which cannot be preserved without observing the laws of nature, the observation of these laws is understood to be imperatively imposed on us.'[45]

In the *Positionum ex jure divino universali*, then, Reitzer was effectively in the process of constructing an introduction to Pufendorfian natural law. This included presenting precisely the aspects of this system which were most controversial at the time: the strict distinction between moral theology and natural law, the strong moral voluntarism and doctrine of imposed statuses or personae, and sociality as the foundation of natural law. The wider significance of this becomes clear when we consider the religious and political aims of Pufendorf's works on natural law. As Ian Hunter has argued, Pufendorf had developed a 'detranscendentalised' theory of natural law to promote the 'secularisation' of the early modern state. In doing so Pufendorf had reformed the discipline of natural law that had held together a philosophical-theological synthesis that was centred in the faculties of theology and helped secure the influence of theologians in the political-religious constitution of the early modern confessional state. Pufendorf's works on natural law thus had important consequences for the nature of the state and were part of a contest between two professional groups about the authority to determine the social and political order of the state, the theologians and the jurists.[46] In adopting the more radical aspects of Pufendorf's and Thomasius's theories of natural law, Reitzer was simultaneously championing this political programme. It would seem that Reitzer was fully aware of the controversial aspects of his endeavour, for although the arguments and definitions offered in the 1694 and 1702 editions of his textbooks were virtually identical, any references to relevant passages in Thomasius were omitted from the former edition whereas they could be found in the latter.

Christian Natural Law: Weghorst's *Compendii juris naturae dissertatio prima*

At first glance, Weghorst's *Compendii juris naturae dissertatio prima* might give the impression that Weghorst was indeed following Grotius or Pufendorf in his theory of natural law. The work begins with a substantial quotation from Grotius's *De iure belli ac pacis* defining *ius naturae*, and contains further quotations from Grotius in key places. Likewise, the structure of the work bears some resemblance to Pufendorf's *De officio hominis et civis*, the first chapter concerning the definition of natural law, followed by chapters on the principle of natural law and on the duties towards God. This structure of discussing duties towards oneself, God and other persons was, however, quite conventional in the Lutheran world.[47] Moreover and more significantly, a closer look at Weghorst's argumentation quickly reveals that his position departed significantly from those of both Grotius and Pufendorf. In fact, as will be shown, Weghorst's *Compendium* exhibited all the characteristics of 'anti-Pufendorfian' works of natural law identified by Thomasius, and this reflected the academic environment in which Weghorst had received his university training.

Weghorst had received his university education at Kiel University in the Duchies of Schleswig-Holstein, where he enrolled in 1670. After some years, he did the usual European tour, to Germany, Italy and France, before before returning to Kiel where he became Dr. Jur. in 1681. Natural law had been taught at Kiel University since it was founded in 1665. During Weghorst's studies there, the professor of natural law was Samuel Rachel, a prominent representative of what has been termed 'Christian natural law'.[48] This tradition, which also included authors such as Johann von Felde, Caspar Ziegler, Johann Adam Osiander and Valentin Alberti, sought to re-establish natural law on a Christian foundation against the secularising theories of natural law developed by Grotius and Hobbes, and later Pufendorf and Thomasius. Rachel was one of the thinkers, also including Pufendorf and Conring, whom Baron von Boineburg approached to produce a system of natural law.[49] Weghorst had ample opportunity to become acquainted with the tradition of 'Christian natural law': according to the *Catalogus lectionum in Academia Christian-Albertina Kiliensi*, Rachel taught courses on 'Jus naturale' in 1671, on 'Jura naturae & arbitraria' in 1672, on Grotius's *De iure belli ac pacis* in 1673, 'Juris naturae & gentium doctrina' in 1674, his *Dissertationes de Jure naturae* in 1675, and 'Jurisprudentia universalis' in 1676–77.[50]

In the construction of his natural law theory, Rachel discussed several 'modern' works, but in particular Hugo Grotius's *De iure belli ac pacis*, which he interpreted through William Grotius's *De principiis iuris naturalis*. Rachel drew extensively on certain scholastic doctrines combined with extensive use of Aristotle and Cicero, as was common to much Protestant natural law theorising in the wake of Grotius. Central to Rachel's theory was the view that certain things or actions were eternally and in themselves good and provided a fundamental framework for God's creation. Natural law was the means by which man was obligated to do those things good in themselves and avoid those bad in themselves:

and hence it is that that which the Law of Nature enjoins or forbids is not, respectively, good or bad merely because God has of his free will decided to enjoin the one or forbid the other; but since the former is in its essence wholly good and the latter wholly bad, God could not but forbid this and enjoin that.[51]

In further determining the specific precepts of natural law, Rachel turned first to discussing the alternative 'systems' for determining these laws. Having presented contemporary theories, including those of Selden, Sharrock, Cherbury, Cumberland and Hobbes, he finally turned to Aristotle's *Posterior Analytics* for a method for the discipline of natural law or 'scientia philosophiae moralis'.[52] Having set down as first principles the existence of God, divine providence and the immortality of the soul, Rachel on this basis developed the laws of nature governing man's society with God and with other humans. In order to determine these, Rachel argued, one must first ask: 'What is the ultimate end of man considered as a political animal by nature, ζῷον φύσει πολιτικόν? That end, I say, is conformity or congruence of the human will, which is the proximate principle of moral conduct, with the Divine will, as expressed in natural laws.'[53] In so doing man would not only express the 'primeval image of God' but also, Rachel asserted with a reference to William Grotius, 'attain the utmost perfection of which he is capable in this life'.[54] In elucidating what this meant in more specific terms, Rachel resorted to the Roman law dictum 'suum cuique tribuere': 'Man, therefore, attains this Assimilation and Perfection when he renders to God, to himself, and to his fellows the things which are due to them respectively, and avoids the contrary.'[55] Finally, in answering the question of what the due – the 'praestanda' – according to natural law amounted to, Rachel found no better answer than piety to God and the Aristotelian virtues to others in human society.[56]

Although Weghorst never cited Rachel in his *Compendium juris naturae*, it would seem that it was significantly informed by his studies in Kiel in the 1670s. Concluding the manuscript with a few reflections on the challenges of writing the work, Weghorst noted that he had based the *Compendium* on his private studies of natural law fifteen years earlier (that is, c. 1679).[57] Indeed, there are, as will be shown, several points of similarity on central issues in Rachel's and Weghorst's theories of natural law. In developing his own theory of natural law Weghorst thus drew on several Grotius commentators from the seventeenth century who had endeavoured to 'Christianise' Grotius's theory of natural law: Caspar Ziegler, Philipp Reinhart Vitriarius and William Grotius, as well as the French jurist Jean Domat. Weghorst was, moreover, undoubtedly aware of Pufendorf's position, as the citations in the work reveal. At one point Weghorst cited Pufendorf's *De officio*, on the issue of innate ideas, only to dismiss discussion of the issue as redundant ('supervacuum').[58] Another paragraph cites a section of Vitriarius's commentary on Grotius, which refers the reader to a part of Pufendorf's *Specimen controversarium circa ius naturale*, 'De origine moralitatis et indifferentia motus physici in actione humana', that discusses the distinction between *entia physica* and *moralia*.[59] It would thus seem that Weghorst was consciously developing an alternative to Pufendorf's theory of natural law which was becoming increasingly in vogue, and which was spearheaded in Copenhagen by his colleague Reitzer.

Grotius's theory of natural law in *De iure belli* fitted Weghorst's purposes in that it allowed him to argue that certain things were necessarily in accordance with 'rational nature' as an objective basis of natural law. In other words, he could use Grotius as an authority for the ('perseitas') doctrine that certain things were morally good or bad in themselves and as such the object of natural law: 'Therefore according to the opinion of Grotius there are actions necessarily conforming or contrary to rational nature, and which by their nature are prior to natural law.'[60] This was a 'necessity' of the 'moral action' which was independent of the determination of any law, but which rather showed which actions the law should determine as obligatory and thus invest with a 'legal necessity'.[61] Weghorst thus insisted, contrary to the Pufendorfian position, that certain moral actions, 'worshipping God' is the example given, are 'necessary in themselves apart from the obligation of law'.[62] As he concluded later in the same chapter: 'thus actions morally good in themselves are the foundation of natural law'.[63] In this regard, Weghorst positioned himself in a line of natural law theoreticians, such as Osiander, Ziegler and Vitriarius, who criticised Grotius's *etiamsi daremus* principle by arguing that the obligatory force of natural law stemmed from the command of God, but likewise, in contrast to Pufendorf, argued that certain actions were good in themselves and therefore the object of natural law.

The further question, however, was in what this 'necessary conformity' with rational nature consisted, in other words, what was the 'principium cognoscendi' of natural law. Here Weghorst's theory of natural law exhibited a second of the scholastic, anti-Pufendorfian characteristics identified by Thomasius, explicitly departing from the position of Grotius (and Pufendorf) in denying that sociality (such 'actions that conserve the society of rational beings') was a sufficient basis for natural law:

As I see it, it is indubitable that those actions without which or by which society among humans is destroyed pertain to natural law. But that all the precepts of natural law have as their end that human society is maintained, I believe should be rejected. No indeed, from the following it will be clear that those precepts which seem to have as their end the maintenance of society do not have this as their final end.[64]

Where Grotius had secularised natural law by positing sociality as a necessary and sufficient foundation and by his *etiamsi daremus* principle, and where Pufendorf had detranscendentalised natural law with his radical voluntarism, Weghorst reinforced the transcendent character of natural law and moved God centre stage by positing the love of God as the foundation of natural law:

Disregarding the opinions of others, I consider that man is created first and foremost for this end: that he should love God. And since the love of God is good in itself, God also obliges man to do so by the natural law. From this it is evident that the basis of natural law should be determined in accordance with the end of man, so that accordingly the basis of natural law is the love of God, of oneself, and one's fellow man. Of these the love of God is the foremost end. . . . Neither indeed do they err, who posit the basis of natural law solely in the love of God, for from this cannot but follow the love of men.[65]

This paragraph succinctly demonstrates the extent to which Weghorst's position was in line with the key doctrines of 'anti-Pufendorfian', neo-scholastic, Christian natural law identified by Thomasius. First, in the quote Weghorst emphasised the realist character of his theory of natural law, that this love of God was 'good in itself' and therefore commanded by natural law, not the other way around. Second, Weghorst's natural law theory was indeed orientated towards the essential nature of man, realising the end – *finis* – for which man has been created. Finally, to Weghorst sociality was not the fundamental principle as it could, he argued, encompass neither man's duties to himself nor his duties to God.[66]

Having appropriated Grotius's use of the *perseitas* doctrine only to argue for an alternative foundation of natural law to sociality, Weghorst continued to further distinguish his position from the aspects of Grotius's position that tended towards a secularised conception of natural law. Against Grotius's argument that natural law would oblige if there were no God, he put forward a voluntarist concept of obligation. Following Caspar Ziegler, he argued that it was God as a supreme legislator that promulgated the law of nature and invested it with obligatory force.[67] Nevertheless, as we have seen, God did so in accordance with the essential goodness of certain actions. In this way Weghorst adopted, again following Ziegler, the scholastic doctrine of an 'eternal law' in accordance with which God acted: 'moreover, we do not deny that the principle of this law [of nature] is the law in God, by which He Himself directs all acts and movements to their ends. See Ziegler on Grotius's Prolegomena, section "Non esse Deum etc.".'[68]

In determining the specific precepts of natural law Weghorst (like Rachel) first discussed the principles commonly advanced: the three established Roman law principles in Ulpian: 'honeste vivere', 'neminem laedere' and 'suum cuique tribuere'.[69] In his interpretation of the Roman law principles, Weghorst drew on Aristotelian virtue ethics: 'of these principles we consider the foremost of all to be that we live honourably [*honeste vivere*]. For to live honourably is to practice any duty of love, be it towards God or man . . . and in this [principle] the precepts of all the virtues are contained.'[70] In the end, however, he settled on a different set of principles more in accordance with the theory of the love of God as the foundation of natural law that he had developed in the previous chapter: '(1) Love in the proper way. (2) Love God from your heart. (3) Love your fellow man as yourself.' The love of God, moreover, could be considered specifically as what was His due and generally as doing everything which God has commanded, including the totality of one's duties according to natural law.[71]

The final chapter discussed the duties specifically towards God: the right knowledge, or contemplation, of God and the worship (*cultus*) of God which Weghorst comprehended under the concept of piety (*pietas*). Although Weghorst concluded the work with the remark that he had shown the knowledge philosophy could obtain even when divorced from Christian faith, his position in this regard was ambiguous. For Weghorst also warned that although it was not the place to explain how God should be contemplated 'according to divine revelation', in fact it was 'not within our powers to comprehend God by means of reason'.[72] Therefore, one should beware not to be led astray by reason, and 'the knowledge of God should be sought in such a way that reason is contained within the bounds of worship, veneration and fear'.[73]

Weghorst's *Compendium* on natural law was an independent work although it shares a number of characteristics with the kind of natural law Samuel Rachel had taught (without referring to him). Weghorst followed Grotius precisely on those issues where the latter had retained scholastic doctrines also found in Rachel: the notion of the *perseitas* of good and evil and an eternal law in accordance with which God obligated man through natural law. Moreover, where Weghorst was the most original in relation to his intellectual background, positing the love of God rather than sociality as the foundation of the law of nature, this had the effect of emphasising the Christian and transcendent aspects of his theory of natural law even further.

Natural Law and Natural Right

Having established that Weghorst and Reitzer developed substantially different theories of natural law in their respective introductions to the subject, we may turn to the question whether such differences also extended to their views on the issue of the relationship between natural law and natural right. The above discussions would suggest that in this regard as well, the relevant context for evaluating the positions of Weghorst and Reitzer is the argumentative framework constituted, in the first instance, by the theories of Hugo Grotius, Samuel Pufendorf and Lutheran 'Christian' natural law. One side was constituted by Grotius's 'radical' position giving primacy to a notion of subjective natural right (however conceived) on the basis of which individuals would negotiate and construct a legal and moral order. The other side was characterised by an emphasis on law and duty common to both Orthodox Lutheran natural law and Pufendorf and Thomasius, who were nonetheless, as we have seen, strongly divided over their respective realist and voluntarist notions of natural law and morality.[74] The following section will argue that, despite the significant differences between Weghorst's and Reitzer's works, they shared the common characteristic of Protestant, post-Grotian natural law that natural right was theoretically subordinated to and derivative of natural law. Both Weghorst's and Reitzer's theories focused on natural law as God's law imposing fundamental duties, obligations and rights on men in their social life, however they might have conceived the fundamental principle of this law.

In the case of Reitzer, the *Positionum* provides sufficient material to determine his position, but in the case of Weghorst it will be necessary to go beyond the printed dissertation, drawing on his manuscript *Compendium juris naturae* and his *Meditationes* on Grotius's *De iure belli ac pacis*. Although the *Meditationes* on Grotius's *De iure belli* is catalogued as 'Anonymous commentary on Grotius . . . interspersed with notes by Henrik Weghorst' at the Royal Library in Copenhagen,[75] the work is very likely Weghorst's own. It is most likely the work mentioned in Albert Thura's 1723 *Idea historiae litterariae Danorum* with the title *Meditationes ad Grotium de J. B. & P. secundum ordinem ipsius Grotii ad singulos paragraphos contextae & connexae*, amongst a list of Weghorst's manuscript works which, Thura writes, Weghorst gave to him before his death.[76] Weghorst's authorship is further corroborated by the fact that it is written in the same hand(s) as the *Compendium*, by substantial overlaps in argumentation as we shall see, and by the fact that Weghorst refers to a commentary of his on Grotius in the *Compendium*.[77] This last point also makes it likely, at least, that the *Meditationes* had been written at the same time as the *Compendium*.

A first indication of Weghorst's view on natural right is that while there are several references to rights in a subjective sense in the (manuscript) *Compendium* on natural law, it is never defined in any substantial way and neither is its relation to natural law. Thus, when Weghorst opens the *Compendium* with a definition of *ius naturae* followed by a quotation of Grotius, it is with the third definition given by Grotius, lending itself most easily to re-interpretation along the lines of Christian natural law.

> The law of nature [*ius naturae*] is the law, which obligates man, by means of right reason, towards the duties towards God and man. It is described by Grotius thus: 'Natural Right is the Rule and Dictate of Right Reason, shewing the Moral Deformity or Moral Necessity there is in any Act, according to its Suitableness or Unsuitableness to a reasonable Nature, and consequently, that such an Act is either forbid or commanded by GOD, the Author of Nature.'

This reading is further reinforced by quoting Vitriarius' definition immediately following: 'natural law is the law which God established through right reason between all men according to the morally good and bad'.[78] Weghorst, then, from the outset focused on Grotius's definition of *ius naturae*, understood as law. This primacy of *ius naturae* as law runs through Weghorst's thinking on natural law.

In summarising man's duties to God, oneself and others in the manuscript *Compendium*, Weghorst included among the latter those due to others in so far as they possess 'certain goods from nature, namely life, soul, body', as well as 'certain common rights of liberty', or in so far as they had rights derived from supervening acts.[79] Earlier, Weghorst had defined such *ius* as a 'facultas moralis', which a person possesses along with other 'bona', but what such a moral faculty was, how and in what sense man might possess this, or its relation to law was not clarified. Instead, Weghorst went on to discuss the rights man holds in and to corporal things, both those capable of being appropriated as private property and those not, broadly following Grotius's account.[80] For a clearer sense of how Weghorst saw the relationship between natural law and natural right it is necessary to turn to the *Meditationes*, where Weghorst explicitly engaged with Grotius's definitions of *ius*.

Weghorst saw both Grotius's definitions of *ius* – first as 'the just' or the not unjust, and second as a 'faculty' or 'moral quality belonging to a person, enabling him to have or do something justly'[81] – as theoretically subordinated to the third sense of *ius* as 'law'. In the first case, noting that Grotius took 'unjust' to mean that which is 'contrary to rational nature and destroys society', Weghorst asserted that a 'more correct' meaning would be that which is 'contrary to the love of God, one's neighbour and oneself, or contrary to the end of and obedience to the law'.[82] And as we saw above, Weghorst precisely defined the first principle of natural law as the love of God, subsidiary of oneself and one's neighbour in the *Compendium*.

Commenting on Grotius's third sense of *ius* as law, as a rule of moral actions obliging to that which is right, Weghorst once again offered his own 'more correct' definition as 'a precept of a superior concerning moral actions, that they should conform to the intention of the lawgiver'.[83] In the following paragraph, Weghorst defined specifically *natural* law as 'divine law revealed to man through right reason, so that by obeying this he would attain the end imposed on him by God'.[84] Moreover, in line with the realist position in the *Compendium*, Weghorst here noted that the proper objects of natural law were the actions in agreement with rational nature, 'in such a way that it cannot not be commanded', such as 'worship God, love parents, refrain from theft'.[85] Furthermore, disagreeing with Grotius's position that there was no such thing as a 'permissive law', Weghorst noted that Grotius himself had in fact operated with permissive natural law, citing his discussion of the right to appropriate property.[86] To Weghorst there was in fact a permissive natural law whose effect was a 'moral faculty', just as the effect of a commanding law was 'moral necessity'.[87] In this way, it would seem correct to say that at least in one sense natural right as a *facultas moralis* was, for Weghorst, an effect of permissive natural law.

This reading of Weghorst's account of the relation between natural law and natural right is in line with the larger structure of his (manuscript) *Compendium juris naturae*, consisting in the first instance of precepts of natural law concerning, as outlined above, man's duties towards God, himself and his fellow men. In the most general terms, the duty to love others meant caring for and not diminishing their *bona*. These included their 'life, soul and body', as well as 'fame, dignity, riches' and rights.[88] From this fundamental precept Weghorst derived specific precepts concerning each of these *bona*, including property rights, right of punishment arising from violation of rights, and the duties pertaining to marriage, servitude and the 'status civitatis'. Weghorst did describe how man might create and receive rights, for instance through contracts or by appropriating property. However, as it would seem, Weghorst conceived these rights as effects of permissive natural law, with the precepts of natural law establishing corresponding obligations of others to respect them. For instance, the precept that one should not harm the right which pertains to another, as the heading of the tenth chapter has it. Whether or in what cases the right of one person should be seen as a permissive effect of one law commanding another to respect this right, or whether rights and obligation were effects of permissive and commanding laws respectively, Weghorst did not make clear in the *Compendium*.[89] In any case, the fundamental structure of the work was the derivation of specific precepts, and duty and virtue remained primary. As Weghorst wrote, introducing the precepts regulating the duties of man towards man:

> there are indeed duties, which man should perform towards another. These indicate the virtues, which commonly direct the actions towards all others, such as justice, liberality, mercy, courage and others. Certainly, if one could do whatever one pleased to another, there would be no order but the utmost disorder, and no distinctions between persons in human society.[90]

In contrast to Weghorst, Reitzer clearly set out the relation between natural right and natural law in the *Positionum*. In the second *positio*, Reitzer clarified the various meanings of the term *ius*, the three principal discussed in the work being law (*lex*), an attribute of a person, and an attribute of an action. Of these, Reitzer further explained in a note, law was primary, as a precondition of the other two: 'for I have a right of doing or having because the law gives or asserts it against others, and an action is said to be just because it agrees with the law'.[91] Having explained in more detail the concept of law, and the moral nature of man as capable of being subject to law, Reitzer then turned to a detailed definition of right as an attribute of a person in *positio* 22.

Expanding on the definition given in Thomasius's *Institutes*, to which the reader is referred along with Grotius and Pufendorf, Reitzer defined right as an attribute thus: 'an active moral quality belonging to a person, always conferred by a superior and relating to human beings, enabling that person to justly receive or do something against other persons with whom he lives in society'.[92] In the first note to the *positio*, Reitzer clarified that while the rights of subjects are dependent on the right of a superior to command, it is only the right of God as creator of the universe, who knows no superior – which is 'most different from human right' – that is truly primary. All human right is ultimately dependent on God's will, and thus has its origin in the law or will of a ruler.[93]

This point is brought home further in the following *positiones*. In *positio* 27, Reitzer discussed natural and what he, following Thomasius, termed innate (*congenitum*) right, which man holds immediately from God. Referring back to the discussion of the state of nature in *positio* 23, Reitzer explained that certain rights pertain to man *qua* possessing reason. 'Thus we have the right, prior to any human acts or pacts, that other men not hurt us without cause, or hold us in contempt, that they perform their duties of humanity towards us, keep their words to us, and in short treat us as in like manner human beings.'[94] The reference back to *positio* 23 served to make the point that such rights reflected man's capacity to recognise God as supreme lawgiver and his obligation to act accordingly.

This account might give the impression that Reitzer was, after law, giving priority to rights over obligations. This would, however, be too hasty a conclusion. The discussion after law of right rather than obligation was not one of logical order, according to which rights would be morally prior to obligations, but purely of an expositional order (explaining first the various meanings of *ius*), in which Reitzer largely followed Thomasius's *Institutes*. On the logical relation between right and obligation, one should take note of a few things. First, Reitzer argued that right and obligation were correlates, that is, one cannot exist without the other so that one person's right always corresponded to the obligation of another, and that neither were possible outside of a society. Thus it was only in a society, whose members were obliged to act towards one another in a certain way in accordance with that society's aim, that it was possible to claim rights.[95] In the most fundamental sense, since all humans recognised God as a supreme ruler they were united in a natural society (or state of nature) whose end was 'the happy and peaceful life of the whole human race'. A society's end could only be obtained, however, if the human beings living therein 'were obliged to perform certain duties towards one another'.[96]

The constellation of natural rights and obligations constituted, then, the duties – *officia* – which men owed each other in accordance with natural law. Imparted by God they constituted man's status, his 'place and condition in common life' in the natural state, and thus his most basic moral person. This was bestowed primarily with the purpose of attaining a certain end, 'the happy and peaceful life' of humanity, and it was for this reason that the innate, natural rights enumerated by Reitzer corresponded so closely to the (absolute) duties derived by Pufendorf from the fundamental principle of natural law, sociality.

Conclusion

Existing scholarship has described the history of natural law in early enlightenment Denmark-Norway as the story of the introduction of 'modern' natural law derived from Grotius and Pufendorf in the generation around 1700. In contrast, this chapter has argued that, while Weghorst and Reitzer both broke new ground relative to Masius's orthodox confessional denial of natural law on the basis of reason, the decades around 1700 in fact saw the rivalry and competition between significantly different traditions within post-Grotian natural law. In so far as the Danish writers on natural law were following the theories of either Grotius or Pufendorf, they had been received and reinterpreted through local discourses of natural law: 'Christian natural law' in Kiel in the case of Weghorst, and Thomasius's Pufendorfian natural law in Halle in the case of Reitzer. As such, Weghorst and Reitzer disagreed significantly over such central questions as the character of natural law and its first principle or foundation, the relation between law and the moral good, and the question of eternal law. Where Reitzer was propounding a theory of natural law based on sociality central to the secularising, anti-confessional agenda of Pufendorf and Thomasius, Weghorst denied precisely the sufficiency of sociality as the basis of natural law, drawing instead on the realist aspects of Grotius's oeuvre to reinforce the transcendental and Christian aspect of his theory of natural law.

Nevertheless, there were also similarities between Weghorst and Reitzer's theories, particularly in their conceptions of the relation between natural law and natural right, as the last section has shown. While they differed profoundly in their understanding of the principle of natural law, neither of them were prepared to take up the aspects of Grotius's theory that arguably tended towards a primacy of natural rights. Weghorst, whose works were to a larger degree orientated towards Grotius, explicitly re-interpreted Grotius's definitions of *ius naturale* as subjective right in a way giving primacy to natural law as God's commands, while retaining its realist and Christian foundations. Having done so, and having furnished his theory of natural law with the appropriate realist, transcendental and Christian foundations, Weghorst was free to engage with the works of classical authors, Grotius and even Pufendorf in his more casuistic discussions of the precepts, rights and duties of natural law. Reitzer for his part was engaged in writing an introduction to divine and natural law fully committed to the positions of Pufendorf and Thomasius. Apart from the supreme right of God the creator and ruler of the universe, and as far as human morality was concerned, law as command, and fundamentally divine natural law, was fundamental. Rights and their corresponding obligations were bestowed on persons by a superior, which constituted the nexus of *officia* that made up social and political life.

As such Weghorst and Reitzer illustrate both the common ground of much Lutheran natural law theorising in the later seventeenth century – a focus on duties as constitutive of social and political life – as well as the competition and decisive differences between a scholastically informed, realist and Christian natural law underpinning the confessional state on the one hand, and Pufendorf's and Thomasius's voluntarist, secularising theories of natural law focusing on the requirements of sociality on the other. Weghorst and Reitzer both continued to set the agenda for natural law theorising in Copenhagen in the first decades of the eighteenth century. Weghorst lectured on Grotius and moral philosophy, and Reitzer, in addition to his teaching, also acted as mentor for a younger generation of thinkers, including Ludvig Holberg and Andreas Hojer, the first professor of natural law at the University.[97] The story of the further competition between these different forms of natural law theory and their wider intellectual and political significance for the early enlightenment in Denmark-Norway still largely remains to be told.

Notes

1. For detailed discussions of the polemics between Masius and Thomasius from a variety of perspectives, see Frank Grunert, 'Zur aufgeklärten Kritik am theokratischen Absolutismus. Der Streit zwischen Hector Gottfried Masius und Christian Thomasius über Ursprung und Begründung der summa potestas', in *Christian Thomasius (1655–1728). Neue Forschungen im Kontext der Frühaufklärung*, ed. Friedrich Vollhardt (Tübingen: Max Niemeyer Verlag, 1997), 51–77; Frank Grunert, '"Händel mit Herrn Hector Gottfried Masio." Zur Pragmatik des Streits in den Kontroversen mit dem Kopenhagener Hofprediger', in *Appell an das Publikum: Die öffentliche Debatte in der deutschen Aufklärung 1687–1796*, ed. Ursula Goldenbaum (Berlin: Oldenbourg Akademieverlag, 2004), 119–74; Frank Grunert, 'Konfessionelle Konkurrenz und politisches Kalkül. Der dänische Hofprediger Hector Gottfried Masius', in *Religion Macht Politik: Hofgeistlichkeit im Europa der Frühen Neuzeit*, ed. Matthias Meinhardt et al. (Wiesbaden: Harrassowitz Verlag, 2014), 323–40.
2. See e.g. Thomas Ahnert, *Religion and the Origins of the German Enlightenment: Faith and the Reform of Learning in the Thought of Christian Thomasius* (Rochester: University of Rochester Press, 2006); Annabel S. Brett, *Changes of State: Nature and the Limits of the City in Early Modern Natural Law* (Princeton: Princeton University Press, 2011); Frank Grunert, *Normbegründung und politische Legitimität: zur Rechts- und Staatsphilosophie der deutschen Frühaufklärung* (Tübingen: Max Niemeyer Verlag, 2000); Knud Haakonssen, *Natural Law and*

Moral Philosophy: From Grotius to the Scottish Enlightenment (Cambridge: Cambridge University Press, 1996); Knud Haakonssen, 'German Natural Law', in *The Cambridge History of Eighteenth-Century Political Thought*, ed. Mark Goldie and Robert Wokler (Cambridge: Cambridge University Press, 2006), 249–90; Tim J. Hochstrasser, *Natural Law Theories in the Early Enlightenment* (Cambridge: Cambridge University Press, 2000); Ian Hunter, *Rival Enlightenments Civil and Metaphysical Philosophy in Early Modern Germany* (Cambridge: Cambridge University Press, 2001); Ian Hunter, *The Secularisation of the Confessional State: The Political Thought of Christian Thomasius* (Cambridge: Cambridge University Press, 2007); Richard Tuck, *The Rights of War and Peace: Political Thought and the International Order from Grotius to Kant* (Oxford: Oxford University Press, 1999).

3. The significance of Thomasius for the universities in Halle and Göttingen has been studied in detail in Notker Hammerstein, *Ius und Historie: ein Beitrag zur Geschichte des historischen Denkens an deutschen Universitäten im spaten 17. und im 18. Jahrhundert* (Gottingen: Vandenhoeck & Ruprecht, 1972).

4. Dominik Recknagel, 'Naturrecht in der Lehre. Naturrechtliche Vorlesungen an der Friedrichs-Universität zu Halle bis zum Jahr 1850', in *'Vernunft, du weiß allein, was meine Pflichten sind!' Naturrechtslehre in Halle*, ed. Dominik Recknagel and Sabine Wöller (Halle [Saale]: Mitteldeutscher Verlag, 2013), 12.

5. Bo Lindberg, *Naturrätten i Uppsala 1655–1720* (Uppsala: Almqvist och Wiksell, 1976); Per Nilsén, *Att 'stoppa munnen till på bespottare': den akademiska undervisningen i svensk statsrätt under frihetstiden* (Lund: Institutet för rättshistorisk forskning, 2001). For the reception of Christian Thomasius in the Baltic, see Hanspeter Marti, 'Christian Thomasius und der Pietismus im Spiegel ihrer Wirkungsgeschichte. Zur philosophiegeschichtlichen Bedeutung der Thomasius-Rezeption im Baltikum', in *Christian Thomasius (1655–1728). Neue Forschungen im Kontext der Frühaufklärung*, ed. Friedrich Vollhardt (Tübingen: Max Niemeyer Verlag, 1997), 235–50.

6. For important suggestions in this direction, however, see Kasper Risbjerg Eskildsen, 'Print, Fashion, and the Making of the Enlightenment Philosopher', in *Northern Antiquities and National Identities: Perceptions of Denmark and the North in the Eighteenth Century. Symposium held in Copenhagen August 2005*, ed. Knud Haakonssen and Henrik Horstbøl (København: Det Kongelige Danske Videnskabernes Selskab, 2008), 126–44; Knud Haakonssen, 'Holbergs Pufendorf – men hvilken Pufendorf?', in *Ludvig Holbergs naturret*, ed. Jørgen Sejersted and Eiliv Vinje (Oslo: Gyldendal Akademisk, 2012), 31–45; Sebastian Olden-Jørgensen, '"Saa at jeg har efterlevet en Historieskrivers uden at overtræde en Borgers Pligt" – naturret og historie i Holbergs behandling af enevældens indførelse 1660', in *Ludvig Holbergs naturret*, ed. Jørgen Sejersted and Eiliv Vinje (Oslo: Gyldendal Akademisk, 2012), 118–39; Sebastian Olden-Jørgensen, 'Scandinavia', in *European Political Thought, 1450–1700: Religion, Law and Philosophy*, ed. Howell A. Lloyd, Glenn Burgess and Simon Hodson (New Haven: Yale University

Press, 2007), 300–31. The standard account of enlightenment philosophy in Denmark is given as a history of the eclipse of a conservative, Aristotelian philosophy by Wolffianism followed by French and British influences as well as Kantianism. Carl Henrik Koch, *Dansk oplysningsfilosofi, 1700–1800* (København: Gyldendal Akademisk, 2003). But see also Koch, 'Dänemark und Norwegen', in *Die Philosophie des 18. Jahrhunderts*, ed. Helmut Holzhey and Vilem Mudroch, Vol. 5: *Heiliges Römisches Reich Deutscher Nation, Schweiz, Nord- und Osteuropa*, Zweiter Halbband (Basel: Schwabe, 2014), 1509–11, which briefly mentions Thomasius's influence as well.

7. Edvard Holm, *Holbergs statsretslige og politiske synsmåde* (Kjøbenhavn: Gyldendal, 1879), 17, 18n1.

8. Kåre Foss, *Ludvig Holbergs naturrett på idéhistorisk bakgrunn* (Oslo: Gyldendal, 1934), 175.

9. Ditlev Tamm, *Juraen på Københavns Universitet 1479–2005* (København: Københavns Universitet, 2005), 65. For an older account in German briefly discussing Reitzer and Holberg, see Ditlev Tamm, 'Pufendorf und Dänemark', in *Samuel von Pufendorf 1632–1982: ett rättshistoriskt symposium i Lund 15–16 januari 1982*, ed. Kjell Å. Modéer (Stockholm: Nordiska Bokhandeln, 1986), 81–9, at 87–8.

10. For an account of political thought and ideology in Denmark-Norway and Sweden, see Olden-Jørgensen, 'Scandinavia'; for the Lex Regia, Wandal and Masius, see 322–6.

11. For an analysis of Masius's confessional agenda, see in particular Grunert, 'Konfessionelle Konkurrenz und politisches Kalkül'.

12. Hector Gottfried Masius, *Interesse principum circa religionem Evangelicam ad serenissimum ac potentissimum Daniæ Regem* (Hafniae: Joh. Phil. Bockenhoffer, 1687), 3f.

13. 1691 draft of new university statutes printed in William Norvin, *Københavns Universitet i Reformationens og Orthodoxiens Tidsalder*, Vol. 2 (København: Gyldendal, 1940), 86.

14. 1732 university statutes printed in ibid., 114. On the statutes, see Tamm, *Juraen på Københavns Universitet*, 70ff.

15. For a general account of the history of the Knights' Academy and the sources pertaining to it, see William Norvin, 'Det ridderlige Akademi i København', in *Historiske Meddelelser om København*, Vol. 2. rk. 5. bd. (København: Københavns Kommune, 1931), 103–235; William Norvin, 'Aktstykker til Oplysning om det ridderlige Akademi i København 1690–1710', in *Danske Magazin*, 6 series, Vol. 5. (København: Det Kongelige Danske Selskab for Fædrelandets Historie, 1930), 1–169.

16. Norvin, 'Det ridderlige Akademi i København', 206; Norvin, 'Aktstykker', 19, 134

17. Norvin, 'Aktstykker', 68. For biographical information, see 'Heinrich Weghorst', *Dansk Biografisk Leksikon Online*, http://denstoredanske.dk/Dansk_Biografisk_Leksikon/Samfund,_jura_og_politik/Jura/Jurist/Heinrich_Weghorst;

Johann Moller, *Cimbria literata* (Hafniae: Gottmann F. Kisel, 1744), I:715; Johann Heinrich Zedler, *Grosses vollständiges Universal Lexicon aller Wissenschaften und Künste*, 1731, 53, 1917f.; Tamm, *Juraen på Københavns Universitet*, 65.

18. The *Compendium* manuscript bears the inscription 'haec scripseram A. 1694', Henrik Weghorst, 'Compendium Juris naturae' (Copenhagen, Det Kongelige Bibliotek, MS Thott 909 4o, 1694), final page.

19. Henrik Weghorst, *Compendii juris naturæ, Dissertatio prima* (Hafniae: Joachim Smetgen, 1696).

20. Ejvind Slottved, *Lærestole og lærere ved Københavns Universitet 1537–1977* (København: Samfundet for Dansk Genealogi og Personalhistorie, 1978), 90, 139, 213.

21. Ibid., 88, 213. For biographical information, see 'Christian Reitzer', *Dansk Biografisk Leksikon Online*, accessed 2 February 2016, http://denstoredanske.dk/Dansk_Biografisk_Leksikon/Kunst_og_kultur/Litteratur/Bogsamler/Christian_Reitzer.

22. *Lectiones publicae Professorum in Universitate Hauniensi* (Hafniae: Ex Typographeo Regiae Majest. & Universit., n.d.), 1700–1.

23. Christian Reitzer, *Positiones ex jure divino, sive universali, sub præsidio Christiani Reitzer defendent nobilissimi alquot & lectissimi juvenes* (Hafniae: Ex. Reg., Maj. & Univers. Typographeo, 1694).

24. Christian Reitzer, *Positionum ex jure divino universali partis primæ caput primum, seu de iis, quæ universo in iure præcognita esse debent* (Hafniae: Ex Reg., Maj. & Univers. Typographeo, 1702).

25. Christian Reitzer, *De obligatione sontium ad subeundam poenam dissertatio* (Hafniae: Joh. Bockenhoffer, 1693).

26. Christian Thomasius, *Institutes of Divine Jurisprudence: With Selections from Foundations of the Law of Nature and Nations*, ed. Thomas Ahnert (Indianapolis: Liberty Fund, 2011), 'Introductory dissertation', 13ff.

27. Decades later Thomasius would recall Reitzer's stay in Halle in conversation with a travelling Danish student; cf. Vello Helk, *Dansk-norske studierejser, 1661–1813*, Vol. 1 (Odense: Odense Universitetsforlag, 1991), 91.

28. Christian Thomasius, 'Christian Thomas [. . .] Eröffnet Der Studierenden Jugend in Halle Ein Collegium Privatum Uber seine Institutiones Jurisprudentiae Divinae', in *Institutionum Jurisprudentiæ Divinæ Libri Tres* (Halæ: Halæ Sumtibus & Typis Viduæ Christophori Salfeldii, Regiminis Reg. Boruss. Typograph, 1710), 74f. For an account of Osiander's 'Christian natural law', see Hans-Peter Schneider, *Justitia universalis: Quellenstudien zur Geschichte des 'Christlichen Naturrechts' bei Gottfried Wilhelm Leibniz* (Frankfurt am Main: Vittorio Klostermann, 1967), 151–9.

29. Thomasius, 'Collegium Privatum', 76.

30. 'wie er denn auch in Definition des Rechts der Natur der Schul-lehrer ihre Doctrin, dass die durch das Recht der Natur verbothene Dinge per se & antecedenter ad voluntatem divinam böse wären / mit beybehalten / auch nach

ihrer Anleitung geschrieben, dass das Recht der Natur die Menschen verbinden würde / wenn gleich kein GOtt seyn oder sich umb die menschlichen Händel nicht bekümmern solte.' Ibid., 76f.

31. Samuel Pufendorf, *De iure naturae et gentium libri octo* (Lund, 1672).

32. 'Alle Scripta Anti-Pufendorffiana zielen dahin / dass die Socialität kein Principium cognoscendi des Rechts der Natur seyn könne. . . . Hiernechst haben die meisten sich angelegen seyn lassen / die ex lege aeterna hergeleitete convenientiam cum sanctitate divina antecedenter ad voluntatem divinam, oder die sogenandte perseitatem turpitudinis & honestatis in objecta Juris naturae, die von dem Herrn von Pufendorff von ihrem Thron ware verstossen worden / wieder auff denselben zu heben.' Thomasius, 'Collegium Privatum', 79.

33. Reitzer, *Positionum ex jure divino*, 1.c. Here, and in the following, references are given to positio (1) and when relevant note (c).

34. Samuel Pufendorf, *De officio hominis et civis juxta legem naturalem libri duo* (Lund, 1673).

35. For an analysis of these issues in Pufendorf, see Hunter, *Rival Enlightenments*, ch. 4, in particular 162ff.

36. For a discussion of the importance of such histories, see Hochstrasser, *Natural Law Theories in the Early Enlightenment*, 66, 137.

37. Reitzer, *Positionum ex jure divino* (first unnumbered page headed 'L.S.').

38. 'Contra quam cum Scholasticis statuere videtur Grotius, dum in *Prolegominis Jur. B. & P. §11. Legem Naturalem obligaturam fore* dicit, *etiamsi daremus non esse Deum.*' Ibid., 5(a).

39. 'Et hinc sequitur, *aeternam* illam *legem*, secundum quam agere Deum Scholastici dicunt (b), merum solummodo esse figmentum.' Ibid., 6.

40. Reitzer here referred the reader to Pufendorf's *De iure* (bk. 1, ch. 1 and bk. 2, ch. 2), *De officio* (bk. 2, ch. 1) and Thomasius's *Institutes* (bk. 1, ch. 2).

41. '*Jus* autem (a) personae competit, non qua illa *physice*, sed qua *moraliter* (b) & quidem tamquam homo in statu aliquo (c) existens consideratur. *Status* enim est *ipse cujusvis hominis in communi vitae locus & conditio*'. Reitzer, *Positionum ex jure divino*, 23.

42. '. . . abstrahendo ab ista *moralitate*, nullum ipsi jus competit, ut ut inde non sequatur, dari hominem, qui in nullo existat *statu*. Eo ipso enim, quo *homo* est, in *statu* quoq; *humanitatis* degit; at hic *status* propria sua etiam habet *jura*.' Ibid., 23(b), cf. dI. Cf. Pufendorf, *De iure*, bk. 1, ch. 2, §§7 and 12.

43. Reitzer, *Positionum ex jure divino*, 23.dI–III.

44. 'Cum enim *socialitas*, qua utique temporaria humani generis continetur felicitas, en eo consistat, ut sarta tectaque mortalibus talia sua sint *jura*, consequens est, *haec in universum* non magis, quam ipsas naturae leges, quae quidem conservandae socialitati[s] sunt latae, *mutari tollique posse.*' Ibid., 32.

45. 'Eo ipso ergo, quo Deus rerum omnium Creator naturam nobis indidit, quae sine observatione legum naturalium salva esse nequit, earum etiam observationem pro imperio nobis injunxisse intelligitur.' Ibid., 33(f).

46. Hunter, *Rival Enlightenments*, 150, 162f, 195; Haakonssen, 'German Natural Law', 261f.

47. Found, for instance, in Samuel Rachel and H. G. Masius.

48. See Hans-Peter Schneider, 'Christliches Naturrecht', in *Die Philosophie des 17. Jahrhunderts*, ed. Helmut Holzhey and Wilhelm Schmidt-Biggemann, Vol. 4: *Das Heilige Römische Reich Deutscher Nation, Nord- und Ostmitteleuropa*, Zweiter Halbband (Basel: Schwabe, 2001), 813–35; Schneider, *Justitia universalis*, for Rachel, 208–23; Hunter, *Rival Enlightenments*, 132–4. Rachel's 1676 *De jure naturae et gentium dissertationes* was included in the Carnegie series on international law as an important alternative to Pufendorf's doctrine of the law of nations. Samuel Rachel, *De Jure Naturae et Gentium Dissertationes (1776)*, ed. Carl Ludwig Bar, trans. John Pawley Bate, 2 vols, Classics of International Law (Washington, DC: Carnegie Institution, 1916).

49. Rachel, *Dissertationes*, I§101; Hochstrasser, *Natural Law Theories in the Early Enlightenment*, 47.

50. *Catalogus lectionum in Academia Kiliensi*, Personal- und Vorlesungsverzeichnis der Christian-Albrechts-Universität zu Kiel, n.d., http://www.uni-kiel.de/journals/receive/jportal_jpjournal_00000001.

51. 'Hujus igitur Legis Aeternae radii sunt Leges Naturales, quas nobis Ratio, divinae particula aurae, indicat, persuadet ac promulgat. Atque hinc est, quod quidquid Jure Naturae, vel praecipitur vel vetatur, illud non bonum nec malum est ideo quod Deus illud libere voluit praecipere, hoc vetare; sed quia intrinsecus illud omne bonum, & hoc omne malum est, Deus illud non potuit non praecipere, hoc vetare. Ut ita simul intelliges, quo pacto hoc jus divinum Naturale, a Jure divino arbitratio differat. Grot I.c.1.n.10 & 15; Wilh.Grot. de.princ.cap.3.n.2.' Rachel, *Dissertationes*, I§32.

52. Ibid., I§114.

53. 'Discipiendum itaque primo omnium erit, quis sit Hominis finis ultimus, quatenus ille ut ζῷον φύσει πολιτικόν, animal natura civile, consideratur. Hunc finem esse dico, conformitatem seu convenientiam voluntatis humanae, quae actionum moralium proximum est principium, cum voluntate divina legibus naturalibus expressa.' Ibid., I§117.

54. 'in quo fine ultimo cum Homo maximam, cujus quidem in hac vita particeps esse queat, consequatur perfectionem'. Ibid.

55. 'Hanc ὁμοίωσιν & τελείωσιν Homo itaq; obtinet, si Deo, sibi, & aliis praestanda praestet, vitetq; contraria.' Ibid., I§118.

56. Ibid., I§121. Rachel also equated piety with religion and the 'duties of the first table of the Decalogue'. Ibid., I§115.

57. Weghorst, 'Compendium', cap. Ultimum §4. Here and in the following I refer to chapter and paragraph as the manuscript is unpaginated.

58. Weghorst, *Compendii*, cap.1§16. Weghorst here also paraphrased the same passage in Aristotle's *Topica* (without reference) that Rachel had used in justifying the existence of first principles that should not be questioned: 'Recte Aristoteles, eum, qui Deum honorandum aut parentes amandos esse

neget, non argumentis sed poena domandum dixit.' Cf. Rachel, *Dissertatio-nes*, I§115.

59. Weghorst, *Compendii*, cap.1§8. Referring to Philippus Reinhardus Vitriarius, *Institutiones juris naturae et gentium [. . .] ad methodum Hugonis Grotii conscrip-tae* (Lugduni Batavorum, 1692), ch. 1, question 12.

60. 'Ergo secundum sententiam Grotii dantur actus naturae rationali necessario convenientes aut disconvenientes, qui sui natura jus naturae antecedent.' Weghorst, *Compendii*, cap.1§4.

61. Ibid., cap.1.§5.

62. 'Ita cultus Dei, etiam seposita obligatione legis, in se necessarius, & recta ratio eum homini necessario convenientem judicate.' Ibid., cap.1§6.

63. 'Fundamentum itaque juris naturae, sunt actus hominum in se moraliter boni & male.' Ibid., cap.1§13.

64. 'Mihi equidem indubitatum est, actus ejusmodi sine quibus, aut per quos societas inter homines evertitur, ad jus naturae pertinere; at omnia juris nat-uralis praecepta ad hunc finem referri, ut societas inter homines salva sit, negandum esse arbitror. Im[m]o ex sequentibus patebit, praecepta illa, quae societatem tanquam finem suum tueri videntur, in eo tanquam fine ultimo non subsistere.' Ibid., cap.1.§9.

65. 'Missis aliorum opinionibus existimamus, hominem primario ob hunc finem esse factum, ut diligat Deum. Cum autem dilectio Dei in se sit bona, Deus quoque hominem per jus naturae ad eam obligat. Unde apparet fundamen-tum juris naturae a fine hominis aestimandum, ut ita fundamentum juris naturae sit, dilectio Dei, sui ipsius, & socii. Ex his dilectio Dei, principalis est finis. [. . .] Neque vero errant, qui fundamentum juris naturae in sola Dei dilectione ponunt, quippe cum hanc non possit non sequi dilectio hominis.' Ibid., cap.1§10.

66. Ibid., cap.1§12.

67. Ibid., cap.1§14.

68. 'Alioqui non negamus principium hujus juris esse legem in DEO, per quam ipse omnes actus ac motus in suos fines dirigit. *Add. Ziegl. ad Grot. in proleg. Vers: Non esse Deum &c.*' Ibid., cap.1§15. Ziegler has the following: 'Interim tamen hoc non nego esse en Deo aeternam aliquam legem, hoc est rationem divinae sapientiae, directivam omnium actionum & motuum in suos fines, & jus aliquod naturale immanens antecedenter ad omnem liberum voluntatis actum, secuncum quod non potest velle juri illi repugnat.' Kaspar Ziegler, *In Hugonis Grotii De Iure Belli Ac Pacis Libros, Quibus Naturae & Gentium Ius Explicavit, Notae & Animadversiones Subitariae* (Wittebergae: Mevius & Schumacher, 1666), 7f.

69. Weghorst, *Compendii*, cap.2§1.

70. 'Ex his primum omnium principium existimamus esse, honeste vivere. Est enim honeste vivere, quodvis amoris officium exercere; sive illud exhiben-dum sit Deo, sive homini [. . .] Unde hoc principio omnia virtutum prae-cepta continentur.' Ibid., cap.2§2.

71. Ibid., cap.2§6–7; and cf. Rachel above at note 58.
72. Weghorst, *Compendii*, cap.3§7.
73. 'Cum nostrorum virium non sit, DEum ratione assequi, cavendum esse, ne proprius accedamus ad lucem illam inacessim, ne radiorum fulgore obruamur. Ita enim cognitio Dei appetenda, ut intra cultus, venerationis & timoris concellos ratio contineatur.' Ibid., cap.3§7.
74. For an account of this argumentative field, see Haakonssen, *Natural Law and Moral Philosophy*, ch. 1; for the emphasis on duty in Protestant natural law (apart from Grotius), see 26; for the commonalities and differences between Pufendorf and Orthodox Lutheran natural law, 35–46. For a different account of the notion of subjective natural right in Grotius, see Knud Haakonssen, 'The Moral Conservatism of Natural Rights', in *Natural Law and Civil Sovereignty: Moral Right and State Authority in Early Modern Political Thought*, ed. Ian Hunter and David Saunders (New York: Palgrave, 2002), 27–42. The most recent account of Grotius's 'focus on individual rights' and Pufendorf's voluntarist construction of law and duty as the central concepts is in Knud Haakonssen and Michael Seidler, 'Natural Law: Law, Rights and Duties', in *A Companion to Intellectual History*, ed. Richard Whatmore and Brian Young (Chichester: Wiley-Blackwell, 2015), 384f and 388f.
75. Henrik Weghorst, 'Anonymi Collegium in Grotium . . . passim Notulae Henr. Weghorst interspersae' (Copenhagen, Det Kongelige Bibliotek, MS Thott 908 4o). I will refer to this work as 'Meditationes' in the following.
76. Albert Thura, *Idea historiae litterariae Danorum* (Hamburg: Theodor Christophor Felginer, 1723), 162.
77. For instance Weghorst, 'Compendium', cap.12§7 and cap.13§5.
78. 'Ius Naturae est lex, qua homo per rectam rationem obligatur ad officia in Deum ac hominem. Grotio sic describitur: *Ius naturae est dictatum rectae rationis, indicans actui alicui ex ejus convenientia aut disconvenientia cum ipsa natura rationali inesse moralem turpitudinem aut necessitatem moralem, ac consequenter ab auctore naturae, Deo, talem actum, aut vetari, aut praecipi: tr. de Jur. B. &. P. l.1. c.1 §.10.* Vitriarius ita: "*Jus naturae est jus, quod Deus per rectam rationem inter omnes homines constituit propter honestatem & turpitudinem.*"' Weghorst, *Compendii*, cap.1§1. I use the translation in Hugo Grotius, *The Rights of War and Peace*, ed. Richard Tuck, 3 vols (Indianapolis: Liberty Fund, 2005).
79. 'quatenus habet bona a natura, puta vitam, animam, corpus #et iura quaedam libertatis communia#'. Weghorst, 'Compendium', cap.ult.§2. The latter in '#'s is a later marginal addition.
80. Weghorst, 'Compendium', cap.10§2.
81. Weghorst, 'Meditationes', I.1§§3–7. As the work is unpaginated I refer to book (I), chapter (1) and paragraph (§).
82. 'Est autem iniustum, quod naturae rationali repugnat et societatem evertit [. . .] Rectius, quod amore Dei, proximis suiq; ipsius, seu quod legis fini eiusq; obsequio contrarium est.' Ibid., I.1§3.

83. 'Rectius dicitur praescriptum superioris circa actiones morales, ut intentione legislatoris congruunt.' Ibid., I.1§9.
84. 'Ius naturae est lex divina homini per rectam rationem indicata ut ex illius obsequio finem sibi a Deo propositum observet.' Ibid., I.1§10.n.1.
85. Ibid., I.1§10.n.2.
86. Hugo Grotius, *De iure belli ac pacis libri tres* (Paris: Nicolaus Buon, 1625), book 2, chapter 3, §5.
87. Weghorst, 'Meditationes', I.1§9.
88. Weghorst, 'Compendium', cap.6§1–2.
89. Weghorst explained the relation between law, right and obligation in greater detail in a later work. In the third unpublished part of his *Labyrinthus moralis jure naturae pervius* (1713), Weghorst explained that a right is a moral faculty conceded by law, the exercise of which others have an obligation imposed by law not to impede. Weghorst, 'Labyrinthus moralis juri naturæ pervius. Pars I et II impressæ, pars III manuscripta' (Copenhagen, Det Kongelige Bibliotek, MS Thott 910 4o), cap.I [second paragraph mistakenly numbered '9']. He also reiterated that all obligation derives from a legislator (cap.II§3).
90. 'Esse etiam officia, quae in alium exerceri debent, ipsae virtutues, quarum fere omnium actus in alium diriguntur, indicant, puta iustitia, liberalitas, misericordia, mansuetudo, et alia. Certe si quodvis in alium liceret, non esset rerum ordo, sed summa confusio, et in societate humana personarum nulla distinctio.' Weghorst, 'Compendium', cap.5§1.
91. 'Nam & *agendi habendiq; ius* mihi est, quoniam *id Lex* adversus alios dat asser-tive, & *iusta* dicitur *actio*, quia cum *Lege* convenit.' Reitzer, *Positionum ex jure divino*, 2(b).
92. 'definietur (b) per *Qualitatem moralem activam* (c) *personae competentem*, & quod ad homines attinet (d), a Superiore semper concessam ad aliquid (e) ab aliis personis, cum quibus in societate degit, iuste habendum vel adversus eas agendum'. Ibid., 22. Compare Thomasius, *Institutes*, I.1§82.
93. This indeed acted as a limiting point to what would otherwise be infinite regress in the account of human legal and moral order, 'nisi forte progredi velimus in infinitum'. Reitzer, *Positionum ex jure divino*, 22(a).
94. 'Ita absque praecedente ullo vel facto vel pacto humano naturaliter id ius habemus, ne alii homines sine causa nos laedent, ne contemnant, ut nobis officia humanitatis praestent, ut fidem nobis datam servent, ut denique nos tamquam aeque homines tractent.' Ibid., 27(c).
95. Ibid., 24. Later in the work, Reitzer noted that what was said about right was held for obligation as well. Ibid., 34. Accordingly, a man alone in the world would have no right, and in so far as he had an obligation to act in a certain way, this was an obligation towards God, whose law commanded man to conserve himself as a 'servant of God', and be a useful member of human society. Ibid., 24(g).
96. 'Eo ipso enim, quo communem Imperantem, Deum scilicet, agnoscunt, [omnes homines] in aliqua etiam *societate*, nimirum *naturali*, existere intel-liguntur.' Ibid., 24(d). 'Ita e.g. in societate naturali beatam & tranquillam

totius humani generis vitam, in civili autem civium omnium felicitatem primarios esse fines novimus. Qui vero obtineri hi fines possent? ni viventes in istis societatibus homines, alter adversus alterum, certa deberent officia. At hoc iterum praesupponit imperium.' Ibid., 24(e).

97. For Weghorst and Reitzer's lecturing activity, see *Lectiones publicae Professorum in Universitate Hauniensi*. For an account of the international circle around Reitzer, see Martin Mulsow, 'Freethinking in Early Eighteenth-Century Protestant Germany: Peter Friedrich Arpe and the "Traité Des Trois Imposteurs"', in *Heterodoxy, Spinozism, and Free Thought in Early Eighteenth Century Europe*, ed. Silvia Berti, Françoise Charles-Daubert and Richard Popkin (Dordrecht: Kluwer Academic Publishers, 1996), 204–8.

Part II

Natural Law and the Philosophers

5

Natural Equality and Natural Law in Locke's *Two Treatises*

Kari Saastamoinen

I

The idea that human beings are equal by nature is a standard topic in modern commentaries on John Locke's political theory.[1] Together with its sister concept natural liberty it is often associated with the idea of Locke as an early representative of liberal political thought. Locke's notions of natural liberty and equality are seen as signs of his commitment to the values of individual autonomy and political equality held central in liberal-democratic societies of today, and his political theory is read as a more or less successful attempt to articulate those values. In this chapter I will argue that such an approach to Locke's remarks on natural equality is historically misleading, and they are best understood when we take seriously the fact that he developed his political theory within the parameters of seventeenth-century natural law.[2]

In recent years the most sophisticated and widely discussed proto-liberal interpretation of Locke's natural equality has been the one proposed by Jeremy Waldron in his monograph *God, Locke, and Equality*.[3] Commentators have paid much attention to Waldron's views concerning the role of Christian religion in Locke's political theory, and to his attempt to square Locke's remarks on human species in *Two Treatises* with the critique of the traditional notion of the species presented in *An Essay Concerning Human Understanding*.[4] What has received less critical attention is Waldron's claim that behind Locke's political theory was a doctrine of 'basic equality'. By basic equality Waldron means that fundamental but abstract commitment to human equality which lies behind all respectable political theories of today, and which enables us to analyse these theories as rival accounts of what it means to treat human beings as equals.[5] Waldron holds that, while Locke's political theory commented on issues which were relevant in late seventeenth-century England, behind those comments was a commitment to basic human equality similar to the one we find in modern moral and political thought.[6] In *God, Locke, and Equality* Waldron, following Ronald Dworkin's formula of fundamental equality, characterises this basic equality as equal respect and concern.[7] However, in the essay 'Basic Equality', written a few years later, Waldron is more cautious, holding now that in Locke's case we shouldn't speak about equal concern, at least in any active sense of the term.[8] This leaves us with equal respect. While this is an idea with obvious Kantian overtones, what Waldron finds in Locke is not the Kantian *Achtung* we owe to all rational beings as ends in themselves, but the idea that we owe equal respect to all human beings as creatures who are able to know God and his law, and to whom God has offered the possibility of life after death.[9]

If we are purposefully reading Locke as an early liberal, equating natural equality with equal respect easily appears as a fruitful way of analysing his political theory. Given the role the idea of respecting humanity plays in much of modern moral and political thought, this approach seems to make Locke's theory highly relevant to our present concerns. If, however, we are interested in understanding Locke's theory historically, things become more complicated. After all, Locke never explicitly mentioned the idea that we owe equal respect to human beings due to their status as God's special creatures, nor did he use the term 'respect' when discussing the natural equality of human beings.[10] This leaves the possibility that equal respect operated as an unpronounced background assumption in Locke's theory. But as Waldron points out, such an idea is difficult to combine with Locke's expressed opinions on issues such as the subordinated position of women in marriage, the bestialisation of criminals, and the class structure of the English constitution.[11] It is equally tricky to see how such an abstract idea of equal respect fits with the fact that Locke explicitly affirmed the existence of non-consensual relations of authority and subjection among human beings, remarking that things such as birth, alliance and benefits can subject a person 'to pay an Observance to those to whom Nature, Gratitude or other Respects may have made it due'.[12]

In what follows I will argue that the relationship between Locke's notion of natural equality and the above elements in *Two Treatises* is best understood if we abandon the Kant-inspired idea of equal respect and pay attention to how natural equality was conceived in seventeenth-century political thought. In this respect, the crucial observation is that the idea of human beings as free and equal by nature was widely shared in early modern Europe, and that these notions usually referred to the idea that natural law gives no individual political power over another. In *Two Treatises* Locke followed this traditional practice, using the notion of natural equality to denote his own particular version of the view that no person has inherent political author-ity over another. To be sure, the version he offered was in some respects novel and unconventional. Yet it did not include or presuppose anything like the idea of equal respect. As has been noted in previous historically ori-ented scholarship, the natural equality Locke defended was noticeably jural in character.[13] Behind such an account of equality was the idea that, while there are non-consensual moral hierarchies among human beings, due to their personal obligation to preserve their own lives, they are all on the same moral footing with respect to issues relevant to life and death.

II

The notions of natural equality and natural liberty (the two concepts were often seen as interchangeable) were no novelties when Locke wrote *Two Treatises*. They had been articulated already in antiquity, the *locus classicus* being *Corpus iuris civilis*, in which Ulpian maintained that according to natural law human beings are free and equal, wherefore slavery is against natural law (though approved by the law of nations).[14] These notions were adapted to the Christian tradition, used in scholastic philosophy, and often mentioned in early modern political thought.[15] The natural liberty and equality of human beings was affirmed, for example, by a line of six-teenth- and seventeenth-century Jesuits, including widely read authors such as Luis de Molina, Robert Bellarmine and Francisco Suarez. While the character of natural equality and liberty varied from author to author, and these concepts were used for multiple purposes, they referred pre-dominantly to the idea that no individual is by nature a servant of another. This was usually not understood to mean that the origin of political power would be in the consent given by individuals, as individual human beings were not seen as possessing rights which could be used as building blocks for political authority. Most often political power was understood to be established by the people as an already existing corporate entity, though Suarez brought up the idea of an agreement between male householders.[16]

Until the first half of the seventeenth century, natural equality and liberty were most often seen as notions which help us to understand the proper character of human power relations, and were not conceived as subversive with respect to prevailing social hierarchies. During the Eng-lish Civil War Leveller pamphleteers such as Richard Overton and John Lilburne used Roman law and Christian formulations of natural liberty and equality to argue that English freemen were politically equal.[17] At the same time a new way of understanding natural equality was intro-duced by Thomas Hobbes, partly perhaps as a reaction to the radicalism expressed in Leveller pamphlets.[18] Hobbes associated notions of natural liberty and equality vividly with the idea that the state is a human artefact which comes into being by a contract between free and equal individuals. To be sure, the equality he attributed to individuals living in the state of nature lacked traditional references to natural law, consisting mainly in their shared capacity to kill each other. However, Hobbes also referred to natural equality when discussing the laws of nature, i.e. the rules of reason needed to achieve peace. Here, he pointed out that irrespective of the possible differences in individual human abilities, all human beings have a strong tendency to regard themselves as equal with others and are not inclined to join a commonwealth unless this happens on equal terms. From this followed a principle of natural law: '*That every man acknowledge other for his Equall by Nature.*' Such recognition meant above all that people do not demand for themselves rights which they are not ready to grant others, admitting that civil hierarchies are established by the sovereign.[19]

The idea that maintaining peace requires us to recognise others as our equals by nature was adopted by the most widely read natural law theorist of the period, Samuel Pufendorf. In his main work on natural law, *De jure naturae et gentium* (1672), Pufendorf defined natural law as a God-imposed rule which is known by natural reason, and which obligates human beings already in the state of nature irrespective of their religious confession. Offering a demonstrative account of natural law, Pufendorf first established that in order to survive and develop the special abilities God has given them, human beings need social life and interaction. For this purpose, they need to act towards each other in a manner which pacifies as much as possible their inherent tendency to aggressive behaviour. Thus, the fundamental principle of natural law is the duty to maintain and promote peaceful sociality (*socialitas*) among human beings. Other precepts of natural law are then demonstrated by showing that they are, given human nature and condition, necessary means for maintaining sociality. A significant observation in this regard is that while individuals vary greatly in their ability to govern their own actions, they are all highly concerned about their status as human beings. As a result, they are incapable of maintaining peaceful relations with persons who claim for themselves a higher ranking as human beings. Since natural law requires us to maintain peaceful sociality with all human beings, everyone 'must esteem and treat other men as his natural equals, or men in the same sense as he'.[20] This happens, above all, by recognising that relations of domination and servitude are never established by nature alone, but always include an element of consent.[21]

Locke was aware of the popularity of natural equality already when he wrote the essay nowadays called 'Second Tract on Government' (c. 1662).

There, he explained how authors discussing the origins of civil power can be divided into two rival camps. One group claims that the origin of government is to be found in paternal right, indicating that 'men are born in servitude'. Others take as their starting point 'an equality between men founded on the law of nature', holding that human beings are born 'to liberty'. In this early writing Locke saw no need to take sides. Yet he commented on the latter position by pointing out that a commonwealth always requires a sovereign who is not accountable to any earthly power, and that 'such power can never be established unless each and every individual surrenders the whole of this natural liberty of his, however great it may be, to the legislator'.[22] In 'An Essay on Toleration' from 1667 Locke had already changed his mind, despite his formal neutrality between the idea that 'monarchy is *jure divino*' and the contractual theory. Now, he ridiculed the first mentioned doctrine, and explained that if political authority is derived 'from the grant and consent of the people', it cannot be assumed that people would give anyone such power 'for any other purpose than their own preservation'.[23] Yet, Locke did not explicitly mention natural equality in this context, and it was only when he needed to confront Robert Filmer in *Two Treatises* that he discussed this topic in any detail.

We know that when Locke was writing *Two Treatises* he was familiar with Pufendorf's *De jure*, and later he expressed his admiration for the book.[24] Yet, while Locke was evidently inspired by several elements in Pufendorf's theory,[25] their accounts of natural law differed in some respects significantly. Above all, Locke did not adopt Pufendorf's pivotal idea of promoting sociality as the fundamental principle of natural law, but gave this status to our duty to preserve our own lives and, when these are secure, the lives of others.[26] The main purpose of Pufendorf's doctrine of *socialitas*, including the duty to recognise natural equality, was to make apparent how all social hierarchies and institutions are founded on human contracts and imposition, and to eliminate moral and religious pretexts for civil strife.[27] In *Two Treatises*, on the other hand, the fundamental principle of natural law offered citizens a moral criterion for evaluating the legitimacy of political authority and a justification for overthrowing a ruler who had lost their trust. Before exploring how such understanding of natural law was connected to natural equality, we should look at the peculiar idea of natural inequality Locke aimed to refute in *Two Treatises*.

It is well established that Locke's main intellectual adversary in both *Treatises* was Robert Filmer, whose works had been republished (or in the case of *Patriarcha* published for the first time) during the Exclusion crisis. In *Patriarcha* Filmer had observed that the idea of human beings as free and equal by nature was widely shared 'by divines as by divers other learned men', referring especially to Bellarmine and Suarez, but also mentioning 'over zelous' Calvinists such as George Buchanan. Filmer claimed that these authors had used notions of natural liberty and equality to justify the view that the people have a right to choose any form of government they please and even a right to punish the king, if he violates the laws of the monarchy.[28] In doing so they had failed to notice that if all human beings truly are free and equal by nature, this means that every individual, not only the organised elite traditionally associated with the term 'the people', is entitled to govern his or her actions independently of others. And Filmer was quick to point out the difficulties involved in any attempt to derive the form of government from the decision of the multitude.[29] The idea of natural inequality Filmer vigorously defended in his works was not the Aristotelian one, in which all relations of domination and servitude in civil life reflect differences in individual virtues and abilities. Instead of the multi-layered natural social hierarchy following from the Aristotelian position, Filmer postulated one grand inequality founded on birth which prevailed between the monarch and his subjects. The power of each king had its origin in the patriarchal power God had given to Adam over his offspring and the whole world. It consisted of the absolute and arbitrary domination over the life, death and material possessions of all his subjects, giving the monarch a full right 'to preserve and to distribute to every subordinate and inferior father, and to their children, their rights and privileges'.[30]

It was this grand inequality with respect to life and death which Locke confronted with his account of natural equality. In order to argue that legitimate political power, i.e. the 'Right of making Laws with Penalties of Death, and consequently all less Penalties',[31] can only be founded on consent and trust, and can never be absolute and arbitrary in character, Locke needed to refute Filmer's claim about the huge innate disparity between the monarch and his subjects. In order to do so, it was not necessary for him to attribute all sorts of equality to human beings. All Locke needed to show was that they are equal in the sense that no one has by nature political power over others. This is, I will argue, all he did, and he did it by claiming that due to their shared God-imposed duty to follow the law of preservation, human beings are all on the same moral footing with respect to life and death. Of course, this alone was not enough to prove that absolute political power could not be established by consent. This element in Locke's argument did not rely on his notion of natural equality, but on the claim that the law of preservation makes any attempt to establish absolute political authority by contractual means morally invalid.[32]

To be sure, Locke also maintained, *pace* Filmer, that the duty of each individual to preserve his or her life gives everyone in the state of nature an equal right to use other creatures for maintaining and improving their lives, and a right to own property. And in the first *Treatise* he associated natural equality with the idea that 'everyone ought to partake in same common Rights and Privileges'. It should be noted, however, that Locke presented this characterisation of natural equality in the middle of his argument for the view that a 'Man has a *Natural Freedom*' in the sense that only 'a Man's own consent subjects him to a Superior'.[33] While we may well say that in Locke's theory human beings are equal with respect to natural rights, his explicit arguments for natural equality were targeted at showing that no one has by nature political power over others.

III

Before exploring Locke's arguments in more detail it should be noted that his much-cited chapter on the state of nature in the second *Treatise* includes formulations which, if read in isolation, appear to indicate that the scope of natural equality is broader than the mere absence of political power relations. First of all, Locke declares that this state is a condition of '*perfect Freedom*' in the sense that everyone has the liberty 'to order their Actions, dispose of their Possessions and Persons as they think fit, within the bounds of the Law of Nature, without asking leave or depending upon the will of any other Man'.[34] A little later he adds that in the state of nature everybody has, in relation to other human beings, 'an uncontroleable Liberty, to dispose of his Person and Possessions'.[35] By strongly emphasising personal autonomy in the state of nature these remarks give the impression that natural liberty and equality rule out not only political power relations but every form of authority one person has over another. Such an interpretation seems to find further confirmation when Locke remarks that the state of nature is a condition of equality in the sense that not only all 'Jurisdiction' but also 'all the Power' is reciprocal, 'no one having more than another'.[36] In the previous chapter Locke has distinguished political power from the power husbands have over their wives and masters over their servants, making it clear that only the first mentioned includes the juridical right of imposing laws sanctioned by punishments.[37] When Locke now says that in the state of nature 'all power' is reciprocal, this could be understood to mean that every sort of authority, not only political power, needs to be founded on consent, especially as he a little later characterises the state of nature as a condition of '*perfect Equality*'.[38]

If the above expressed Locke's considered view on the issue, natural equality could not be a moral precept interlocked with the fundamental principle of preservation, but would need an independent moral foundation, such as equal respect. But as is well known, at the beginning of the chapter on paternal power Locke explicitly remarks that when in the chapter on the state of nature he declared that 'all Men are by Nature Equal', he did not mean 'all sorts of *Equality*', specifying that 'the Equality I there spoke of, as proper to the Business in Hand', was equality 'in respect of Jurisdiction or Domination one over another'.[39] It is significant to note that this is not a reassessment Locke makes after realising that he may have been too egalitarian in the chapter on the state of nature. Already that chapter includes passages which strongly suggest that remarks indicating total personal autonomy should be seen as overstatements, motivated perhaps by a wish to repudiate Filmer's grand natural inequality with an equally bold declaration of natural liberty and equality. The most obvious example is the observation that human beings remain in the state of nature until they 'by their own Consent make themselves Members of some Politic Society; other Promises and Compacts, Men may make one with another, and yet still be in the State of Nature'.[40] As households precede civil society both theoretically and historically, this statement indicates that the domestic subjection of wives and servants does not remove them from the condition of liberty and equality, a positon which makes perfect sense if liberty and equality refer here to the absence of political power.

The jural character of natural equality is also implied in the much-cited remark that 'there is nothing more evident than that Creatures of the same species and rank, born to the same advantages of Nature, and the use of same faculties, are equal amongst another without Subordination or Subjection'.[41] After the publication of Waldron's *God, Locke, and Equality*, it has been popular to ponder how this passage should be understood in the light of what Locke says in *An Essay Concerning Understanding* about the idea of the species, and about the human capacity to make abstractions and to have the idea of God.[42] Recently, Timothy Stanton has pointed out that we should be careful when using philosophical ideas formulated in the *Essay* to explicate Locke's views in *Two Treatises*. In the *Essay* Locke uses terms such as 'man' and 'person' to denote well-defined ideas which abstract clear-cut features from our sensory ideas, whereas in *Two Treatises* he is relying on what he in the *Essay* calls the '*civil Use*' of words.[43] This consists of terms which get their meaning in everyday conversation and represent ideas which are less precise than the ones used in the *Essay*. While the use of well-defined ideas is necessary for the philosophical purposes of the *Essay*, the civil use of words is better suited for 'the upholding of common Conversation and Commerce, about the ordinary Affairs and Conveniences of civil life, in the societies of men, one amongst another'.[44] They definitely offer appropriate vocabulary for a work which aims at convincing a larger group of readers, many of them unfamiliar with the *Essay*, of the legitimacy of overthrowing a monarch. Therefore, in *Two Treatises* Locke does not hesitate to speak about the human species and to use the term 'man' in the everyday sense of 'a thinking or rational Being' which has 'a Body, so and so shaped, joined to it'.[45]

I find Stanton's observation about Locke's civil use of words extremely valuable in this context. Yet, I do not entirely agree with his suggestion that in the case of natural equality Locke still relies on the philosophical idea of a human being as a creature subject to law. Stanton refers here to Locke's remark that 'God having given Man an Understanding to direct his Actions, has allowed him freedom of the Will, and liberty of Acting . . . within the bounds of that Law he is under.'[46] From this, Stanton concludes that when Locke speaks about human beings belonging to the same species and being born to the use of the same faculties, this means nothing more than that they are 'equally capable of grasping and following' the law God has imposed on them.[47] If taken literally, this would mean that it is the mere ability to know and observe God's law, irrespective of the content of this law, which makes human beings equal by nature. Such a proto-Kantian interpretation would make it problematic to claim that Locke's natural equality only refers to the absence of political power in the state of nature, but it would also leave us wondering why Locke bothers to point out that human beings are 'born to the same advantages of Nature'. In my view, we can make better sense of Locke's various remarks on this issue once we notice that they rely not only on the human capability of knowing and observing natural law. What is equally important is the central content of this law, the duty of each individual to preserve his or her life.

It may be tempting to assume that since God has raised human beings above other creatures by endowing them with intellectual and moral abilities, it follows that God also wants them to preserve their lives. Yet scholars have had difficulties in finding justifications for the duty of self-preservation or the immorality of suicide in the *Essay*, where Locke analyses moral agency in terms of well-defined ideas.[48] Of course, Locke famously explains how any corporeal creature with an ability 'to understand general Signs, and to deduce Consequences about general *Ideas*' should be regarded as a 'Man' in the moral sense of being a creature 'subject to Law'.[49] But the fact that a creature is subjected to law does not give us the content of this law. Moreover, even if we understand that the law God has imposed on us aims to promote our happiness, how do we know for sure that it forbids us to terminate our earthly existence? In the essay 'Morality' (1677–8) Locke remarks 'that man is capable of some degrees of happiness and great degrees of misery in this life', adding that it is 'possible that there may be a state after this life wherein men may be capable of enjoyments or suffering'.[50] If our rational faculties give us such a gloomy picture of our worldly existence, why should we conclude that we have a duty to preserve our lives?

In *Two Treatises* this question is answered when Locke in the first *Treatise* explains how we know that God has given every individual a right to use other creatures for preserving and improving their lives. Locke points out that, while God has endowed human beings with special intellectual and moral abilities, he has also planted in them, 'as in all other Animals, a strong desire of Self-preservation, and furnished the World with things fit for Food and Rayment, and other Necessaries of Life'. It is only when we pay attention to all these aspects of God's creation that we become aware of God's 'design, that Man should live and abide for some time upon the Face of the Earth, and not that so curious and wonderful a piece of Workmanship, by his own Negligence, or want of Necessaries, should perish again, presently after a few moments continuance'. A person reflecting on all these things understands that the 'strong desire of Preserving his Life and Being' has been 'Planted in him, as a Principle of Action by God himself'. Therefore, his reason cannot but 'assure him' that by following this natural inclination he obeys 'the will of his Maker'.[51]

In the second *Treatise* Locke explains that since small children are incapable of knowing and observing the law of preservation, they must live under the quasi-juridical authority of their parents. It is important to note that it is not the lack of reason alone which submits children to the authority of their parents. The crucial thing is that due to their inadequate rational abilities children are incapable of preserving themselves. If God had made the world such an amicable place in which children could survive and develop without any help and instruction from an adult, their lack of reason would not give parents similar authority over them. Parental power is needed because the world into which a child is born is a place in which the 'Necessities of his Life, the Health of his Body, and the Information of his Mind . . . require him to be directed by the Will of others and not his own'.[52] Accordingly, children emancipate from parental authority when their rational abilities make them capable of knowing the law of preservation and observing it of their own accord. When Locke declares that 'God having given Man an Understanding to direct his Actions, has allowed him freedom of the Will, and liberty of Acting . . . within the bounds of that Law he is under',[53] he is not speaking about law as an abstract idea, but is referring to the law of preservation. The freedom 'of Man and Liberty of acting according to his own Will' is not founded on rational abilities as such. It 'is *grounded on* his having *Reason*, which is able to instruct him in that Law he is to govern himself by', i.e. the law of preservation.[54] The fact that all normal adults are capable of and entitled to observe this law independently of others means, first and foremost, that they are personally accountable to God for preserving their own lives.

In the chapter on the state of nature Locke takes the above observations as given. When he says that human beings are 'Creatures of the same species and rank', he points out that while they share with other animals a strong desire for self-preservation, they are also endowed with intellectual and moral abilities which raise them above other earthly creatures. By noting that human beings are 'promiscuously born to all the same advantages of Nature', Locke reminds his readers of the fact that God has furnished the world with creatures which they can use to maintain their lives and that everyone is by nature entitled to do so. By adding that human beings are born to the use of 'the same faculties', he emphasises that every adult has an ability to know and a right to observe natural law of their own accord. Together all these observations indicate that every human being is personally accountable to God for preserving his or her life. Therefore, no one is obliged to obey another person in matters important for preservation, and no one is entitled to impose his or her will on others by using the threat of punishment.

It might be protested that the above makes Locke's argument overdetermined, that the conclusion is too obviously implied in the premises. But this is exactly the point. Locke is not making an overstatement but merely stating the obvious when he declares that 'there is nothing more evident' than that creatures with the above natural and moral characteristics are equal in the sense of being 'without Subordination or Subjection'. That the absence of natural subjection refers here solely to political power finds further confirmation in Locke's remark that relations of authority in the state of nature would be different only if it could be shown that God has given some individual 'an undoubted Right to Domination and Sovereignty'.[55] Nothing less than such a God-given power over life and death could alter the character of the state of nature.

When Locke in paragraph II.6 explains why the state of nature is not a state of license, he re-states that it is governed by natural law, adding now that 'Reason, which is that Law, teaches all Mankind, who will but consult it, that being all equal and independent, no one ought to harm another in his Life, Health, Liberty, or Possessions'.[56] By this Locke is not saying that the duty to abstain from harming others would be founded on natural liberty and equality. His idea is that the same principles which make human beings free and equal in the state of nature also impose moral restrictions on their behaviour in that state. The rest of the paragraph consists of three different formulations of this one idea. The first is the much-cited remark that we are all God's property and servants, 'sent into the World by his order, and about his business'. In the first *Treatise* Locke has made it clear that the most elementary worldly business for which God has sent human beings into the world is the preservation of their own lives. Here, he points out how this fact imposes moral norms on how we should behave towards others, as God wants everyone 'to last during his, not one another's Pleasure'. Accordingly, while the fact that we are creatures who share 'one Community of Nature' and are 'furnished with like Faculties' makes it evident that we are equal in the sense that there is no natural political power among us, these features also indicate 'that there cannot be supposed any such *Subordination* among us, that may Authorize us to destroy one another'. Finally, just as we know that God has imposed on us a duty of self-preservation, so 'by the like reason' we can conclude that God has done so to every human individual. Thus, when a person's 'own Preservation comes not in competition, ought he as much as he can, *to preserve the rest of Mankind*'. This means that we should abstain not only from killing other human beings but also from harming things which advance their preservation, including their liberty in the sense of freedom from arbitrary coercion, which Locke characterises as 'the Fence' to their preservation.[57]

The above makes it easier to understand Locke's infamous statement that a person who violates central precepts of natural law can be 'destroyed as a *Lyon* or a *Tyger*'.[58] Timothy Stanton has suggested that Locke is here relying on the functional moral idea of humanity or 'man', defined in the *Essay* as a creature who not only knows a law but also observes it.[59] This assessment should, however, be specified by the observation that the law in question is the law of preservation. Murderers are to be 'treated as Beasts of Prey' not simply because they disobey God's law, but because the law they violate is the one God 'has set to the actions of Men, for their mutual security'.[60] By violating the law of preservation murderers abandon the rule which makes humankind 'one Community' and 'one Society distinct from all other Creatures'.[61] It may not be self-evident that all this necessitates the conclusion that we should treat those who violate the law of preservation like people in the seventeenth century treated wolves, lions and tigers. Locke's choice of words may be motivated not only by a wish to demonise rulers with absolutists aspirations, but also by an awareness of the fact that when he argues for a natural right to execute natural law, he is offering every individual a right which is traditionally seen as belonging solely to God.[62] The important thing in this context is that once some people leave the human community founded on the law of preservation, Locke's notion of natural equality includes no deeper idea of respect which could still constitute a moral tie between them and us.

IV

In Locke's theory, human beings are equal by nature because they are all personally accountable to God for preserving their own lives, wherefore no one has by nature a right to impose on others laws sanctioned by punishments. Such equality does not preclude the existence of non-consensual forms of authority which are not concerned with issues vital for life and death and do not include a right to punish. In such a moral relationship I have a duty to obey the wishes of another, or at least to take them very seriously, but the other person is not entitled to punish me, if I fail to fulfil his or her request.

The existence of such moral forms of authority and obedience is explicitly affirmed when Locke in paragraph II.54 remarks that by natural equality he does not mean 'all sorts of *Equality*'. He clarifies this point by making a distinction between two ways in which human beings are subjected to another person. They may be under the 'Jurisdiction or Domination' of another, or they are subjected 'to pay an Observance' to someone else. The latter form of authority does not require the consent of the subjected party, as Locke points out how '*Birth* may subject some, and *Alliance* or *Benefits* others, to pay an Observance to those to whom Nature, Gratitude, or other Respects, may have made it due'.[63]

In *Two Treatises* Locke is interested in the origin and character of political power and has no reason to say much about moral forms of authority and subjection. But as we shall see below, the work includes at least three short references to such moral relations. They all seem to be founded on natural law, and might perhaps be understood in terms of imperfect rights and duties Locke presumably knew from Pufendorf's *De jure*.[64] Yet, in one of the three instances, Locke's remarks seem to imply that moral authority can be strengthened by civil laws, which is against the idea of imperfect rights and duties as explained by Pufendorf.[65] In any case, Locke's decision not to bother his readers 'with the particulars of the Law of Nature' makes it difficult to be more specific on this issue.[66] From what he says about the law of opinion in the *Essay* we can gather that such moral relations of authority can be powerfully sanctioned by the social pressure established by other people's approval and condemnation. In fact, Locke holds that for most people these sanctions offer a stronger motive for obedience than the sanctions associated with civil law or divine law.[67]

John Marshall has suggested that when Locke refers to moral authority founded on 'Alliance or Benefits' he is supporting one of the central elements of social cooperation in late seventeenth-century England, namely that of giving favours and subjecting others through gratitude. This was a practice so familiar to the social classes Locke had in mind 'that it simply did not need to be expressed at any length in the *Treatise*'.[68] Such practice seems to be assumed when Locke remarks that a person may owe 'gratitude to a Benefactor, to such a degree, that all he has, all he can do, cannot sufficiently pay it'.[69] When he continues by emphasising that even in such extreme cases the benefactor has no right to impose laws on the person who owes him or her gratitude, the observation gets its meaning from the idea that duties associated with gratitude are powerful and may include an obligation to take the wishes of the benefactor extremely seriously. In a culture where moral norms related to favours, gifts and gratitude are less demanding and not sanctioned by strong social pressure, such a comparison between duties of gratitude and political power hardly makes any sense.

That gratitude is a part of natural law can be gathered from Locke's remark that the honour matured children owe to their parents follows from gratitude and is imposed by 'the Law of God and Nature'.[70] Moral authority founded on gratitude is explicitly mentioned when Locke points out that the honour grown-up children owe to their parents includes not only respect, reverence and support, but 'compliance too'.[71] The same idea is implied in the remark that in the case of adult children the 'Duty which is comprehended in the word *honour*, requires less *Obedience*' than in the case of small kids, but for the grown-ups 'the obligation is stronger'.[72] Nothing here gives us a reason to conclude that less obedience would mean no obedience at all. While parents have no juridical or quasi-juridical authority over their full-grown offspring, they are not without moral authority on issues not directly related to life and death, such as who to marry or what profession to choose. Thus, Locke does not contradict his account of natural equality when in *A Letter Concerning Toleration* he points out how no one complains if their neighbours manage their private domestic affairs badly, offering as an example the observation that no 'man is angry with another for an Error committed in sowing his Land, or in marrying his Daughter'.[73] That parents use moral authority over their offspring in marital issues is fully in accordance with the juridical equality which prevails between them, provided parents remember that they are not entitled to punish their adult sons and daughters if they refuse to obey their wishes.[74]

The best-known example of moral authority and subjection in *Two Treatises* is Locke's claim that a marital relationship needs one head, and that it is the husband as 'the abler and the stronger' of the spouses who should enjoy the dominant position. In so far as Locke is here analysing marriage in the state of nature, he is not contradicting his account of natural equality. As is well known, Locke carefully explains that the authority the husband has over his wife is restricted to issues important for the purpose of their union. It includes no political or juridical authority over the wife, and gives 'the Husband no more power over her Life, than she has over his'.[75] Things become more complicated when Locke in the first *Treatise* tells us that this arrangement is generally ordered not only by 'customs of Nations' but also by 'the Laws of Mankind'.[76] Of course, Locke could argue that in political societies wives have given their consent to civil authority, and that it serves the common good to strengthen the authority of the husband by civil laws. Yet it is difficult to see how such legislation would be compatible with Locke's statement that civil laws should be the same for everyone.[77] At this point Locke seems to depart from the idea that all human beings, men and women alike, are on a similar moral footing in respect of issues relevant to life and death. It is important to bear in mind, though, that with his remarks on marriage Locke is not defending the women of his time from domestic abuse, but refuting Filmer's claim that the marital relationship gives the husband political authority over his wife.[78]

The ambivalence in Locke's remarks on marital authority appears to be connected to the exclusion of women from political rights. On this issue, Locke accepts the mainstream prejudices and social conventions of his time. Yet, it should be noted that in *Two Treatises* the precise form of government and the extent of political representation are largely questions of expediency and convention. Nothing in the natural equality of human beings makes one form of government inferior to another, save absolutism, which is incompatible with natural law. In the early innocent days of humankind pure monarchy was a perfectly suitable form of government for people connected by kinship ties. After the invention of money, kings became vain and greedy and the people found 'their Properties not secure under the government' of one man. As a result, 'the Legislature was placed in collective Bodies of men, call them Senate, Parliament, or what you please'.[79] The reason for establishing such institutions was not a wish to make the government more democratic, but the idea that they would make it easier for the citizens to control those using political power. The male-dominated English constitution, with its House of Lords and forty-shilling freeholders, is not demanded by natural equality, but nor does it contradict this principle. What is important is that the government does its job in protecting life, liberty, limbs and possessions. The one feature in Locke's doctrine of well-ordered political community which may be seen as partly dictated by his account of natural equality is the view that civil laws should be the same for everyone (though Locke fails to explain how this applies to women).[80] The reason for this is not that civil laws should reflect equality as a political value. It is rather their aim to advance the common good and the fact that due to the character of their ultimate sanction, all civil laws are 'laws of Life and Death'.[81]

V

Above I have argued that there is no conception of basic equality to be found behind Locke's remarks on natural equality. In *Two Treatises* natural equality was not an independent moral principle with a philosophical foundation of its own. Nor was it understood as a value which should be actualised in political society as much as possible. Natural equality was a label Locke used to denote the moral fact that no one has by nature political power over others, and, more generally, that everyone is on the same footing with respect to things relevant to life and death. There was no deeper and more abstract idea of equality, such as equal respect, behind Locke's use of the term. In fact, Locke could have presented the propositional content of his political theory without mentioning natural equality at all. He could have merely stated that due to their God-imposed duty to preserve themselves and others, human beings in a state of nature have a right to use other creatures for their survival and to own property. Everyone has a right to observe the law of preservation independently of others, no one has legislative power over another, and all are entitled to punish violations of natural law. The reason why Locke used the notion of natural equality to denote such absence of natural political power relations and the moral facts related to it was that in seventeenth-century Europe this was the conventional thing to do.

Notes

1. I would like to thank Sami-Juhani Savonius Wroth for commenting on an earlier version of this essay.
2. On Locke as a natural law theorist, see Knud Haakonssen, *Natural Law and Moral Philosophy: From Grotius to the Scottish Enlightenment* (Cambridge: Cambridge University Press, 1996), 51–8. For recent case studies exploring the natural law background of Locke's views on toleration, see Timothy Stanton, 'Natural Law, Nonconformity, and Toleration: Two Stages on Locke's Way', in John Parkin and Timothy Stanton, eds, *Natural Law and Toleration in the Early Enlightenment* (Oxford: Oxford University Press, 2013), 35–58, and Ian Harris, 'John Locke and Natural Law: Free Worship and Toleration', in ibid., 59–106.
3. Jeremy Waldron, *God, Locke, and Equality: Christian Foundations in Locke's Political Thought* (Cambridge: Cambridge University Press, 2002).
4. On these themes, see Timothy Stanton, 'Christian Foundations; or Some Loose Stones? Toleration and the Philosophy of Locke's Politics', *Critical Review of International Social and Political Philosophy*, 14:3 (June 2011), 323–47. My essay is indebted to Stanton's insightful analysis, though my account of Locke's natural equality slightly departs from his formulations.

5. Waldron follows here Ronald Dworkin's influential account of the character of modern political thought. See Ronald Dworkin, *Taking Rights Seriously* (London: Duckworth, 1977), 180; *Laws' Empire* (Cambridge, MA: Harvard University Press, 1986), 296–7. Cf. Alexander Brown, 'An Egalitarian Plateau? Challenging the Importance of Ronald Dworkin's Abstract Egalitarian Rights', *Res Publica*, 13 (2007), 255–91.

6. Waldron, *God, Locke, and Equality*, 9–12.

7. Ibid., 1–10. It is worth noting that Dworkin associates equal respect and concern with the question of how the state should treat its citizens, whereas in Waldron's reading of Locke equal respect has to do with universal moral norms which govern human relations even in the state of nature.

8. Jeremy Waldron, 'Basic Equality', *New York University Public Law and Legal Theory Working Papers*, Paper 107 (2008), 43; at http://lsr.nellco.org/nyu_plltwp/107.

9. Waldron, *God, Locke, and Equality*, 75–81.

10. In *Two Treatises* II.69–70 Locke remarks that adult children owe honour and respect towards their parents and explains how we 'may owe *honour* and respect to an ancient, or wise Man'. John Locke, *Two Treatises of Government*, ed. Peter Laslett (Cambridge: Cambridge University Press, 1988), 313–14. He never expresses the idea that we would owe respect to others due to some characteristic shared by all human beings. In *Some Thoughts concerning Education* §117, Locke mentions respect as a component of civility which enables a gentleman to maintain good relations with 'inferiours, and the meaner sort of People, particularly Servants'. Young gentlemen should be taught that if they avoid treating servants with 'Domineering Words, Names of Contempt, and an imperious Carriage; as if they were another Race, and Species beneath them', no 'part of their Superiority will be hereby lost, but the Distinction increased, and their Authority strengthened, when Love in Inferiors is join'd to outward Respect, and an Esteem of the Person has a Share in their Submission'. John Locke, *Some Thoughts concerning Education*, ed. John W. and Jean S. Yolton (Oxford: Oxford University Press, 1989), 182.

11. Waldron, *God, Locke, and Equality*, 6, 109.

12. *Two Treatises* II.54, 304.

13. The jural character of Locke's natural equality is observed in John Dunn, *The Political Thought of John Locke: An Historical Account of the Argument of the 'Two Treatises of Government'* (Cambridge: Cambridge University Press, 1969), 121. It is also emphasised in John Marshall, *John Locke: Resistance, Religion and Responsibility* (Cambridge: Cambridge University Press, 1994), 298–9.

14. *Digest* I.I.4, *Digest* 50.17.32.

15. For a short summary of the intellectual history of natural equality prior to Thomas Hobbes, see Kinch Hoekstra, 'Hobbesian Equality', in S. A. Lloyd, ed., *Hobbes Today: Insights for the 21st Century* (Cambridge: Cambridge University Press, 2013), 94–9.

16. See Harro Höpfl, *Jesuit Political Thought: The Society of Jesus and the State, c. 1540–1630* (Cambridge: Cambridge University Press, 2004), 204–62.

17. John Lilburne, 'The Free-man's Freedom Vindicated', in Andrew Sharp, ed., *The English Levellers* (Cambridge: Cambridge University Press, 1998), 31; Richard Overton, 'An Arrow Against All Tyrants and Tyranny', in ibid., 55.

18. The most elaborated analysis of Hobbes and equality is now Hoekstra, 'Hobbesian Equality'.

19. Thomas Hobbes, *Leviathan*, ed. Richard Tuck (Cambridge: Cambridge University Press, 1991), 107.

20. Samuel Pufendorf, *De jure naturae et gentium* III.ii.1. The English translation is from *The Political Writings of Samuel Pufendorf*, ed. Graig L. Carr, trans. Michael Seidler (Oxford: Oxford University Press, 1994), 159.

21. See Kari Saastamoinen, 'Pufendorf on Natural Equality, Human Dignity, and Self-Esteem', *Journal of the History of Ideas*, 71:1 (2010), 39–62.

22. John Locke, *Political Essays*, ed. Mark Goldie (Cambridge: Cambridge University Press, 1997), 69–71.

23. Ibid., 135–6.

24. *Some Thoughts concerning Education*, §186, 239.

25. See Haakonssen, *Natural Law and Moral Philosophy*, 52–5.

26. *Two Treatises*, II.6, 271, II.16, 278–9, II.135, 358.

27. For an insightful, if somewhat extreme formulation of this point, see Knud Haakonssen, 'Natural Law and Personhood: Samuel Pufendorf on Social Explanation', Max Weber Lecture, European University Institution, 2010; at http://hdl.handle.net/1814/14934.

28. Robert Filmer, *'Patriacha' and other Political Writings*, ed. Johann P. Sommerville (Cambridge: Cambridge University Press, 1991), 2–3. On the character of Filmer's argument, see Ian Harris, 'Robert Filmer', in S.-J. Savonius-Wroth, Paul Schurman and Jonathan Walmsley, eds, *The Bloomsbury Companion to Locke* (London: Bloomsbury, 2014), 57–61. Cf. Cesare Cuttica, *Sir Robert Filmer (1588–1653) and the Patriotic Monarch: Patriarchalism in Seventeenth-Century Political Thought* (Manchester: Manchester University Press, 2012).

29. Filmer, *'Patriacha' and other Political Writings*, 19–21.

30. Ibid., 12.

31. *Two Treatises*, II.3, 268.

32. Ibid., II.135, 357–8.

33. Ibid., I.67, 190.

34. Ibid., II.4, 269.

35. Ibid., II.6, 270–1.

36. Ibid., II.4, 269.

37. Ibid., II.2–3, 268.

38. Ibid., II.7, 272. In *God, Locke, and Equality*, 137, Waldron points out how in paragraph II.123, 350, Locke describes a person living in the state of nature as an 'absolute Lord of his own Person and Possessions, equal to the greatest, and subject to no Body'. In so far as Locke speaks here about an absolute

lord, this is of course an overstatement, as human beings are all God's property. The status of a worldly lord is, for Locke, a legal construction which in no way liberates its holder from whatever moral obligations he or she has towards others as a human being. Thus, to be a lord of one's own person and possessions means nothing more than not to be under anyone's legislative power.

39. Ibid., II.54, 304.
40. Ibid., II.14–15, 276–8.
41. Ibid., II.2, 269.
42. For Waldron's use of the *Essay*, see *God, Locke, and Equality*, 49–81.
43. Stanton, 'Christian Foundations', 325, 340.
44. John Locke, *An Essay Concerning Human Understanding*, ed. Peter H. Nidditch (Oxford: Oxford University Press, 1975), III.ix.3, 476.
45. Ibid., II.xxvii.8, 335.
46. *Two Treatises*, II.58, 306.
47. Stanton, 'Christian Foundations', 338.
48. See George Windstrup, 'Locke on Suicide', *Political Theory*, 9:2 (May 1980), 169–82.
49. *An Essay Concerning Human Understanding*, III.xi.16, 517.
50. *Political Essays*, 267–8.
51. *Two Treatises*, I.86, 204–5.
52. Ibid., II.61, 308–9.
53. Ibid., II.58, 306.
54. Ibid., II.63, 309.
55. Ibid., II.4, 269.
56. Ibid., II.6, 271.
57. Ibid., II.6, 271, II.17, 279.
58. Ibid., II.11, 274.
59. Stanton, 'Christian Foundations', 336.
60. *Two Treatises*, II.8, 272.
61. Ibid., II.128, 352.
62. Haakonssen, *Natural Law and Moral Philosophy*, 55–6.
63. *Two Treatises*, II.54, 304.
64. On reading Locke's views on ownership in terms of imperfect duties, see Robert Lamb, 'Locke on Ownership, Imperfect Duties and "the Art of Governing"', *The British Journal of Politics and International Relations*, 12 (2010), 126–44.
65. See Pufendorf, *De jure*, I.i.19; *The Political Writings of Samuel Pufendorf*, 19.
66. *Two Treatises*, II.12, 275.
67. *An Essay Concerning Human Understanding*, II.xxviii.12, 356–7.
68. Marshall, *John Locke*, 299, 159–63.
69. *Two Treatises*, II.70, 314.
70. Ibid., II.66, 311.
71. Ibid., II.67, 312.

72. Ibid., II.68, 313.
73. John Locke, *A Letter Concerning Toleration and Other Writings*, ed. Mark Goldie (Indianapolis: Liberty Fund, 2010), 25.
74. Locke admits that the right of the father to decide his inheritors establishes, among the landed classes, a form of authority which can be said to be sanctioned by punishments. He is worried that since this practice mainly takes place in the context of the family, 'it passes in the World for a part of *Paternal Jurisdiction*', and could be seen as supporting Filmer's doctrine of paternal power. It is, therefore, important for Locke to emphasise that this practice is not a part of parental power, but a separate right, common to all human beings, 'to *bestow their Estates* on those who please them best'. *Two Treatises*, II.72, 314–5.
75. *Two Treatises*, II.82, 312.
76. Ibid., I.47, 174.
77. Ibid., II.142, 363. Locke's expression 'one Rule for Rich and Poor' may suggest that he has only different social positions in mind and doesn't want to say anything about gender.
78. For different assessments on marital power, most of them made from the perspective of modern liberalism, see Nancy J. Hirschmann and Kristie M. McClure, eds, *Feminist Interpretations of John Locke* (University Park: Pennsylvania State University Press, 2007).
79. *Two Treatises*, II.94, 329.
80. Ibid., II.142, 363.
81. Ibid., I.129, 236.

6

Dignity and Equality in Pufendorf's Natural Law Theory

Simone Zurbuchen

This chapter will provide a fresh account of the notion of dignity and the meaning Samuel Pufendorf assigned to it in his treatise *The Law of Nature and Nations* as well as in his manual *On the Duty of Man and Citizen According to Natural Law*.[1] There are several reasons for taking up this issue. First, since human dignity and the way it is related to human rights have recently become a much-debated issue in contemporary theories of human rights, scholars are also interested in the history of these notions.[2] Second, intellectual historians and historians of philosophy are discussing how Pufendorf's notion of dignity fits into his overall account of moral entities and of the law of nature.[3] The third motivation for dealing with dignity in Pufendorf's work has to do with the close link the latter establishes between dignity and equality. If it is correct to hold – and I will argue for this below – that in Pufendorf's view human individuals have to respect each other as equals in virtue of their dignity, it becomes very surprising that he readily subscribes to social hierarchies in the domain of the civil society as well as in that of the family. In this chapter, I will take issue with the family or the household, which Pufendorf conceives – like other representatives of modern natural law in the seventeenth and eighteenth centuries – along the lines of the *oikos*. It therefore comprises the relationships between man and woman, between parents and children, and between master and servant, or slave. From a contemporary perspective, it seems contradictory to consider an individual as a dignified human being and at the same time as a servant, or slave. We thus have to inquire why this was not so in Pufendorf's view.

The chapter is divided into three parts. In the first part, I will deal with Pufendorf's foundation of *socialitas*, i.e., the principle of natural law, and expose the duties and rights of men, which he deduces from this principle. Special attention will be paid to the duty of equality. Two notions of dignity – which correspond to the Latin notions *dignitas* and *dignatio* – will be considered in this context. In the second part of the chapter, I will turn to Pufendorf's theory of the state of nature, to which he refers in order to demonstrate why men needed to leave this state and to found civil societies or states. Here I will take issue with his concept of the family and with the status of the servant, or slave, in particular. This will allow me to show why we have good grounds for thinking that Pufendorf's account of dignity and natural equality marks an important turning point in the history of modern natural law. In the third part of the chapter I will deal with Pufendorf's theory of esteem or reputation (*existimatio*), which renders his concept of dignity highly ambiguous and precludes any direct link with Kant's understanding of dignity as an intrinsic value, or with the notion of the inherent dignity of man as we find it in the Universal Declaration of Human Rights of 1948. Despite this, I will conclude that in virtue of the attention Pufendorf pays to the relational or comparative account of dignity (*dignatio*), his natural law theory remains a notable text of reference in debates about dignity and equality.

Natural Law, Dignity and Natural Equality

According to Pufendorf, *socialitas* is imposed on men as a duty. It can be recognised through reason by considering the nature and inclinations of man. Pufendorf first points to self-love, which in human beings is closely connected to the inclination to harm others.[4] While in animals, self-love is limited by needs such as hunger and thirst or the reproductive drive, the satisfaction of these needs has no natural limit in man, and the latter is also subjected to a great number of passions and desires (such as avarice, ambition, vanity, envy, jealousy, resentment, or thirst for revenge) that are unknown to animals. The second characteristic of man is the variety of dispositions that manifests itself in differing occupations, habits and modes of life.[5] The third peculiar trait of man is his weakness (*imbecillitas*): while animals are able to feed themselves soon after being born, men remain for a very long time in a helpless condition. Deprived of help, a child could not survive until adult age without a miracle. The fiction of the miserable condition of a man, who without education and communication survives in a deserted place, illustrates how important it is for men to enter into commerce with each other and to lead a sociable life.[6] According to Pufendorf, the foundation of natural law can easily be grasped on account of this human condition:

> Man, then, is an animal with an intense concern for his own preservation, needy by himself, incapable of protection without the help of his fellows, and very well fitted for the mutual provision of benefits.

Equally, however, he is at the same time malicious, aggressive, easily provoked and as willing as he is able to inflict harm on others. The conclusion is: in order to be safe, it is necessary for him to be sociable; that is to join forces with men like himself and so conduct himself towards them that they are not given even a plausible excuse for harming him, but rather become willing to preserve and promote his advantages.[7]

As this citation shows, Pufendorf proposes to derive *socialitas* from self-love. This implies that he originally conceives it as a maxim of prudence. In order to establish the latter as a principle of law, he refers to the will of God who imposes *socialitas* on man as a duty and obligates him to respect this duty.[8] This idea connects with his account of the position man is assigned by God in the world. Considering man in relation to God, his creator, he identifies the immortal soul, endowed with intelligence and judgement, as the property by which man distinguishes himself from the rest of animals. Invoking the dignity (*dignitas*) and pre-eminence (*praestantia*) of human nature, he argues that man could not properly exist without law, that he could not remain *exlex*.[9] This is the first way in which natural law is related to the notion of dignity.

It is important, however, not to confound this notion of dignity (*dignitas*) with the one Pufendorf introduces in the chapters devoted to the duties imposed on man by the law of nature.[10] In this context, *socialitas* functions as a general law from where specific laws are derived in the form of means deemed to realise an end. There are well-known discrepancies between *The Law of Nature and Nations* and *On the Duty of Man and Citizen* in regard of Pufendorf's classification of duties. This is however of no concern here, since I only consider the duties of man towards others, i.e., the class of duties Pufendorf deals with in both of his works and in all of their editions.[11] The first duty incumbent on man requires not inflicting any damage to others. If damage occurs, it has to be repaired.[12] God imposed this duty on all men in virtue of their being human. Unlike a hypothetical duty a man owes to another under certain specific circumstances, the duty not to harm others is absolute. Pufendorf refers here to the *neminem laedere* principle of Roman law, adding however that he applies a broad notion of damage. Hence, he observes that while 'damage' is usually related to goods or external things one possesses, he would apply it to everything a man can rightfully pretend to.[13] Accordingly, the duty not to harm others protects what naturally belongs to us such as our life, body, limbs, honour or liberty on the one hand, and what belongs to us in virtue of a human institution or a contract on the other. It is also noteworthy that Pufendorf deals with this duty as a reciprocal duty and explains it by referring to the rights corresponding to it. While the rights to our life, body or liberty are natural rights, goods we may own count as acquired rights that are founded on contract.[14]

The second absolute duty concerns the equality among men.[15] Instead of explaining the duty by focusing on its object (what men ought or ought not to do), Pufendorf first refers to the delicate self-esteem (*delicata quaedam sui aestimatio*) inherent in man, which human beings would care about no less than their body or goods.[16] Since the mere word 'man' would convey a certain dignity (*dignatio*), we could silence a person who insults us by means of the simple and highly efficient argument: after all, I am not a dog but a man just like you.[17] As Pufendorf goes on to explain, humanity belongs to all men in the same way, and for this reason no one likes to live in peaceful society with any other who would not consider him an equal man and as sharing in a common nature.[18] The second absolute duty thus requires that each one respects and treats all others as beings sharing in the same nature or being equally men like him.[19] Against Hobbes, Pufendorf argues that equality is neither related to physical strength nor to the faculties of the mind, but to the state and condition of man considered simply as man. This general equality implies that however far a man may surpass his fellow beings in bodily or intellectual endowments, he has to comply with the law of nature in the same way as he expects this from others.[20]

Having considered how Pufendorf introduces the duty of equality, I now turn to its object.[21] The first thing Pufendorf observes is that each one who lays claim to the services of others has to render himself useful to them as well. The person who readily grants to others what he asks for himself is best suited for society. Those who feel superior to others, who claim a higher esteem and a greater share in common goods, are considered to be unsocial beings. In consequence, no one can claim more for himself than he equally grants to others.[22] The duty of equality teaches, secondly, how right has to be distributed among men: all of them need to be treated as equals, and no one shall be preferred. Otherwise, one commits an injustice, insulting the disregarded and depriving them of the dignity (*dignatio*) bestowed on them by nature. For this reason, common property (*res communis*) needs to be distributed in equal shares, or, in cases where this is impossible, to be conveyed to all having a share in it in common, proportional or alternating use. Should this also be impossible, compensation is due.[23] Thirdly, pride (*superbia*), i.e., valuing oneself more highly and despising others as unequal, is excluded by the duty of equality.[24] Pufendorf adds, however, that there might be good grounds for a man to enjoy priority. We will look at these grounds below. The duty of equality requires, fourthly, not expressing contempt towards others through one's behaviour, words, countenance, scornful laughter or other insults.[25]

The third absolute duty men owe each other in virtue of their common humanity consists in the promotion of the others' well-being, in so far as this can be easily done.[26] Since nature would have instituted a kind of kinship between men, Pufendorf argues, it is not enough that men do not harm and despise each other. They also need to lend each other services, and this is the source of their reciprocal benevolence.[27] The advantage of others can be promoted in two different ways: first, in an indefinite way, when a man, through the cultivation of his soul and body, makes himself a useful member of human society.[28] Second, a man promotes the benefit of others in a determinate way when he lends services to others that do not cost him anything (for example, letting another take fire from one's own, giving him honest advice on demand), or when he aids another in a situation of necessity, gratuitously and out of goodwill, even if this causes him troubles and expenses. The latter are good deeds in the proper sense of the term.[29] Unlike the rights corresponding to the duty of justice (i.e., the duty not to harm others), the rights corresponding to the duty of humanity are imperfect rights. The latter duty is not sufficient for promoting everybody's advantage and needs therefore to be supplemented by promises and treatises suitable for guaranteeing a regular exchange of services.[30]

In my presentation of the duty of equality, I deliberately highlighted the elements suitable for demonstrating the contemporary appeal of Pufendorf's doctrine. Thus, when he holds that a delicate 'esteem and value for himself' is 'deep-seated' in man's mind, that 'human nature agrees equally to all persons', or when he argues that the word 'man' carries 'somewhat of dignity in its sound', one naturally thinks of the inherent dignity of man that features prominently in the 1948 Universal Declaration of Human Rights and also plays an important role in the contemporary literature on human rights.[31] Scholarly debates about this doctrine of Pufendorf's show, however, that it needs to be interpreted with great circumspection. While Knud Haakonssen holds that equality should not be mistaken as something given or rooted in human nature, Stephen Darwall believes it possible to find in the passages we have looked at above the seeds of a contemporary understanding of human dignity.[32] Darwall's position rests on the claim that in Pufendorf's theory the idea of reciprocity (of duties and rights) is not implicit in the fundamental natural law itself, which is imposed on man by God, but is spelled out on a different basis, i.e. that of dignity. While Saastamoinen stresses in the same vein that in Pufendorf's theory the duty to promote *socialitas* is distinct from the duty to esteem others as one's equals, he claims that Pufendorf advocates not a Kantian, but a traditional Ciceronian concept of dignity.[33]

In order to clarify how Pufendorf understands 'humanity' and 'dignity' in the chapter on the duty of equality, I briefly turn to the epistemological foundations of his theory of natural law. So far, I only observed that in Pufendorf's view natural law is imposed on man by God's will. It needs to be added that this account of the law is closely connected to the distinction between physical and moral entities he develops at great length in the first book of his treatise.[34] While the former belong to the material world and form the object of the physical sciences, the latter are invented by reflective beings and 'superadded' or 'imposed' on physical things in order to give direction to free and voluntary human acts. Moral entities are imposed on the world either by God or by men. There are four kinds of moral entities: (1) condition or status, (2) substances and modes, (3) moral qualities, and (4) moral quantities.[35]

If we now come back to the duty of equality and the way Pufendorf introduces it, it turns out that he deals in this context with the state and condition of man (considered simply as man), which is imposed on him by God. When he holds that human nature 'agrees equally to all persons', he thus does not refer to men's physical or mental endowments, which are part of the physical world, but to the moral status of man. This is exactly what he stresses in his critique of Hobbes. It thus comes as no surprise that he concludes his discussion of the latter's position by observing that the equality he has in mind is an *equality of right*, which has its origin in the fact that an obligation to cultivate a social life is 'equally binding upon all men'.[36] It seems, however, problematic to conclude from this that Pufendorf would not consider the common humanity all persons equally agree in as something given. For he holds the obligation to a social life as 'an integral part of human nature as such',[37] and for illuminating the equality he has in mind in a popular and plausible way he also points to the common 'stock' from where we derive our lives and invokes several features human beings share, such as the frail and brittle matter of which their bodies consist, the method of propagation, etc.[38] Like the phrase that self-esteem is 'deep-seated' in man's mind, these illustrations confirm the impression that common humanity is somehow given and that the duty of equality is deemed to bring out what it implies.

Pufendorf makes this even clearer in a rarely considered paragraph in the chapter on moral entities. He explains there that he uses the term 'humanity' for denoting the condition in which his creator places man.[39] Adding that this status obliges man to certain duties and also gives him a title to certain rights, he then inquires when this state begins in individual men. Arguing that this does not depend on the perfection of his nature or the full use of reason, he fixes the beginning at the moment when a yet unborn child shows life and sensation, which coincides for him with the being in the womb having taken on a human form. While admitting that the fetus cannot yet fulfil his obligations, since he does not yet understand his own nature and is unable to conform his actions to a rule, Pufendorf insists that he is entitled to rights from the very beginning of his being. It follows from this that if the fetus in the womb suffers from any unlawful violence, the injury is not done to the parents, but to the child, and that the latter may demand justice in his own name once he comes to an age of discretion. Pufendorf resumes this thought by observing that '(c)onsidered *in its relation to other men*, the natural state of man is when men order their lives on nothing but a simple universal kinship resulting from the similarity of their physical nature'.[40]

I conclude from this that Pufendorf takes the moral status he calls 'humanity' to be something given. Although it would be wrong to understand it as a physical entity, it is nevertheless not something humans may dispose of at liberty. Quite to the contrary, they owe something to others in virtue of the status they have in common from the beginning of their very existence as human beings. As the example of the fetus illustrates, respecting the humanity of the other may imply an asymmetry of rights and duties. This is, however, not Pufendorf's concern in the chapters on the absolute duties of men. Here he deals with the reciprocity of rights and duties, and he introduces the notion of 'dignity' in order to spell out what equality of status implies. To conclude this section, let us recall that Pufendorf accounts for the human condition from two different perspectives: when considering man in relation to God and the world the latter created, he deals with the dignity (*dignitas*) and pre-eminence of human nature, which makes man inapt for remaining without law. This is the classical notion of dignity as Cicero defined it.[41] When considering the relationship between men, taken simply as men, Pufendorf introduces the notion of *dignatio*, which refers to their common humanity. The latter founds their equality and the reciprocity of their rights and duties.

The meaning of this latter notion of dignity will be further explored in the next section. In order to understand the function Pufendorf assigns to it in the structuring of social relationships, we need to account for his distinction between the natural state imposed on man by God and the artificial or adventitious states imposed on men by themselves via contracts. While the duties and rights originating in the former are absolute, those originating in human institutions are conditional.[42] As the example of the adventitious states within the household, and in particular the master-servant relationship, will show, the social inequalities created by contracts strongly contrast with natural equality but nevertheless do not supersede it.

Natural Equality and Social Inequality

Even though Pufendorf declares dignity (*dignatio*) to found equality between human beings in the way just described, his doctrine is very far from supporting an egalitarian notion of dignity as it is understood today. In the present understanding, status equality is intrinsically linked with non-discrimination in all spheres of human life, private as well as public ones.[43] This is certainly not how Pufendorf saw it. In order to properly assess the implications of his doctrine of equality, we need to examine how he conceived of the state of nature in opposition to the various adventitious states. This theory is fairly complex,[44] and for the present purposes I will provide only a brief sketch of it. In Pufendorf's view, the state of nature can be considered from three different angles: *first*, in relation to God, man appears as a being whose status remarkably differs from that of animals. We have seen above that Pufendorf mentions in this context the *dignitas* and pre-eminence of man. *Second*, considered in itself (*in se*), i.e. by imagining the condition of a solitary human being who manages to survive without the aid of others, the state of nature is opposed to civilised life. *Third*, seen in relation to others, the state of nature features the relationship between men, which is instituted by God or, as he also says, by their common nature. The state of nature in the third sense is opposed to the civil state.[45] In order to conceive it this way, one needs to abstract it from any kind of social relationship instituted by men through contract.

The third concept of the state of nature is of prime importance here. In this context, it is crucial to account for an equivocation in Pufendorf's theory of the state of nature, which is also present in that of Hobbes', albeit not as clearly visible: the state of nature in relation to others can on the one hand be conceived as a fiction, and on the other as a reality.[46] As a fiction, the state of nature is a state of liberty in the sense that no one is subjected to any other. Every human being has a right to independence and is equal to all others; it is neither master nor servant. On the basis of this concept Pufendorf aims at demonstrating that the state of nature is a state of profound insecurity and that out of prudence men need to leave this state and to institute civil societies. He leaves no doubt, however, that in reality the state of nature has never existed. Men have always lived together in families, i.e., in social units held together by domination and instituted (like civil society) by contract. The family or household comprises the relationship between man and woman (marriage), between parents and children, and between master and servant, or slave.[47] In each case, Pufendorf attempts to show on what grounds the persons in question enter the contract legitimating domination, the consent being either explicit, or tacit (as for instance in the contract between parents and children).

As we have seen, Pufendorf holds that in reality the state of nature (in the third sense of the term) does not obtain between individual human beings, but rather between families. In consequence, he also assumes that (exceptions barred) only the *patres familiae* participate in the social contract and become citizens. Women, children and servants are integrated into the civil society as members of the family. This is why, after dealing with the duties and rights of men considered simply as men, Pufendorf first proceeds to consider the duties and rights incumbent on men as members of the family before he gets to their status as citizens. I don't have the space here for dealing extensively with domination in the context of the family. In order to show how Pufendorf proposes to resolve the tension between natural equality on one hand and social inequality on the other, I will focus on the relationship between master and servant, or slave.[48]

In eighteenth-century English translations of *De iure belli ac pacis*, 'servant' instead of 'slave' usually translates the Lain term *servus*. This seems to be due to the influence of Jean Barbeyrac,[49] who translated *servus* by *serviteur*.[50] The translation of *servus* and *servitus* still constitutes a problem. As Gustaaf van Nifterik has rightly observed in an article devoted to Grotius, for the modern reader 'the word "slavery" is above all connected to the North-American slavery, characterized by its racial basis and a brutal exploitation of black slaves',[51] while Grotius rather had in mind a form of unfreedom he would prefer to translate as 'perpetual service'. It seems difficult to establish what kind of reality early modern authors had in mind when dealing with the *servus*.[52] While Jean Bodin, for instance, in his *Six Books of the Republic*, speaks out at great length against the cruelty perpetrated against enslaved humans from antiquity up to his own time and denounces those who make a thriving business out of the slave trade,[53] Pufendorf alludes neither to the slave trade nor to slavery in the New World in either of his treatises on the law of nature.

Translation problems stem from the fact that early modern natural law theories of *servitus* remained heavily indebted to Roman law and even tended, out of veneration for that law in general, 'to present Roman slave law – the law that was known to them – more kindly than the Roman legal sources themselves'.[54] As Alan Watson observed, the Roman jurists had a kind of 'tunnel vision' regarding slavery to the extent that they dealt with it as an abstract category detached from policing issues, law reform or the actual condition of the poorer sort of slaves, such as those who worked in the silver mines or in chains in the fields. According to Watson, the slaves that appear in the *Digest* are the relatively affluent ones, approaching the types of slaves at the upper end of the scale like those who were engaged by their owners 'as doctors, ship masters, bankers or business entrepreneurs with even hundreds of other slaves in their *peculium*'.[55]

Grotius's theory of the *servus*, which remained influential throughout the seventeenth and eighteenth centuries, was indeed indebted to Roman law.[56] Without any ambition of presenting the details of Grotius's theory, let us just recall how he conceives of *servitus* in relation to the law of nature and nations. Grotius – and indeed all his followers – rejected the Roman concept of natural law in the sense of an unchangeable law common to animals and men. Law proper is the natural law of men, dictated by right reason. According to Grotius, this law can be easily discovered, is found in all civilised nations, and is always right.[57] The law of nations (*ius gentium*) has two meanings. In the primary meaning, it is the same as the law of nature; in the secondary meaning it constitutes a kind of civil or voluntary law and corresponds to what we now call international law.[58] These basic distinctions are important regarding Grotius's theory of *servitus*. Hence, he distinguishes between two types of *servitus*, the first based on natural law, the second on the law of nations (*ius gentium*).[59] Like Pufendorf later on, Grotius rejects the Aristotelian doctrine of natural slavery when he argues that the first type of slavery originates in a voluntary act whereby a man subjects himself to a master, either for life ('perfect slavery') or for a limited period, or under certain conditions ('imperfect slavery').[60] Since in the case of 'perfect slavery' the relationship between master and *servus* rests on an agreement, 'whereby one person (the future *servus*) commits himself to perpetual services, the other (the future master) to providing of the necessities of life', and since this type of *servitus* is not cruel in any other sense, van Nifterik opines that it is better to translate it as 'perpetual service' than as 'slavery'.[61]

The second type of *servitus* is based on the law of nations. In this context, Grotius refers to Roman law, stating that the law of nations encourages, as an act of mercy, the enslavement of prisoners of war instead of killing them. He also confirms the etymology of the word slavery established by the Romans according to which *servi* are so called because commanders save (*servare*) rather than kill their captives.[62] Specialists of Grotius's theory of *servitus* such as John Cairns and Gustaav van Nifterik disagree about the proper interpretation of the first kind of *servitus* and its limits.

They seem however to agree that according to Grotius the second kind of *servitus* implies that the authority of the master over the slave is unlimited, i.e., that the former can inflict on the latter any cruelty. What is more, the master owns anything captured with the slave, and his ownership (*dominium*) extends to the slaves' descendants; the master may transfer his right to others, just as the ownership of things.[63]

Turning now to Pufendorf, we can see that Grotius's basic outline of the theory of *servitus* is still present in his works, although he does not explicitly refer to *De iure belli ac pacis*. Hence Pufendorf also distinguishes between two types of slavery, the first originating in voluntary consent, the second in war. Two noteworthy differences, however, need to be highlighted here. First, instead of insisting on the distinction between *servitus* according to the law of nature and to the law of nations, Pufendorf establishes a temporal sequel between the two kinds of *servitus* by first pointing to the 'early ages of the world' and then to the 'succeeding times', when it became customary to grant captives life and corporeal liberty, on condition that they would yield perpetual service to the conqueror.[64] Regarding the early ages of the world, where the poorer and more helpless persons would have entered servitude by contract, Pufendorf explains that the power of the master over the servant derives from the ends of instituting such a society and that it can therefore not be a power over life and death. The highest degree of punishment a master is authorised to inflict on his servant is the expulsion from the family. Before civil societies were instituted, the master had indeed the right to kill his servant when the latter attacked either him or his family, not in virtue of his sovereign power however, but as an enemy, by the right of war.[65] If we consider that Grotius also held that in the case of voluntary servitude the master does not have the *ius vitae ac necis* over the *servus*, Pufendorf seems to agree with much of what Grotius had to say about this type of *servitus*.

There subsists, however, a major disagreement between the two authors concerning the other type of *servitus*, which originates in war. This is the second difference I wish to highlight. It needs to be stressed that Pufendorf does not criticise Grotius in any direct way, for his main reference in this context is Hobbes's *De cive*. Pufendorf fully agrees with Hobbes's distinction between the condition of *servi* who are held captive and those who enter into their condition by contract.[66] While the former remain in a state of war with their preserver and therefore retain a right to escape or even slay him, the latter owe obedience to the master, not in virtue of mere force, but in virtue of mutual faith, i.e., a 'moral tye'.[67] Referring to the terminological distinction between the 'slave' and the 'servant' Hobbes introduces in this context,[68] I will now use the term 'servitude' when considering how

Pufendorf disagrees with Hobbes regarding of the nature of dominion, or the master's right of governing the servant. Pufendorf insists, firstly, that the master does not own the servant like a thing or cattle. This is why he cannot be transferred to another master without his consent, and the master does not become the owner of the things the servant possessed before entering this condition without the latter's agreement.[69] Secondly, Pufendorf holds that a master can do an injury to the servant, for instance when he denies him the things necessary for life, or when he mistreats or kills him. In this context, he speaks out against the very rude handling of servants and criticises the law of states, which would impose greater hardship on servants than the law of nature permits. He also deplores that public laws would seldom afford servants relief from their master, unless in cases of most barbarous severity and cruelty.[70] In *On the Duty of Man and Citizen*, Pufendorf summarises this critique in the following way:

> since humanity bids us never to forget that a slave is in any case a man, we should by no means treat him like other property, which we may use, abuse and destroy at our pleasure. And when one decides to transfer to another a slave of this kind, one should take even more pains than the slave deserves to ensure that he is not sent somewhere where he will be treated inhumanely.[71]

These reflections on servitude show quite nicely what function Pufendorf assigns to the state of nature and the equality of human beings. Although this state is fictitious, it nevertheless serves as a basis for identifying the aspects of the relationships between human beings which refer to their common humanity.[72] This in no way excludes that in reality human beings are at the same time involved in social relationships such as the family and civil society. While they are equal in virtue of their condition or status as human beings, they are unequal in virtue of their social status. So understood, the duty of men to esteem and treat each other as equals does not exclude social hierarchies, but rather defines the moral limits within which domination is deemed legitimate.

The Value of Human Beings

Given what has so far been established, it is somewhat surprising that Pufendorf argues in a later chapter in *De jure naturae et gentium* that the condition or status of human beings, considered simply as such, comes at a price. The crucial notions he uses in this context are *existimatio* and *valor*, which are distinct from the *aestimatio* and *dignatio* he mentions in the chapter on equality we have considered earlier. As I noted above, the expression *dignatio* is intrinsically linked with one of the four kinds of moral entities, namely the condition or status of man which is imposed on him by God and is also called 'humanity' or 'human nature', common to all men. While *existimatio* also denotes a moral entity, it is an entity of a different kind, namely a moral quantity that serves as currency for comparing and making distinctions among men. The word has been variously translated into English, either as 'esteem' or as 'reputation'.[73] In what follows, I will only deal with 'simple' reputation in the state of nature, which Pufendorf distinguishes from both 'simple' and 'intensive' reputation among those who live in civil society.[74]

As Joachim Hruschka has shown in a paper on central notions in Kant's *Metaphysics of Morals* and its antecedents in modern natural law, Pufendorf was the first author who dealt extensively with *existimatio*, first in the *Elementa jurisprudentiae universalis* (1660), then in the dissertation *De existimatione* (1667) and finally in his two treatises on the law of nature we are considering here. Hruschka argues convincingly that it would be wrong to translate *existimatio* as 'estimation' (*Schätzen*) or 'judgement' (*Beurteilen*), for this would not allow a correct rendition of Pufendorf's own definition of the term, which is: 'the value of persons in common life [*vita communis*] by which they may be measured against others or compared with them and either preferred or put after them'.[75] Referring to Gottlieb Gerhard Titius's commentary of *De officio hominis et civis* as well as to early French and German translations of Pufendorf's works, Hruschka suggests that Pufendorf's *existimatio* means something like 'probity' (*Rechtschaffenheit*), 'dignity' (*Würde*), 'respectability' (*Achtbarkeit*) or 'worthiness' (*Würdigkeit*).[76] He justifies these proposals by pointing to the passage in the *Digest* Titius mentions in his commentary: 'Reputation is the condition of unimpaired dignity approved by law and custom, which is either diminished or destroyed by legal authority on account of some offence which we have committed.'[77] Knud Haakonssen criticises this proposal because it would wrongly suggest that Pufendorf's *existimatio* somehow anticipates Kant's concept of dignity. Referring to Pufendorf's proposal to understand 'simple reputation' in the state of nature to consist 'in this: That a man deport himself and be regarded as a person with whom you may treat as with a good man (*vir bonus*), who is also therefore ready, to the best of his ability, to observe natural law in his relations with others',[78] Haakonssen attempts to show why a moralistic reading of the expression 'good man' would be mistaken. The notion *vir bonus* rather corresponds to the neutral notion of innocence and designates 'the human being's most basic standing in the state of nature'.[79]

In my view, these precautionary remarks are fully confirmed by Hruschka himself, who shows in his paper that *existimatio* was broadly discussed and re-defined in the later natural law literature, and that it is therefore impossible to establish any direct link between Pufendorf's simple 'existimatio' and Kant's *Würde*. Contemporary readers may be tempted to draw too hasty comparisons between Pufendorf's and Kant's theories, since both of them compare the value of persons with the price of things. The way in which Pufendorf draws the comparison shows, however, that he does not conceive the standing of a person as an 'intrinsic value' or dignity which admits of no equivalent. Unlike Kant, who opposes dignity to price,[80] Pufendorf draws an analogy between the price of a thing and the value of a person. Observing that we say of a thing which is of use in common life that it is of value, and of a useless thing that it is worth nothing, he argues that one may say as well that a person is a man of some value, who deserves to be treated as social creature, while a man who plainly proves to be unfit for society, by disregarding the law of nature, may deservedly be looked upon as a man of no worth or value.[81] As we have already seen, Pufendorf explicitly acknowledges the comparative trait of *existimatio* or *valor* by taking it as a moral quantity serving as currency for making distinctions between men.

This is further confirmed by the fact that *valor* admits of degrees. Hence Pufendorf explains that *existimatio* can be impaired or even destroyed. In doing so, he does not make a normative argument but rather explains how others usually treat a person who lessens or loses his or her moral standing as a sociable being. Firstly, a person impairs or lessens his or her reputation by violating the law of nature through criminal malicious actions, especially those of more than ordinary guilt, and which are committed with the intention to disquiet other men. In consequence, such a deceiver will be mistrusted, and no one will engage in important affairs with him without great caution. Pufendorf adds however that in this case a person's value in common life is not absolutely lost. He or she may recover it by voluntarily repairing the damages caused (or providing an equivalent), and by showing sorrow and repentance.[82]

Secondly, a person may destroy or lose her standing as a sociable being by choosing a pattern of life that causes harm to others and profiting from the injuries done. Pufendorf mentions as examples 'pirates, freebooters, highway robbers, assassins, cutthroats and the like'.[83] In his view, these people fall into the category of 'common enemies of all' (*communes omnium hostes*). They deserve public contempt, even though they may have 'some resemblance of justice' among them.[84] He goes on to explain that in the state of nature the destruction or loss of reputation has the effect that unless these criminals leave off their unjust and bloody way of life, other men will treat them with no more mercy than beasts of prey. If they are apprehended, they will be treated more severely than other kinds of ene-mies, and looked upon as not deserving the common offices of humanity. Moreover, they are incapable of receiving obligations of good faith from other men. Like in the case of the impairment, Pufendorf observes that it is possible for those having destroyed their reputation to regain it, when they forsake their wicked profession and live again as honest men.

It is not easy to properly account for Pufendorf's theory of reputation and the concept of 'common enemies of all' he introduces in this context. It is certainly noteworthy that he does not address these issues in the chap-ters on dignity and natural equality, where he rather attempts to distance himself from Hobbes by insisting on the common humanity all persons agree on. The fact that Pufendorf discusses the reputation, or value, of human beings in book VIII of his treatise, where he deals with the power of sovereigns and related matters, may well indicate that he was not aware of the profound tension between his doctrine of man's moral condition or status on one hand, and that of his comparative value on the other. There are, however, sufficiently clear indications that the latter doctrine is not intended to undermine the former. Hence, Pufendorf explains that any man who does not, by an act of deliberate malice and out of wicked design, violate the law of nature to the prejudice of another person, deserves repu-tation. Since the frailty of human nature would excuse sins of infirmity, a man does not by them forfeit the reputation of being an honest man. As a general rule, a man is supposed to deserve this reputation until his own evil actions deprive him of it. Pufendorf thus asserts that 'it must be said to belong by nature to every man in equal share, and, when no evil deed has preceded, all men must be judged to be equally honourable'.[85] As we have seen, Pufendorf also holds that reputation, once impaired or lost, may be recovered through appropriate action. We can conclude from this that the notion 'common enemy of all others' does not denote a moral condition or status comparable to the one he calls 'humanity' or 'dignity'. It rather serves to indicate the conditional loss of a person's standing as a sociable being. Despite this, there is no doubt that the doctrine of *existimatio* renders Pufendorf's theory of dignity and natural equality highly ambiguous. The latter stands in clear contradiction to the contemporary understanding of the inherent dignity of man, deemed to make sure '[t]hat the moral community is not a club from which members may be dropped for delinquency'.[86]

Conclusion

When discussing Pufendorf's theory of 'dignity' (*dignatio*) and natural equality, I variously referred to the contemporary appeal of his doctrine by invoking, for instance, the inherent dignity of man in the Universal Declaration of 1948, or to Kant's notion of dignity as incomparable intrinsic value. By focusing on the example of the relationship between master and servant, or slave, I attempted to show that Pufendorf's theory remains compatible with the justification of a kind of social hierarchy and domination that clearly contradicts the contemporary understanding of dignity and equality. We may thus be tempted to conclude that his natural law theory took on an ideological function in the sense that it constituted a general framework apt for legitimising social hierarchies existing in his own time instead of criticising them. This is indeed what Jean-Jacques Rousseau suggested in the *Social Contract*, where he reduced to absurdity Grotius's theory of slavery originating in war. Even though Pufendorf accounts for this kind of slavery in a slightly different way than Grotius, it certainly does not escape Rousseau's critique. For the main argument Rousseau advances is that the victor does not have the right to kill the prisoner of war. This is why it would be absurd to make the latter buy his life in exchange for his liberty.

It is however also possible to account for Pufendorf's theory of servitude from a different angle by highlighting, as we did above, the implication of his theory of dignity and natural equality. While Pufendorf does not criticise servitude or slavery in any direct way, he nevertheless insists on the moral limits of domination. As we have seen, he invokes in this context the idea of humanity common to all men. In comparison with Grotius and Hobbes, his theory of 'humanity', 'dignity' and natural equality does indeed mark a turning point in the history of modern natural law. An interesting historical question would be how this theory was further developed in the natural law literature up to the American and French revolutions, and how it was used to question social inequalities within the family.

Regarding Pufendorf himself, it is worth pointing to the uneasiness he expresses in regard to the inconveniences attending a state of personal servitude, 'which, in the Opinion of most People, passeth for the greatest Misery incident to Mankind'.[87] Reflecting on the difference between the status of freemen and servants, he observes that free subjects are only obliged to obey the supreme power and the general law of the state, whereas servants are subject to private commands and the coercive power of their fellow subjects. Pufendorf considers it to be the greatest hardship that the servant has to bear even the master's most stubborn and impious humour. This would make his bondage all the more grievous because of the frequent intercourse with his master and lack of relief granted by public laws. When he finally observes that a man must be the more afflicted under these circumstances, the more 'soft and gentle' his nature is, and that pride makes the yoke of servitude truly unbearable,[88] Pufendorf seems to admit that there are good moral grounds for questioning the institution of servitude which he nevertheless justifies. Speculations about the emancipatory potential of Pufendorf's doctrine of dignity and equality may serve as an invitation for further research on its reception in eighteenth-century natural law theory.

Notes

1. Samuel Pufendorf, *De jure naturae et gentium*, trans. C. H. and W. A. Old-father, 2 vols (Oxford: Clarendon Press, 1934), henceforth cited as ING; *On the Duty of Man and Citizen According to Natural Law*, ed. James Tully, trans. Michael Silverthorne (Cambridge: Cambridge University Press, 1991), henceforth cited as OHC.

2. The notion of dignity plays an important role in so-called 'naturalistic' or 'orthodox' accounts of human rights. Such accounts are notably defended by James Griffin, *On Human Rights* (Oxford: Oxford University Press, 2008), and by John Tasioulas, 'Human Dignity and the Foundations of Human Rights', in Christopher McCrudden, ed., *Understanding Human Dignity* (Oxford: Oxford University Press, 2013), 291–314. I discuss these theories and highlight their weaknesses by drawing on Pufendorf's theory of dignity and natural equality in Simone Zurbuchen, 'Menschenrechte, Menschenwürde und Gleichheit', in Daniel Bogner and Cornelia Mügge, eds, *Natur des Menschen: Brauchen die Menschenrechte eine Menschenbild?* (Fribourg: Academic Press, 2015), 45–66.

3. Important recent contributions on this issue are Kari Saastamoinen, 'Pufendorf on Natural Equality, Human Dignity, and Self-Esteem', *Journal of the History of Ideas*, 71:1 (2010), 39–62; Knud Haakonssen, 'Natural Law and Person-hood: Pufendorf on Social Explanation', Max Weber Lecture No. 2010/06, at http://cadmus.eui.eu/bitstream/handle/1814/14934/MWP_LS_2010_06.pdf?sequence=1; Stephen Darwall, 'Pufendorf on Morality, Sociability, and Moral Powers', *Journal of the History of Philosophy*, 50:2 (2012), 213–38; Vanda Fiorillo, 'Der Andere – "ut aeque homo": Gleichheit und Menschenwürde in der politischen Anthropologie Samuel Pufendorfs', *Archiv für Rechts- und Sozialphilosophie*, 99:1 (2013), 11–28.

4. ING II, 1, §6; OHC I, 3, §1, 4.

5. ING II, 1, §7; OHC I, 3, §6.

6. ING II, 1, §8; OHC I, 3, §3.

7. OHC I, 3, §7; see ING II, 3, §14–15.

8. ING II, 3, §20; OHC I, 3, §11.

9. ING II, 1, §5.

10. As we will see, in the chapter on equality Pufendorf does not speak of *dignitas*, but of *dignatio*. I do not want to suggest that these notions refer to different moral entities. Both of them denote the peculiar condition or state of man, but each from a different angle, either 'absolutely', or 'in relation to other men' (ING I, 1, §7). In his otherwise very insightful paper 'Pufendorf on Natural Equality, Human Dignity, and Self-Esteem', Saastamoinen does not properly account for these two notions of dignity. In consequence, he almost desperately tries to detect from where Pufendorf derives the reciprocity of duties and rights.

11. In ING Pufendorf focuses on the duties of man towards others. In the second revised edition (1684) he also deals with the duties of man towards himself. In OHC he deals in addition with the duties of man towards God, which are part of natural religion.

12. ING III, 1; OHC I, 6.

13. OHC I, 6, §5.

14. OHC I, 6, §3.

15. ING II, 2; OHC I, 7.

16. ING III, 2, §1, Vol. 2, 330: 'In addition to that love which every man cherishes for his life, his person, and his possessions, by which he cannot avoid repelling or fleeing before everything that tends to their destruction, there is to be observed, deep-seated in his soul, a most sensitive self-esteem; and if any one undertakes to impair this, he is rarely less and often more disturbed than if an injury were being offered his person and property.'

17. ING II, 2, §1; OHC I, 7, §1.

18. ING II, 2, §1, Vol. 2, 330: 'Now since human nature belongs equally to all men, and no one can live a social life with a person by whom he is not rated as at least a fellow man, it follows, as a precept of natural law, that "Every man should esteem and treat another man as his equal by nature, or as much a man as himself."'

19. Ibid.

20. ING III, 2, §2.

21. ING III, 2, §4–8. Pufendorf argues in this context against the Aristotelian doctrine that some men are slaves by nature (see section 2 below). Saastamoinen is however right to point out that Pufendorf relies on the disparity of natural abilities when explaining why men would need to accept social hierarchies. 'Pufendorf on Natural Equality', 42–4.

22. ING III, 2, §4.

23. ING III, 2, §5.

24. ING III, 2, §6.

25. ING III, 2, §7.

26. ING III, 3; OHC I, 8.

27. ING III, 3, §1.

28. OHC I, 8, §2.
29. OHC I, 8, §4–5.
30. OHC I, 9, §2.
31. Some may also think of Immanuel Kant's concept of human dignity. For the differences between Pufendorf and Kant, see Saastamoinen, 'Pufendorf on Natural Equality', 48–53.
32. Darwall claims that Pufendorf would understand esteem or respect for human dignity 'perhaps more explicitly than Kant' as a form of sociability or interpersonal relating ('Pufendorf on Morality, Sociability, and Moral Powers', 224). The main problem with this interpretation is that it rests on a misunderstanding of Pufendorf's notion of *existimatio* (see section 3 below).
33. Saastamoinen, 'Pufendorf on Natural Equality', 55, 51–2.
34. ING I, 1.
35. For a more detailed account of the theory of moral entities see, for instance, Michael Seidler, 'Pufendorf's Moral and Political Philosophy', The Stanford Encyclopedia of Philosophy (Winter 2015 edition), ed. Edward N. Zalta, at http://plato.stanford.edu/archives/win2015/entries/pufendorf-moral; Saastamoinen, 'Pufendorf on Natural Equality', 45; and Haakonssen, 'Natural Law and Personhood', 1–4.
36. ING III, 2, §2, Vol. 2, 333.
37. Ibid.
38. ING III, 2, §3, Vol. 2, 334.
39. ING I, 1, §7, Vol. 2, 7.
40. ING I, 1, §7, Vol. 2, 8.
41. Saastamoinen, 'Pufendorf on Natural Equality', 51–2. On the stoic origin of Pufendorf's notion of dignity see also Fiorillo, 'Der Andere – "ut aeque homo"', 16–24. Referring to the *Thesaurus Linguae Latinae* Fiorillo recalls (23 n. 86) that *dignatio* was used as synonym of *dignitas*, but could also mean respect, esteem, recognition, benevolence, favour or clemency towards others.
42. OHC II, 1, §2.
43. Allen Buchanan has argued convincingly that any theory of human dignity and human rights which pretends to be philosophically interesting should be able to account for the salient egalitarian features of the existing global legal-institutional phenomenon of human rights. 'The Egalitarianism of Human Rights', *Ethics*, 120:4 (2010), 679–710. On the importance of the relational or comparative aspect of dignity see also Jeremy Waldron, *Dignity, Rank, & Rights*, ed. and introduced by Meir Dan-Cohen (Oxford: Oxford University Press, 2012).
44. See Fiammetta Palladini, 'Pufendorf Disciple of Hobbes: The Nature of Man and the State of Nature: The doctrine of *socialitas*', *History of European Ideas*, 34 (2008), 26–60.
45. OHC II, 1, §3–5.
46. This distinction is clearly drawn in OHC II, 1, §6–7.
47. ING VI, 1–3; OHC II, 2–4.

48. The foundation of the social relationships within the family in the tradition of modern natural law has been most comprehensively treated by scholars interested in the theory and critique of patriarchalism on the one hand (Gordon Schochet, *Patriarchalism in Political Thought* (Oxford: Blackwell, 1975)), and by feminist philosophers on the other (Carol Pateman, *The Sexual Contract* (Stanford: Stanford University Press, 1988)); on Hobbes see also Nancy J. Hirschmann and Joanne H. Wright, eds, *Feminist Interpretations of Hobbes* (University Park: Pennsylvania State University Press, 2012), chs 5–6; on Locke, Nancy J. Hirschmann and Kirstie M. McClure, eds, *Feminist Interpretations of John Locke* (University Park: Pennsylvania State University Press, 2007), chs 1–4, and Simone Zurbuchen, 'Ist Lockes politische Philosophie "sexistisch" und "rassistisch"? Formen der Herrschaft im häuslichen Verband der Familie', in Michaela Rehm and Bernd Ludwig, eds, *John Locke, Zwei Abhandlungen über die Regierung* (Berlin: Akademie Verlag, 2012), 17–34. For the concept of marriage in particular see Alfred Dufour, *Le mariage dans l'école allemande du droit naturel moderne au XVIIIe siècle. Les sources philosophiques, de la Scolastique aux Lumières – La doctrine* (Paris: Librarie Générale de Droit et de Jurisprudence, 1972), and *Le mariage dans l'école romande du droit naturel au XVIIIe siècle* (Geneva: Librairie de l'Université, Georg & Cie, 1976). The concept of servitude and/or slavery, on which I will focus here, is often treated in isolation from the rest of the other relationships within the family and with a view on the application of the theories considered. See for instance David Brion Davis, *The Problem of Slavery in Western Culture* (Oxford: Oxford University Press, 1966); Jean Allain, *Slavery in International Law: Of Human Eploitation and Trafficking* (Leiden, Boston: Martinus Nijhoff Publishers, 2013), ch. 1; for theories of slavery in the seventeenth and eighteenth centuries, see Bernd Franke, *Sklaverei und Unfreiheit im Naturrecht des 17. Jahrhunderts* (Hildesheim: Olms, 2009) and John W. Cairns, 'Stoicism, Slavery, and Law', *Grotiana*, 22/23 (2001/2002), 197–231, and 'The Definition of Slavery in Eighteenth-Century Thinking: Not the True Roman Slavery', in Jean Allain, ed., *The Legal Understanding of Slavery: From the Historical to the Contemporary* (Oxford: Oxford University Press, 2012), chap. 4. On the social relationships between the family see also Simone Zurbuchen, 'La famille, une société naturelle?', *Rousseau Studies* (forthcoming).
49. See Franke, *Sklaverei und Unfreiheit*, 28–9.
50. In his translation of Pufendorf's *De iure naturae et gentium*, both expressions are used. Barbeyrac rendered *De potestate herili* (ING VI, 3) as 'Du pouvoir des Maîtres sur leurs serviteurs, ou leurs esclaves'. See Samuel Pufendorf, *Le droit de la nature et des gens, ou système général des principes les plus importans de la morale, de la jurisprudence, et de la politique*, trans. Jean Barbeyrac, Vol. 2, book VI, ch. 3.
51. Gustaaf van Nifterik, 'Hugo Grotius on "Slavery"', *Grotiana*, 22/23 (2001/2002), 234.

52. For this reason, John W. Cairns' discussions of the Scottish civil cases concerning slavery in the eighteenth century are very important. They allow us to understand how Grotius's natural law concept of slavery influenced Scottish lawyers and judges. See Cairns, 'Stoicism, Slavery, and Law', and 'The Definition of Slavery in Eighteenth-Century Thinking'.
53. Jean Bodin, Les six livres de la république, book I, ch. 4.
54. Alan Watson, 'Seventeenth-Century Jurists, Roman Law, and the Law of Slavery', Chicago-Kent Law Review, 68/3 (1993), 1346.
55. Ibid., 1347–8.
56. Ibid. As Cairns has pointed out in 'Stoicism, Slavery, and Law', his theory was also indebted to the Stoics, especially to Seneca.
57. Hugo Grotius, The Laws of War and Peace, ed. with an introduction by Richard Tuck, from the ed. Jean Barbeyrac, 3 vols (Indianapolis: Liberty Fund, 2005), book I, ch. 1, §10–11; henceforth cited as IBP; Watson, 'Seventeenth-Century Jurists', 1349.
58. IBP Discursus praeliminaris, §18; I, 1, §13–14.
59. Cairns, 'Stoicism, Slavery, and Law', 206; van Nifterik, 'Hugo Grotius on "Slavery"', 234.
60. IBP II, 22, §11, III, 8, §1 (rejection of slavery by nature); II, 5, §27 ('perfect slavery'), §30 ('imperfect slavery'). See also Cairns, 'Stoicism, Slavery, and Law', 207; Van Nifterik, 'Hugo Grotius on "slavery"', 236; Franke, Sklaverei und Unfreiheit, 108–17. I omit here slavery originating in punishment (IBP II, 5, §32) as well as the question concerning the status of slaves' children and hence of slavery by birth. See Franke, Sklaverei und Unfreiheit, 117–19; Cairns, 'Stoicism, Slavery, and Law', 208–9.
61. van Nifterik, 'Hugo Grotius on "Slavery"', 236.
62. IPB III, 7, §1–5; Cairns, 'Stoicism, Slavery, and Law', 200, 211.
63. Cairns, 'Stoicism, Slavery, and Law', 211; van Nifterijk 'Hugo Grotius on "Slavery"', 241.
64. ING VI, 3, §4–5.
65. ING VI, 3, §4.
66. Thomas Hobbes, De cive, ch. 8, §1–4.
67. ING VI, 3, §6, 617a.
68. In order to clearly distinguish the two kinds of conditions, Hobbes (De cive, ch. 8, §2–3) calls the former kind of servi 'slaves' ('esclave', 'serf'), the latter 'servants' ('serviteur'). See also Franke, Sklaverei und Unfreiheit, 172–4.
69. ING VI, 3, §7. Hobbes (De Cive, ch. 8, §5–6) holds, to the contrary, that the master owns the servant and his possessions, and that he can transfer his right of ownership to another person.
70. ING VI, 3, §8. According to Hobbes (De cive, ch. 8, §7), the master cannot be unjust to the slave, just as the sovereign cannot do any injustice on the subject.
71. OHC II, 4, §5, 130
72. On this point, I fully agree with Franke, Sklaverei und Unfreiheit, 221–8.

73. In the translation I am referring to in this chapter, *existimatio* is translated as 'esteem'. In what follows, however, I will rather use 'reputation'.
74. For a more detailed account of esteem or reputation, see Michael Seidler's chapter in this volume. While I stress here the difference between dignity (*dignatio*) and value (*valor*), Seidler identifies 'human dignity' with 'simple esteem'.
75. OHC II, 14, §1, 163.
76. Joachim Hruschka, 'Existimatio: Unbescholtenheit und Achtung vor dem Nebenmenschen', *Jahrbuch für Recht und Ethik*, 8 (2000), 188–9, 191.
77. *Digest* 50.13.5.1: 'Existimatio est dignitatis inlaesae status, legibus ac moribus comprobatus, qui ex delicto nostre auctoritate legume aut minuitur aut consumitur'; Hruschka, 'Existimatio', 189.
78. ING VIII, 4, §2, Vol. 2, 1230.
79. Haakonssen, 'Natural Law and Personhood', 8.
80. Immanuel Kant, *Grundlegung zur Metaphysik der Sitten*, 2nd ed., AA IV, 1911, 434–5.
81. ING VIII, 4, §2, Vol. 2, 1230.
82. ING VIII, 4, §4.
83. ING VIII, 4, §5, Vol. 2, 1232.
84. Ibid.
85. ING VIII, 4, §3, Vol. 2, 1230.
86. Gregory Vlastos, 'Justice and Equality', in Richard B. Brandt, ed., *Social Justice* (Englewood Cliffs: Prentice-Hall, 1962), 48.
87. ING VI, 2, §10, 620a.
88. Ibid., 621a.

7

Theory and Practice in the Natural Law of Christian Thomasius

Ian Hunter

As with other early modern natural- and public-law thinkers, the modern reception of Christian Thomasius has been significantly shaped by the retrospective application of a post-Kantian conception of the relation between theory and practice. According to Kant, knowledge of law is characterised by a fundamental division between a domain of theory – in which universal a priori principles are formally intelligised independent of all 'material' ends and actions – and a domain of practice, in which these principles 'ought' to be empirically executed by a will conformed to them.[1] Such is the historical shadow cast by Kant's formulation of the relation between theory and practice that, together with its post-Kantian derivatives, it has played a key role in the interpretation of Thomasius's natural law. Thomasius's natural law has thus been interpreted as if it were a theory of his jurisprudential practice, giving rise to an anachronistic post-Kantian reception of it, especially during the second half of the twentieth century.[2]

At the beginning of his most complete natural law work, the *Institutiones jurisprudentiae divinae* (Institutes of Divine Jurisprudence) of 1688, Thomasius argues explicitly that the relation between understanding and will in juristic matters should not be framed as a relation between the theoretical and practical intellect, proposing instead that it be understood in terms of the habitus of *prudentia* or practical understanding.[3] Here prudence governs actions not in accordance with rational a priori laws but with actual laws that have issued instead from a human or divine legislator, such that actions governed by them are 'honest' or upright. Jurisprudence thus does not concern the practical execution of a theoretical moral law but the practical understanding as applied to actions governed by legislated laws: 'That *prudence* which is concerned with honest actions in general is jurisprudence in the broad sense, and that which is concerned in particular with the honest actions of others in the past is judicial prudence in the *strict* sense, or jurisprudence in the strict sense' (IDJ, I.i.17, 63).

The notion that the theoretical faculty is grounded in contemplation or speculation, and should thus be privileged over the practical understanding whose object is action, must therefore be rejected as a scholastic error rooted in in the 'false opinion of the Gentiles [Greeks], who believed that the essence of God consisted in contemplation' (IDJ, I.i.24, 64).

In ignoring his prudential understanding of law in favour of a renewed theoretical conception, the post-Kantian reception of Thomasius has relied on two basic hermeneutic strategies. In the first place, this reception has deployed a textual hermeneutics in which Thomasius's natural law works are read as if they were attempts to provide a theoretical construction of formal legal or moral norms that might then be applied in practice. Forgetting Thomasius's methodological warning that legal norms should be derived not from a *theoria* that intelligises formal principles but from a *prudentia* that governs the will in accordance with legislation, this strategy has read Thomasius's positive jurisprudence and legal pedagogy as if they were an (only partially successful) attempt to put his natural law 'theory' into empirical practice.[4] Secondly, this reception has relied on the historical hermeneutics of dialectical philosophical history. By using the opposition between theory and practice – norms and facts, formal and instrumental reason – to conceive of 'history' as the unfolding of reason in time, dialectical philosophical history produces a template account in which ideal norms are limited by their factual determination, while promising that these limits might be overcome through the historical actualisation of rational freedom.[5] When this template was applied to Thomasius, then his prudential understanding of natural law norms – as laws capable of being legislated by an early modern territorial prince – assumed a new and anachronistic hermeneutic significance: namely, as the historically conditioned failure to realise the moral norms of self-legislating rational beings in a democratic 'public sphere'.[6] Far from holding the key to understanding the kind of thinker that he was, Thomasius's historical position as academic jurisconsult providing *jurisprudentia* to a princely territorial state now appeared as an index of what prevented him from becoming the kind of thinker that he could (and should) have been: that is, were he to have anticipated the realisation of theory in practice and morality in politics. In other words, despite his explicit rejection of the doctrine that empirical history is the domain in which a priori normative theory is realised, this metaphysics of history has been foisted onto Thomasius's natural law discourse, retrospectively turning it into a failed attempt to realise a theory that he never held in a history that he never lived.

In what follows I shall show how these problems endemic to the post-Kantian reception of Thomasius's natural law can be avoided by adopting a different historiographic approach. It will be argued that Thomasius's natural law works should be viewed not as the theoretical foundation of his 'practical' jurisprudential and pedagogical works, but as post-facto works of abstraction performed on and with these latter works for particular programmatic purposes. These purposes were those of providing a legal pedagogy and a mode of receiving imperial positive law suited to a particular kind of legal order: namely, the 'secularised' or multi-confessional imperial constitutional order that had grown from the treaties of Augsburg (1555) and Westphalia (1648).[7] This programme was in turn anchored in Thomasius's role as an academic jurisconsult or *Gelerhte Rat* to the princely territorial state of Brandenburg-Prussia, with whose religious and political interests he could directly engage through the academic training of its juristic elite.[8] Placed in this context, Thomasius's natural law was not the theory of his jurisprudential practice, but a particular part of this practice: namely, the part concerned with imbuing his students with a certain understanding of and attitude towards a specific legal order. In developing this approach, we first need to say something about the historical circumstances in which natural law could have this kind of role (section 2), then move on to discuss the specific form of Thomasius's natural law in this context (section 3). After that we can discuss the relation between his natural law teaching and his work on the philosophy curriculum and on the historical reception of positive law (section 4), before concluding with some reflections on the relation between morality and law in Thomasius (section 5).

Natural Law in Protestant States and Universities

The importance of natural law in early modern German universities resulted from the central role played by positive law and religion in the constitutional order of the Holy Roman German Empire.[9] Unlike England and France, which were monarchically governed political kingdoms, the German Empire was the umbrella constitutional-legal order for a conglomerate of political entities.[10] The most important of these were the imperial estates – the cities, nobilities and knights circles – and the dynastic princely territorial states whose jurisdictional claims over 'their' estates were a source of protracted struggles and conflicts, particularly following the splitting of the imperial church at the beginning of the sixteenth century. The disputed rights and entitlements of these overlapping political entities were increasingly adjudicated by imperial public law as enunciated by the *Reichskammergericht* (Imperial Chamber Court) and the *Reichshofrat* (Aulic Court).[11] This constitutional order ensured the centrality of law in the various imperial polities, and it accounts for the importance of the law faculties in their universities. It also resulted in the great diversity of forms of juridical and political thought characteristic of the German Empire, which varied with the interests of the diverse forms of polity.

This diversity was further intensified by the manner in which the multiplex order of estates was permeated by religious culture and, in the wake of the Lutheran and Calvinist 'reformations', fractured by confessional disputes. Not only did the churches play a direct role in the pastoral and pedagogical governance of populations, but they and their clergies were incorporated in the system of estate rights. Moreover, their theologies continued to play a key role in providing religious or moral intelligibility for the exercise of juridical and political power, especially via the 'Christian natural law' taught in university theology faculties.[12] The religious wars that convulsed the German Empire during the middle of the sixteenth century and again during the first half of the seventeenth were thus the direct result of the confessional fracturing of the already conflict-prone imperial constitutional order. The two great peace treaties that followed these periods of conflict – the Treaty of Augsburg in 1555 and the Westphalian treaties of 1648 – brought about major changes to the religious and political constitution of the German Empire. Nonetheless, they were executed within the treaties, statutes and institutions of imperial public law. This continued to locate the Empire's centre of constitutional gravity at the nexus of the rival confessions and the conflicting estates and states.[13]

One can see the way this worked in the case of the Treaty of Augsburg. Here, in order to reach a peace, the Habsburg Emperor Ferdinand I had to concede significant religious-political rights to Protestant cities and territorial princes, despite the victory of the Catholic imperial forces over the Protestant estates. These included the so-called *jus reformandi* – the right to carry out a Protestant reformation within their jurisdictions, encapsulated in the *cuis regio eius religio* formula. This entailed major changes to territorial religious and political orders.[14] In Protestant ecclesial jurisdictions the link to the bishop of Rome was severed and the political ruler assumed a dual public-law persona, becoming both highest bishop and civil sovereign. This state of legal and religious affairs was formalised in the fundamental *Zwei-Personen-Lehre* of Protestant *Staatskirchenrecht*. At the same time, the governance of Protestant churches was territorialised through the establishment of consistories. These were territorial ecclesial administrative bodies composed of secular and religious notables, and capable of exercising ecclesial jurisdiction in areas such as marriage and inheritance, in lieu of the former canon law courts.[15] The Augsburg treaty thus demonstrates how profoundly the constitutional order of the Empire continued to be determined by the institutions of imperial public law and by the religious cultures and ecclesial institutions that permeated this legal order.

It is in this setting that we can understand the importance of Protestant natural law, for whose scholarly recovery we are indebted to the work of Knud Haakonssen.[16] The historical importance of Protestant natural law arose not from its character as formal theory, but from its key role as the academic nexus for the juridical and religious cultures of Protestant states and cities in the German Empire and in Protestant Europe more generally. Natural law was the academic clearing house that permitted the various sources of positive imperial law – imperial public law (*Staatsrecht*), public church law (*Staatskirchenrecht*), Romano-canon law and German common law – to be harmonised with the moral theology and metaphysics of the churches, and with an array of 'regional' political doctrines that had been developed for the variegated political entities of the Empire. Protestant natural law – which began as a theological discipline but became increasingly juridical and secular during the seventeenth century – was thus itself a highly variegated discipline. Its intellectual configurations and religious and political purposes varied with the contexts in which it was developed and the interests that it served.

The term natural law itself indicates the hybrid theological-juridical character of the discipline. It refers to a law that is natural in the dual sense of being acceded to via natural as opposed to revealed knowledge, and in being inscribed in man's own nature, for example as the norms required to perfect his 'rational and sociable being'. Far from constituting a stable theoretical foundation, however, this broad understanding of natural law only set the outer parameters for a disciplinary field characterised by continuous innovation and conflict. Situated on the shifting terrain formed by the overlapping of the university's law, theology and philosophy faculties, its exponents differed radically over the character of 'natural' reason and its relation to the revealed truths of Christianity, and hence over the kind of norms that could qualify as natural law, and the kind of intellect or persona who could accede to them.[17]

In its theological form, known generically as 'Christian natural law', Protestant natural law drew heavily on metaphysical philosophy, particularly the metaphysics of spiritual substance that had been elaborated in association with the definitive Lutheran confession, the Formula of Concord (1557).[18] The university metaphysician played a key role in this kind of natural law, as it was through the spiritual renewal of his intellect – the *usus in renatis* – that the metaphysician was supposed to be able to participate in divine intellection and community, thereby acquiring rational natural knowledge of specifically Christian natural law norms, including those of the Decalogue. This permitted him to mediate these transcendent norms to the civil realm and the civil authorities, where they could shape the reception of positive civil law – the *usus paedogogicus*.[19] In addition to composing one of the key works of Lutheran metaphysics,[20] the Saxon metaphysician Balthasar Meisner (1587–1626) thus published an influential natural law work in which an intellectualist anthropology holds the key to the theological derivation of natural law and its use as a justification for the civil punishment of sinners and heretics – the *usus politicus* – Calvinists in particular.[21] Understood as the ultimate source of all norms, the divine law originates as the form of divine intellection and willing, which is then accessed by man via natural law as interpreted by (Protestant) theologians and philosophers, rather than jurists.[22] In his dual (Protestant) persona as sovereign and highest bishop, the prince then enacts the norms of divine and natural law as civil law, and delegates the promulgation of ecclesiastical law to the (confessional territorial) church, through which it maintains theological orthodoxy and religious discipline.[23]

During the first half of the seventeenth century there were two main reasons why the kind of Christian-metaphysical natural law expounded by Meisner played a key role in such Lutheran confessional states as Saxony. First, Saxony had made the militantly anti-Calvinist and highly metaphysical Formula of Concord into the state confession during the 1580s. Meisner's metaphysics of spiritual substance offered a philosophical explication of the interaction between Christ's divine and human natures that lay at the heart of this confession. Second, during the same period, Saxony had established a centralised legal system whose several positive-law sources – Romano-canon law, Saxon common law and imperial public law – could be received in accordance with the theological imperatives of the Lutheran state via metaphysical Christian natural law.[24] The most important Saxon positive jurist of the seventeenth century, Benedict Carpzov (1595–1666) could thus draw on Meisner's natural law to help frame a legal code in which the prince issued laws as God's vice-regent, acting in the dual persona of highest bishop and civil sovereign that had been created by the Treaty of Augsburg.[25] This facilitated the reception of the Romano-canon law crimes of heresy, blasphemy and witchcraft in Saxony's theocratically oriented legal order. Meisner's metaphysical form of Christian natural law thus served the twin purposes of legal reception and legal pedagogy within the religious and political context of the Lutheran confessional state. It served these ends, however, not through the abstract concepts that it theorised – God's divine intellection of transcendent norms acceded to by man through natural law and reason – but through the role of these abstract constructions in the moral and intellectual grooming of the theologian-jurists – the purificatory *usus in renatis* – in the context of the public law *jus reformandi* that Augsburg had bestowed on Protestant princes.

In broad historical terms, Thomasius had a good deal in common with Carpzov.[26] He too was one of the Protestant *Gelehrte Räte* who combined the roles of law professor and court jurisconsult, although not with Carpzov's political clout. Further, parallel to the metaphysical natural law on which Carpzov relied, Thomasius developed a natural law whose role was to frame the reception of positive law and shape the legal pedagogy for a particular kind of Protestant princely territorial state. The natural law that Thomasius elaborated, however, differed radically from the metaphysical form of Christian natural law. So too, following the eclipsing of the *jus reformandi* and the *cuius regio* doctrine under the terms of the Treaty of Osnabrück of 1648, the religious and political constitution of the state in which Thomasius worked – Brandenburg-Prussia – differed markedly from that of neighbouring Saxony. In contradistinction to Christian natural law, the natural law that Thomasius developed through his studies of Hugo Grotius (1583–1645) and Samuel Pufendorf (1632–94) has been called 'modern'.[27] This presentist ascription can be misleading, however, as the metaphysical form of natural law not only remained a potent rival to Pufendorfian natural law, but would resurface in Kant's *Rechtslehre*, which would also be hailed as 'modern'. It is more useful to characterise Thomasius's Protestant natural law as anti-scholastic or as 'secular' in a circumscribed sense of that promiscuous term: namely, in being designed to depose metaphysicians and theologians from their privileged place as mediators of natural law and to transfer this role to jurists, understood as operating within the revised multi-confessional religious constitution instituted by the Treaty of Osnabrück.[28]

Thomasius, however, did not develop his version of secular natural law on the basis of pure intellectual insight into his opponents' theoretical errors, as an exemplary representative of a modernising rational *Aufklärung*.[29] He did so rather by engaging them in an intellectual 'war of position'. Owing to the pivotal role of universities in staffing the juridical, theological and political offices of the German imperial and territorial-state orders, academic arguments directly engaged powerful religious and political forces. The character of the disputes through which Thomasius developed his natural law is shown by the response of his opponents at the Saxon University of Leipzig, who had him charged before the Lutheran Superior Consistory for religious 'indifferentism' and then banned from lecturing by the Saxon court itself.[30] We can bring this small yet bitterly divided intellectual world into focus by observing that if Benedict Carpzov's theocratic legal code was a central target for Thomasius's attack, then the phalanx of metaphysicians and theologians who engineered his expulsion from Saxony included Johann Benedict Carpzov (1639–99), Benedict's nephew, who, together with Valentin Alberti (1635–97), was a leading exponent of the Christian natural law earlier elaborated by Meisner. It is by situating it in this context – as a combative discipline designed to transform legal pedagogy and the reception of positive law – that we will understand the natural law that Thomasius advanced during his time at Leipzig and then carried with him to Halle when, in 1690, he fled across the border of Saxony into neighbouring Brandenburg-Prussia.

Thomasius's Natural Law

The normative bearing of Thomasius's natural law came not from a priori principles that he was attempting to put into juridical practice, but from his reshaping of the discourse of natural law into the instrument of a particular cultural and political programme: namely, the creation of a legal culture and pedagogy suited to the reception of the 'secular' or multi-confessional constitution that had been instituted by the two great imperial public-law treaties of the sixteenth and seventeenth centuries. In this regard, Thomasius was standing on the shoulders of a giant, Samuel Pufendorf, whose works had been dedicated to just this kind of cultural and political reshaping of natural law by altering both its basic intellectual architecture and also the substantive doctrines that it contained. Thomasius lectured on Pufendorf's central works on natural and church law throughout his teaching career at Halle, and drew on them selectively in his primary natural law work, the *Institutiones jurisprudentiae divinae* of 1688 and its emended sequel, the *Fundamenta juris naturae et gentium* of 1705.[31]

Thomasius took many of his basic natural law concepts – the juridical concepts of obligation, right and law, and the political concepts of church, society, state and sovereignty – directly from Pufendorf. Even more importantly, Pufendorf also supplied his follower with his fundamental intellectual outlook regarding the character and role of natural law as such. This was not the outlook of the university metaphysicians like Meisner, who approached natural law as the means by which man acceded to divine concepts of justice through his own natural reason. Rather, it was the 'Hobbesian' one that viewed natural law as the form in which man discovered the rules of sociability required for his security through observation of his (fractious) nature and (threatening) circumstances.[32] Once it was understood as a deportment to which man had to be obligated by the laws of a civil superior – rather than as one to which he acceded through his own 'rational and sociable nature' – then sociability held the key to the displacement of the metaphysicians and theologians as mediators of natural law. Pufendorfian sociability was thus not the object of a new theory of natural law so much as a symptom of a changed attitude towards political and juridical authority, brought about by a discourse that viewed sociability as the 'worldly' product of such authority rather than its transcendental foundation.[33]

At the same time, however, Thomasius significantly altered the architecture of Pufendorf's natural law by adding two disciplines which he took from other sources and used to inflect the new anti-scholastic form of Protestant natural law in accordance with his own intellectual background and regional circumstances. The first of these disciplines was a fideist moral anthropology, as elaborated in the second chapter of book I of the *Institutiones*. According to this anthropology, for the purposes of deriving natural law, man is to be considered in his postlapsarian or fallen condition: that is, as a creature whose darkened intellect and passion-corrupted will mean that he can no longer govern himself through an intellect shared with God, and must instead be governed by imposed laws which are the source of obligation and rights (IDJ, I.i.28–156, 65–85). In relegating Pufendorf's conception of man's natural condition (*status naturalis*) in favour of this conception of his ruined condition (*status corruptis*) as the terrain of natural law, Thomasius sought to engage more frontally with such local opponents as Valentin Alberti, Johann Benedict Carpzov and Albrecht Christian Roth. These Leipzig metaphysicians and Christian natural jurists derived natural law from man's prelapsarian condition of innocence (the *status integritatis*) – hence from man's society with God – whose (religious) norms of sociability and rationality could still be discerned through the spark of reason fanned by the metaphysical theologian himself, who could in turn prescribe these norms to civil authority.[34]

By insisting that man's society with God had lapsed, and that the spark of divine reason had been extinguished with the ruin of man's faculties, Thomasius could argue that jurisprudential norms should not be derived from metaphysical participation in divine thinking and willing and thence prescribed to the prince: 'They clearly err . . . who believe that divine forensic law prescribes a norm to princes, to which they must adapt the laws of their commonwealths' (IDJ, I.ii.136, 112). Rather, such norms had to be learned by a residual empirical reason that gathered them from two experiential sources: either from observation of the fallen nature that taught man the laws of sociability required for civil society, or – when such laws failed in the face of man's corrupted will and intellect – from the positive laws that God had revealed and published in the Bible (IDJ, I.ii.42–5, 95). With regards to the latter 'divine positive laws', Thomasius maintains a division between law and theology by stipulating that jurists are concerned only with the laws that God has 'published' pertaining to man's 'external conduct in civil society' – for example, laws pertaining to marriage and family life – while those laws pertaining to salvation are the preserve of the theologians (IDJ, I.ii.1–12, 88–9). Jurists thus have the right to interpret both natural law and the relevant 'civil' divine positive law, as the Fall that was responsible for man's present condition is a matter of 'history' – not theology or metaphysics – and the damage it inflicted on human reason and will means that these faculties are now only capable of the kinds of prudential reflection exercised by jurists (IDJ, I.ii.16–19, 90). This was in direct opposition to the kind of argument mounted by such Christian natural jurists as Meisner, who argued that because of their renovated intellects theologians rather than jurists had the right to interpret natural law.

Despite appearances, the net effect of Thomasius's theological moral anthropology was thus to 'secularise' natural and biblical law, in the restricted sense of transferring disposition over them from theologians to civil jurists in accordance with the multi-confessional imperial religious constitution. It is clear that Thomasius used this anthropology to restrict 'juridical' biblical laws to those concerned with 'external' civil conduct and thereby grant disposition over such laws to civil rather than ecclesial jurists. More fundamentally, though, in viewing divine law as positive, and in denying that natural law is a mediation of supra-positive theo-rational norms, Thomasius collapsed the hierarchy of divine, natural and civil law characteristic of Christian natural law. He thus treated both divine law and natural law as subordinate to the end of civil sociability, hence as dual sources for norms restricted to this civil end (IDJ, I.ii.137–41, 112–13).

In doing so, Thomasius was acknowledging that the Bible remained a source of positive law in Protestant jurisdictions, specifically in the consistories that had taken over the regulation of marriage, inheritance and sexual matters from the Catholic canon-law courts. At the same time, he was arguing that biblical law should now be administered in the consistories by 'secular' jurists, whose sole concern would be with the regulation of external conduct in accordance with the natural law end of sociability or civil peace. In his characteristically provocative manner, Thomasius could thus declare that 'We believe that this doctrine [of the natural juristic character of divine positive law] conforms to the common practice in the territories of the Protestant princes, and among us to the practice of the consistories and the regulations issued by the princes' (IDJ, I.ii.139, 112). In this regard, the *Institutes* may be regarded as a natural law text designed to remould Protestant legal culture into a form that would exclude the salvational laws and ceremonies of the confessional churches from the sphere of civil authority, in accordance with the new multi-confessional imperial religious constitution.

The second discipline that Thomasius added to the architecture of Pufendorf's natural law was a historiography of philosophy to which his father, Jacob, had been a pioneering contributor.[35] Thomasius had elaborated this historiography in his *Philosophia aulica* (Civil Philosophy) published in the same year as the *Institutiones* (1688), where he had used it to convict his metaphysical opponents of a 'sectarian philosophy' arising from the confusion of pagan metaphysics with Christian faith.[36] In the *Institutiones* – especially in chapter 4 of book I dealing with the derivation of natural law norms – he deployed this history of philosophy as a means of discrediting the metaphysical derivation of such norms from 'right reason'. In particular he targeted the doctrine dear to such metaphysical opponents as Alberti and Roth that reason is the image of God (*imago Dei*) in man, through which he is supposed to participate in the divine intellection of the transcendent archetype of justice and right. Were this to be true, Thomasius argued, it would mean that 'natural law is also based on this archetype, and therefore to conform to right reason is the same as conforming to divine sanctity and justice' (IDJ, I.iv.21, 132).

It is this 'rationalist' way of acceding to the norms of natural law – as norms of divine justice devolving into civil law via metaphysical reason – that Thomasius sought to undermine by using his father's historiography of philosophy. He did so by treating his conception of reason as something that originated in the teachings of the Greek philosophers and their Patristic inheritors – that is, as a product of a particular pagan culture and time – thereby historicising it and depriving it of its purported universal validity:

I believe, however, that this belief of the Scholastics in the conformity of natural law with the divine essence owes its origin to pagan philosophy. For Augustine and Clement of Alexandria mention that Plato defined the supreme good and the essence of virtue as man becoming similar to God. The ineptitudes of the Stoics, who compared their wise man to God, are widely known. (IDJ, I.iv.27, 133)

Once he has used this historiography to suspend the form of reason and 'holy' virtue through which his metaphysical opponents claimed insight into theological norms of natural law, Thomasius could put a different kind of reason and intellectual comportment in its place. He thus argues that natural law norms agree with sound reason in the sense that man possesses sufficient reason to derive these norms from observation of his actual condition and general constitution (IDJ, I.iv.39, 136). Thomasius points to the direction of this argument in his comment that to derive norms from a quasi-divine reason 'is obviously not suitable for civil life', as here we are concerned 'not with abstract ideas of men, but with actually existing humans', which means that the 'remedies to be used are those that will preserve them' (IDJ, I.iv.45, 137).

Thomasius thus argued that the norms of natural law should be derived from a use of reason that observes what is needed to preserve man in his historical fallen condition. In this way, man discovers that the norms of natural law are in fact the rules of sociability required to govern the passion-driven conduct that threatens his society, just as Pufendorf taught. The norm of sociability agrees with sound reason not because (theoretical) reason permits it to be recovered through participation in divine intellection and community, but because (empirical) reason can gather the norm from observation, and because such reason is itself is nothing more than social discourse in the context of social intercourse (IDJ, I.iv.49–56, 138–9). In short, in deploying a civil rather than a metaphysical reason, man discovers the norms of natural law not through pure ideas that link him to divine justice, but through the observation of a fallen nature that requires laws be legislated for him to live sociably with his fellows. The norm of sociability agrees with sound reason not because reason is the spark of divinity in man through which he participates in a divine society, but because man has just enough empirical reason to gather that he must be sociable to survive. From this Thomasius derives the central principle of natural law as: 'Do that which necessarily conforms to the social life of man and omit that which is contrary to it' (IDJ, I.iv.64, 141).

Above all, though, by using his reason to gather the norm of sociability in this way, man does not himself become rational: that is, rational in the metaphysical sense of recovering the self-legislating intellect that he shares with God and thereby achieving free self-governance. On the contrary, what he discovers through this use of reason is how incapable he is of rational self-determination and how much he is in need of a 'superior' to govern his fractious, passion-impaired will. As a result of the fact that man is a being whose conduct can only be governed through obligations imposed on him by a superior, the prime practical principle is not to act in accordance with reason but to 'Obey him who has the power to command you' (IDJ, I.iii.34, 118). This means the civil sovereign in the case of natural law and, in the case of divine positive law, scriptural commands as interpreted by civil jurists. All the juridical rights and liabilities of which men are capable thus derive not from a personal rational capacity for free conduct, but from the laws of a sovereign that imbue men with various capacities for civil action in accordance with the end of civil peace.

Despite Thomasius's claim that his prime practical principle arises from the definitions of a superior (as one with the power to obligate), the law (the command of a superior that obligates a subject) and obligation (as that which is imposed by the superior's command) (IDJ, I.iii.35–7, 118), it is clear that these definitions are not formal axioms for a theory of natural law. Rather, they derive from the substantively normative discourses assembled in the *Institutiones* and from the programmatic purposes they were intended to serve. In fact they come from Pufendorf's 'Hobbesian' discourse on the obligative power of civil sovereignty, and from the moral anthropology and historiography of philosophy through which Thomasius sought to transform Pufendorfian natural law into a weapon capable of countering the natural law of the Protestant scholastics.

Thomasius's natural law thus should not be approached as an attempt to provide a theoretical deduction of supra-positive norms for civil or positive law. In this regard, he explicitly and self-consciously refused to follow the Thomist path of deriving such norms through rational access to the divine law inscribed in man's 'rational and sociable nature'. Neither, though, can his natural law be understood in accordance with Kantian canons: as an attempt to theorise an a priori principle of right intended as a supra-positive norm for the legal 'practice' of the empirical republic. In fact Thomasius's norm of sociability is not supra-positive in any sense, as it is derived in such a manner that it can only be rendered effective through the obligative commands of a superior; that is, as positive law (IDJ, I.i.134–6, 83). In treating the commands of a civil sovereign as the means by which the norm of sociability is turned into a binding obligation, Thomasius was seeking to free civil law from destabilising transcendent confessional norms of justice whose obligation is supposed to flow from the supra-civil sources of reason or holiness. At the same time and by the same strategy, he was also seeking to restrict civil law and civil authority to the scope delimited by the norm of sociability: that is, the preservation of external civil peace to the exclusion of all concern with the citizen's inner moral or religious condition. In this way he used his reworked Pufendorfian natural law to shape a religious and legal culture suited to a constitutional order in which the civil sovereign maintains social peace among a plurality of religious communities.

Philosophical Therapeutic and Reception Propaedeutic

We are thus coming close to inverting the post-Kantian understanding of the relation between theory and practice with regards to Thomasius's natural law. Rather than regarding it as the formal theory of his academic and jurisprudential practice, Thomasius treated natural law as a preparatory discipline for law students that was itself in need of reform, specifically through the inclusion of perspectives derived from his history of philosophy and his positive-law reception histories.[37] In this regard, Thomasius's natural law theory was shaped by his pedagogical and jurisprudential programme, rather than the other way around. The discursive structure and propaedeutic function of Thomasius's natural law was derived from the transformation of the philosophy or arts curriculum that he sought to effect, and from the mode of receiving positive constitutional law that he hoped this transformation would facilitate. In order to understand Thomasius's natural law as a propaedeutic discipline, we thus need to provide a brief overview of his campaign to reform the arts curriculum, and his jurisprudential work on the reception of positive public law in Protestant territorial jurisdictions.

Thomasius's continuous reworking of the Protestant 'philosophy' or arts curriculum was undertaken with a view to transforming the persona of the Protestant jurist. This aim was pursued through continuous lecturing and writing at Halle, and culminated in a private or fee-based seminar that he offered to senior students oriented to a career as law academics.[38] This seminar distilled the results of his reform work in the form of a model arts curriculum, which was in turn published as a compendium whose title speaks to its purpose: *Cautelae circa praecognitia jurisprudentiae* (Cautions regarding the Preparatory Studies for Jurisprudence, 1710); in German: *Cautelen zur Erlernung der Rechtsgelehrtheit*.[39] The *Cautelen* offered advice on how to teach everything in the arts curriculum: from poetics to physics, from mathematics to oratory. But, for our present concerns, we can say that its programmatic form was signaled in its opening remarks on scholarship or wisdom, and its intellectual centre of gravity lay in the chapters dealing with ethics, metaphysics and jurisprudence.

In his opening chapters on scholarship in general, Thomasius begins this extended piece of pedagogical advice and curriculum reform by advising his law students that they should not seek knowledge (*Wissenschaft*) as such, and especially not the contemplative or speculative knowledge advocated by the scholastics. Rather they should cultivate erudition (*Gelehrsamkeit*) in the form of wisdom (*Weisheit*) or 'living knowledge', understood as knowledge that is morally transformative and beneficial for life (CRG, 1–15).[40] Wisdom in its turn is characterised as seeing with two eyes: those of history and philosophy. Understanding *historia* in the early modern sense of all knowledge based on testimony – both the testimony of the senses and that of written records – Thomasius recommends it to his students as the basis of all knowledge of the temporal and physical world.[41] For its part, philosophy (in the narrow sense) is to be understood not in terms of the recovery of a priori concepts, but as the means by which general principles are derived from historical knowledge and used to guide it (CRG, 82–108). In short, via his conception of erudition as wisdom, Thomasius was seeking to shift the entire axis of the arts curriculum away from theoretical philosophy and towards *historia* in the form of a fallibilistic and probabilistic 'learned empiricism'.[42]

In the ethics chapter of the *Cautelen*, Thomasius summarised the *Affektenlehre* or doctrine of the passions which had displaced the theological moral anthropology of the *Institutiones* and had filled this vacated space in the revised sequel, the *Fundamenta juris naturae et gentium*. In keeping with his *Ausübung der Sittenlehre* (Practice of Ethics, 1696), in the *Cautelen*, Thomasius treats ethics as a therapeutics organised around the restraint of the passions and governed by the ends of achieving the inner tranquility that comes with 'reasonable love' (CRG, 325–63). Thomasius is explicit that his aim is not to provide a theory of the rational principles of a good will, but to induce his students to change the way in which they relate to themselves as ethical subjects and care for their ethical selves.[43] In fact the point of his ethics teaching is to encourage his students to give up the view of themselves as rational beings capable of governing their wills through a self-determining intellect. They should instead learn to relate to themselves instead as creatures of their ruling passions – of lust, avarice and ambition – thence to begin the task of restraining their passions in accordance with the ends of inner tranquility and outer civil peace.[44]

In his chapters on 'sectarian philosophy' and metaphysics, Thomasius provided his students with a crash course in his father's anti-metaphysical historiography of philosophy and theology (CRG, 108–36).[45] Here they learned about the origins of Catholic and Protestant university metaphysics in the primal miscegenation of Greek metaphysics and Christian faith, and about the hubristic claims of the metaphysicians to derive norms of justice from their own rational holiness. Not only does such metaphysics purport to provide theoretical knowledge of God as a pure intelligence thinking itself and the universe – thereby applying pagan metaphysics to matters of faith – but in doing so it tempts its practitioners with the thought that by 'participating' in this knowledge they become god-like or holy and capable of rational self-governance. This in turn has led metaphysicians like Veltheim and Alberti to claim access to transcendental norms for ethics and natural law, thereby allowing a pagan natural theology to impose its pursuit of holiness on a civil domain whose proper end is sociability (CRG, 260–79).

Such teachings were particularly dangerous for law students, Thomasius warned his audience. Not only do they delude students regarding their own 'miserable' inability to govern their wills through reason, but they are incompatible with the persona of the jurist. To cultivate this persona, Thomasius tells his seminarians, they must view the law not as that which governs disembodied intellects in their community with God, but as that which maintains peace in the historical society of fallen men. Jurisprudence is thus the science that explicates divine and human law, and, in accordance with this, preserves good order and external peace and prevents tumult (CRG, 63–71). In this way, Thomasius sought to relegate the metaphysical jurist – who mediates transcendent (confessional) norms in the civil domain – in favour of the civil jurist, whose norm of sociability is realised in the commands of a civil sovereign restricted to the end of social peace.

As far as Thomasius's work on legal reception is concerned, this was carried out in his public lecture courses on Roman law – a central part of his professorial duties at Halle – and in the continuous cycles of lectures and disputations that he conducted and supervised. In these lectures and disputations Thomasius traversed the entire domain of positive law: private, criminal, public and church law. Here he approached the question of justice not by deriving it from a natural law theory but via historical accounts of the reception of various kinds of positive law and treaties within the multiple jurisdictions of the German Empire.[46] In this regard he followed in the footsteps of other Protestant humanist jurists, Hermann Conring in particular, who had broken with the glossatorial reception of Roman and canon law and its assumption of a timeless universal church and empire. Focusing instead on the historical emergence of confessionally divided states within the empire, Conring had provided law with an historical and political intelligibility. He treated it not in terms of the execution of a priori natural law norms, but in terms of the history of imperial public laws and peace treaties and their reception within the jurisdictions of territorial states and estates.[47] This legal humanism was the basic approach to public law and politics that informed Thomasius's work on legal reception.

We can exemplify this approach by briefly looking at Thomasius's reception studies in the areas of criminal and public law – specifically his celebrated and notorious disputations dealing with the crimes of heresy and witchcraft.[48] In these disputations he tracks the origins of the modern statutes back to the Italian glossators who had incorporated the 'superstitious' canon-law decretals of the popes into the statutes. This allowed the twin crimes to be specified in terms of the violation of divine majesty, thereby introducing inquisitorial trial involving torture, and capital punishment for those found guilty.[49] These Romano-canon-law crimes were received in German jurisdictions, initially in the imperial *Constitutio Criminalis Carolina* promulgated for the empire by Charles V in 1532, but then in various territorial jurisdictions. The latter included Catholic jurisdictions where canon law was still in force, but also (to their shame) Protestant jurisdictions, which Thomasius exemplifies by citing the relevant statutes of Benedict Carpzov's criminal code for Saxony: the *Practica nova imperialis saxonica rerum criminalium* or New Imperial Saxon Practice of Criminal Law of 1635.[50] Thomasius thus points out that in addition to carrying forward the 'papalist' construction of the capital crime in terms of the violation of divine majesty, Carpzov's heresy statute receives the (Augustinian) canon-law specification of the crime as obstinate error regarding fundamental articles of the faith.[51] For its part, Carpzov's witchcraft statute adopts the 'papalist' specification of the *Carolina* whereby the crime is an apostasy whose elements are a pact with the devil, consummated in sexual intercourse with him, and the assumption of diabolical powers to harm.[52] Thomasius viewed these twin acts of reception as instances of the manner in which the confessional theologians and their juristic minions had eroded the fundamental rights of Protestant princes, which consist in their sovereign and exclusive authority to determine the criminality of conduct on the basis of the threat posed to civil peace.[53]

It is striking that in his discussion of the historical process by which these Romano-canon-law crimes were received into the jurisdictions of both Catholic and Protestant territories, Thomasius ascribes a key role to university metaphysics or 'sectarian philosophy'. In the case of heresy, through its mixing of philosophy and theology, the Aristotelian and Platonic metaphysics of the scholastics had transformed religion into a body of enforceable theological articles. What should have been a 'simple active faith' in the divine word was thus converted into the most elaborate philosophical doctrine, exemplified for Thomasius in that egregious 'manual of coercion', the Lutheran Formula of Concord. In claiming privileged metaphysical access to these doctrinal truths, the clergy duped the civil authorities into exercising a murderous juridical power over dissenters.[54] In the case of witchcraft, by purporting to show how (angelic and diabolic) spiritual beings could communicate with humans without assuming corporeal form, Protestant metaphysics continued to facilitate reception of the 'papalist' crime and thereby perpetuate the clerical erosion of civil sovereignty in such states as Saxony. In the *Cautelen*, Thomasius thus cites Alberti's pneumatology as complicit in the reception of the crime of witchcraft in Saxony, while referring his students to his own sorcery disputation for a more detailed explanation (CRG, 282–4). This again displays the reciprocal relations between Thomasius's reform of the philosophy curriculum and his secularising reception treatises.

Thomasius's work on the philosophy curriculum and the reception of positive law can thus be envisaged as forming a dual and reciprocating strategy with regard to the academic and legal culture of the Protestant confessional state. On the one hand, through his anti-metaphysical reconstruction of *Schulphilosophie* he sought to dissolve the nexus of philosophy and theology through which Protestant metaphysicians had claimed a privileged role in mediating transcendent confessional norms in civil laws. By deploying his fideist moral anthropology and therapeutic *Affektenlehre* in tandem with his anti-metaphysical historiography of philosophy, Thomasius sought the complete destruction of this nexus. Turning his back on all natural theology, he wished to leave the theological-philosophical field divided between a faith that saved independently of all philosophical doctrine, and a philosophy tethered to history and restricted to the domain of fallibilistic generalisations from experience. On the other hand, through his historical approach to the reception of positive law, Thomasius sought to destroy the nexus of ecclesial and civil authority that characterised the confessional state. In treating justice in terms of the commands that a civil sovereign issues for the preservation of social peace – rather than in terms of the mediation of theo-rational concepts – his objective was to remove the power of the churches from the legal apparatus of the state, while simultaneously ensuring that the sovereign could not exercise his power for religious purposes.[55] The natural law that Thomasius elaborated on this basis did not supply his programme with a theoretical foundation – he was quite clear that such a foundation was inimical to the programme itself – but with the propadeutic form in which it would be transmitted to law students.

Concluding Remarks on Morality and Law

We began by discussing the post-Kantian conception of the relation between theory and practice and its effects on the academic reception of Thomasius's natural law in the second half of the twentieth century. Now we can observe that this conception is inseparable from a parallel understanding of the relation between morality and law, and morality and politics. On this view, if theory represents the deduction of a priori principles subsequently put into practice, then morality is understood as theoretical insight into pure norms, while law and politics must be understood as the forms in which these norms obtain (partial) realisation in the empirical republic. We have noted that natural law is an apt vehicle for this understanding of the relation between morality and (positive) law, and, indeed, that many natural jurists have understood themselves in just this way – as mediating transcendent norms to the civil domain – although not Thomasius and the other anti-scholastic Protestant natural jurists. When, after Kant, the community of self-willing rational beings was identified with the citizens of an ideal republic, it became possible to assess empirical law and politics against their supposed historical mission of actualising this ideal republic in the real one. This republic was understood as a democratic community of rights-bearing free individuals destined to assume a cosmopolitan form.[56] Once Thomasius's natural law is placed in this anachronistic perspective then he appears to have failed to fully realise morality in a democratic rights-based law and politics, apparently owing to his 'entrapment' within the merely historical world of the early modern dynastic princely state[57] – as if he actually could or should have tried to achieve such an outcome.

This way of interpreting Thomasius – which of course treats his natural law as if it were the theoretical foundation of his programme – finds a particular anchorage in commentary on his second main natural law work, the *Fundamenta juris naturae et gentium* of 1705, in which he had incorporated his *Affektenlehre* or doctrine of the passions. Commentators have thus argued that because here Thomasius specifies *honestum* or uprightness in terms of the inner calming of the passions – thereby distinguishing it from justice as the coercive disciplining of external conduct – he had begun to open a space of inner freedom, beyond the reach of law and politics, hence a possible sphere of subjective rights against the external power of the state.[58] Once this theoretical advance has been imputed, Thomasius's unfortunate adherence to the normative power of the princely state and its positive laws – his insistence, for example, that justice derives from the commands of the civil sovereign – can be treated as his failure to fully execute his admirable theoretical gains in practice, owing to the unripeness of his princely territorial place and time.[59]

In light of the preceding discussion, however, we can advance a quite different interpretation of Thomasius's doctrine of the passions and its role in his natural and positive law. In fact this doctrine was not used to open a space of inner moral freedom as a foundation for supra-state individual rights. Rather, even in the *Fundamenta*, Thomasius's *Affektenlehre* remained focused on providing his students with a moral therapy designed to groom the juristic persona that he regarded as required by a multi-confessional princely territorial state. If we look at the heresy disputations, for example, Thomasius does not argue for a right to individual religious freedom in the civil sphere based on an inner capacity for moral freedom.[60] His argument rather is that in attempting to 'coerce conscience' through the civil imposition of what are in fact metaphysical doctrines, the heresy statutes are inimical to both inner 'Christian freedom' and the outer civil order.[61] As Thomasius makes clear in another important treatise, however, the right that is infringed in this regard does not belong to individual Christians, since the Christian freedom of individuals pertains only to spiritual relations between members of an 'invisible church' which cannot give rise to civil injuries and juridical rights of redress.[62]

In fact, the juridical right that is infringed by the existence of heresy statutes and their clerical and metaphysical proponents thus belongs to the Protestant prince alone.[63] Heresy prosecutions and persecutions infringe the prince's sovereign right to determine the conduct deserving of criminal sanction in accordance with his office of preserving social peace; for this authorises him to tolerate religious dissenters regarded as 'heretics' by the ruling confession, to the extent that the dissenters remain law-abiding.[64] Thomasius never sought to construct religious toleration as an individual right inhering in a space of inner moral freedom grounded in his *Affektenlehre*, and thus may not be historically understood as 'failing' to achieve this. Rather, for Thomasius the *jus tolerandi* or right of toleration belonged to the prince alone. It had been constructed for him by an imperial public-law constitution that recognised freedom of worship for a limited plurality of confessions in so far as they were civil associations under the supervision of a princely territorial state that was prohibited from enforcing any particular confession.[65]

We can conclude then that Thomasius's natural law – including its later variant in the *Fundamenta* – was not the source of a foundational moral theory that could only achieve partial practical realisation in the historical world of the princely territorial state. I have argued to the contrary that the normative demeanour of his natural law was itself the product of the philosophical and jurisprudential work that Thomasius carried out on behalf of what he took to be the interests of a particular variant of this kind of state: the post-Westphalian religious and political order of Brandenburg-Prussia in which toleration was an instrument for governing a fractious multi-confessional society. The 'detranscendentalising' of philosophy and the 'secularising' of law that Thomasius achieved in the course of his remarkable programme were not the result of a theoretical breakthrough to a natural law based on inner morality or reason. Rather, they were the product of his tireless reconstruction of the philosophical pedagogy and positive jurisprudence of the Protestant university in accordance with his deconfessionalising programme. To the extent that Thomasius's programme succeeded, then this depended not on its philosophical truth, but on the degree to which its cultural and juridical agenda found anchorage in imperial Germany's multi-confessional religious constitution, and in the *Religionspolitik* of the polity that would become Germany's pre-eminent *Machtstaat*, Brandenburg-Prussia.[66] So too we might say that to the extent that Thomasius's programme has been perceived to 'fail', then this is not the result of its alleged philosophical shortcomings, but of the degree to which an inimical metaphysical form of natural law persisted in the academic culture of this same state: a persistence that we encounter in the post-Kantian reception of Thomasius's natural law.

Notes

1. Immanuel Kant, 'On the Common Saying: That may be correct in theory, but it is of no use in practice', in *Practical Philosophy*, ed. M. J. Gregor, trans. M. J. Gregor (Cambridge: Cambridge University Press, 1996), 279–81. For the standard German text, see Immanuel Kant, *Kants Gesammelte Schriften* (Berlin: Preußische Akademie der Wissenschaften/de Gruyters, 1902–), VIII, 275–7.

2. Cf. the similar warnings against imposing Kantian categories on Thomasius in Frank Grunert, *Normbegründung und politische Legitimität. Zur Rechts- und Staatsphilosophie der deutschen Frühaufklärung* (Tübingen: Max Niemeyer, 2000), 238–40.

3. Christian Thomasius, *Institutes of Divine Jurisprudence, with Selections from Foundations of the Law of Nature and Nations*, trans. T. Ahnert (Indianapolis: Liberty Fund, 2011), I.i.1–21, 61–4. Future references given in text, abbreviated as IDJ.

4. See, for example, Wolfgang Röd, *Geometrischer Geist und Naturrecht: Methodengeschichtliche Untersuchungen zur Staatsphilosophie im 17. und 18. Jahrhundert* (Munich: Bayerischen Akademie der Wissenschaften, 1970), 151–84. More recently, Klaus-Gert Lutterbeck, *Staat und Gesellschaft bei Christian Thomasius und Christian Wolff: Eine historische Untersuchung in systematischer Absicht* (Stuttgart: Frommann-Holzboog, 2002), 42–88. For an argument that Thomasius attempted to reform jurisprudence on the basis of theoretical natural law norms but failed, owing to his inclusion of positive law within natural law, see Georg Steinberg, 'Praxis und Theorie: Positives Recht im Naturrecht von Christian Thomasius', in H. Lück, ed., *Christian Thomasius (1655–1728): Wegbereiter moderner Rechtskultur und Juristenausbildung* (Hildesheim: Georg Olms, 2006), 353–68.

5. Immanuel Kant, 'Idea for a Universal History with a Cosmopolitan Purpose', in *Kant: Political Writings*, ed. H. Reiss, trans. H. B. Nisbet (Cambridge: Cambridge University Press, 1970), 41–3; *Gesammelte Schriften*, VIII, 15–32. Cf. Jürgen Habermas, *Between Facts and Norms: Contributions to a Discourse Theory of Law and Democracy*, trans. W. Rehg (Cambridge, MA: MIT Press, 1996), 82–131.

6. For this interpretation, see Jutta Brückner, *Staatswissenschaften, Kameralismus und Naturrecht: Ein Beitrag zur Geschichte der Politischen Wissenschaft im Deutschland des späten 17. und frühen 18. Jahrhunderts* (München: C. H. Beck, 1977), 112–48, 175–211. Cf. also Lutterbeck, *Staat und Gesellschaft*, 13–41.

7. For this, see in particular the seminal study by Horst Dreitzel, 'Christliche Aufklärung durch fürstlichen Absolutismus. Thomasius und die Destruktion des frühneuzeitlichen Konfessionsstaates', in F. Vollhardt, ed., *Christian Thomasius (1655–1728). Neue Forschungen im Kontext der Frühaufklarung* (Tübingen: Niemeyer, 1997), 17–50.

8. As I have argued at greater length in my *The Secularisation of the Confessional State: The Political Thought of Christian Thomasius* (Cambridge: Cambridge University Press, 2007).

9. Horst Dreitzel, 'Naturrecht als politische Philosophie', in H. Holzhey and W. Schmidt-Biggemann, eds, *Die Philosophie des 17. Jahrhunderts, Band 4: Das heilige Römische Reich deutscher Nation, Nord- und Ostmitteleuropa* (Basel: Schwabe, 2001), 836–48, at 837–41.

10. For a helpful overview, see Robert von Friedeburg and Michael J. Seidler, 'The Holy Roman Empire of the German Nation', in H. A. Lloyd, G. Burgess and S. Hodson, eds, *European Political Thought 1450–1700: Religion, Law and Philosophy* (New Haven and London: Yale University Press, 2008), 102–72.

11. Michael Stolleis, *Geschichte des öffentlichen Rechts in Deutschland. Erster Band: Reichspublizistik und Policeywissenschaft 1600–1800* (Munich: C. H. Beck, 1988), 126–224; and Joachim Whaley, *Germany and the Holy Roman Empire: Volume I: Maximilian I to the Peace of Westphalia, 1490–1648* (Oxford: Oxford University Press, 2012), 457–61.

12. Dreitzel, 'Naturrecht als politische Philosophie', 841–5.

13. Gabriele Haug-Moritz, 'Protestantisches Einungwesen Und Kaiserliche Macht: Die Konfessionelle Pluralität Des Frühneuzeitliches Reiches (16. Bis 18. Jahrhundert)', *Zeitschrift für Historische Forschung*, 29 (2012), 189–214.

14. For an overview, see Martin Heckel, *Deutschland im konfessionellen Zeitalter* (Göttingen: Vandenhoeck & Ruprecht, 1983), 33–69.

15. Martin Heckel, 'Kirchenreformfragen im Verfassungssystem. Zur Befristung von Leitungsämtern in einer lutherischen Landeskirche', in K. Schlaich, ed., *Martin Heckel: Gesammelte Schriften. Staat, Kirche, Recht, Geschichte* (Tübingen: J. C. B. Mohr, 1997), 553–94.

16. See in particular, Knud Haakonssen, 'Divine/Natural Law Theories in Ethics', in D. Garber and M. Ayers, eds, *The Cambridge History of Seventeenth-Century Philosophy* (Cambridge: Cambridge University Press, 1998), 1317–57; Knud Haakonssen, 'Protestant Natural-Law Theory: A General Interpretation', in N. Brender and L. Krasnoff, eds, *New Essays on the History of Autonomy: A Collection Honoring J. B. Schneewind* (Cambridge: Cambridge University Press, 2004), 92–109; Knud Haakonssen, 'German Natural Law', in M. Goldie and R. Wokler, eds, *The Cambridge History of Eighteenth-Century Political Thought* (Cambridge: Cambridge University Press, 2006), 251–90. In addition to these

agenda-setting studies, Knud Haakonssen has been responsible for making the classics of Protestant natural law newly accessible, through his general editorship of the Liberty Fund's *Natural Law and Enlightenment Classics* series. Many natural law scholars, not least the present writer, owe Knud an immense debt of gratitude for enabling them to work on and with this series.

17. Michael Stolleis, 'The Legitimation of Law through God, Tradition, Will, Nature and Constitution', in L. Daston and M. Stolleis, eds, *Natural Law and Laws of Nature in Early Modern Europe: Jurisprudence, Theology, Moral and Natural Philosophy* (Farnham: Ashgate, 2008), 45–56.

18. See Hans-Peter Schneider, 'Christliches Naturrecht', in Holzhey and Schmidt-Biggemann, eds, *Die Philosophie des 17. Jahrhunderts, Band 4*, 813–35.

19. See Dreitzel, 'Naturrecht als politische Philosophie', 840.

20. Balthasar Meisner, *Philosophia sobria*, 3 vols (Wittenberg, 1611–23).

21. Balthasar Meisner, *Dissertatio de legibus in quatuor libellos distributa* (Wittenberg, 1616).

22. Ibid., 85–92, 119–22, 140–2.

23. Ibid., 249–84, 433–51.

24. On the centralisation of the Saxon legal system around the Leipzig *Schöffenstuhl* – central court or legal bureau – see Heiner Lück, 'Benedict Carpzov (1595–1666) und der Leipziger Schöffenstuhl', in G. Jerouschek, W. Schild and W. Gropp, eds, *Benedict Carpzov: Neue Perspektiven zu einem umstrittenen sächsischen Juristen* (Tübingen: Diskord, 2000), 55–72.

25. See Peter Landau, 'Carpzov, das Protestantische Kirchenrecht und die frühneuzeitliche Gesellschaft', in Jerouschek et al., eds, *Benedict Carpzov*, 227–56.

26. On their similarities, see Hinrich Rüping, 'Thomasius und Carpzov', in F. Grunert and F. Vollhardt, eds, *Aufklärung als praktische Philosophie* (Tübingen: Max Niemeyer, 1998), 187–96.

27. Richard Tuck, 'The "Modern" Theory of Natural Law', in A. Pagden, ed., *The Languages of Political Theory in Early-Modern Europe* (Cambridge: Cambridge University Press, 1987), 99–122.

28. On this delimited sense of secularity, in which the separation of civil from spiritual authority is quite compatible with deep religious conviction, see Martin Heckel, 'Das Säkularisierungsproblem in der Entwicklung des deutschen Staatskirchenrechts', in G. Dilcher and I. Staff, eds, *Christentum und modernes Recht. Beiträge zum Problem der Säkularisation* (Frankfurt am Main: Suhrkamp, 1984), 35–95.

29. In fact it is not Thomasius but his metaphysical opponents who can best be characterised as 'rationalist', as shown in the important study by Thomas Ahnert, *Religion and the Origins of the German Enlightenment: Faith and the Reform of Learning in the Thought of Christian Thomasius* (Rochester: University of Rochester Press, 2006).

30. On this, see Rolf Lieberwirth, 'Christian Thomasius' Leipziger Streitigkeiten', *Wissenschaftliche Zeitschrift der Martin-Luther-Universität Halle-Wittenberg*

(*Gesellschafts- und sprachwissenschaftliche Reihe*), 3 (1953), 155–59; and for a broader view, Frank Grunert, 'Zur aufgeklärten Kritik am theokratischen Absolutismus. Der Streit zwischen Hector Gottfried Masius und Christian Thomasius über Ursprung und Begründung der summa potestas', in F. Vollhardt, ed., *Christian Thomasius (1655–1728). Neue Forschungen im Kontext der Frühaufklärung* (Tübingen: Niemeyer, 1997), 51–78.

31. For a detailed account of Thomasius's use of Pufendorf's works in his lecture programmes, see Georg Steinberg, *Christian Thomasius als Naturrechtslehrer* (Cologne: Carl Heymann, 2005).

32. For the Hobbesian dimension of Thomasius's natural law thought, see Fiammetta Palladini, *Samuel Pufendorf discepolo di Hobbes. Per una reinterpretazione del giusnaturalismo moderno* (Bologna: Il Mulino, 1990). See also Peter Schröder, *Naturrecht und absolutistisches Staatsrecht: Eine vergleichende Studie zu Thomas Hobbes und Christian Thomasius* (Berlin: Duncker & Humblot, 2001), 131–62.

33. See Michael Seidler's discussion of the Pufendorfian sociality in this volume. See also Fiammetta Palladini, 'Pufendorf Disciple of Hobbes: The Nature of Man and the State of Nature: The doctrine of *socialitas*', *History of European Ideas*, 34 (2008), 26–60.

34. See, for example, Valentin Alberti, *Compendium Juris Naturae, orthodoxae Theologiae conformatum* (Leipzig, 1676), 22–4, 196–214; and Albrecht Christian Roth, *Thomasius Portentosus* (Leipzig, 1700).

35. See in particular, Ralph Häfner, 'Jacob Thomasius und die Geschichte der Häresien', in Vollhardt, ed., *Christian Thomasius (1655–1728)*, 141–64; and Sicco Lehmann-Brauns, *Weisheit in der Weltgeschichte: Philosophiegeschichte zwischen Barok und Aufklärung* (Tübingen: Niemeyer, 2004), 308–54. See also Hunter, *Secularisation of the Confessional State*, 61–82.

36. Christian Thomasius, *Introductio ad philosophiam aulicam* (Leipzig, 1688), I.2.

37. On the reciprocal relations between the historiographic disciplines and the new secularised form of natural law, see Notker Hammerstein, *Jus und Historie: Ein Beitrag zur Geschichte des historischen Denkens an deutschen Universitäten im späten 17. und im 18. Jahrhundert* (Göttingen: Vandenhoeck & Ruprecht, 1972); and, with specific regard to Thomasius, Hammerstein, 'Thomasius und die Rechtsgelehrsamkeit', *Studia Leibnitiana*, 11 (1979), 22–44. On the role of 'histories of morality' in framing Thomasius's natural law, see the important study by T. J. Hochstrasser, *Natural Law Theories in the Early Enlightenment* (Cambridge: Cambridge University Press, 2000).

38. See Steinberg, *Christian Thomasius als Naturrechtslehrer*, 159–64.

39. Thomasius's *Cautelen zur Erlernung der Rechtsgelehrtheit* (Halle, 1713; repr. Hildesheim: Olms 2006) is the German translation of his *Cautelae circa praecognitia jurisprudentiae* (Halle, 1710). Cited in text as CRG, followed by page numbers. For a contextual overiew, see Friedrich Vollhardt, '"Abwege" und "Mittelstraßen": Zu Intention and Programmatik der *Höchstnötigen Cautelen zur Erlernung der Rechts-Gelahrtheit*', in Lück, ed., *Christian Thomasius*

(1655–1728), 173–98; and for the pedagogical character and purposes of Thomasius's *collegium privatissimum*, see Kasper Risbjerg Eskildsen, 'Christian Thomasius, Invisible Philosophers, and Education for Enlightenment', *Intellectual History Review*, 18 (2008), 319–36. See also, Hunter, *Secularisation of the Confessional State*, 76–82.

40. See Frank Grunert, 'Die Pragmatisierung der Gelehrsamkeit. Zum Gelehrsamkeitskonzept von Christian Thomasius und im Thomasianismus', in U. J. Schneider, ed., *Kultur der Kommunikation: Die europäische Gelehrtenrepublik im Zeitalter von Leibniz und Lessing* (Wiesbaden: Harrassowitz, 2005), 131–53.

41. On this array of uses of the term, see the illuminating study by Arno Seifert, *Cognitio Historica. Die Geschichte als Namengeberin der frühneuzeitlichen Empirie* (Berlin: Duncker & Humblot, 1976). See also the helpful introduction to Gianna Pomata and Nancy G. Siraisi, eds, *Historia: Empiricism and Erudition in Early Modern Europe* (Cambridge, MA: MIT Press, 2005), 1–38, from whence I borrow the phrase 'learned empiricism'.

42. For a different view of this, see Frank Grunert, 'Der Jurist als Philosoph. Zur Disziplinendifferenzierung und Disziplineninterferenz bei Christian Thomasius', in Lück, ed., *Christian Thomasius*, 151–72.

43. A helpful discussion of Thomasius's *Affektenlehre* or doctrine of the passions, as an Epicurean practice of 'care of the self', is provided by Dorothee Kimmich, 'Lob der "ruhigen Belustigung": Zu Thomasius' kritischer Epikur-Rezeption', in F. Vollhardt, ed., *Christian Thomasius (1655–1728)* (Tübingen: Max Niemeyer, 1997), 379–94.

44. For the pioneering discussion of Thomasius's ethics, see Werner Schneiders, *Naturrecht und Liebesethik. Zur Geschichte der praktischen Philosophie im Hinblick auf Christian Thomasius* (Hildesheim: Olms Verlag, 1971). Schneiders discusses Thomasius's *Affkektenlehre* on 183–239 and, while focusing on its therapeutic role, treats this as indicative of Thomasius's failure to provide a proper philosophical grounding for his ethics.

45. This history is taken directly from Jacob Thomasius, *Schediasma historicum* (Leipzig, 1665). For helpful commentary see Häfner, 'Jacob Thomasius und die Geschichte der Häresien'.

46. Gertrud Schubart-Fikentscher, 'Ein Beitrag zum Usus Modernus Pandectarum inbesondere nach dem Dissertationen von Samuel Stryk und Christian Thomasius', *Eranion in honorem Georgii S. Maridakis*, 35 (1963–4), 297–324.

47. For more on this, see Horst Dreitzel, 'Hermann Conring und die Politische Wissenschaft seiner Zeit', in M. Stolleis, ed., *Hermann Conring (1606–1681). Beiträge zu Leben und Werk* (Berlin: Duncker & Humblot, 1983), 135–72; and Michael Stolleis, 'Hermann Conring und die Begründung der deutschen Rechtsgeschichte', in M. Stolleis, ed., *Herman Conring. Der Ursprung des deutschen Rechts* (Frankfurt am Main: Insel, 1994), 253–67.

48. The most important disptutations are *An haeresis sit crimen?* (*Praeses* Christian Thomasius, *respondent* Johannes Christoph Rube, Halle, 1697);

in English: 'Is Heresy a Punishable Crime?', in I. Hunter, T. Ahnert and F. Grunert, eds and trans., *Christian Thomasius: Essays on Church, State, and Politics* (Indianapolis: Liberty Fund, 2007), 148–206. *De jure principis circa haereticos* (*praeses* Christian Thomasius, *respondent* Johannes Christoph Rube, Halle, 1697); in English: 'On the Right of Protestant Princes regarding Heretics', in the appendix to Hunter, *Secularisation of the Confessional State*, 168–206. And *De crimine magiae* (*praeses* Christian Thomasius, *respondent* Johannes Reiche, Halle, 1701); in English: 'On the Crime of Sorcery', in Hunter et al., eds, *Christian Thomasius: Essays*, 207–54. I shall cite from the English versions.

49. Thomasius, 'Heresy a Crime?', 148–58, 178–89; Thomasius, 'Right regarding Heretics', 171–86; Thomasius, 'Sorcery', 208–10, 228–30, 239–46.

50. Benedict Carpzov, *Practica nova imperialis saxonica rerum criminalium* (Frankfurt, 1635).

51. Thomasius, 'Heresy a Crime?', 160–1, 189. See Carpzov, *Practica nova*, part I, qu. 44.

52. Thomasius, 'Sorcery', 210, 220–29. See Carpzov, *Practica nova*, part I, qu. 48–9.

53. Thomasius, 'Right regarding Heretics', 193–205.

54. Ibid., 177–8.

55. The most compact and perspicuous formulation of this dual strategy is to be found in Christian Thomasius, *De jure pincipis circa adiaphora* (*praeses* Christian Thomasius, *respondent* Enno Rudolph Brenneisen, Halle, 1695); in English: 'The Right of Protestant Princes regarding Indifferent Matters or Adiaphora', in Hunter et al., eds, *Christian Thomasius: Essays*, 49–127.

56. See, for example, Jürgen Habermas, 'The European Nation-State: On the Past and Future of Sovereignty and Citizenship', *Public Culture*, 10 (1998), 397–416; and more generally, Habermas, *Between Facts and Norms*.

57. See, for example, Lutterbeck, *Staat und Gesellschaft*, 140–3.

58. As argued, for example, by Klaus Luig, 'Von Samuel Pufendorf zu Christian Thomasius', in F. Palladini and G. Hartung, eds, *Samuel Pufendorf und die europäische Frühaufklärung. Werk und Einfluß eines deutschen Bürgers der Gelehrtenrepublik nach 300 Jahren (1694–1994)* (Berlin: Akademie Verlag, 1996), 137–46.

59. For various versions of this interpretation, see Lutterbeck, *Staat und Gesellschaft*, 140–3; Steinberg, 'Praxis und Theorie', 360–2; and Martin Kühnel, *Das politische Denken von Christian Thomasius: Staat, Gesellschaft, Bürger* (Berlin: Duncker & Humblot, 2001), 65–7, 322–8.

60. For the opposed view, see Simone Zurbuchen, 'Gewissensfreiheit und Toleranz: Zur Pufendorf-Rezeption bei Christian Thomasius', in Palladini and Hartung, eds, *Samuel Pufendorf und die europäische Frühaufklärung*, 169–80; and Steinberg, 'Praxis und Theorie'.

61. Thomasius, 'Heresy a Crime?', 189–200.

62. Christian Thomasius and Enno Rudolph Brenneysen, *Das Recht evangelischer Fürsten in theologischen Streitigkeiten* (Halle, 1696), ch. xiv, §3, 171.
63. For more, see Ian Hunter, 'The Tolerationist Programmes of Thomasius and Locke', in J. Parkin and T. Stanton, eds, *Natural Law and Toleration in the Early Enlightenment* (Oxford: Oxford University Press, 2013), 107–37.
64. Thomasius and Brenneysen, *Recht evangelischer Fürsten*, ch. xiv, §1, 167; and Thomasius, 'Heresy a Crime?', 198.
65. For a rare appreciation of this crucial point, see Matthias J. Fritsch, *Religiöse Toleranz im Zeitalter der Aufklärung. Naturrechtliche Begründung — konfessionelle Differenzen* (Hamburg: Felix Meiner, 2004), 48–65.
66. See Hinrich Rüping, 'Thomasius und seine Schüler im brandenburgischen Staat', in H. Thieme, ed., *Humanismus und Naturrecht in Berlin-Brandenburg-Preussen* (Berlin: Walter de Gruyter, 1979), 76–89; and more recently, Rüping, 'Christian Thomasius und seine Schule im Geistesleben des 18. Jahrhunderts', in H. Lück, ed., *Recht und Rechtswissenschaft in mitteldeutschen Raum* (Cologne: Böhlau Verlag, 1998), 127–36.

8

The 'Iura Connata' in the Natural Law
of Christian Wolff

Frank Grunert

If one is interested in Wolff's concept of the 'iura connata' one has to state at once that there is a long and vivid discussion among – mostly – German scholars[1] about the theoretical status and the practical function of innate rights in the natural law theory of Christian Wolff. It began in the past and is still going on; for the moment, the last contributions to the dispute were published in 2014 and 2015.[2] The crucial point of the discussion was and is the question of whether Wolff's concept of innate rights is a substantial contribution to the development of the concept of human rights or not. The given answers to this question could not be more antagonistic. On the one hand we have significant scholars like Diethelm Klippel and Louis Pahlow, who warn strongly against confusing Wolff's idea of innate rights with the concept of human rights because the iura connata are rights which only belong to the 'status naturalis', and they are completely given up in the 'status civilis'. So in Klippel's view the iura connata in the natural law theory of Wolff – and other natural lawyers before and after him – have in fact no practical significance for the relationship between the citizen or the subject and the government. Iura connata – Klippel explicitly states – are 'lost rights of human beings'.[3] On the other hand we have enthusiastic partisans of Christian Wolff like Marcel Thomann, Hanns-Martin Bachmann and others who defend the idea that Wolff's concept of innate rights belongs to the 'milestones of the history of the general human rights'.[4] While Bachmann claims that Wolff is 'the real founder of the modern catalogue of human rights',[5] Thomann even believes that Wolff is in fact 'the early advocate of a liberal constitutional state'.[6] So in the light of this controversy, there is no doubt that it might be interesting to have a closer look at Wolff's concept of the iura connata, especially with regards to the relationship between natural law and human rights, keeping in mind Klippel's acknowledgement that Wolff's idea of innate rights seem to be – at first glance – somehow similar to the concept of human rights.[7]

The question thus is: what is the theoretical and practical meaning, and what is the function, of the concept of the iura connata within the natural law of Christian Wolff? Moreover, since one cannot expect the concept of human rights to be fully developed in the work of Christian Wolff – that is, in the middle of the eighteenth century in Germany – it might be interesting to consider which elements of the definition of human rights are already given in Wolff's idea of innate rights and which elements are missing, even though Knud Haakonssen may be right in the end when he states that 'Wolff's idea of the innateness of rights was in fact very different from the modern idea'.[8]

In comparing Wolff's concept of 'iura connata' with human rights, it is necessary to begin by providing a suitable definition of human rights. Apart from all of the theoretical problems the concept of human rights may be connected with, they are commonly defined as rights which every human being has because of the mere fact that he or she is a human being. Therefore human rights are universal, i.e. equally applicable to every human being, and inalienable, i.e. they are valid in any circumstance and cannot be revoked or divested. Human rights are real rights and not moral rights,[9] which means that they are enforceable by legal proceedings. They are usually subdivided into defensive rights against illegitimate demands of the state, rights of political participation, and social rights which grant a life under humane conditions.[10]

With regard to Wolff's natural law theory[11] one can state that the concept of innate rights holds a significant position within the Wolffian *Ius naturae* – explicitly in contrast to other natural law theories. Christian Thomasius, for example, is not interested in the possible consequences of the division between 'ius connatum' and 'ius acquisitum'. Thomasius uses both terms and certainly knows the differences between them, yet he does little more than state the division while exemplifying 'innate right' with the power of parents towards their children in contrast to the 'summa potestas' as an acquired right which is created by contract.[12] Wolff however gives a proper definition of the iura connata and presents an extensive catalogue of these rights. In reviewing Wolff's approach, five points can be highlighted.

1. Natural Rights and Natural Obligation

Unlike other natural lawyers, Wolff strengthens the iura connata by transforming the duties commanded by natural law into explicit rights. Natural law obliges men to act in a way such that actions contribute to the perfection of themselves and their circumstances.[13] In order to be able to fulfil this obligation men receive together with the (natural) obligation the (natural) right to all actions which are necessary to achieve the obligatory aim. Thus the right is definitely based on obligation.[14] That means on the one hand that there would not be any natural right without natural obligation, and on the other hand that the right men receive by the obligation is an instrument to fulfil the demands of the natural law. So the rights are conditions for obeying the natural law of perfection. It is very striking that Wolff sets value on this transformation, while other natural lawyers – such as Thomasius and Samuel Pufendorf – divorced duties ('officia') from the goal of perfection, in accordance with a different normative and theoretical viewpoint.

2. The Necessity and Immutability of Natural Law/Rights

According to Wolff, the supreme obligation of natural law – i.e. for humans to seek perfection of themselves and their circumstances – is founded in the nature and the essence of men.[15] This has three important consequences. First, since the nature and essence of men is unchanging and unchangeable, the law of nature and the demands based on it are necessary and immutable.[16] Second, because of the immutability of human nature and the necessity of natural law, every human being is obliged in the same way and no one can be exempted from natural law.[17] That means, third, that the validity of the law of nature is universal, and in combination with certain metaphysical reasons – every man as man has the same nature and essence as any other man – all human beings are equal in respect to their natural law duties.[18] Since the obligations of the natural law are the source of natural rights, these rights themselves are immutable and universal, and all men are equal in respect of their rights which are created by natural law obligation.

3. Iura Connata – Iura Absoluta

Natural law obligation is innate because it arises from the nature of man and is immediately given by the pure natural existence of men.[19] The rights that are immediately and directly caused by this innate obligation are innate themselves, which means that Wolff is speaking of innate rights, iura connata: 'Jus connatum dicitur, quod ex obligatione connata oritur.'[20] Wolff gives the following definition in §74 of the German translation of the *Institutiones Iuris Naturae* which appeared in 1754, the year of his death:

Das angebohrne Recht (jus connatum) nennt man dasjenige, welches aus einer angebohrnen Verbindlichkeit entstehet. Es ist aber eine angebohrne Verbindlichkeit (obligatio connata) diejenige, welche aus der Natur und dem Menschen nothwendig erfolget, und davon nicht getrennet werden mag. Da nun diese wegen der Unveränderlichkeit des Wesens und der Natur unveränderlich ist, davon sie gar nicht getrennet werden kann; so ist auch das angebohrne Recht so genau mit dem Menschen verbunden, daß es ihm nicht genommen werden kann; denn er hat dasselbe um seiner Verbindlichkeit ein Genüge zu leisten.[21]

The remarkable sentence 'Jus quoque connatum homini ita inhaeret, ut ipsi auferri non possit'[22] is in the Latin original of the text, published in 1750, emphasised by being printed in italics. This remark in connection with the following one – 'datur nimirum ad satisfaciendum obligationi' – indicates that the iura connata are unalienable. The iura connata are instruments to fulfil the demands of the natural law created by the natural obligation itself – 'Jus connatum cum obligatione connata simul ponitur.'[23] They can't be taken away by someone else, and they can't be given away by the owner of these rights, because the obligation which creates the innate rights is necessarily and intrinsically connected with the nature and essence of human beings. Such rights could only be alienated if it were possible to alienate the nature and essence of man, which means that the division between the iura connata and the nature and essence of man is simply not possible: 'Quamobrem cum esssentia hominis immutabilis sit; nec ulli hominum jus connatum auferri potest.'[24] So when Wolff states that the iura connata cannot be taken away, he means that it is no less impossible for the owner of the rights to relinquish them than it is for someone else to seize them.[25]

Wolff is emphasising this idea when he demonstrates that the iura connata derived from the obligationes connata and based on the human nature[26] are jura absoluta. He defines 'Jus absolutum' as a right which belongs to the human being 'per se': 'Jus absolutum dicitur, quod homini per se, nullo supposito facto humano, competit', and he adds in the following paragraph: 'Jus, quod ex obligatione connata oritur, absolutum est.'[27] So the iura connata are not just moral claims but are explicitly regarded as perfect rights: since the iura connata derive from natural law, they have the same validity as natural law. Wolff thus states:

Das Recht, welches uns das Gesetze der Natur giebt, damit wir unserer Verbindlichkeit ein Gnüge thun können, da diese nothwendig und unveränderlich ist, und wir folglich nicht leiden dörffen, daß wir in

dem Gebrauch unsers Rechtes von einem andern gehindert werden,
ist ein vollkommenes Recht; denn es entstehet aus der vollkommenen
Verbindlichkeit, niemanden in dem Gebrauch desselben zu hindern,
mit dieser ist das Recht verbunden, nicht zu leiden, daß wir in dem
Gebrauch unsers Rechtes verhindert werden. Da nun dieses ein
vollkommenes ist; so muß auch dasjenige Recht, von dem es seinen
Ursprung hat, ein vollkommenes Recht seyn. Es ist also ein jedes ange-
bohrnes Recht ein vollkommenes Recht.[28]

This explicit statement has to be taken seriously, especially when one discusses the role of the iura connata within the status civilis.

4. The Catalogue of Innate Rights

Which rights does Wolff actually have in mind when he develops the concept of innate rights? In §95 of the *Institutiones iuris naturae et gentium*
Wolff gives a list of the rights which are required to obey the innate obligation. He thus enumerates: 'aequalitas, libertas, jus securitatis, [. . .] jus
defensionis & jus puniendi', and in §97 he adds the 'jus alterum ad certas
praestationes sibi obligandi', which is in fact the ius contrahendi.[29] We find
this first list in the third chapter of the *Institutiones* called 'De obligatione
& Jure hominum universali in genere', and it is completed by explanations
in the following chapter with the title 'De officiis hominis erga seipsum &
cum iis connexis Juribus'. Here Wolff strikingly does not explicitly speak
of innate rights, but the title of the chapter already shows that the deductive idea is similar: man is by natural law obliged to perfect his body and
his soul, so he gets all the necessary rights to achieve this aim,[30] with Wolff
always adjoining the phrase 'man has the right to . . .' ('homini igitur jus
est ad ea. . .'). On this basis Wolff develops an expansive list of rights: the
right to everything which preserves his life and health, which means food,
beverage and medicine; everything which is necessary to produce clothes
and houses, and even everything needed to preserve or to create the
beauty of the body.[31] Wolff seems to regard all of these rights – including
the right to work according to one's capacities[32] – as contained within an
overarching right to everything which contributes to human happiness:
'Der Mensch muß also besorgt seyn, daß er glückseelig wird, nicht aber
unglückseelig; folglich hat er ein Recht zu demjenigen, was etwas zu seiner
Glückseeligkeit beytragen kann.'[33] If we consider this list, which of course
has to be discussed in detail, there is no doubt that it looks very like an
early catalogue of human rights, especially when we consider the construction of its philosophical basis.

5. Iura Connata: More Than Lost Rights and Less Than Human Rights

If we compare the iura connata in Wolff's natural law with the definition of human rights given above,[34] we can state that the similarity between them is simply astonishing. This is especially so if one keeps in mind that Wolff's first volume of his 'Jus naturae' including his ideas on the iura connata was published in Germany in 1740, the year when Frederic II became the king of Prussia and the political discussion was dominated by debates on various concepts of 'enlightened absolutism'. Since innate rights are necessary rights – 'iura absoluta' – based on natural law and inscribed by nature in man, Wolff regards them as valid rights. The crucial question now becomes: do these absolute natural rights keep their validity when man passes from the natural to the civil state (status civilis)? It is clear that the concept of innate rights is at first developed for and within Wolff's theory of the status naturalis, so it is reasonable to ask whether innate rights retain their validity with the normative change that occurs when the natural state is given up and the status civilis is entered. Are innate rights simply eliminated by civil law – as asserted by several scholars[35] – or do they continue to exercise their authority within the status civilis?[36] This poses the question of the practical and theoretical relationship between natural law and civil law. Wolff's answers to this question are not simple, and while they may point in a certain direction, they might not escape contradiction. I would like to point out the following four aspects.

1. The strict immutability and the necessity of the iura connata which are based on innate obligation and intrinsically connected with the nature and the essence of man seem to indicate that they retain their normative validity even in the status civilis. Since the nature of man does not change, the obligation which is strictly based on this nature cannot change either, and so the rights which are deduced from this obligation are also immutable. The iura connata are in Wolff's view 'iura absoluta', and that means they are absolutely – without any reserve – valid: they cannot depend on facts made by men.[37] Wolff is in this respect very clear and explicit, so it has to be taken seriously when he claims in a philosophical sense that the innate rights are absolute rights.

2. Since natural obligation is immutable the civil laws may not contradict the laws of nature,[38] so in principle the innate rights as a result of the natural obligation cannot be set aside by the civil law. Wolff intends to demonstrate by his entire natural law theory that civil law originates from natural law, such that natural law works as the normative benchmark of civil law. He even

states that if civil law errs – e.g. by ignorance – it has to be revoked or adapted to natural law.[39] In this context it is striking that Wolff repeats on several occasions that he does not want to be a 'story-teller' who only tells about customary practices, but that he rather speaks as a 'philosopher', who points out what must happen when reason is put into practice.[40] So on the one hand it seems to be obvious that Wolff is able to maintain a critical distance from the political status quo by adopting the standpoint of the natural lawyer: the personage who knows and describes the difference between the given political reality and the normative requirements postulated by a philosophy accountable to the truth alone.[41] On the other hand the asserted dominance of natural law creates a problematic point in respect to the validity of innate rights. This arises when Wolff defines public welfare and security not only as the principal aims of the state but also as the supreme and ultimate law, which itself is an expression of natural law. That means: civil law serving public welfare and security is justified by natural law as the supreme and ultimate law which in fact enriches its normative value. The effect is that civil law supported by the supreme and ultimate law may be able to subordinate norms of natural law in order to prevent greater damage.[42] In this case – in case of danger – these natural norms may be devaluated by civil law because they then belong to a lower normative level. Referring at least to perfection as the last goal Wolff creates a hierarchy of norms not only between civil law and natural law but also within the set of natural law norms. This astonishing, and almost utilitarian construction may help to preclude any rivalry between different legal domains, but it also introduces a serious danger for the realisation of the iura connata: supported by the supreme law, civil law is able to abolish any other law or right – actually justified by natural law.[43]

3. There is no doubt that Wolff derives the concept of innate rights from the general obligation of natural law. Since it is clear that natural liberty is restricted when the state is founded, it seems – on the one hand – that the validity of the innate rights is restricted to the status naturalis and simply given up within the status civilis. On the other hand, Wolff emphasises that natural obligation – man is obliged to make himself and his conditions more and more perfect – and innate rights as the means of fulfilling this obligation are, by definition, immutable. The only way to abolish this contradiction and to reconcile the natural validity of innate rights with their civil restriction is to construct the state as a free person who is inaugurated by a mutual and voluntary contract of its members with the aim of securing at least the iura connata. When Wolff points out that the purpose of the state is internal subsistence, law and order and security against external threats, it becomes obvious that the normative substance of the innate

rights is preserved and perpetuated by the state. By asserting that men in the status naturalis are not able to require everything which is necessary to fulfil the obligations of the natural law, Wolff claims that the nature of man – and that means the natural law itself – necessitates the civil state as the means of realising the normative substance of innate rights and natural law by guaranteeing subsistence and inner and outer peace.[44] In this respect innate rights retain their normative substance in the civil condition, and remain necessary in order to fulfill the obligations of the natural law. At the same time, innate rights are also changed by their transposition into the civil state, since here Wolff does not treat them as rights at the disposal of individuals, viewing them instead as rights invested in social institutions.

This transformation is explicitly reflected in Wolff's account of the difference between the status naturalis and the status adventitius (to which the status civilis belongs) in his *Grundsätze des Natur- und Völkerrechts*. In order to realise the difference between the two states one has to be aware that men may have a certain right in the status naturalis which later can only be exercised by someone else in the status civilis:

Damit man aber nicht in der Unterscheidung des ursprünglichen Zustandes von dem entstandenen zuweilen zweifle; so muß man mercken, daß der Mensch im ursprünglichen Zustande an und vor sich selbst ein Recht haben könne, dessen Ausübung aber nicht anders, als in dem entstandenen statt findet, in so weit nämlich die Handlung eines andern macht, daß es statt finden kann.

And he adds as an explanation: 'Ein Exempel finden wir in dem Rechte uns zu wehren, oder zu vertheidigen, und dem Rechte zu strafen.'[45] The idea that the exercise of a particular right depends upon the activity of someone else – in this case the authorities – leads to a certain alienation of this right as a personal capacity of the original owner. Nevertheless, although the original owner of the innate right does not exercise his right himself, he still enjoys the beneficial use of its normative substance, because it has to be preserved by the authorities as an agent of the state who now is responsible for the actualisation of the (formerly personal) rights. Since the original normative aims of the necessary and immutable innate rights have to be kept and can be kept, there is at least no need for an active role of the owner of the innate rights.[46] So Klaus-Gert Lutterbeck is correct in stating that in Wolff's natural law theory the basic rights of a person were reformulated as purposes of the state.[47] But he is not right in asserting that the basic rights were simply given up when the power of the sovereign was created.[48] Instead one has to consider that Wolff's construction necessarily requires that the original normative substance of the innate rights is preserved, and that leads to a permanent normative claim of the subjects towards the authorities.[49]

4. Since it seems to be clear that the innate rights in Wolff's natural law theory have certain similarities with human rights, one has to consider how far these similarities actually reach. In this context it seems to be a crucial question whether the normative claims of innate rights can be rendered legally enforceable. It is striking that there seems to be no clear and really satisfactory answer to this question. If one surveys Wolff's political theory, then, on the one hand, it seems clear that the body politic is created by a contract that excludes the political participation of the subjects. The contract between the authorities and the subjects includes a double promise: the authorities promise to do everything to establish welfare and security and the subjects promise that they will accept as their own will everything that the authorities arrange to achieve the state's purposes.[50] So there is at least – per definitionem – no difference left between the will of the authorities and the will of the subjects.[51] From this point of view the stated normative claim towards the authorities based on the normative substance of the immutable innate rights cannot be enforced by legal proceedings. On the other hand, however, Wolff concedes a large range of possibilities in instituting a political government. Since sovereignty is originally possessed by the people, they have the right to define all conditions of the political government,[52] and they even have the right to resist when the 'rector civitatis' infringes the rights of the people or the elites, as far as they are defined by the fundamental law:

> Weil auch der Oberherr kein Recht hat, etwas zu befehlen, so wider die Grundgesetze streitet; so darf man ihm auch nicht gehorsamen, wenn er etwas wider die Grundgesetze befiehlet, ja es ist erlaubt sich dem Regenten zu widersetzen, und ihn im Zaum zu halten, wenn er das Recht, so dem Volck, oder den Vornehmsten vorbehalten ist, einen Eingrif thut.[53]

According to this there are in principle certain political and legal arrangements possible which may create the legal capacity to judge even the prince. One has to consider however that the violation of the fundamental laws ('Grundgesetze', 'leges fundamentales') is a special political case, which has to be discussed in respect to the still-feudal political structure of eighteenth-century Germany. If one additionally considers that on the one hand Wolff states that the subject is allowed to disobey the authorities if they violate the natural law, and on the other hand asserts that the disobedient subject has to suffer the punishment for his disobedience[54] – because of the high value of security granted by the state – then it becomes clear that Wolff was not intending to safeguard the validity of the innate rights by making them part of the fundamental laws. Although that might be in principle a way to make the normative claim based on the innate rights enforceable by legal proceedings.

Conclusion and Further Perspectives

The result of the preceding discussion is somewhat ambivalent: on the one hand we can state that in Wolff's natural law theory the iura connata are strongly defined as 'iura absoluta' which are intrinsically and immutably connected to the nature of man; they are consequently by definition not alienable. These are aspects of Wolff's natural law theory that are shared with later theories of human rights. At the same time, we can see that Wolff's efforts to preserve the normative substance of the necessary and immutable innate rights by transforming them into a purpose of the state lead to the loss of their character as individual rights. For Wolff's theory it seems to be crucial that the reconciliation between the necessary rights of a human being on the one hand and the function of the state on the other is not achievable in a convincing way. In the end, German natural law at that time – Wolff is typical in this respect – always emphasises the supreme purpose of a state: it is security by law and order which subordinates any other rightful claims, and from this point of view it becomes clear that political decisions within the political theory neutralise the more progressive aspects of the law theory. So in sum it may be obvious that in comparison with human rights Wolff's concept of the iura connata already possesses a significant number of semantic elements which are suited to the later idea of human rights. Wolff's innate rights, however, cannot be identified as 'les droits naturel, inaliénables et sacrés de l'Homme' which found expression in a number of political statements and claims in the French Déclaration des Droits de l'Homme et du Citoyen.

Wolff's concept of the iura connata is nevertheless, in comparison with other natural law theories in his time, rather elaborated. Although the reception of the concept of the iura connata in Wolff's natural law theory is still unknown,[55] the natural law theory of Georg Friedrich Meier may be an interesting example of a theory which explicitly deals with the idea of innate rights after Wolff, but which develops it from a different explanatory background with – in fact – less radical implications. Meier

is regarded to be, to some extent, a follower of Christian Wolff. As a professor of philosophy he taught natural law at Halle University for many
years, not least on the basis of the textbooks of Christian Wolff, Alexander Gottlieb Baumgarten and Heinrich Köhler. So one can presume that
Meier knew Wolff's natural law theory very well when he published his
Recht der Natur in 1767.[56] Meier explicitly distinguishes between iura connata and iura acquisita, and gives an interesting list of innate rights which
belong to men from their birth without any further voluntary actions as
requirements of their existence. He specifies the right to life, the right to
physical integrity, the right to freedom and equality, the right not to be
offended in one's reputation, and the right to be virtuous combined with
the right to commit inner sins. The last one is the consequence of his principle of natural law which is focused on the avoidance of damage of one's
external self ('suum'): the first duty of the natural law is therefore not to
offend one's external self, and the first right is to defend oneself against
damage. Since inner sins – which stay in one's internum – cannot offend
someone else, individuals have the right to commit these sins. All these
rights belong to the status naturalis, so again the typical question arises:
what happens to them when the status civilis is established? Are they in
principle unalienable, or is it possible to give them up voluntarily? With
reference to the first part of Meier's later *Lehre von den natürlichen gesellschaftlichen Rechten und Pflichten des Menschen* (Halle, 1770), Dominik
Recknagel convincingly demonstrates that Meier asserts that innate
natural rights are given up within the state. Meier explicitly claims that
natural law is limited and modified by civil law, so men can get additional
rights on the one hand and lose parts of their natural rights on the other
when they enter the status civilis.[57] This idea is already prepared in his
Recht der Natur, which exclusively deals with the status naturalis, when
Meier definitely holds that my belongings can only be given up when I
agree: 'Nichts hört auf das Meine zu seyn, ohne meine Einwilligung.'[58] So
Recknagel seems to be right when he states the following: 'Begreift man
Menschenrechte als durch Geburt verliehene und unverlierbare Rechte
des Menschen, so kann bei Meier in diesem Sinne von Menschenrechten
keine Rede sein.'[59] If we compare Meier's concept with that of Wolff we
have to state that Meier stays behind his predecessor: while Wolff tries
to preserve the innate rights by transforming them, Meier is claiming the
facility to give them up voluntarily. So in his view innate rights are given
by birth but they are not as necessary as they are in Wolff's concept. The
crucial difference between the two concepts is the connection between
the iura connata and the nature and essence of man: Meier only distinguishes the iura connata and the iura acquisita for systematical reasons;

the innate rights are given by birth without any additional voluntarily act, the iura acquisita are constituted later and require volition. They both belong to the 'suum' of someone and have in normative regards the same status. Wolff in contrast links the iura connata intrinsically to the nature and essence of men; since the nature and essence of men are unchangeable, the innate rights are necessary and unalienable, and their surrender would clearly imply the abandonment of the essence of man. Thus it is quite clear that Wolff's statement of the necessity of innate rights marks an important step within the whole discussion – although it has still no political consequences. And it is noteworthy, as we can learn from Meier's example, that Wolff's successors did not follow him in taking this step, in spite of its theoretical significance.

But times and theories were changing. Thirty years after Wolff's death and seventeen years after Meier's *Recht der Natur* we find in Johann August Schlettwein's book *Die Rechte der Menschheit oder der einzige wahre Grund aller Gesetze, Ordnung und Verfassungen* everything we missed before. Schlettwein's book is an early example of a long list of publications which combine a catalogue of human rights with certain political claims.[60] These publications appeared in Germany during the 1780s and were without doubt already influenced by Rousseau, who argued in his *Du Contrat Social* (1762) against the possibility of renouncing one's natural liberty.[61] The title of Schlettwein's book is programmatic: while Meier uses the term 'Rechte der Menschheit'[62] only once and somewhat unspecifically, in Schlettwein's book the normative substance and political consequences of the term are fully elaborated. In regard to the discussion above, the following three aspects are especially striking: 1) Schlettwein follows Wolff in connecting the innate rights – which are now explicitly human rights – to the nature and the substance of man, and therefore these rights cannot be given up as long as man keeps being man. Schlettwein emphasises:

Diejenigen Rechte und Pflichten, welche der Menschheit selbst, als solcher, vermöge ihres Wesens eigen sind, können weder ganz, noch zum Theil verlohren werden, so lange der Mensch ist. Es kann auch kein Mensch diese Menschen-Rechte und MenschenPflichten ganz, oder zum Theil fahren lassen, wenn er nicht der Bestimmung der Menschheit zuwider handeln will.[63]

2) This is considered when Schlettwein defines the purpose of the state: it is no longer happiness determined by a superior, but is now the full guarantee of the human rights of each citizen.[64] In this context Schlettwein picks up the Wolffian idea of perfection and ties it to the actualisation of human

rights: a civil society is not perfect if it is not able to guarantee the human rights of each of its citizens. 3) These two insights have directly political consequences: Schlettwein conceptualises a sort of sovereignty of the people which is constituted by the members of the society and which stays as a potentially active power in the background of any state.[65] Although it is still not clear how this basic power ('Grundgewalt') actually works, the idea of this construction becomes obvious when Schlettwein describes the juridical obligation and responsibility of the regent towards the rights of a citizen or the rights of the state as a whole: if the regent damages the citizen's rights he can be brought to justice, and the permanently existing 'Grundgewalt' of the people even gives rise to the capacity to change a regime.

Schlettwein's in many respects practically and theoretically vague concept – which of course cannot be discussed further here – may nevertheless be an interesting example of the reception of some elements of Wolff's idea of the iura connata which were put into a completely different political frame. Within this frame Wolff's concept of innate rights comes closer to the idea of human rights. Decades earlier, in contrast, Wolff had been quite careful concerning the political consequences or even political requirements flowing from his concept of innate rights, not least because he was convinced that an enlightened state with the help of enlightened science was able to guarantee the welfare and the security of its citizens. Nevertheless, in spite of his own political constraints, by defining innate rights as necessary, immutable and absolute rights based on the immutable nature and essence of men, Wolff created the theoretical preconditions for further developments.

Notes

1. Although one gets the impression that the discussion of Wolff's concept of innate rights is purely German, one has to admit that Knud Haakonssen's contribution to the issue is at least one significant exception, see Haakonssen, 'German Natural Law', in Mark Goldie and Robert Wokler, eds, *The Cambridge History of Eighteenth-Century Political Thought* (Cambridge: Cambridge University Press, 2006), 251–90, esp. 268–78.
2. See Dirk Effertz, *Menschenrechte und Staatstheorie. Wolffs zweiter Aufenthalt in Halle* (Perspektiven der Aufklärung, Vol. 5) (Halle: Universitätsverlag Halle-Wittenberg, 2014); Nele Schneidereit, 'Angeborene Rechte – Bürgerrechte – soziale Rechte: Christian Wolffs Lehre von den iura connata', *Jahrbuch für Recht und Ethik – Annual Review of Law and Ethics*, 22 (2014), 159–81. See also the short version of the former: Nele Schneidereit, 'Christian Wolffs Lehre von den iura connata', in Tilmann Altwicker, Francis Cheneval and

Oliver Diggelmann, eds, *Völkerrechtsphilosophie der Frühaufklärung* (Politika, Vol. 12) (Tübingen: Mohr Siebeck, 2015), 165–74.

3. Diethelm Klippel, *Politische Freiheit und Freiheitsrechte im deutschen Naturrecht des 18. Jahrhunderts* (Paderborn: Schöningh, 1976), 75. See also Louis Pahlow, 'Die verlorenen Rechte der Menschen. Rechtscharakter und Funktion der "iura connata" bei Christian Wolff', in Jürgen Stolzenberg and Oliver-Pierre Rudolph, eds, *Christian Wolff und die europäische Aufklärung*, Part 3 (Hildesheim, Zürich, New York: Georg Olms, 2007), 311–25. In Pahlow's view, the innate rights only have an analytical and logical function; Wolff wants only to demonstrate the origin and legitimacy of further norms which in fact limit the innate rights in his natural law theory (324).

4. Hanns-Martin Bachmann, *Die naturrechtliche Staatslehre Christian Wolffs* (Berlin: Duncker und Humblot, 1977), 100. See also Effertz, who explicitely affirms the positive view of Bachmann, Thomann and Ernst Cassirer (*Menschenrechte und Staatstheorie*, 28).

5. Bachmann, *Die naturrechtliche Staatslehre Christian Wolffs*, 107.

6. Marcel Thomann, 'Christian Wolff', in Michael Stolleis, ed., *Staatsdenker der Frühen Neuzeit* (Munich: C.H. Beck, 1995), 259.

7. See Klippel, *Freiheitsrechte*, 75. Klippel also somewhat distantly states that the earlier German natural law plays a 'certain role' (78) in the development of human rights.

8. Haakonssen, 'German Natural Law', 271.

9. For the distinction between real and moral rights, see Andreas Niederberger, 'Are Human Rights Moral Rights?', in Matthias Lutz-Bachmann and Amos Nascimento, eds, *Human Rights, Human Dignity and Cosmopolitan Ideals. Essays on Critical Theory and Human Rights* (Farnham: Ashgate, 2014), 75–92.

10. See, e.g., with more references to the enormous literature: Anja Mihr and Mark Gibney, eds, *The SAGE Handbook of Human Rights* (London: Sage, 2014); Dinah Shelton, ed., *The Oxford Handbook of International Human Rights Law* (Oxford: Oxford University Press, 2013).

11. For the discussion of Wolff's theory, especially in comparison to the natural law theory of Christian Thomasius, see, e.g., Timothy J. Hochstrasser, *Natural Law Theories in the Early Enlightenment* (Cambridge: Cambridge University Press, 2000), 150–86, esp. 159–70; Klaus-Gert Lutterbeck, *Staat und Gesellschaft bei Christian Thomasius und Christian Wolff. Eine historische Untersuchung in systematischer Absicht* (Stuttgart-Bad Cannstatt: Frommann-Holzboog, 2002); Haakonssen, 'German Natural Law', 251–90, esp. 268–78. For Wolff's natural law theory in general see: Bachmann, *Die naturrechtliche Staatslehre Christian Wolffs*; Bénédict Winiger: *Das rationale Pflichtenrecht Christian Wolffs. Bedeutung und Funktion der transzentalen, logischen und moralischen Wahrheit im systematischen und theistischen Naturrecht Wolffs* (Berlin: Duncker und Humblot, 1992).

12. Christian Thomasius, *Institutiones Jurisprudentiae divinae* (Halle, 1688), I, 1, §114. See also his later and more original approach to natural law, *Fundamenta iuris naturae et gentium* (Halle, 1705), where we also find no further discussion of the difference between 'iura connata' and 'iura acquisita'.

13. 'Selbst durch die Natur wird der Mensch verbunden, die Handlungen zubegehen, welche seine und seines Zustandes Vollkommenheit befördern.' Christian Wolff, *Grundsätze des Natur- und Völkerrechts* (Halle, 1754), §36, see also §43. 'Lex naturalis nos obligat ad committendas actiones, quae per se ad perfectionem nostram statusque nostri tendunt, & ad omittendas actiones, quae per se ad imperfectionem nostram statusque nostri tendunt.' Christian Wolff, *Jus naturae methodo scientifica pertractatum. Pars prima, in qua obligationes et jura connata ex ipsa hominis essentia atque natura a priori demonstratur* (Frankfurt and Leipzig, 1740), §170. See Haakonssen who explains: 'The notion of human perfectibility is complex and can only be understood through Wolff's metaphysics, but three central characteristics indicate its nature. It is a gradual realisation of our natural abilities in such a way that they are in harmony with each other, both in ourselves and in others, which in turn is the same as our progress in happiness guided by a divine and transhuman ideal of perfect happiness, beatitude, and signalled to us through pleasure.' Haakonssen, 'German Natural Law', 270.

14. 'Daher erhellet, daß das Recht aus der leidenden Verbindlichkeit entstehe; und daß kein Recht seyn würde, wenn keine Verbindlichkeit da wäre; wie auch, daß uns durch das natürliche Gesetze ein Recht zu allen denjenigen Handlungen gegeben werde, ohne welche wir die natürliche Verbindlichkeit nicht erfüllen können.' Wolff, *Grundsätze*, §46. 'Si nulla esset obligatio, nec jus ullum foret. Etenim jus oritur ex obligatione. Habet igitur rationem sui, cur sit & cur tale sit, in eadem, adeoque non ponitur, nisi posita obligatione. Nullum igitur jus foret, si nulla esset obligation.' Christian Wolff, *Jus naturae* I, §25.

15. 'Daß also die natürliche Verbindlichkeit diejenige ist, welche ihren hinreichenden Grund selbst in dem Wesen und der Natur des Menschen und der übrigen Dinge hat.' Wolff, *Grundsätze*, §38. '[U]t ideo obligatio naturalis sit, quae rationem sufficientem in ipsa hominis rerumque essentia atque natura habet.' Christian Wolff, *Institutiones Iuris Naturae et Gentium* (Halae, 1750), §38. See also Wolff, *Jus naturae* I, §2.

16. 'Quoniam lex naturae rationem sufficientem in ipsa hominis rerumque natura habet, ideoque obligationem naturalem continent, haec autem immutabilis & necessaria est, lex etiam naturae immutabilis & necessaria est.' Wolff, *Institutiones*, §40.

17. 'Auf gleiche Weise beweisen wir, daß das Gesetz der Natur alle Menschen verbinde; und daß von der natürlichen Verbindlichkeit kein Mensch befreyet werden könne; weil nämlich das natürliche Gesetz den hinreichenden Grund in der Natur des Menschen und der Dinge selbst hat, und die Verbindlichkeit, welche dasselbe in sich begreift, also bald statt findet, wenn man die

Natur und das Wesen der Menschen und der übrigen Dinge annimt.' Wolff, *Grundsätze*, §42. 'Similiter quia lex naturalis sufficientem in ipsa hominis rerumque essentia atque natura habet, & obligatio, quam continet, ponitur ista posita; lex naturae omnes homines obligat, nec ab obligatione naturali ullus hominum liberari potest.' Wolff, *Institutiones*, §42.

18. '[S]o ist die Verbindlichkeit, die der Mensch als ein Mensch erfüllen muß, bey allen Menschen einerley; und folglich sind auch die Rechte, die dem Menschen zukommen, insofern als er ein Mensch ist, bey jedem Menschen einerley. Also ist klar, daß es allgemeine Verbindlichkeiten und allgemeine Rechte gebe.' Wolff, *Grundsätze*, §69.

19. 'Jus connatum homo natura habet. Etenim jus connatum omne ponitur posita essentia & natura hominis, adeoque per essentiam & naturam suam ipsi competit.' Wolff, *Jus naturae* I, §33.

20. Ibid., §26.

21. Wolff, *Grundsätze*, §74. 'Jus connatum dicitur, quod ex obligatione connata oritur. Est autem obligation connata, quae cum essentia & natura hominis ponitur. Quamobrem cum haec propter essentiae ac naturae immutabilis sit, utpote ab ea inseparabilis; Jus quoque connatum homini ita inhaeret, ut ipsi auferri non possit: datur nimirum ad satisfaciendum obligationi.' Wolff, *Institutiones*, §74.

22. Ibid., §74.

23. Wolff, *Jus naturae* I, §27.

24. Ibid., §64.

25. See in contrast, e.g., Bachmann, who states that the innate rights cannot be taken away, but can be given away by a voluntary decision of the owner of these rights. *Die naturrechtliche Staatslehre Christian Wolffs*, 110–12. See also Schneidereit, 'Angeborene Rechte – Bürgerechte – soziale Rechte', 162, and Haakonssen, who asserts: 'Although basic rights are innate, this only means that they cannot be taken away, not that they cannot be given away.' 'German Natural Law', 272. They all underestimate the fact that the innate rights are – in the view of Wolff – intrinsically necessarily linked with the immutable nature and essence of man, which simply cannot be taken or given away.

26. 'Posita essentia & natura hominis, ponitur etiam omne jus connatum.' Wolff, *Jus naturae* I, §28.

27. Ibid., §48f.

28. Wolff, *Grundsätze*, §81. 'Jus, quod lex naturae dat ad satisfaciendum obligationi, cum ea necessaria sit & immutabilis sit, consequenter pati non tenearis, ut in ejus usu ab altero impediaris, perfectum est. Oritur nimirum ex perfecta obligatione ejus usum non impediendi, cui respondet jus non patiendi, ut is impediatur, quod cum sit perfectum, jus quoque, unde ortum suum trahit, perfectum esse debet. Ac ideo jus connatum perfectum est.' The last four words are emphasised by being printed in italics. Wolff, *Institutiones*, §81.

29. Ibid., §§95, 97.

30. See Wolff, *Institutiones/Grundsätze*, §§103, 107.
31. See ibid., §§114–17.
32. See ibid., §124.
33. Wolff, *Grundsätze*, §118. 'Homo igitur curae habere debet, ut sit felix & ne infelix fiat [. . .], consequenter ipsi jus est ad ea, quae ad felicitatem quidpiam conferunt.' Wolff, *Institutiones* §118. See also Wolff, *Jus naturae* I, §§280, 284. For Wolff's concept of happiness see Clemens Schwaiger, *Das Problem des Glücks im Denken Christian Wolffs. Eine quellen-, begriffs- und entwicklungsgeschichtliche Studie zu Schlüsselbegriffen seiner Ethik* (Forschungen und Materialien zur deutschen Aufklärung, Dept. II, Vol. 10) (Stuttgart-Bad Cannstatt: Frommann-Holzboog, 1995).
34. See notes 9 and 10.
35. See e.g. Pahlow, 'Rechtscharakter und Funktion', 324, see also Effertz, who points out that the validity of the iura connata may change within the status civilis (*Menschenrechte und Staatstheorie*, 19).
36. See, e.g., Bachmann: 'Andererseits stellen die dem Menschen von Natur aus zustehenden angeborenen Rechte nicht lediglich ein Gut dar, das etwa mit Beendigung des paradiesischen Urzustands entfiele, vielmehr behält das Naturrecht einschließlich der angeborenen Rechte bei Wolff entgegen einer vielfach wiederholten Legende seine Gültigkeit auch und gerade im sogenannten zukömmlichen Zustand, ja schließlich auch im gesellschaftlichen, also staatlichen Zustand.' H-M. Bachmann, 'Zur Wolffschen Naturrechtslehre', in Werner Schneiders, ed., *Christian Wolff 1679–1754* (Hamburg: Felix Meiner, 1986), 163.
37. Wolff explicitly states: 'Ab obligatione connata nemo hominum liberari potest, seu ea constanter in eundum cadit. Obligatio enim connata homini natura inest, adeoque per essentiam & naturam suam eidem competit. Quamobrem eodem modo patet, ab obligatione connata neminem hominum liberari posse, consequenter eandem constanter in hominem cadere, quo paulo ante evicimus, jus connatum homini auferri non posse.' Wolff, *Jus naturae* I, §68.
38. 'Da die natürliche Verbindlichkeit unveränderlich ist, und sich kein Mensch davon losmachen kann; so müssen die bürgerlichen Gesetze denen natürlichen gebietenden und verbietenden nicht zuwider seyn; folglich kann das bürgerliche Gesetz aus dem, was man natürlicher Weise schuldig ist, nicht etwas unerlaubtes, und aus dem, was natürlicher Weise unerlaubt ist, nicht eine Schuldigkeit, oder etwas erlaubtes machen.' Wolff, *Grundsätze*, §1069, see also Wolff, *Jus naturae* VIII, §973.
39. 'Weil aus dem bisherigen erhellet, daß aus natürlichen Gesetzen die bürgerlichen gemacht werden; so muß man verhüten, daß der Gesetzgeber nicht gewisse gemeine Irrthümer für das Recht der Natur halte: Wenn folglich durch Unwissenheit der Zeiten einige Irrthümer in die bürgerlichen Gesetze eingeschlichen, oder einige aus andern an dieser Kranckheit liegenden durch eine Folge herausgezogen wären, so müssen dieselben entweder abgeschaffet,

oder der Wahrheit gemäß geändert werden.' Wolff, *Grundsätze*, §1074, see also Wolff, *Jus naturae* VIII, §992.

40. Christian Wolff, *Vernünfftige Gedancken von dem gesellschaftlichen Leben der Menschen und insonderheit dem gemeinen Wesen*, 4th edition (Frankfurt and Leipzig, 1736), Preface, §§270, 379.

41. See Wolff, *Institutiones/Grundsätze*, Praefatio/Vorrede.

42. Ibid., §1071.

43. See Frank Grunert, 'Absolutism(s): Necessary Ambivalences in the Political Theory of Christian Wolff', *Tijdschrift voor Rechtsgeschiedenis – Revue d'Histoire du Droit. The Legal History Review*, LXXIII: 1–2 (2005), 149.

44. 'Wir erkennen sehr leicht, daß eintzele Häuser sich selbst dasjenige nicht hinreichend verschaffen können, was zur Nothdurft, Bequemlichkeit und dem Vergnügen, ja zur Glückseligkeit erfordert wird, noch auch ihre Rechte ruhig geniessen, und was sie von andern zu fordern haben, sicher erhalten, noch auch sich und das ihrige wider anderer Gewaltthätigkeiten schützen können. Es ist also nöthig, dasjenige durch gemeinschaftliche Kräfte zu erhalten, was eintzele Häuser vor sich nicht erhalten können. Und zu dem Ende müssen Gesellschaften errichtet werden. Eine Gesellschaft, die zu dem Ende gemacht wird, heisset Staat (civitas). Daher erhellet, daß durch Verträge der Menschen Staaten entstanden, und die Absicht eines Staats bestehe in hinlänglichen Lebensunterhalt (in sufficientia vitae), d.i. im Überfluß alles dessen, was zur Nothdurft, zur Bequemlichkeit und zum Vergnügen des Lebens, auch zur Glückseligkeit des Menschen erfordert wird, in der innern Ruhe des Staates (tranquillitate civitatis), d.i. in der Befreyung von der Furcht für Unrecht, oder Verletzung seines Rechts, und der Sicherheit (securitate) oder der Befreyung von der Furcht vor äußerer Gewalt.' Wolff, *Grundsätze*, §972. 'Fines civitatis sunt vita sufficientia, tranquillitas & securitas.' Wolff, *Jus naturae* VIII, §13, see also §§4, 9, 17, 26.

45. Wolff, *Grundsätze*, §102.

46. In this perspective Haakonssen is right when he emphasises that the precondition of relinquishments of the innate rights is 'that such an action is in our best interests in pursuing the overall good, our perfection'. 'German Natural Law', 272.

47. 'Die Grundrechte werden in Staatszwecke umgedeutet.' Lutterbeck, *Staat und Gesellschaft*, 196. See also Schneidereit: 'Die iura connata der Individuen gehen auf den Staat als künstliche Person über, ohne dass die Individuen auf ihrer Grundlage gegen den Staat vorgehen könnten.' 'Angeborene Rechte – Bürgerrechte – soziale Rechte', 173.

48. See Lutterbeck, *Staat und Gesellschaft*.

49. See Jörn Garber, who is right when he asserts the following with Wolff in mind: 'Dem Staat ist durch diese Staatszweckkategorien die Einlösung jener materialen Anspruchsrechte aufgegeben, die sich (vom Blickpunkt des Staatsglieds) darstellen als materiale Anspruchsrechte des Individuums an das "gemeine Wesen".' Garber, 'Vom "ius connatum" zum "Menschenrecht".

Deutsche Menschenrechtstheorien der Spätaufklärung', in *Spätabsolutismus und bürgerliche Gesellschaft. Studien zur deutschen Staats- und Gesellschaftstheorie im Übergang zur Moderne* (Frankfurt am Main: Keip, 1992), 160.

50. 'Es ist demnach zwischen der Obrigkeit und den Unterthanen ein Vertrag, nehmlich die Obriget verspricht alle ihre Kräffte und ihren Fleiß dahin anzuwenden, daß sie zur Beförderung der gemeinen Wohlfahrt und Sicherheit diensame Mittel erdencke, und zu deren Ausführung nöthige Anstalten mache: hingegen die Unterthanen versprechen dargegen, daß sie willig seyn wollen alles dasjenige zu thun, was sie für gut befinden wird.' Wolff, *Vernünfftige Gedancken von dem gesellschaftlichen*, §220 [recte: §230.].

51. See, e.g., Frank Grunert, 'Paternalismus in der politischen Theorie der deutschen Aufklärung. Das Beispiel Christian Wolff', in Michael Anderheiden, Peter Bürkli, Hans Michael Heinig, Stephan Kirste and Kurt Seelmann, eds, *Paternalismus und Recht. In memoriam Angela Augustin (1968–2004)* (Tübingen: Mohr Siebeck, 2006), 9–27.

52. See Wolff, *Institutiones/Grundsätze*, §982.

53. Wolff, *Grundsätze*, §1079. See also Wolff, *Jus naturae* VIII, §1047: 'Si superior involat in jus populo, vel optimatibus reservatum; injuriam populo facit & illi resistere eumque coërcere licet.'

54. See Wolff, *Grundsätze*, §1079, and Wolff, *Jus naturae* VIII, §1045.

55. The history of the reception of Wolff's concept of 'iura connata' has to be reconstructed step by step. The more comprehensive studies of Klippel and Garber give an important starting point for a history like this. It may review Schneidereit's assertion that Wolff's concept of 'iura connata' remained nearly without any impact: 'Rezeptionsgeschichtlich ist Wolffs iura connata-Lehre fast ohne Echo geblieben.' 'Christian Wolffs Lehre von den iura connata', 173.

56. G. F. Meier, *Recht der Natur* (Halle, 1767). Reprint: Christian Wolff, *Gesammelte Werke, III. Abteilung, Materialien und Dokumente, Band 141* (Hildesheim, Zürich, New York: Georg Olms, 2014). For Meier in general see Frank Grunert and Gideon Stiening, eds, *Georg Friedrich Meier (1718–1777). Philosophie der Aufklärung twischen populärer Reproduktion und theoretischer Innovation* (Berlin, Boston: De Gruyter, 2015).

57. See Dominik Recknagel, 'Vorwort', in Meier, *Recht der Natur*, 25f. See also Dominik Recknagel, 'Meiers "Recht der Natur" im Kontext des halleschen Naturrechtsdiskurses', in Grunert and Stiening, eds, *Georg Friedrich Meier (1718–1777)*, 255.

58. Meier, *Recht der Natur*, 363.

59. Recknagel, 'Vorwort', 23. See also Klippel (*Freiheitsrechte*, 83f.), who concedes that the obvious gap between the political reality of the status civilis on the one hand and the description of innate rights in the status naturalis on the other may have created the opportunity to discuss the limitations of human rights within the status civilis. Klippel asserts that Meier in this way created 'Denkmöglichkeiten' for the further discussions.

60. See Klippel, *Freiheitsrechte*, 120.

61. Jean-Jacques Rousseau, *Du Contrat Social; ou, Principe du Droit Politique*, in *Œuvres completes, Vol. III: Du Contrat Social, Écrits politiques* (Paris: Gallimard, 1991), 356.

62. Meier, *Recht der Natur*, 27.

63. Johann August Schlettwein, *Die Rechte der Menschheit oder der einzige wahre Grund aller Gesetze, Ordnungen und Verfassungen* (Giessen, 1784, Reprint: Frankfurt am Main: Scriptor, 1980), 27.

64. 'Dies soll nach dem gesunden MenschenSinne in der bürgerlichen Gesell- schaft die HauptAbsicht seyn, daß ein jeder die vollkommenste Garantie aller seiner MenschenRechte, und des Genusses derselbigen darinnen findet.' Ibid., 451.

65. Ibid., 360f.

9

Hume's Peculiar Definition of Justice

James A. Harris

I

Justice as Hume usually speaks of it consists in respect for rights of property.[1] The first example given of an act of justice in Book 3 of *A Treatise of Human Nature* is the repayment of a loan: the return by a borrower of property to its owner. Sometimes, Hume observes later, it is a requirement of justice that a poor man must repay what he owes to a rich man who has no need of it. Sometimes justice requires that the labour of the poor and industrious be bestowed on the rich and dissolute. Sometimes justice requires putting into the hands of the vicious the means of harming both themselves and others. The work of justice is no more (and no less) than the enforcement of rules which articulate the distinction between possession and property. Thus far Hume's approach to justice appears to be consonant with what he terms the 'vulgar' definition of justice, the definition popular among the Roman lawyers and given classic formulation by Ulpian as '*constans et perpetua voluntas ius suum cuique tribuendi*': in Hume's translation, '*a constant and perpetual will of giving every one his due*'.[2] But, Hume is quick to point out, there is contained in this definition 'such things as right and property, independent of justice, and antecedent to it' (T 526). And Hume takes himself to have removed the basis for rational belief in those things. He has argued that there is no means of measuring rules of justice against 'natural' principles of right. Rules of justice, as Hume understands them, *define* the distinction between possession and rightful ownership. An act is just, therefore, to the extent that it does not violate those rules. Justice as such cannot be distinguished from justice as it is defined in a particular system of law. Although Hume himself is not as clear about the matter as one might wish, it is an implication of such an approach to justice that, conceived of as a virtue, it is a virtue of abstention and omission. The justness of an individual agent lies in her *not violating* the rules of justice. It lies in not stealing or otherwise appropriating what is not hers.

Sometimes Hume includes in his definition of justice the obligation to respect promises and contracts. Thus he talks in *Treatise* 3.2.6 of 'the three fundamental laws of nature, *that of the stability of possession, of its transference by consent*, and *of the performance of promises*' (T 526). But it is much more common for the scope of justice to be restricted to, as Hume puts it in the second *Enquiry*, 'laws for the regulation of property'.[3] In the essay 'Of the Original Contract' Hume talks in terms of 'justice, or a regard to the property of others' as distinct from 'fidelity or the observance of promises'.[4] Fairly frequently Hume speaks of 'equity' as if it were part of justice as he understands it, but the context in almost all cases makes it clear that he is using 'equity' as a synonym of 'justice', rather than using it in its technical sense as a principle of moral insight that may be used by judges, in Kames's words, 'to correct and mitigate the rigour, and what even in a proper sense may be termed the *injustice of common law*'.[5] In the *Treatise* Hume includes 'equity', presumably meant in the technical sense, among the natural virtues (cf. T 578). Justice is thus for Hume remarkably limited in its domain. This has been noted and regretted by a succession of commentators, beginning with some of Hume's most notable philosophical contemporaries, including Adam Smith and Thomas Reid. More recent writers, such as John Mackie, Jonathan Harrison and David Raphael, also remark on the oddness of Hume's definition of justice[6] – though others proceed as if there were nothing remarkable at all in it.[7] My purpose in what follows is to use the context provided by the modern natural law tradition in order to show just how peculiar Hume's definition is, and then to offer an explanation of why he restricts the scope of justice in this way. In Hume's day it was usual, I shall show, to include in a definition of justice a much wider set of rights than rights of property. Hume focuses on property, I shall argue, because he believes, first, that prosecuting the case for a sympathy-based theory of moral judgement, and against a special moral sense, requires an account of the historical origins of justice; and, secondly, that rules concerning property must have been, historically speaking, the first rules to have been developed by human beings wanting to live in society with each other. In conclusion I shall make a brief comparison between Hume's theory of justice and the rather broader theory developed by Adam Smith in *The Theory of Moral Sentiments*. Hume and Smith share a hostility to the idea of a special sense of justice, and analyse the moral sentiments in general in terms of the operations of sympathy, but Smith does not follow Hume in pursuing a historical examination of justice in the course of his explication of the moral sentiments. I shall suggest that this is to Smith's credit.

II

The natural jurisprudence that had flourished in Europe since the publication of Grotius's *De Iure Belli et Pacis* in 1625 was an attempt to give a scientific character to the teaching of morality by showing how moral and political duties could be derived from principles of reason.[8] As in natural philosophy, the goal in modern moral philosophy was to do away with the jargon and obfuscation of scholasticism, and, as far as possible, to replace it with the clarity bestowed by the geometrical method of proof. Particularly influential in Scotland were the versions of natural law put forward by Samuel Pufendorf in *De Iure Gentium et Naturae* (1672) and by Johann Gottlieb Heineccius in *Elementa Iuris Naturae et Gentium* (1737). A translation of Pufendorf's abbreviation of his system of natural law, *De Officio Hominis et Civis* (1673), together with copious 'supplements and observations', was published by Glasgow's first professor of moral philosophy, Gershom Carmichael, in 1718, with a second edition six years later. George Turnbull, until 1727 regent at Marischal College, Aberdeen, translated Heineccius 'with supplements and a discourse' in 1741. These systems divided the duties of human beings into three kinds: duties to God, duties to others and duties to self. Duties to others were in turn divided into two classes: perfect duties and imperfect duties. Carmichael explains:

> There are some duties which are so absolutely necessary to social life that human society itself would be unsociable in their absence, and therefore they are rightly enforced even on those who do not want to do them. But there are other duties, which pertain to the comfort or ornament of social life, and are therefore left to the discretion and honor of each individual.[9]

The duties of beneficence and humanity are imperfect in this sense, while the duties of justice are perfect. Without beneficence and humanity, social life would be uncomfortable; without justice, it would be impossible.

The perfect duties of justice, according to Heineccius, 'may be reduced to *not injuring any one, and rendering to every one his due*'.[10] An explication of the particular perfect duties to others proceeded by means of an enumeration of the various kinds of harm that could be counted as *injuries*. An injury in this technical sense of the word was understood to be a violation of a *right*, and some writers in the natural law tradition – though not

Pufendorfians or Wolffians – explained duties in terms of rights, perfect and imperfect. Thus Hutcheson in his *Philosophiae Moralis Institutio Compendaria* (1745; translated into English as *A Short Introduction to Moral Philosophy* in 1747) asserts that 'the several duties of life may be naturally explained by explaining the several *rights* belonging to men, and the corresponding obligations, in all the several states and relations they stand in to each other'.[11] Hutcheson begins by distinguishing between natural rights and adventitious rights. Natural rights are then divided into three classes, '*private, publick,* and *common to all*'. Private rights are the rights of individuals, public rights are the rights of a particular society or body of people, and common rights are the rights of '*mankind* in general as a great community'.[12] The duties of justice as ordinarily understood protect private rights, and are divided into the perfect and imperfect. There are eight *perfect* private rights: (i) to life, and not to be injured in body; (ii) to preserve chastity; (iii) to reputation; (iv) to liberty, to being able to act according to one's own judgement; (v) over life, i.e., to be able to sacrifice oneself to public good; (vi) to private judgement; (vii) to what is common to all, to acquire adventitious rights, and to equal treatment; (viii) to marriage. It is a matter of *imperfect* right that 'each one may justly claim such offices as are profitable to him, and no burden or expense to the performer. Nay every innocent person has a right to such offices of others, as are of high advantage to him, and of small burden or expence to the performers.'[13] Then Hutcheson comes to adventitious rights, that is to say, to rights which are acquired, rather than which pertain to human beings as such. Adventitious rights are either 'real' or 'personal': 'The real terminate upon some certain definite goods: the personal terminate upon some person, not peculiarly respecting one part of his goods more than any other.'[14] The principal real adventitious right is to property, a right which has its ground in a combination of the right to self-preservation and the necessity of labour. We see, then, that on this account, the rights of property make up only one part of a complex and variegated analysis of the concept of justice.

It is very much in the spirit of Hutcheson's analysis of private rights that Reid, in the course of his critique of Hume's account of justice, notes that:

A man may be injured, *first*, in his person, by wounding, maiming or killing him; *secondly*, in his family, by robbing him of his children, or any way injuring those he is bound to protect; *thirdly*, in his liberty, by confinement; *fourthly*, in his reputation; *fifthly*, in his goods or property; and, *lastly*, in the violation of contracts or engagements made with him.[15]

The first four of the rights corresponding to these injuries are natural in the sense of being 'innate', 'founded on the constitution of man, and antecedent to all deeds and conventions of society'.[16] The last is acquired, 'not grounded upon the constitution of man, but upon his actions'.[17] But it is still *natural* in the sense that it may be acquired even in a state of nature, prior to and independent of positive legislation. Reid expresses puzzlement, as well he might, as to why, in the light of this well-established way of analysing the rights and duties of justice, Hume in his account of justice 'had in his eye only two particular branches of justice', pertaining to rights to property and the fidelity to contracts.[18] In the rest of this paper I offer an explanation of why Hume limited his analysis of justice in this way. But first it is worth noting that there is yet more that appears to be missing from Hume's treatment of justice. There is nothing, for example, about the notion of *desert* that is usually taken to underwrite the justice of punishment. And Reid points out that also absent is the *distributive* dimension to justice. Reid argues, as Locke had done in the second of the *Two Treatises of Government*, that the right to the acquisition of property of one individual can be restricted by the right to subsistence of another individual. He says that 'justice, I think, as well as charity, requires, that the necessities of those who, by the providence of God, are disabled from supplying themselves, should be supplied from what might otherwise be stored for future wants'.[19] The reason for Hume's omission of this aspect of justice is given in the second *Enquiry*, where Hume, in the manner of Hobbes, argues that where human life is threatened, the rules of justice no longer apply. On the usual view, by contrast, what happens in such circumstances is that one right trumps another, and Reid sharply criticises Hume for diverging from this view. Our question, however, is why in his account of justice Hume gives almost exclusive attention to rights of property.[20]

III

In Book 3 of the *Treatise*, though not in the second *Enquiry*, Hume's analysis of morals is organised around the distinction between 'artificial' and 'natural' virtues. What distinguishes these two groups of virtues from each other is the fact that in the case of the former group it is implausible, so Hume argues, to regard the practices in question as the result of innate principles of action. They are not expressions of human nature as it might manifest itself in a state of nature. We human beings are fitted with self-interest and a concern for those related to us, but neither of these principles of action prompts us to the virtues of justice, promise-keeping and allegiance. These virtues are 'artificial', then, in the sense of being the work of human invention. In order to solve problems set for them by a combination of human need, unfriendly circumstance and limited generosity, human beings developed conventions regarding possessions, reciprocal exchange and the subordination of most to the will of a chief, conventions that, as we will see, Hume regards as essential enabling conditions of social life as such. Now, it might be thought that Hume focuses on rights of property to the exclusion of other aspects of justice as usually defined because such rights are easier to portray as questionable in their naturalness than, for example, the rights not to be physically harmed and imprisoned. After all, as we have seen already, rights of property were generally accepted to be *adventitious*, and, in Reid's words, 'not grounded upon the constitution of man, but upon his actions'. So perhaps it was with a view to highlighting the artificiality of justice that Hume gives such importance to rights of property. I think this is implausible. There is no reason to think that showing the artificiality of justice was one of Hume's primary intentions. That is indeed where his argument leads him, but it is not, I think, what he started out to show. The main agenda of Book 3 of the *Treatise* is, rather, the demonstration that, once rationalism in ethics is dispensed with, we are not forced to accept Hutcheson's postulation of a special moral sense, but can explain the moral sentiments in a more parsimonious and (as we would say now) naturalistic manner, in terms of the operations of sympathy. The thesis of the artificiality of justice is simply part of the case for the sympathy theory, in the sense that it explains how and why justice is a virtue without recourse to some special instinct. Several of Hume's early critics focused on the artificiality thesis because it seemed to them to be evidence of Hume's 'licentious' intention to loosen the hold of morality upon his readers. But there is no reason whatsoever to think that Hume actually had such an intention.

Hume wrote the *Treatise* in geographical and intellectual isolation in provincial France. Could it be that it is out of pure ignorance or carelessness that he fails to consider justice in its full extent? This too is implausible, most obviously because Hume does in fact give an *argument* for his prioritisation of property. The argument is given in the course of the explication of the 'interested' obligation in *Treatise* 3.2.2, when Hume comes to explain the danger posed to the 'new-establish'd' social union by the fact that 'each person loves himself better than any other single person, and in his love to others bears the greatest affection to his relations and acquaintance' (T 487). This fact sets the passions of each of us against the passions of (almost) everyone else; and this in turn creates a serious problem for peaceful social life, when we consider the general scarcity of many of the things we desire for ourselves and our relations and friends. Hume writes:

> There are three different species of goods, which we are posses'd of; the internal satisfaction of our minds, the external advantages of our body, and the enjoyment of such possessions as we have acquir'd by our industry and good fortune. We are perfectly secure in the enjoyment of the first. The second may be ravish'd from us, but can be of no advantage to him who deprives us of them. The last only are both expos'd to violence of others, and may be transferr'd without suffering any loss or alteration; while at the same time, there is not a sufficient quantity of them to supply every one's desires and necessities. As the improvement, therefore, of these goods is the chief advantage of society, so the *instability* of their possession, along with their *scarcity*, is the chief impediment. (T 487–8)

Hume's claim, put crudely, is that that there is nothing to be gained from robbing people of their peace of mind or from physically abusing them. And so there is no need – at this early stage of social life, at least – to postulate prohibitions against such things, nor to postulate a 'natural' sense of rights that would be violated were people to be so harmed. There is surely an implicit response to Hobbes here. It is not true, Hume is saying, that in a 'state of nature' man is a wolf to man. We are not so naturally fearful of each other that without the safeguards provided by the state and its law-enforcement apparatus, we would pre-emptively strike against others to prevent them from striking against us. We are not naturally disposed, out of fear, to terrorise and maim and rape and kill. The reason for Hume's rather more optimistic conception of pre-political human nature is surely to be found in his sense of the way our passions are shaped from the beginning by life in the (extended) family. This is an aspect of Hume's theory of nature that has been vividly brought out by Annette Baier. As she says, Hume pictures us as social from our very first days, and creatures thus socialised will not generally be aggressive and bloodthirsty: 'What Hume's convenors of justice aim to eliminate is not a climate of violence against persons, but a climate of incommodious insecurity of possession of material goods.'[21]

It might be thought that there is plenty of empirical evidence to suggest that we are in fact rather more pointlessly violent than Hume is prepared to admit here. Don't we, after all, have whole bodies of law arising from cases of slander and libel (and now also 'hate speech'), and from cases of assault, rape and murder? And are these not obviously part of justice on any plausible understanding of it? Of course they are. But Hume's concern in 3.2.2, and indeed throughout Book 3 of the *Treatise*, is with justice considered as a condition of social life – specifically, as a condition of the possibility of the peaceful coexistence of families or tribes. As we have seen, natural ties of kinship and friendship bind small groups together. Problems arise that need to be solved by conventions when those groups have to interact with each other. And these problems have, in the first instance, to do with the instability and scarcity of possessions. Hume's concern here, that is to say, is *historical*. He is tracing the development of human society as such. And the importance of the fixing of conventions to do with property for the possibility of human society is what explains his focus on property to the exclusion of other aspects of justice as we ordinarily conceive of it – and as his precursors in the tradition of natural jurisprudence ordinarily conceived of it. The fact that we have no natural instinct for justice sets Hume off on a historical journey that takes him back to the origins of human sociability, and he never returns from that journey to engage in a full consideration of justice as it is understood in the kinds of societies that he and we actually live in. But, as Duncan Forbes pointed out in his book on Hume's politics, this does not mean that Hume's theory could not have been developed to encompass a larger set of rights: the point is that, given his conjectural-historical objectives in 3.2.2, 'there was no need for Hume to go any further at that juncture'.[22]

It is thus perfectly consonant with Hume's approach to justice in the *Treatise* that he should in other works appear to be working with a much more commonsensical notion of what justice amounts to. Annette Baier has drawn attention to more ordinary Humean conceptions of justice in recent work on *The History of England*. Baier points, for example, to Hume's praise of various acts of 'justice' on the part of James I. James is referred to as having introduced 'justice' to Ireland, where that meant, in Baier's words, 'a fair return for one's labor, as well as fixed tenure of one's land'.[23] In another 'laudable act of justice' James insisted on the proper sentence (of death) for a nobleman convicted of murder. Baier remarks that '[o]nce wrongful death counts as an injustice . . . English history becomes a long string of injustices, since many who ended on the scaffold or the gibbet can be seen as wrongly convicted, and of course many died at the hands of ordinary murderers'.[24] James I was as guilty of injustice in this sense as any of his predecessors and successors. For reasons of geopolitical expediency, after all, James executed Sir Walter Raleigh. Hume comments:

No measure of James's reign was attended with more public dissatisfaction than the punishment of Sir Walter Raleigh. To execute a sentence, which had been originally so hard, which had been so long suspended, and which seemed to have been tacitly pardoned by conferring on him a new trust and commission, was deemed an instance of cruelty and injustice.[25]

And we move on in the last two volumes of the *History* through the unjust executions of the Earl of Strafford and Archbishop Laud to the execution of Charles I. As Baier notes, Hume refrains from condemning Charles's execution as unjust, but his long and careful discussion of the case of Charles Stuart is coloured by a scrupulous – excessively and wilfully scrupulous, Hume's Whig critics would say – consideration of the demands of justice. For present purposes, all that needs to be said about Hume's use of the language of justice in the *History* is that the society he is describing is at some unspecified (and unspecifiable) distance from the primal stages analysed in *Treatise* 3.2.2. In developed societies, Hume can allow as components of justice rights other than rights of property. They are absent from the *Treatise* discussion because, to repeat, Hume's concern there is exclusively with the necessary conditions of social life as such.

IV

This concern with the necessary conditions of social life is most explicit in *Treatise* 3.2.6, where, as has already been noted, Hume describes '*the stability of possession,* . . . *its transference by consent,* and . . . *the performance of promises*' as 'the three fundamental laws of nature'. ''Tis on the strict observance of those three laws', Hume continues, 'that the peace and security of human society entirely depend; nor is there any possibility of establishing a good correspondence among men, where these are neglected' (T 526). Here, it may be felt, Hume's affinities with modern natural law are most obvious. But in the same section there is a reminder of the fact that there is a fundamental difference between Hume and other modern natural lawyers, in the form of Hume's decision to formulate his treatment of justice in terms, not of rights, but of virtues. Rights appear in Hume's discussion of justice only in the context of one of this section's 'new arguments' to prove that justice is an artificial, not a natural, virtue. The argument is not easy to make sense of. It proceeds by way of a distinction between vices and virtues, on the one hand, and 'rights, and obligations, and property', on the other. Hume lays down two principles that he thinks no one will disagree with. The first is that virtue and vice come in degrees. '[A]ll kinds of vice and virtue', according to Hume, 'run insensibly into each other, and may approach by such imperceptible degrees as will make it very difficult, if not absolutely impossible, to determine when the one ends, and the other begins' (T 529). The second principle is that rights, and obligations, and property, do not come in degrees. Either one has a right to something, or has an obligation to do something, or owns something, or one does not. 'A man that hires a horse, tho' but for a day', Hume observes, 'has as full a right to make use of it for that time, as he whom we call its proprietor has to make use of it any other day; and 'tis evident, that however the use may be bounded in time, the right itself is not susceptible of any such grada- tion, but is absolute and entire, so far as it extends' (T 529–30). These two principles force one to make a choice about justice and injustice, defined as what rights, and obligations, and property, 'depend upon'. These things 'depend upon' justice and injustice in the sense that, as Hume puts it, 'Where the justice is entire, the property is also entire: Where the justice is imperfect, the property must also be imperfect' (T 530). Either one must say that justice and injustice are virtues and vices like other virtues and vices, and come in degrees; and then one contradicts the second principle. Or one must say that justice and injustice do not come in degrees; and then one contradicts the first principle.

To contradict the first principle, and to assert that justice and injustice 'are not susceptible of degrees', is, Hume goes on to claim, the same as to assert that justice and injustice 'are not *naturally* either vicious or virtu- ous' – 'since vice and virtue, moral good and evil, and indeed all *natu- ral* qualities, run insensibly into each other, and are, on many occasions, undistinguishable' (T 530). The reader might well feel at this point that what Hume has uncovered is not so much the artificiality of the virtue of justice and of the vice of injustice as the difficulty of making sense of justice and injustice using the language of virtue and vice – while, at least, justice and injustice are defined in terms of rights, and obligations, and property. Hume has himself, in his genealogy of justice in 3.2.2, shown that there is a sense in which justice, in the form of rules regarding property, is perfectly natural. It is in no sense arbitrary that human beings frame and then enforce respect for such rules. Compelled as they are to live in society with each other, human beings must develop, and enforce, conventions which fix possession and turn it into property. These conventions are arti- ficial in the sense that they are the product of reflection and invention, but they are natural in the sense that they are entirely what was to be expected, given our nature and our circumstances. Why not then, one might ask, simply define justice as the following of rules regarding property and its transfer, and injustice as the violation of those rules? There need be nothing interesting to say about the state of mind, or trait of character, that prompts one to follow the rules. Morally speaking, in fact, it may not matter at all *why* one follows, or violates, the rules. It matters simply, when the interests of society as a whole are taken into account, that one does follow them. The virtue of justice, then, if you want to carry on using that language, could be said to consist in acting in accordance with certain rules. The vice of injustice could be said to consist in violating them. One might then wonder whether anything interesting is being said of someone when she is called 'just'. One might wonder whether, in fact, justice is not better predicated of the rules themselves, or of the institutions that define and enforce them, rather than of individual moral agents. But, however that may be, there is at least a sharp distinction here, and no possibility of justice turning 'insensibly' into injustice, or into anything else for that matter. Thus it would seem eminently possible to combine the principle that the constituent elements of justice are not susceptible of gradation with the principle that the difference between justice and injustice is the difference between moral good and evil, without needing to insist on the artificiality, in this case, of that difference. All that is necessary to this end is to give up on the idea that justice and justice are the names of particular traits of character. This would be in the spirit of Grotius's declaration, in the Prolegomena to *De iure belli ac pacis*, that 'The very Nature of Injustice consists in nothing else, but in the Violation of another's Rights; nor does it signify, whether it proceeds from Avarice, or Lust, or Anger, or imprudent Pity, or Ambition.'[26]

The question arises why Hume felt it necessary to examine the morality of justice and the immorality of injustice using a language, that of virtue and vice, which was inherently at odds with such fundamental elements of jurisprudence as right, obligation and property.[27] One explanation is suggested by a remark Hume makes before he moves on to his next argument for the artificiality of justice. He notes a contradiction between the way in which right, obligation and property are treated of technically, in philosophy and in law, and the way in which we conceive of them 'in our common and negligent way of thinking', when we find it hard to accept that they do not admit of degrees, 'and do even *secretly* embrace the contrary principle' (T 530). '[W]hen we consider the origin of property and obligation', he continues, 'and find that they depend on public utility, and sometimes on the propensities of the imagination, which are seldom entire on any side; we are naturally inclin'd to imagine, that these moral relations admit of an insensible inclination' (T 531). This is puzzling for more than one reason. It suggests that Hume's view is that 'our common and negligent way of thinking' about property and obligation includes both reflection upon their origins in public utility and also acknowledgement of the role of the imagination, described in *Treatise* 3.2.3, in specifying the rules which determine property. Hume usually writes as if these are aspects of justice revealed by the anatomy of the mind, rather than being conscious aspects of ordinary thought. The more fundamental point, however, seems to be that there is something about ordinary thought, or, to be more precise, ordinary feeling about property and obligation, that disposes us to assume that approval of respect for property and for contracts is approval of a trait of character that issues in such respect. And this is, of course, an instance of a principle that is central to Hume's analysis of the operation of the moral sentiments more generally. Hume takes it as a given that moral assessment is assessment of motives, taken as indications of character. We call actions morally good or morally evil just in so far as we take them to have been caused by good or evil motives. That, for Hume, is simply how the mind works. He reaffirms this feature of moral common sense in the further argument for the artificiality of justice to which he turns in the remainder of 3.2.6. 'No action can be either morally good or evil', he declares, 'unless there be some natural passion or motive to impel us to it, or deter us from it' (T 532). The problem with justice is that, as Hume sought to show in 3.2.1, there is no 'natural' passion or motive to impel us to it or deter us from it. That made it a puzzle why there is such a thing as justice at all, and it was to solve that puzzle that Hume, in 3.2.2, offered a conjectural history of conventions regarding property. If he had not been so sure that moral assessment is in the first instance assessment of motives, it would not have been necessary to offer a theory of the origins of justice.

It is arguable, therefore, that it is Hume's certainty that moral sentiments are excited solely by beliefs as to what an action tells us about the agent's character that sets him off on the way towards defining justice in terms of property and the rules which protect it. Hume was probably confirmed in his confidence about the centrality of motives to moral estimation early on in his intellectual development, by Hutcheson's analysis of the operation of the moral sense in *An Inquiry into the Original of Our Ideas of Beauty and Virtue*. Our ideas of moral goodness, Hutcheson claims, are ideas of the benevolence that prompts moral agents to pursue the happiness of others, regardless of the consequences for themselves. Even respect for 'perfect' rights, those which 'are of such necessity to the publick Good, that the universal Violation of them would make human Life intolerable', is, according to Hutcheson, approved of as a virtue in so far as it is taken to manifest a benevolent concern for the well-being of all.[28] Hume disagrees with this, on the grounds that he does not think that human beings are capable of such extensive benevolence. Benevolence cannot, therefore, be what we approve of, when we approve of respect for rights of this kind. What is it, then, that we approve of? It must be, Hume believes, some motive or other. There is room for disagreement when it comes to Hume's characterisation of the motive to justice, and to the explanation given by Hume as to how that motive comes to be morally approved of. It could be that Hume is proposing a kind of error theory, according to which moral goodness is projected onto what is in reality nothing more than self-interest. It could be that Hume has an explanation to give of how respect for rights of property as such, while not 'naturally' something the moral sense can approve of, becomes recognisable as a virtuous motive in the context of general adherence to the conventions regarding property.[29] Alternatively, it could be that the case of justice pushes Hume towards an implicit acknowledgement that, to the extent that common sense contains a commitment to the principle that moral assessment is always assessment of motives taken as signs of traits of character, common sense is misleading. Hume's engagement with modern natural law could have led him, without his being fully aware of it, to the Grotian conclusion that the morality of justice and injustice is different in kind from the morality of virtue and vice.[30] Certainly, as the argument described above makes clear, Hume was sensitive to the differences between the language of rights and the language of virtue. Here there might be a further example of the kind of clash in which Hume is so keenly interested elsewhere in his writings, between common sense, on the one hand, and accurate philosophising on the other.

The conjectural history of justice described in 3.2.2 foregrounds the utility of rules of property. It is self-interest on the part of every member of society that prompts the development of such rules, and what is in the interest of every individual is, necessarily, in the interest of society taken as a whole. There is no need to suppose that justice developed as a result of concern for the interest of society as a whole. The general utility of the system of rules concerning property can be seen, rather, as an unintended consequence of the universal pursuit of private interest.[31] The utility of justice, irrespective of whether or not it is intended by those who develop and follow the rules by which justice is constituted, can then be shown to be the key to answering the question of how it is that we come to regard justice as a virtue in the first place. That is the question which Part 2 of Book 3 of the *Treatise* begins with, the possibility having been raised in Part 1 that not all impressions of moral goodness and evil arise naturally in the mind as a product of an innate sensitivity to the difference between virtue and vice. When the public utility of justice is taken together with the incontestable fact of a sympathetic awareness on the part of human beings to the pains and pleasures of others, we have, Hume argues, the beginning of an explanation of how it is that distinctively moral sentiments are excited by respect for and violation of the conventions of justice. The importance of the possibility of such an explanation, for Hume's purposes, is that it makes it unnecessary to appeal, in the manner of Hutcheson, to a special sense in an account of the morality of justice. And then the stage is set for the general claim, made in Part 3 of Book 3, that the faculty of sympathy can be used to explain *all* moral approbation and disapprobation. Establishing this, I think, is the major ambition of the moral philosophy of A *Treatise of Human Nature*. The goal, as I suggested above, was to reformat Hutcheson's moral sense theory so that it was compatible with Hume's distinctive understanding of the goals and method of a science of man worthy of the name.[32]

V

By the time he rewrote his moral philosophy in An *Enquiry concerning the Principles of Morals*, it had come to seem to Hume that putting Hutchesonian moral philosophy on a properly scientific footing did not require the kind of elaborate conjectural history that is such a prominent feature of *Treatise* 3.2.[33] Concomitantly, it no longer mattered that the virtues be divided into the 'natural' and 'artificial'. The agenda remains that of undermining the case for a special moral sense, but the means to that end are different. Hume describes his project in Section III, on justice, as that of showing '[t]hat public utility is the *sole* origin of justice, and that reflection on the beneficial consequences of this virtue are the *sole* foundation of its merit' (E 183). And he moves towards a conclusion of that project as follows:

> As justice evidently tends to promote public utility and to support civil society, the sentiment of justice is either derived from our reflecting on that tendency, or like hunger, thirst, and other appetites, resentment, love of life, attachment to offspring, and other passions, arises from a simple original instinct in the human breast, which nature has implanted for like salutary purposes. If the latter be the case, it follows, that property, which is the object of justice, is also distinguished by a simple original instinct, and is not ascertained by any argument or reflection. But who is there that ever heard of such an instinct? Or is this a subject in which new discoveries can be made? We may as well expect to discover, in the body, new senses, which had before escaped the observation of all mankind. (E 201)

The supposed need of a 'simple original instinct' is now obviated by the possibility of explaining the moral merit of justice more simply, in terms of reflection upon its obvious utility. Note, though, that justice is still defined as it was in the *Treatise*, in terms of rules of property. This, I believe, is a by-product of Hume's continuing tendency to think of the 'origins' of justice in historical terms. When he says that 'public utility is the *sole* origin of justice', he must surely be talking about a *historical* origin, the origin of justice in the development of human society, not the origin of the concept of justice in the experience and sentiments of each and every human individual. And there is no sign given in the second *Enquiry* that when Hume now considers the history of human society, he has changed his mind as to the plausibility of taking conventions regarding property to have come before the other elements of justice.

It is sometimes said that Hume toned down the radicalism of his moral philosophy for more general public consumption in the second *Enquiry*, and that is why, for example, there is no insistence on the artificiality of certain of the virtues.[34] This is unconvincing for a number of reasons, one of which is the fact that Hume in the second *Enquiry* draws attention to a consequence of his understanding of justice that he did not mention in the *Treatise* and that he must have known would be shocking to his contemporaries. It is unsettling even now. In the course of a series of counterfactual considerations designed to make the case for his account of the origins of justice, Hume argues that there are obligations of justice only between those who are sufficiently equal in strength to be able make each other 'feel the effects of their resentment' (E 190). Where one party is 'incapable of all resistance' in the face of the superior strength of another, the former are reliant for gentle treatment solely on the checks provided by compassion and kindness. Hume's point here is that it makes no sense to imagine the strong making conventions and compacts regarding property with the weak. The strong have no need to do so. They are not threatened by the weak, and can take whatever they want, when they want. Conventions of justice will not naturally develop between two such unequal parties because there is no need for them. 'This is plainly the situation of men, with regard to animals', Hume says; it has been thought to be the situation of 'civilized Europeans' with regard to 'barbarous Indians'; and '[i]n many nations' it is the situation of women with regard to men (E 191). Nothing could make it plainer that Hume rejects absolutely the idea of what we now call 'human rights', rights to equal and fair treatment possessed by human beings as such. Obviously, he rejects natural 'animal rights' as well. It is conceivable, from the Humean point of view, that rights might come to be accorded to animals, Indians and women through positive legislation. What Hume will have no truck with is the notion that such rights can be thought of as *natural* as opposed to conventional. And even where the right kinds of convention do exist, they will be rather late historical developments. Reid comments that 'If Mr. Hume had not owned this sentiment as a consequence of his Theory of Morals, I should have thought it very uncharitable to impute it to him.'[35] There can be no better evidence of the falsity of a moral theory, Reid says, than the fact that it subverts the rules of practical morality. Hume would deny that he *subverts* practical morality, since he is quick to stress the work that benevolence does in the protection of the weak. But it is surely true that he is here working with a conception of justice that is *at odds with* ordinary moral conceptions.

The reason why Hume denies that ('civilized') men are under duties of justice with respect to animals, non-Europeans and women is that he continues to think of justice in terms dictated by the focus of modern natural law on the primary and enabling conventions of human social life. In fact, his hostility to the idea of a natural, innate or instinctual regard for justice pushes him close to embracing the Hobbesian position that there can be no injustice where there has been no prior covenant. It is therefore not surprising that Hume's first critics accused him of Hobbism. An anonymous French reviewer called Book 3 of the *Treatise* 'le Système de Hobbes habillé dans un goût nouveau'.[36] The compiler of the charges against Hume that helped to bar him from the Edinburgh chair in moral philosophy accused Hume of going even further than Hobbes had: after all, 'Mr. *Hobbs*, who was at Pains to shake loose all other natural Obligations, yet found it necessary to leave, or pretended to leave, the Obligation of Promises or Pactions; but our Author strikes a bolder Stroke. . .'.[37] As regards the argument from the second *Enquiry* just described, Reid suggests that Hume is merely repeating Hobbes's doctrine 'that right has its origin from power', and remarks that here, despite his official disavowal of the selfish hypothesis, Hume 'founds justice solely upon utility to *ourselves*': 'Mr Hobbes could have said no more.'[38] In Appendix 3 of the second *Enquiry* Hume tries to distance himself from Hobbes by explicitly rejecting the view of those who, like Hobbes, had portrayed justice as arising from a promise – while at the same reaffirming the *Treatise* view that it arises from unspoken conventions adopted by self-interested individuals (cf. E 306). Hume is being very careful here. He would have known that most of Hobbes's critics had fixed in particular on the claim that the duties of justice might be resolved into the terms of explicit promises. Pufendorf, for example, had claimed that the opinion that justice is 'nothing else but a keeping of Faith, and fulfilling of Contracts' was something that Hobbes 'borrow'd from Epicurus'.[39] 'Indeed,' Pufendorf had continued, 'so far is it from being rational to resolve all of Justice into Performance of Cov-enants, that, on the contrary, before we can know whether any Covenant is to be perform'd, we ought to be certain that it was entred upon, either by the Command, or with the Permission of the Laws of Nature; that is, that it was *justly* made.'[40] Hume is attempting to navigate a way between Hobbes and Pufendorf: neither covenants nor divine commands are the basis of justice as he understands it.

In a footnote to Appendix 3 of the second *Enquiry*, Hume claims that 'This theory concerning the origin of property, and consequently of justice, is, in the main, the same with that hinted at and adopted by Grotius's' (E 307 fn). He then quotes (in Latin) the following passage from *The Rights of War and Peace*:

4. From hence we learn, upon what Account Men departed from the antient Community; first of *moveable*, and then of *immoveable* Things: Namely, because Men being no longer contented with what the Earth produced of itself for their Nourishment; being no longer willing to dwell in Caves, to go naked, or covered only with the Barks of Trees, or the Skins of Wild Beasts, wanted to live in a more commodious and more agreeable Manner; to which End Labour and Industry was nec-essary, which some employed for one Thing, and others for another. And there was no Possibility then of using Things in common; first, by Reason of the Distance of Places where each was settled; and after-wards because of the Defect of Equity and Love, whereby a just Equal-ity would not have been observed, either in their Labour, or in the Consumption of their Fruits and Resources.

5. Thus also we see what was the Original of Property, which was derived not from a mere internal Act of the Mind, since one could not possibly guess what others designed to appropriate to themselves, that he might abstain from it; and besides, several might have had a Mind to the same Thing, at the same Time; but it resulted from a certain Com-pact and Agreement, either expressly, as by a Division; or else tacitly, as by a Seizure.[41]

In his notes to Grotius's text, Jean Barbeyrac claims that by 'a certain Com-pact and Agreement' Grotius meant a *contract*, and that is probably right. However, for Hume, I think, the really important aspect of this passage was Grotius's attack on the idea that property might have its origin in 'a mere internal Act of Mind'. That is, it is the negative dimension of the argu-ment that struck a chord with Hume, along with the way Grotius looks to the material circumstances of early humanity, rather than to a God-given moral sense, for the origins of property, and, as Hume says, 'consequently of justice'. This was the decisive move made by Grotius – as far as both Hobbes and Hume were concerned. It followed that a historical story had to be told of how humankind moved from a primal pre-political state of nature to a state in which compacts and agreements were possible. Hume's way of telling that story, even though purely conjectural, is intended to be more historically (and philosophically) plausible than Hobbes's. Civil society does not come into existence all at once, with the universal surrender of rights to a sovereign power. The process is a gradual one, and its first stage is the establishment of conventions regarding property.

VI

My suggestion is that there is a connection to be drawn between Hume's definition of justice in terms of rights of property and his critique of the idea of special moral sense. Having rejected a Hutchesonian moral sense as the faculty of moral judgement, Hume finds himself faced with a puzzle as to the origins of justice, and he solves that puzzle with a conjectural history of human sociability which gives pride of place to property among the conditions of the possibility of social life for human beings. Hume defines justice as he does because of the historical character of his analysis. There was no need for him to go any further: no need, that is, to explore the history of the other rights that were generally brought under the heading of justice by his contemporaries. Once the origins of justice, in the form of respect for property rights, had been uncovered, sympathy could be put to work to explain the moral dimension of respect for property. And once that had been done, Hume thought he had completed the task he had set himself. At this point, a comparison with Adam Smith's treatment of justice in *The Theory of Moral Sentiments* is fruitful. Smith follows Hume in rejecting Hutcheson's notion of a special moral sense, and he follows Hume also in believing that the faculty of sympathy provides a better, more parsimonious, account of the origin of the moral sentiments. But, even though Smith was keenly interested in the historical origins of property rights, he does not follow Hume down the path of conjectural history in *The Theory of Moral Sentiments*. And justice as it is analysed in that book is – I suggest, *as a result* – considerably broader in scope than justice as it is treated of in the *Treatise* and second *Enquiry*. Smith gives detailed attention to the justice of punishment and its basis in sympathy with proper resentment. Smith is explicit about justice being a *negative* virtue: he says that 'We may often fulfil all the rules of justice by sitting still and doing nothing.'[42] But he has a more complete description to give than does Hume of the injuries that the unjust may do:

> The most sacred laws of justice, . . . those whose violation seems to call loudest for vengeance and punishment, are the laws which guard the life and person of our neighbour; the next are those which guard his property and possessions; and last of all come those which guard what are called his personal rights, or what is due to him from the promises of others.[43]

As we have seen, there is nothing in the *Treatise* and second *Enquiry* about the laws which guard the life and person of our neighbour. Hume's historical orientation distracts him from a proper examination of this very considerable aspect of justice as it is ordinarily understood.

Smith sees more clearly than does Hume the difference between two questions regarding the origins of justice. One of these questions concerns the historical origins of justice, and the other concerns how it is that human individuals at later times come to think in terms of the just and the unjust. Both are questions for one who rejects a special moral sense able to provide us with ideas of justice. But they are different questions nonetheless. For it is highly implausible to imagine that the conjectural history of property that Hume gives in *Treatise* 3.2.2 describes a process that each of us must go through in order to be able to have a concept of justice. We are given our ideas of justice by sympathy with the consequences of the conventions of justice – or, more precisely, by sympathy with those harmed as a result of the violation of those conventions. But if sympathy attuned to already existing conventions is the origin of our ideas of justice, and if we as individuals do not beforehand have to go through the process of establishing conventions with other individuals, then it is not clear why the idea of justice that is the object of moral philosophy is restricted in the way that Hume's idea of justice is restricted. Moral philosophy concerns itself, or should concern itself, with morality as we understand it now, rather than with morality's historical origins. In *The Theory of Moral Sentiments* Smith addresses the question of how it is that each of us, in highly developed civil society, thinks in terms of the just and the unjust. Smith saves the other question, concerning the historical origins of justice, for a different kind of philosophical enquiry, pursued on the basis of a stadial model of the human development in his *Lectures on Jurisprudence*.[44] And for the most part, the philosophers of the Scottish Enlightenment followed Smith, and respected the difference between the history of justice and the analysis of the moral faculty. Some, like Reid, concentrated on the latter and ignored the former. Others, like John Millar, concentrated on the former and ignored the latter. Still others, like Lord Kames and Adam Ferguson, sought to do both – but not at the same time. Hume asked questions that the later Scottish writers found they needed to answer. In his own writings on justice, however, Hume tried to answer too many questions at once.

Notes

1. This essay can be thought of as a series of reflections prompted by the opening chapter of Knud Haakonssen's *The Science of a Legislator: The Natural Jurisprudence of David Hume and Adam Smith* (Cambridge: Cambridge University Press, 1981). Haakonssen's question 'What is the relation, in Hume's theory, between justice and historical evolution?' (37) is my question too. Prof. Haakonssen's comments on an earlier version of this essay much improved the final result, but I alone am responsible for all remaining errors and infelicities.

2. David Hume, *A Treatise of Human Nature*, ed. L. A. Selby-Bigge, rev. P. H. Nidditch (Oxford: Clarendon Press, 1978), 526. All subsequent citations from this edition will be given in the text abbreviated as 'T'.

3. David Hume, *Enquiries concerning Human Understanding and the Principles of Morals*, ed. L. A. Selby-Bigge, rev. P. H. Nidditch (Oxford: Clarendon Press, 1975), 195. All subsequent citations from this edition will be given in the text abbreviated as 'E'.

4. David Hume, *Essays Moral, Political and Literary*, ed. Eugene F. Miller (Indianapolis: Liberty Fund, 1987), 480.

5. Henry Home, Lord Kames, *Principles of Equity*, second edition (Edinburgh, 1767), 44.

6. See J. L. Mackie, *Hume's Moral Theory* (London: Routledge and Kegan Paul, 1980), 94; Jonathan Harrison, *Hume's Theory of Justice* (Oxford: Clarendon Press, 1981), 28ff.; Haakonssen, *The Science of a Legislator*, 13; and David Raphael, *Concepts of Justice* (Oxford: Clarendon Press, 2001), ch. 9. See also James Moore, 'Hume's Theory of Justice and Property', *Political Studies*, 24 (1976), 103–19, 119: 'the experience of the two centuries of social life that have passed since Hume wrote requires us to recognize that social justice involves more than security for owners of property'.

7. Examples include David Miller, *Philosophy and Ideology in Hume's Political Thought* (Oxford: Clarendon Press, 1981); Stephen Buckle, *Natural Law and the Theory of Property: Grotius to Hume* (Oxford: Clarendon Press, 1991); Russell Hardin, *David Hume: Moral and Political Theorist* (Oxford: Oxford University Press, 2007); Rachel Cohon, *Hume's Morality: Feeling and Fabrication* (Oxford: Oxford University Press, 2008).

8. See Jean Barbeyrac's *An Historical and Critical Account of the Science of Morality, and the Progress it has made in the World, from the earliest Times down to the Publication of this Work*, trans. Carew, 'prefixed' to Samuel Pufendorf, *Of the Law of Nature and Nations*, trans. Basil Kennett, 4th edition (London, 1729), 79ff.

9. James Moore and Michael Silverthorne, eds, *Natural Rights on the Threshold of the Scottish Enlightenment: The Writings of Gershom Carmichael* (Indianapolis: Liberty Fund, 2002), 44.

10. Johann Gottlieb Heineccius, *A Methodical System of Universal Law, with Supplements and a Discourse by George Turnbull*, ed. Thomas Ahnert and Peter Schröder (Indianapolis: Liberty Fund, 2008), 132.

11. Francis Hutcheson, *Philosophiae Moralis Institutio Compendaria, with A Short Introduction to Moral Philosophy*, ed. Luigi Turco (Indianapolis: Liberty Fund, 2007), 127.

12. Ibid., 128.

13. Ibid., 131.

14. Ibid., 133.

15. Thomas Reid, *Essays on the Active Powers of Man*, ed. Knud Haakonssen and James A. Harris (Edinburgh: Edinburgh University Press, 2010), 312.

16. Ibid., 313.

17. Ibid., 315.

18. Ibid., 314.

19. Ibid., 319.

20. Buckle claims that 'Hume's account of justice is . . . thoroughly in tune with the natural jurists' (*Natural Law and the Theory of Property*, 287). This is untrue. What is true is that there are important affinities between Hume's account of *property* and the natural jurists – though there are important differences as well. I briefly consider the relation between Hume and Grotius as regards property below (section V).

21. Annette Baier, *A Progress of Sentiments* (Cambridge, MA: Harvard University Press, 1991), 223.

22. Duncan Forbes, *Hume's Philosophical Politics* (Cambridge: Cambridge University Press, 1975), 89.

23. Annette Baier, 'Hume's Enlargement of his Concept of Justice', in *The Cautious Jealous Virtue: Hume on Justice* (Cambridge, MA: Harvard University Press, 2010), 86.

24. Ibid., 87.

25. Hume, *The History of England*, ed. Eugene F. Miller, revised edition (Indianapolis: Liberty Fund, 1983), Vol. 5, 79.

26. Hugo Grotius, *The Rights of War and Peace*, trans. John Morrice, ed. Richard Tuck (Indianapolis: Liberty Fund, 2005), 88–9.

27. Haakonssen offers an explanation of Hume's rejection of the language of rights in 'The Structure of Hume's Political Theory', in David Fate Norton and Jacqueline Taylor, eds, *The Cambridge Companion to Hume*, second edition (Cambridge: Cambridge University Press, 2009), 341–80, esp. 360–62.

28. Francis Hutcheson, *An Inquiry into the Original of Our Ideas of Beauty and Virtue*, ed. Wolfgang Leidhold, revised edition (Indianapolis: Liberty Fund, 2008), 183 [2.7.6].

29. For a selection of important contributions to the debate about Hume's conception of the moral motive to justice, see Knud Haakonssen and Richard Whatmore, eds, *David Hume*, International Library of Essays in the History of Social and Political Thought (Farnham: Ashgate, 2013).

30. This possibility is explored in James A. Harris, 'Hume and the Moral Obligation to Justice', *Hume Studies*, 36 (2010), 25–50.

31. This aspect of Hume's theory of justice is given particular attention in chapter 1 of Haakonssen, *The Science of a Legislator*. See esp. 12–21. 'To see justice in this way, as an unintended consequence of individual human actions,' Haakonssen comments, 'must be one of the boldest moves in the history of the philosophy of law' (20).

32. For the case for such an interpretation of Book 3 of the *Treatise*, see James A. Harris, *Hume: An Intellectual Biography* (Cambridge: Cambridge University Press, 2015), 121–39.

33. A full account of Hume's treatment of justice in the second *Enquiry* is given in James A. Harris, 'Justice in *An Enquiry concerning the Principles of Morals*', in Jacqueline Taylor, ed., *Reading Hume on the Principles of Morals* (Oxford: Oxford University Press, forthcoming).

34. This way of reading the second *Enquiry* is rejected in Harris, *Hume: An Intellectual Biography*, 250–65.

35. Reid, *Essays on the Active Powers*, 322.

36. *Bibliothèque Raisonnée des Ouvrages des Savans de l'Europe*, 26 (1741), 427.

37. 'A Letter from a Gentleman to his Friend in Edinburgh', in David Hume, *A Treatise of Human Nature*, ed. David Fate Norton and Mary Norton (Oxford: Clarendon Press, 2007), 424.

38. Reid, *Essays on the Active Powers*, 322.

39. Pufendorf, *Of the Law of Nature and Nations*, I.vii.13, 84.

40. Ibid., I.vii.13, 85.

41. Grotius, *The Rights of War and Peace*, II.ii.4–5, 306–7.

42. Adam Smith, *The Theory of Moral Sentiments*, ed. D. D. Raphael and A. L. Macfie (Indianapolis: Liberty Fund, 1982), II.ii.1.10, 82.

43. Ibid., II.ii.2.2, 84.

44. There is, of course, much more to say than this about the connection between *The Theory of Moral Sentiments* and *Lectures on Jurisprudence*. See Haakonssen, *Science of a Legislator*, *passim*, but especially 99–104.

Part III

Rights and Reform

10

Economising Natural Law: Pufendorf on Moral Quantities and Sumptuary Legislation

Michael Seidler

Introduction: Natural Law and Economics

The influence of the Protestant natural law tradition on economic thinking has been noted by historians for some time. Thus, Jeffrey Young observes that '[t]he value and price theory these [natural law] authors developed is embedded in chapters concerned with oaths, obligations, promises, and contracts. As such, economic analysis is couched in a legal/moral discourse.'[1] In contrast to more recent (especially, twentieth-century) views, natural lawyers regarded '[t]he market ... not as an impersonal mechanism, but as a social phenomenon embedded in a structure of property rights and legal restrictions. To the extent that these serve the common good, they have the sanction of natural law behind them.'[2]

A similar tie between natural law and economics has been noted by social choice theorists, albeit in reverse. That is, instead of seeing natural law as the formative matrix of economic thinking, they consider it to be deeply influenced thereby already. Thus, Wulf Gaertner says of Pufendorf that he reasons 'in economic categories', and that his 'emphasis is on the community based on social action and human interaction'. In Pufendorf, conduct is 'open to rational interpretation' in the sense that '[h]umans have learned to weigh and compare, and consideration is taken of the means best suited to the end'. More specifically, Gaertner justifies the moniker 'Pufendorf, [t]he economist' by pointing out the latter's interest in probable and doubtful conscience, his general cautionary approach, his awareness of externalities and the future discounting of gains and losses (including the asymmetry between these), his attention to different kinds of in/equality in society, and his acknowledgement of the various contingencies (e.g., scarcity) and arbitrary valuations (e.g., snobbery) that influence people's assessments of both persons and things, and thus structure their social lives.[3]

Daniel Brühlmeier, too, has referred to Pufendorf's 'astonishingly proto-classical economic understanding of human life and human institutions', suggesting that he 'clearly subscribes to rule-utilitarianism'.[4] Moreover, Brühlmeier claims, Jean Barbeyrac shared this understanding of society and 'clearly emphasized the economic dimension of Pufendorf's treatise [De officio]'[5] – indeed, embodying it in the very language of his French translation. For Barbeyrac speaks there about the 'commerce de services qui fait le lien & et l'agrément de la Société'. This may seem, at first, an interpretive interpolation, in that *commerce de services* renders Pufendorf's *mutua officia*.[6] Yet a closer examination of Pufendorf's text supports such a reading – at least if one understands economics (like natural law) broadly enough as an empirical account of the pragmatic social transactions whereby humans negotiate the value of persons and things, rather than as the more abstract, formalised and narrowly focused construct it has become over the past two centuries.[7]

Rousseau, who was deeply influenced by natural law – Pufendorf's in particular – understood some of this,[8] and his third *Discourse* (1755) identifies yet another, more direct way in which that discipline involves economics. He distinguished there between two kinds of political economy, one public and the other private: the former is the business of the state (specifically, 'government' in the sense of legislative authority), while the latter involves the management of households and families (§§7–8, 5–6).[9] The public or general economy concerns not only 'the government of persons' but also 'the administration of goods', because (in the state) it is necessary not only to protect citizens but also to sustain them (§41, 23). In fact, these two civic functions are interconnected, and not merely parallel, as appears from the following: the administration of goods attends not only to 'the right of property . . . the most sacred of all the rights of citizens', but also to the necessary costs and expenditures of government (§42, 23); it affects the relative equality of fortunes among the citizens – including that 'middle range' where politics is genuinely participatory, the force of the laws fully effective (§s 34–5, 19), and the condition of natural equality or freedom maximally restored (§19, 10); and, finally, it impacts the very ability of the government to govern at a fundamental, psychological level. For, 'if government limits itself to [mere] obedience it will be difficult to get itself obeyed', Rousseau observes; also, '[w]hile it is good to know how to use men as they are, it is much better still to make them what one needs them to be'. That is, 'form men if you want to command [them]'. This is the idea – also found in Pufendorf (DJN VII.1.4) – that good citizens are not born but made, that sociality is an obligation and an achievement (not a presupposition), and that humans must be disciplined and trained in order to live successfully together. Such social formation is achieved,

Rousseau suggests, by public education, by civil religion, by rulers' modeling of virtuous behaviour, and by sumptuary laws.[10]

This conclusion sounds fairly conservative and intrusive in the context of Rousseau's moralising critique of eighteenth-century society, yet it was anything but that in Pufendorf's radical 'de-ethicising' of natural law thinking a hundred years earlier.[11] For the latter's understanding of natural law as a broadly conceived socialising tool, and its articulation in so-called economic terms, was more empirical, conditioned, pragmatic and self-limited than Rousseau's (and, in his own way, Kant's) rationalistic pronouncements. Indeed, Pufendorf's minimalist juridical approach to the establishment of social boundaries may be seen as paradoxically more liberal or emancipatory, and intellectually more transparent, than the alternative strategies focusing on non-negotiable (individual or group) rights – including claims to property and legally unconstrained consumption – that gradually emerged during the eighteenth century. Herein lies, I think, the novelty and the strength of Pufendorf's voluntarist (and 'positivist') natural law position, its so-called 'Protestant' modernity, as well as the value of Knud Haakonssen's distinctive take on that wider tradition.[12]

Natural Law Positivism

Given Pufendorf's later apologies for his *Elements of Universal Jurisprudence* (EJU, 1660) as an immature work (DJN, 1672, Preface), it is easily neglected by those who consult DJN and DO as the main guides to his philosophical views. Yet EJU is often refreshingly direct and concise – perhaps precisely because of its youthful indiscretion – and thus useful for highlighting Pufendorf's bolder claims. Thus, in characterising moral (vs. natural, or nonimputable) actions and their objects (i.e., 'all that with which those [actions] deal'), Pufendorf propounds a radical voluntarism which asserts that morality is derivative rather than intrinsic; that it

> depends on *imposition*, i.e. on the determination of free agents as such, who have thereby, either from sheer choice [*mero arbitrio*] or some congruence of a thing's nature with imposed morality, and also from a tacit or express agreement mutually entered into, imposed morality on things and persons, and made it so that certain effects would follow from it. (EJU I.D2.1: GW 3, 9; DJN I.2.5)[13]

That is, moral distinctions and their normative 'effects' are not found in the world but fashioned for it; they are willed constructs issuing from various kinds of agreements among those actually sharing (more or less, and in different ways) certain purposes, interests or concerns. The objects thus moralised are divided by Pufendorf (following Roman law) into two general kinds: suppositive and positive, with the former referring to 'status' and the latter to 'persons and things'.[14]

Lest the radicality of this position be questioned because of morality's so-called 'congruence' with nature, note that the congruence does not replace imposition but merely (sometimes) guides it. Thus, even when morality is said to be 'in' (*inesse*) certain actions or things, this means not that it

> results from the physical principles of the thing or from the very nature of the action in itself; but that it does not derive its origin from the arbitrary imposition of men, but rather [*verum*] from the disposition of God himself, who has so formed the nature of man that certain actions necessarily are or are not congruent with it. (EJU I.D2.1: GW 3, 9)

The insertion of a divine (vs. human) disposer into the scheme does not strengthen the challenge but *seems*, merely, to tame Pufendorf's voluntarism, whose emphasis is on the consistency of actions with the *de facto* givenness of (human) nature, such as it is. The latter is not intrinsically moralised by being essentially, teleologically or theologically front-loaded, as it were, but only empirically consulted and descriptively articulated through the unsanitised reports of human history and first-hand experience. Thus, the distinction between divine and human imposition (both of them arbitrary [*mero arbitrio*]) does not demarcate a gulf between objective and subjective morality, but merely distinguishes less and more debatable claims *within* Pufendorf's moral 'positivism'. The latter remains basically a *human* exercise. After all, God's creative purpose 'has not yet been designated with sufficient clearness' (DJN II.3.12: GW 4.1, 143; also, II.3.5), and humans must therefore derive or presume the demands of morality on their own, by means of concrete, *in situ* reasoning about the actual condition of nature and the specific requirements of human affairs (EJU Obs. II.4.1 and 4.3; DJN IV.1.1). Even with the addition of broadly providential considerations from natural theology – which do not fit well with Pufendorf's anti-metaphysical approach – God (whether as hypothesis or object of belief) functions more like a theoretical picture preference than an explanation: He is always present but does little work.

This basic outlook remained in place more than a decade later – after the methodological transition (see the section 'Conclusion: Doing the Math' below) of the *Dissertationes* and *Monzambano* – in the corresponding DJN chapters on so-called 'moral entities' (DJN I.1–9). These are famously presented there as 'certain [*quidam*] modes superadded to physical things or motions by intelligent beings, mainly to direct and temper the freedom of voluntary human actions, and to bring a certain [*aliquem*] order and decorum into human life' (DJN I.1.3: GW 4.1, 14). As in EJU, some moral entities 'flow naturally, as it were [*velut*], from things themselves', while others are added thereto by the power of (human) intelligence. In the latter case (both, actually), intelligent beings – relying on a reflective understanding and comparison of things – devise (*formare*) notions suited for directing human faculties in a consistent (*homogeneam*, i.e. non-self-destructive) way. In the former, especially, where entities flow from the nature of things themselves, one 'could refer' (*dixeris*) again to God as their 'first author', because 'surely' (*utique*) He did not wish humans to live like beasts, without culture (*cultu*) and custom (*more*), but wanted rather that they achieve a certain 'perfection' – understood as the realisation of a distinctively human (non-brutish) life that both befits (*decori*) and benefits (*commodum, proficuum*) them (DJN I.1.3–4).

Once more, the supposed anchor in the nature of things and the presumptive reference to 'God' merely reveal the human factor at work, as it tries to distinguish more or less (not absolutely) 'necessary' moral entities,[15] and to superimpose on the so-called natural order (i.e., the world as is) a normative grid that suits human life. This is the point of moral imposition, after all, which, though free or arbitrary in both its divine and human instances, should not be random or wanton but foster social life and improve human affairs (DJN I.1.15; I.2.5). The presumed compatibility between God's creative (of human nature) and legislative (for human actions) roles – both of them filtered through actual human experience and cognition – is merely a way of articulating the hypothetical or conditioned nature of morality, its inescapable dependence on the world actually encountered (DJN I.2.6); and the lingering voluntaristic premise, in both the divine and human case, signifies – at least, and perhaps no more than – the radical contingency of that world, which humans are left to figure out on their own.

The Moral Grid

Humans collectively establish (*instituti*) moral entities to order their life, an end requiring certain kinds of mutual regard (*habeant*), control (*regant*) of actions, and conduct (*gerant*) towards things useful in human life, whether natural or artificial (DJN I.1.5). As action-guides regulating social demeanour and relations, moral entities might thus be distinguished according to their inherence in humans themselves, in their actions, and (by extension) in the things with which they deal. However – for ease of exposition and out of (itself a) social concern (i.e., comprehension by others) – Pufendorf explicitly adopts the more practised and familiar (albeit superficially more static, and thus misleading) descriptive terminology of the physical sciences, and divides moral entities into four main categories: states, persons, qualities and quantities.[16] Though the first three have received more attention, this essay focuses mainly on the last; for it is where the real work of moral assessment takes place, and the 'economic' aspect of natural law is most apparent.

Status is analogous to (Einsteinian, not Newtonian) space: it designates a moral geography of *when* and *where* that exists only in relation to things operative within it (DJN I.1.6). Comprising several natural and many artificial varieties (all 'arbitrarily' imposed, though some more necessarily or more freely than others), which overlap and thus agree or disagree to various degrees (DJN I.1.11), 'states' both describe and normatively condition the agents within them.[17] And they are affected by these in turn, as when (some or all) humans previously at peace turn hostile, or a deterioration of human affairs due to sociality failure produces other versions of the so-called natural state (i.e., barbarism and/or bestiality).[18] All states involve 'a kind of respect and bearing [*habitudo*] . . . toward others' entailing rights or obligations (DJN I.1.8),[19] and the general concept highlights the situational, relational and thus shifting character of human action, or its layered concreteness. Ideally, states and obligations would/should not conflict (DJN I.1.11); in reality, of course, they do.[20]

There are many more kinds of moral *personae*, i.e. moral entities introduced to assign, differentiate and impute moral agency: simple (individual) and composite (collective), private and public, civil and ecclesiastical – all of them with peculiar, distinct, overlapping and thus potentially conflicting identities, roles, rights and responsibilities, depending on their place, function and importance in social life. The constitutive feature of persons at all levels – especially collective personae – is their degree of unity: whether they comprise 'one system [*systema*]' (DJN I.1.12) and have an effective decision procedure allowing them to act *as* one.[21] Despite the flexibility of the notion, its imposition on diverse pluralities is – like that of other moral entitities – not 'so free' (*ita libera*) as to be random or frivolous, but should rather be guided by a basic concern to produce 'a beneficial [*solidus*] effect in human life' – the sort of thing missing, so Pufendorf claims, in the supposed consular designation of Caligula's horse, the postmortem deification of Roman emperors and, of course, papist canonisation practices (DJN I.1.15: GW 4.1, 21).[22]

Moral qualities and quantities are more difficult notions. Both are, and are conceived as, modes rather than substances. Qualities are termed affective modes because persons are 'understood to be affected by them in a certain way [*certa ratione*]' (DJN I.1.17: GW 4.1, 22), and they are distinguished according to the nature of such effects. Accordingly, there are *formal* qualities or simple attributes, exemplified by the titles assigned to individuals in civil life – which vary, change, and are often contested. More important, however, are *operant* moral qualities, divided into active and passive kinds. The main (*nobilissimae*) *active* qualities are authority or moral power (*potestas*), right (*ius*) and obligation. By virtue of *potestas*, a person is able to do something 'legitimately and with [a] moral effect' (DJN I.1.19: GW 4.1, 23), in the sense that others become obligated to some performance (*exequendi*), or obliged to allow or not hinder someone else's. In terms of its efficacy or force, *potestas* is either perfect or imperfect; in terms of who has or wields it (its subject), it is either personal or communicable (delegable). And in terms of its object, it is experienced in a fourfold way: as *libertas* (the faculty of 'disposing over oneself and one's actions as one chooses'), as *dominium* (authority over one's own things), as *imperium* (authority over other [moral] persons), and as *servitus* (authority over others' things). *Passive* moral qualities, in turn, enable (*potest*) someone 'rightly to have, suffer, allow [*admittere*], or receive something'. Exemplified mainly by rights (*iura*), they also – like active powers – allow us 'rightly to command persons or take hold of [*tenemus*] things' (DJN I.1.19–20: GW 4.1, 24). Indeed, powers and rights are largely correlative or counterpart notions that express the same normative relationship from different positions or perspectives: the former better indicating specific kinds of authority over persons and things, and the latter more clearly connoting the 'rightful' (*recte*) manner in which that authority is acquired and retained. Obligations are qualities making it 'morally necessary' for moral persons 'to do [*praestare*] or allow, or suffer [*pati*] something' (DJN I.1.21: GW 4.1, 25).

As a group, moral qualities articulate the different kinds and degrees of normativity that are imposed on, or attributed to, human actions and (indirectly) persons and things. They allow us to distinguish modalities of moral urgency or 'necessity', provide different ways of assigning or claiming value, and thereby enable us to (self-)regulate and order the interactions of human beings. They constitute the abstract machinery and language in terms of which moral claims are made and understood, and anyone untutored in their use suffers from ethical illiteracy and its effects. In themselves, however, they constitute only a general, adaptive scheme awaiting application; or empty categories needing content, guidance and confirmation from experience. Such concretisation and specification depends entirely on the fourth kind of moral entity, namely moral quantities or modes of estimation. These differ from physical and mathematical quantities as such, in also arising from 'the imposition and determination of a rational power' (DJN I.1.22: GW 4.1, 25) which must weigh, calculate, apportion and compare the experienced substrate of human life, so that it may be appropriately subsumed under the other categories. As noted already, imposed moral quantities register the value of persons and things, something called esteem (*existimatio*) in the former case and price (*pretium*) in the latter; their presence in actions does not have a specific name.

Calculating Moral Quantities

One of the most difficult and esoteric sections of Pufendorf's EJU discusses the so-called 'moral sphere', an integrative mathematical representation of the qualitative and quantitative dimensions of morality.[23] We read there that '[m]oral actions are estimated either *absolutely* and in themselves, or *relatively* and in comparison with one another [*ad se mutuo*]'. The former perspective (emphasised by the Stoics) denies gradations of good or evil, holding all actions of either sort to be equivalent: 'considered formally and precisely, one good action is not better than another' (EJU I.D18.1: GW 3, 103). The absolute moral goodness of an action – which depends on complete and proper performance, and on the intention of the agent – is known only to God (at the centre of the sphere).[24] Materially considered, however, actions are compared and contrasted, said to be 'superior or inferior, or more harmful [*praestantior aut deterior vel nocentior*]', and accordingly preferred one to another (EJU I.D18.12: GW 3, 108; DJN I.8.5).[25] In EJU Pufendorf identifies five (variable) factors involved in such comparisons: the nobility or preciousness of the object (e.g., God, humanity, individuals, life, modesty); the status and condition of the agent (e.g., priest, enemy, magistrate, child); the demands of the action (performative ease or difficulty); its good or bad consequences (both as to number and gravity); and its temporal and spatial circumstances (e.g., public, private, tavern, temple, holiday). In addition, negative precepts trump positive ones, imperfect obligations yield to perfect ones, gratitude outranks benevolence, and affirmative precepts respect the propinquity of persons or special relationships. It matters, too, whether those whom we help are likely to help others in turn (EJU I.Df.18.12–17). These are the familiar calculations of any moral life.

Though Pufendorf apologises later (DJN I.8.1) for this youthful foray into Weigelian moral geometry, he retains the absolute/relative distinction and the focus on moral quantities. At the end of the DJN chapter (I.8.5) dealing with these, he gestures ahead towards 'the relative estimation of actions' in DJN VIII.3, the long discussion of punishment. Punishment, he says there, belongs to 'the prudence which is connected with the duty of ruling others', and 'is seen to be necessary in order to preserve a social life between men' (DJN VIII.3.5, 3.7: GW 4.2, 766–7). Contra Grotius and Locke, it cannot be exercised by individuals as such (vs. rulers), and its proper infliction depends on the sorts of material factors already distinguished in the EJU discussion of moral quantities: 'in a human court crimes should be weighed primarily by their object, by the amount of damage which they cause to the commonwealth, and by the intention and wickedness [*malitia*] of the transgressor, which last are inferred by means of various conjectures' (DJN VIII.3.18: GW 4.2, 782). There is no absolute measure, no general formula or geometrical proportion, between punishments and their objects; rather the appropriate gauge is always 'the welfare of the state' and 'the discretion [*prudentiam*] of the supreme sovereignty', which has 'considerable [*insignis*] latitude' (DJN VIII.3.24: GW 4.2, 791; DJN VIII.3.23: GW 4.2, 788).[26] A similar latitude and discretion are needed in other moral reflections as well, and the great bulk of DJN is due to the 'quantitative' analysis by which different moral options are compared and weighed.

The use of mathematics in EJU is an expository device for depicting the relation of qualitative and quantitative aspects of morality, not an attempt to mathematise, rationalise, or absolutise natural law (see the Epilogue to this chapter). This also appears from Pufendorf's distinction between mathematical and moral demonstration, and the exactitude possible in each case (DJN I.2.10). To be sure, he does seek to establish morality as a science resting on demonstrations that are valid and sound (I.2.3), assuring us that 'that discipline, which considers what is upright and what base in human actions, the principal portion of which we have undertaken to present, rests entirely upon grounds so secure, that from it can be deduced genuine demonstrations which are capable of producing a solid science' (DJN I.2.4: GW 4.1, 28). Moreover, he claims, such demonstrations are not undermined by 'the variety of circumstances', since 'there are definite principles according to which it can be shown how much force any circumstance may have in affecting or varying an action' (DJN I.2.5: GW 4.1, 29). Indeed, circumstances may not affect the moral quality of an action at all (by changing it from good to evil, for instance, or from permitted to required), since some are (deemed) trivial or indifferent; and even when they do have an effect, it does not produce moral uncertainty but merely a different kind of certainty – just as, in geometry, 'a line which varies in the slightest degree from straightness, tends to curvature, but that fact does not produce any uncertainty' (DJN I.2.9: GW 4.1, 34).[27] Moral demonstration and the principles determining the role of circumstances look to actions and persons 'considered in general', and 'no sane person' can doubt them (DJN I.2.8: GW 4.1, 33).[28]

Nonetheless, moral actions also exhibit 'degrees of necessity', even when legally required (and thus qualitatively equivalent), and there are situations where one good must (because of a greater benefit) be chosen over another (DJN I.2.8: GW 4.1, 34). Such latitude or variability is especially pronounced when dealing explicitly with moral quantities. These resemble physical quantities in their attention to concrete details, but differ from them in that they 'arise from imposition, and the judgement of intelligent and free agents'. Fortunately, the purpose for which they are introduced does not demand the same subtlety or 'straining after details [*minutiarum consectationem*]', but it suffices 'that persons, things and actions be [only] roughly rated and compared' (DJN I.2.10, 35; also I.1.22). Beside the variant proportionality between crimes and punishments already noted, a similar latitude is required in regard to 'the value of persons [esteem], . . . the prices of different commercial things and actions, . . . and [,indeed,] in many [other] affairs of human life' (DJN I.2.10: GW 4.1, 35). This is because the moral sciences cannot remain purely theoretical and deal only with definitions, but must 'turn their findings to some practical use [*in usum*]'. That is, beside showing 'the rectitude of human actions in their order according to laws', they must also undertake 'the skillful management [*dextram gubernationem*] of one's own actions and those of others, with an eye to the security and welfare primarily of the public'. This requires adaptation to the flux, the inconstancy, the chance or randomness, and the contingency of human affairs, which often defeat 'the nicety of demonstrations' and even 'the wisest circumspection' (DJN I.2.4: GW 4.1, 28).

This view is also supported by Pufendorf's characterisation of the law of nature. That law is not eternal, not consistent, not transcendental, and not for its own sake. Rather, much of it arises 'gradually out of the conventions and institutions of men' (DJN 4.4.13: GW 4.1, 367); actions opposed to it do not generate an abstract logical or mathematical 'contradiction' (DJN 1.2.6: GW 4.1, 31); the good it serves is not considered 'in an absolute way . . ., so that every entity, actually existing, may be considered good', but 'only in so far as it has a respect to others, and . . . is understood to be good for some person [*alicui*] or for something [*pro aliquo*]' (DJN I.4.4: GW 4.1, 49);[29] and it presumes certain conditions facilitating the attainment of that end, so that goodness exploited or sociality frustrated is not, as such, required.[30]

In EJU Pufendorf describes the natural law as 'certain conclusions, understood by reason, concerning things to be done and to be avoided', and says that it can be 'gathered or presumed by a process of reasoning' from 'the condition of nature, or that of the activity to be undertaken [*negotii, quod gerendum*]' (EJU II.Obs.4.3: GW 3, 135). This corresponds to DJN's claim that 'the law of nature should be deduced from the reason of man himself, and should flow from that source, provided it is not perverted [*recte se habentis*]' (DJN II.3.13: GW 4.1, 144). Pufendorf often

makes this point in terms of *sana* or *recta ratio*, using the notion not as
a substantive middle term between subjective (human) and objective
(cosmic) rationality, as in Stoicism, but in a functionalist sense of proper
reasoning about actual things: 'we call the law of nature a dictate of right
reason [only] in the sense that the human mind has the faculty of being
able clearly to discern, from the observation [*contemplatione*] of the human
condition, that it is necessary for us to live according to the norm of that
law . . .' (DJN II.3.13: GW 4.1, 144). We understand that 'human condition' when we appreciate the diversity and strength of human desires,
discern the beneficial and harmful qualities of things, and recognise 'when
man needs assistance and when he needs restraint' (DJN II.3.14: GW 4.1,
146). The 'necessity' resulting from such observation refers not (as noted
above) to the formalistic framing discourse of divine voluntarism, but to
the hypothetical requirement or demand that humans enact forms of sociality allowing them to realise the kind of life that they (and others) are
capable of and actually desire. This conditional or instrumental relationship is especially clear in Pufendorf's frequent criticisms of Hobbes, whom
he accuses of exceeding the bounds of sane reason and thinking in a perverted (*prave, inepte*) fashion when he ascribes to natural law remedies for
human problems that Pufendorf finds, in fact, either excessive or counter-
productive (DJN VII.1.7: GW 4.2, 635; I.7.13).

Also important to the argument, surely, is the fact that Pufendorf reasons
often about whether actions benefit or harm humans, really or apparently
only, permanently or temporarily, collectively or individually, and in more
or less important ways.[31] Such consequentialistic analysis about results or
outcomes and their comparative value is peculiar to reasoning about moral
quantities. To be sure, Pufendorf explicitly distinguishes morality from utility, assigning the latter to 'another branch of learning [*disciplinam*]' (DJN
I.3.7: GW 4.1, 40); yet he also follows Cicero in consistently associating
one with the other (DJN II.3.10), calling prudence the 'benignant sister'
(*suavissimam sororem*) of natural law (DJN VI.1.18: GW 4.2, 576). The
apparent conflict is easily resolved, however, by clarifying or anatomising
(as Hume would say) 'the ambiguous word "utility"' (DJN II.3.10: GW 4.1,
140) – in the fashion of Bentham's hedonic categories – and by distinguishing the respective recommendations of sound and depraved reason. The
former have the same status in relation to morality as the divinely imposed
moral entities which 'flow' from the nature of things, so to speak, in comparison to merely human (i.e., arbitrary) impositions that are asserted
more tentatively. In short, utility is at the heart of Pufendorf's calculations
about relative accordance with nature. Benefits and harms are not equal,
after all, and those utilities regarded on the basis of experience as more
important, indispensable or desirable – in the sense of sociality-maximising,

security- and welfare-enhancing, and need- and desire-satisfying – are deemed 'necessary' in comparison to the rest, or rationally more *recta* or *sana* as opposed to those labelled *absurda* or *prava*.[32] That is, this distinc-tion, too, is fundamentally empirical and prudential, guided by human experience rather than by unmediated divine commands or rationalistic assumptions. Such an interpretation is also supported by Pufendorf's discus-sions of history and international law (*ius gentium*, explicitly conceived as a continuation of natural law [DJN II.2.23]) in *Monzambano*, *Einleitung* and other historical works, as well as various dissertations, which are conducted primarily in terms of different kinds of human interest that, of course, may conflict with one another.

The Moral Marketplace: Price and Esteem

Among the most consequential imaginary goods that 'depart from nature' in the sense of not serving human interests, and whose value is measured not by sane reason but by human foolishness (*stoliditas*), vanity and per-versity (*pravitas*), is 'vainglory[,] or the opinion that one is more excellent than others, insofar as it is not based on virtue or adjoined to anything useful' (DJN VIII.3.19, GW 4.2, 783).[33] Indeed, conflicts about relative, positional goods necessitate both the natural law itself as well as the politi-cal condition [*status*] that it enjoins humans to enter. Thus, comparing humans with beasts (which need no clothes), Pufendorf notes that the former have used the need for covering as an occasion 'to flaunt [their] vanity and pride'. Indeed, they are constantly stirred by a mass of affects and desires unknown to animals, including: 'a lust for superfluities, ambi-tion, a craving to glory and surpass others, envy, a struggle of wits' (DJN II.1.6, GW 4.1, 110), all of which involve a comparative assessment of self and others.[34] Unless these desires and their pursuits are regulated by (natu-ral) law, sociality becomes impossible and humans (who both need and fear each other) would be more miserable than animals (DJN II.1.8, 152). The same reasoning precedes the introduction of the sovereign state in DJN VII, which necessity (*necessitatis vim*) 'compelled' (*compulit*) humans to enter in order to leave or avoid even less desirable non- or pre-civil conditions. Here, too, the list of inclinations (after hunger and lust) set-ting humans against one another begins with 'an insatiable craving for superfluous things, and ambition, that most vicious of evils' (DJN VII.1.4, GW 4.2, 631).[35] The central problem remains the contested valuation and possession of both things and persons. Notably, the two are connected, since 'in general[,] men scarcely ever consider a thing valuable [*pro bono*] which does not yield to the holder some distinction and position [*praecipui & eximii*] above that possessed by others [*caeteri*], and by reason of which they cannot vaunt themselves above these' (DJN V.1.6, GW 4.2, 681).

There are explicit parallels between Pufendorf's separate discussions of the value of things (*pretium*, price) and of persons (*existimatio*, esteem) respectively – in both their civil and non-civil conditions (including the relations among sovereign states).[36] Things vary in their ability to relieve human needs and must be exchanged (by differently situated human beings) in order to be maximally useful, and such exchanges require a kind of artificial (i.e., 'imposed') equalisation of things fundamentally unequal or different (DJN V.1.1–2, 4). Persons, too, cannot maintain a posture of simple or negative equality towards one another if they are to benefit from social interaction, for this requires them to be compared and ranked according to their respective functions in society – many of which also involve disposition over unequal things (DJN VIII.4.1: GW 4.2, 1229–30). Thus, Pufendorf offers us not a discourse about abstract worth or equality, but an analysis of how, concretely and usefully, to manage inequality in the possession of things and the treatment of persons.

In both instances, the starting point is not some absolute or positive value, but rather its shared absence or lack: i.e., negative communion in the case of property or ownership, and dignity or simple esteem in the case of human beings (or persons more generally).[37] The former refers simply to common availability or (juridically unobstructed) access to as yet unclaimed or (collectively, by agreement) unassigned objects, which anyone may use as he or she wishes. There are no normative distinctions at this point – prior to shared imposition – as Pufendorf repeatedly shows by noting the *reductio* created by Hobbes's use of juridical language (viz., everyone's 'right' [*ius*] to everything) in that state.[38] A similar situation obtains in regard to human dignity or simple esteem, which is also demanded or assigned, rather than given or found. Thus, dignity is not the *basis* of humans' claims to have their interests equally considered; rather, it merely *is* that claim – supported by the natural law's injunction that 'everyone should esteem and treat [any] other man as if [*tanquam*] naturally equal to himself, or as [*ut*] equally a man' (DJN III.2.1: GW 4.1, 226) – itself rooted in the simple fact that, otherwise, there will (most likely) be conflict and other nasty things, which nobody wants.[39] The so-called *equality of right* (*aequalitatem juris*) in any sort of natural state (i.e., states insufficiently or ineffectively structured by imposed moral distinctions) is actually a shared *obligation* to cultivate a social life, one that is equally binding, as it were, upon all men who have interests and seek to satisfy them by living together.[40] As Pufendorf says of simple esteem, linking it to price via the notion of utility: 'as we say of a thing which has a kind of use in human life, that it is of some value [*pretii*], and refer to that which is entirely useless as of no value, so you may say that at least some sort of value [*valorem*] attaches to him with whom one can somehow [*utcunque*] deal as if he were [*tanquam*] a social being' (DJN VIII.4.2: GW 4.2, 803). That is, simple esteem is a necessarily presumed capacity for moral action, and anyone who does not have it, or is (without sufficient cause) unwilling to attribute it to others, is socially 'useless' and may be treated as such.[41]

The exchange of things owned requires shared evaluation, and so this – like property itself – does not await the formation of the civil state but begins as soon as humans interact. Property, exchange and price, as well as intensive esteem, are found in any actual (i.e., relative or mixed – vs. ideal, absolute or pure) state of nature.[42] The methods for assigning value to *res* and *personae* may differ there, but common to both is its imposition by those who attribute it, rather than by those who receive it, as it were: that is, 'as the price of wares is set by the ultimate purchaser, how highly [*quanti*] a man is regarded by others is for them to determine' (DJN VIII.4.11: GW 4.2, 810). This basic relationship does not change within civil states but merely becomes more complicated through the introduction of more and different kinds of moral entities and agents, including the state itself, which exercises a unique sort of impositional authority.

In the valuation of things, Pufendorf distinguishes a so-called common or ordinary (*vulgare*) price from that called eminent. The former 'is seen in things and in actions or activities [*operis*] entering into exchange [*commercium*], insofar as they afford men some use and satisfaction [*delectatio*]' (DJN V.1.3: GW 4.2, 446); the latter refers to money, which serves as a common standard virtually containing any other price. Ordinary price outside of states varies according to many considerations (all subject to moral assessment), and it exhibits 'some latitude within which more or less can be demanded and given' (DJN V.1.9: GW 4.2, 453). Here modern economists have noted with interest Pufendorf's attention to scarcity and abundance, the value-adding role of labor, externalities and transaction costs, opportunity cost, the notion of price-less goods and non-market value, the suitability of different objects for embodying eminent price, and, of course, his concerns about the vanity, fancy and 'overweening luxury of men', which 'has imposed enormous values [*pretia*] upon things which human life could very easily do without' (DJN V.1.6: GW 4.2, 449). Given the complexity of such consider-ations, where latitude and discretion must always remain, the just price is 'commonly set by those who are sufficiently acquainted with both the merchandise and the market' (DJN V.1.9: GW 4.2, 453).

This pricing method continues in civil states. Here, however, there may also be a legal price; this is set by 'a decree of superiors, or by law . . . at a στιγμῆ or definite point, and it has no latitude' (DJN V.1.8: GW 4.2, 452). Pufendorf does not prefer such price controls, he acknowledges that they may be abused by authorities, and he cautions rulers about interfering with commerce, particularly the valuation of money – which should not change 'unless the highest interest of the state advises it' (DJN V.1.15: GW 4.2, 459).[43] Still, this sometimes obtains, since money not only facilitates commerce within states but also among them; that is, it affects foreign relations. A similar continuity and variation (both outside and inside states) may be seen in the assignment of intensive esteem, by which 'persons otherwise equal in terms of simple esteem are preferred one to another, according as there reside in one, more than in the other, things that usually move others' minds to show honor' (DJN VIII.4.11: GW 4.2, 810). Here, too, there comes a point in civil life when sovereigns may, for the sake of the state, 'introduce inequality among men' by differentially assigning honours and dignities according to their service to the state. Such civil preferments do not undermine or eliminate the informal, extra-legal foundations of intensive esteem; they merely override them (DJN VIII.4.23: GW 4.2, 821; also VIII.4.24).

Governing (Moral) Economics: Sumptuary Laws

The twofold authority (and obligation) of the state regarding the valuation of things and persons – which is critical to the pacification of its members – is set out in DJN VIII.4–5. There Pufendorf acknowledges the limits of the state's power over people's possessions (i.e., only so much as 'flows of itself from the nature of supreme sovereignty', or as is needed to attain the state's basic objectives)[44] and divides it into three categories. These concern '(1) the right to pass laws about accommodating property use to the state's welfare; (2) the right to impose taxes; [and] (3) the exercise of eminent domain' (DJN VIII.5.3: GW 4.2, 833). The first power is wielded through sumptuary laws, i.e., regulations about the 'unnecessary expenses' of citizens which affect the strength and material well-being of the state, including its comparative advantage vis-à-vis other states, especially those potentially hostile. Such regulations are important not only because they enable the state as such to function and perform its duties (*pecunia nervus rerum*),[45] but also because they regulate people's escalating contestation over positional goods, both material and personal, which motivates the establishment of states in the first place.[46] That is, the policing of both kinds of purported *propria* is not an illicit expansion of the state's admittedly limited powers, but rather their necessary and appropriate exercise.

The relatively brief discussion of sumptuary laws in DJN (VIII.5.3) summarises a much longer discussion of the topic found in a dissertation appearing almost simultaneously. 'De legibus sumtuariis' (DLS, 1672) is – among the fourteen dissertations known to us – one of those produced by Pufendorf at Lund. It was defended there in March 1672 by a Daniel Lossius of Stade, and may in fact have been written by him rather than by Pufendorf himself.[47] That possibility is supported not only by stylistic considerations but also by the essay's heavy reliance on textual analysis as an entry into the subject matter, and by its relatively non-polemical approach. That is, unlike other dissertations by Pufendorf, including those at Heidelberg, DLS does not exude his aggressive self-confidence and seems not to engage any contemporary opponents.[48] Indeed, the immediate context is unclear, and the piece cites – beside Montaigne, Famianus Strada (d. 1649), Pierre Matthieu (d. 1621) and Grotius – mostly early Christian and especially classical authors. It reflects no awareness of the more recent history of sumptuary legislation, since the Middle Ages,[49] nor of challenges to such laws that became increasingly common during the seventeenth century.[50] Still, the piece addresses a topic important to Pufendorf's general outlook and complements his earlier, Heidelberg dissertation *De existimationibus* (1667), on various forms of esteem.

DLS begins with the challenge of controlling 'the great multitude of men' contained in the state, so as to maintain the latter's 'vigor and health'. The problem is familiar enough: 'mortals are stirred by desires that are not only numerous but also often in conflict with one another', and these are capable of upsetting the tranquillity of civil society. Pufendorf refers specifically to people's 'insatiable desire to have [*habendi*]' and to the 'insane craving to dissipate one's wealth through inanities'. The state must control 'that torrent' not only because of the dangers it poses in itself, but also because it generates additional vices – such as threatening others' goods (after one has wasted one's own) – and 'leads citizens to bicker terribly [with one another]' (§1, 513). That is, the problem goes beyond people's unbounded desire to enjoy 'the delicacies of throat and palate' (as well as other real and imagined goods) for their own sakes, inasmuch as the 'prime source' of profuse spending on luxuries is 'ambition, the display of power and wealth [*opum*], [and] the obsession for pomp and magnificence'. As noted above (after n. 35), it is human nature 'to flaunt itself with that deemed to contain some evidence of superiority' (§17, 532), and the 'chief fruit' of luxury is, ultimately, 'to be seen [*conspici*]' (§25, 542). So, clearly, the regulation of luxury and consumption involves both the valuation and control of things, and the estimation of persons, both of which are central to social and civil life and thus a proper concern of law.

There follows a lengthy review (§§2–7) of the main sorts of things on which – both at Rome and 'today[,] in many parts of Europe' – such 'immense or superfluous expenditures' (§2, 514) have been lavished, touching on almost every area of life: food, dishes, parties, celebrations (of birth, death, engagement, marriage, achievement), dwellings, furnishings, servants, decorations, art, clothes, jewellery, gardens, ponds, carriages, zoos and so on – now extensively surveyed by what may seem, itself, an immoderately indulgent historiography of consumption.[51] Most such objects minister to ostentation, pleasure, ambition, pomp, arrogance, promiscuity, affectation and the like, rather than being necessary or useful, as it were; indeed, some are practically required by 'laws' of luxury (§4) that convention has introduced in different places; and many involve the strange and arbitrary factors affecting the ordinary price of things: rarity, fragility, antiquity, difficulty (of production), fame (of artisans) and other external associations. For expository purposes, Pufendorf simply relies here on a detailed passage from Tacitus' *Annals* and, in the case of female extravagance, on that knower of the other sex, Tertullian.[52] And he returns to these formal divisions towards the end of the dissertation, in briefly applying his proposed solutions to the separate types of consumption.

Over-consumption harms individuals, the households to which they belong, and also the state. Individual alimentary excesses have familiar consequences: 'mental dullness, diminished [*fractus*] vigor, incapacity for exertion, an endless plague of illnesses, premature or feeble old age, [and] a hastened death' (§8, 517). Squandering the inherited wealth of households leads to destructive borrowing[53] and may eventually ruin even the greatest of families, whose members are then unable to devote themselves to 'worthy [*dignis*] arts' and, because of their poverty, become either a burden or a threat to the state through 'depraved' ones (§9, 518). Inconveniences to the state come in two varieties: those where squandered resources stay within its borders and are simply redistributed, as it were, and mercantilist worries about the export of money (i.e., precious metals containing an eminent price) and valuable products to other countries.[54] In each case, Pufendorf presents formal counterarguments to his own position, to which he then responds.

Thus, defenders of luxury may object that spending is better than useless hoarding, that the benefits of money are increased by circulation, and that appropriate tolls and taxes on expenditures may actually benefit the treasury – responses that became increasingly common in the eighteenth century. Moreover, just as it is not generally necessary according to natural law that particular states survive (DJN VIII.11.4), so it seems to matter little to the state 'if some families are destroyed by luxury, since by their ruin [*fractis tabulis*], as it were, other families may be able to gain an increase'. In fact, people have always used the foolishness of others to their own advantage, and even rulers have employed luxury as a weapon to weaken and dominate possible opponents (§10). However, Pufendorf maintains, such arguments only suit rulers who acquire and maintain their rule by force, and that a prince who has acquired sovereignty 'in a legitimate manner and with the consent [*volentibus*] of the citizens' should wish to preserve it by corrupting them is 'neither permissible [*fas*] nor profitable [*proficuum*]' (§11, 520). Lest it appear otherwise, he adds, a strong state depends on a flourishing citizenry (something undermined by luxury), a good prince need not extort money from (good) citizens, and – most important of all – luxury spawns other vices which also threaten the state. Thus, those who have impoverished themselves burden rather than bolster the state; if they happen to occupy official roles they become venal and sap both public and private wealth; and if driven to desperation by their creditors, they may decide to remedy their ills by unsettling or disturbing the state, expecting 'to extinguish a private conflagration with public ruin' (§12, 521).

In cases where money or other important resources are transferred out of the country in exchange for imported luxuries, especially from potential enemies, Pufendorf notes that 'money is necessary for accomplishing anything',[55] referring to the famous comment of Flamininus (in Plutarch) about a numerous and well-armed, albeit impoverished, opponent: 'he has arms [*manus*] and legs, but no belly'.[56] Also, and in line with his general mercantilist assumptions, Pufendorf mentions the unequal exchange of armour between Glaucon and Diomedes in the *Iliad*,[57] and warns about the consequences of a negative trade balance (§13, 525). Finally, he critically dissects arguments based on a supposed link between public and private magnificence, denies that those who have laboured for the state should be allowed to enjoy (and fritter away) their wealth, and dismisses as uninformed the idea that private ownership of things should be entirely immune to state requisitions (§14), as presented in the rhetorical challenge (by Duronius) in Valerius Maximus: 'what need is there for liberty, if those who so wish are not permitted to perish by luxury?' (§16, 531) – an ancient equivalent of the purported right to unlimited consumption.[58]

In the Tacitus passage noted earlier,[59] Tiberius resists the Senate's request to resurrect the old sumptuary laws by suggesting that 'mature vices' (*adulta vitia*) should be left alone, lest one merely reveal one's inability to control them and appear ludicrous in the attempt. Instead, he advises, luxury and consumption should be managed by a combination of shame (for princes), necessity (for the poor), and satiety (for the rich) (§15). Pufendorf agrees that laws long ignored with impunity cannot simply be reinstituted with effect, but he rejects Tiberius' recommendation as inadequate. For it is difficult to experience shame in regard to things commonly regarded as splendid, necessity does not always improve the poor, and 'satiety' often comes only after everything has been spent. Therefore, he suggests, these other means must be supplemented by sumptuary laws, so long as these are 'always cautiously enacted'. Because few people have the probity of mind to wish, on their own (*ultro*), to be cured of some enticing vice, such laws cannot be dismissed as vain (*supervacuus*) or as 'an instance of puerile discipline invented by morose superiors . . . [merely] to molest the citizens' (§16, 530–1).

Pufendorf provides some general examples of such laws in the latter part of DLS (§§19–26), where he returns to the initial categories from Tacitus. It is impossible there, perhaps, to avoid all silliness given the magnitude of the concrete regulatory challenge.[60] Thus, Pufendorf suggests that servants, cooks and sweepers be dressed in high fashion (*habitu superbi*), so as to make this less appealing to clothes-horses and other competitive dressers (§24); that women – if they insist on continuing to wear imported sable furs – be forced to wear them inside out (for warmth and not display); and that a practice of wearing cheap (fake) jewellery be introduced at court ([*r*]*ecipiatur in aulam mos*) so as to reduce the cost of adorning 'our Junos' (§26, 542). Still, he recognises early on that some of these measures will not work, and that 'laws and punishments [alone], no matter how severe, will not entirely eliminate the evil [*malum*]'; for 'men's depraved ingenuity will always find a way to cheat the laws' (§17, 532). Indeed, as in the case of other irrationalities that influence people's valuations (e.g., they buy things *because* they cost a lot, and higher prices only incite them *more*), sumptuary legislation may only dignify the very things it wishes to forbid. Therefore, Pufendorf returns almost immediately to the 'other remedies' just mentioned.

This approach hinges on changing people's valuation of things, and it relies on the same imitative and competitive inclinations that, acording to Pufendorf, basically drive the problem of over-consumption: instead of trying to eradicate these, it seeks rather to redirect them.[61] The method is also in line with Pufendorf's more general recognition that a state cannot be held together 'by force and fear alone' (DJN VIII.1.5: GW 4.2, 748), and that overcoming 'the natural variation of wills and their tendency to oppose each other' depends on more than fear of punishment and external compulsion (DJN VII.2.5: GW 4.2, 642). What is needed, as well, is the kind of citizen-formation mentioned above in relation to Rousseau. This suggests, in the present instance, a sort of transvaluation of values: 'so that the opinion of superiority is removed from [wasteful] expenditures of this sort, and the opposite opinion of vanity, crudeness, fatuity, [and] inelegance may be associated with them'; and, conversely, that citizens be brought to value 'moderate accoutrements, discreet outlays, concern about the future, the preservation and increase of their patrimony; [and] the administration of their affairs [rem] in such a way that when difficult times rush in they are able both to satisfy themselves and to succor the commonwealth' (§18, 533–4).

How? By having the sovereign function as a sort of *arbiter* (or *magister*) *elegantiae*,[62] both through the power of personal example and by (re)ordering court manners in such a way that people compete for the right things, in the right ways, etc. It is the prince's own authority, both real and symbolic, that drives such reforms: 'Thus obedience toward the prince and the desire [*amor*] to emulate him are stronger than legally stipulated punishment and fear' (§18, 535, quoting Tacitus). They also rely on shame (*pudor*) and internalised feelings of inadequacy, which result from the realisation that one values things other than those highly regarded (or not) by the ruler and his circle – whom one seeks of course to please and emulate (for competitive reasons).[63] In support of this top-down transvaluation of values, as it were, Pufendorf refers explicitly to the general view, discussed above, that 'it belongs to the rulers of states to assign [*ponere*] value to persons, money, and merchandise; and, thus, to add or subtract dignity [*dignatio*] from certain things' (§18, 534). That is, rulers have the right or, rather, the obligation of moral imposition, and given human weaknesses and shortcomings (DJN VII.2.5) they must sometimes exercise it, according to their own best lights, for the benefit of the state.

Conclusion: Doing the Math

Here is where Pufendorf's economics and politics converge, in both of the ways noted at the beginning. For not only does the sovereign exercise a directive and enabling control over his subjects' economic or consumptive activities, but his or her own assessment of what is allowable depends also on a sort of consequentialist 'economic' calculation about the needs of the state and the requirements of social life. Indeed, natural law more generally, at least Pufendorf's, is also a sort of 'economic' exercise of identifying, weighing, comparing, prioritising, maximising, minimising, discounting, aggregating, sharing, selecting and deciding about (only) more or less similar preferences, all ordered or focused by humans' *de facto* needs and desires (also a matter of more or less), in order to create some kind of decent (*honesta, decora*, etc.) and mutually beneficial (*utile, commoda*, etc.) life together. That is, it does not merely shape, structure or enable economics from the outside by providing the basic legal/moral vocabulary in terms of which the latter is conducted, but it itself embodies a so-called 'economic' way of thinking, both as a general and, as it were, moral perspective, and as a particular way of thinking about politics at all associational levels including international relations.[64]

This is what Pufendorf's concern with moral quantities is about. As a type of moral entity, they are imposed on the world by humans in the process of valuing things or persons, and in assessing actions – their voluntaristic character being most evident in the application to particular cases, where they appear as contextual, decisional solutions to often untidy, conflicting, differently categorised or incompletely theorised situations.[65] They are required of human beings at all levels of their association, both in the pre- and post-civil natural states, and in civil society where sovereigns have special obligations to employ them usefully in governing individual and collective human behaviour. Also, they pertain to all kinds of human interaction, including those widely termed 'economic' and 'political'. In fact, as we have seen, it is impossible to keep these categories from overlapping, both before and after the creation of the state, in so far as different forms of social power impact and potentiate one another.

Sumptuary laws are but one example of moral quantities at work. Thus, the notion of 'luxury' itself is a general descriptor with a certain latitude, always applied against a background of other normative and factual assumptions.[66] These include particular conceptions of the public/private divide, of real and imaginary (non-moral) goods, of human needs and wants, and the like; as well as determinations of whether and when certain contracts have been fulfilled, and sovereigns or subjects have done their respective duties well 'enough' (*sufficit*). All such distinctions are variant, overlapping, and contested or subject to dispute. Accordingly, a close examination of Pufendorf's language reveals a tentativeness of assertion that implicitly acknowledges this, as we find there a pervasive presence of seemingly ineluctable expressions (merely sampled here) like the following: 'surely' (*utique, sane, plane, nimirum*), 'regularly presumed' (*regulariter praesumitur*), 'sound reason' (*sana ratio*), 'right reason' (*recta ratio*), 'common reason' (*communis ratio*), 'seems absurd' (*absurdum videtur, incongruum videtur*), seem best fitted (*expeditissima videantur*), plain as day (*manifestissimum*), 'sufficiently clear' (*sat dilucide*), 'properly observed' (*probe observata & examinata*), 'to weigh the force of arguments' (*argumentorum momentum ponderare*), 'sufficiently acquainted with' (*sat gnari*), 'weighty reasons' (*graves causas*), and many more.[67] This is not the language of absolutism or presumption, but the cautious, conditioned, only more-or-less confident discourse of ground-level moral imposers trying to get their quantities right.

Epilogue: Natural Law as Casuistry and Probabilism[68]

In his Booker Prize winning novel *The Sense of an Ending*, Julian Barnes offers a diary excerpt of a character who had committed suicide. It is written in a tortured, Wittgensteinian style (with decimal numbers at the front of each paragraph) that seems itself, in its attempt at precision, to indicate a desperate attempt to calculate life's quantities or, more colloquially, to figure things out. Section 5.5 begins:

> So a) To what extent might human relationships be expressed in a mathematical or logical formula? And b) If so, what signs might be placed between the integers? Plus and minus, self-evidently; sometimes multiplication, and yes, division. But these signs are limited. Thus an entirely failed relationship might be expressed in terms of both loss/minus and division/reduction, showing a total of zero; whereas [. . .]. But what of most relationships? Do they not require to be expressed in notations which are logically improbable and mathematically insoluble?
>
> 5.6 Thus how might you express an accumulation containing the integers [standing for persons] b, a^1, a^2, s, v? $b = s - v\ ^x/_+\ a^1$ or $a^2 + v + a^1 \times s = b$?
>
> . . . 5.7 Or is that the wrong way to put the question and express the accumulation? Is the application of logic to the human condition in and of itself self-defeating? What becomes of the chain of argument when the links are made of different metals, each with a separate frangibility?[69]
>
> 5.8 Or is 'link' a false metaphor?
>
> 5.9 But allowing that it is not, if a link breaks, wherein lies the responsibility for such breaking? On the links immediately on either side, or on the whole chain? But what do we mean by 'the whole chain'? How far do the limits of responsibility extend?
>
> 6.0 Or we might try to draw the responsibility more narrowly and apportion it more exactly. And not use equations and integers but instead express matters in traditional narrative terminology. So, for instance, if. . .[70]

A similar though less personal passage occurs in Rousseau's *Social Contract* (III.1.16), where he seeks to determine the proper 'ratios' between sovereign, government and citizens. Sensing criticism of his language, he responds:

> If, in order to reduce this system to ridicule, it were said that, according to me, finding this mean proportional and forming the body of the Government requires no more than taking the square root of the number of people, I would reply that I am here using this number only as an example; that the ratios about which I am speaking are measured not only by numbers of men, but more generally by the amount of activity, which is the combined result of a great many causes; that, besides, if in order to express myself in fewer words I momentarily borrow the language of geometry, I am nevertheless not unaware of the fact that geometric precision does not obtain in moral quantities.[71]

But this concedes too much. To be sure, mathematics can operate as a mere shell, an external shorthand or notation for expressing relationships not themselves numerical. And in such a role it does seem artificial, ironic, almost taunting, its very use revealing its inadequacy to the task. Yet on a deeper, more 'realistic' level which acknowledges different metals and frangibilities, as it were, the association is anything but fanciful. For it is not the isolated or abstract certainties of 'pure' mathematics that attract here and seem so apropos, nor its symbolic efficiency, but its situated calculations: namely, the concrete 'addition' and 'subtraction' (not to mention 'multiplication' and 'division') of details, the constant equilibration of shifting weights and quantities on Vermeerian scales of life.[72] That is, as in Barnes's story, we (must) try continually to estimate, compare, apportion, trade and bargain, even guess, precisely (*sic*) because there is no final, syllogistic certainty. Even when a life is over, others typically disagree about how it should be tallied. To dismiss this phenomenon as mere metaphor, misleading, or unnecessary is to miss something important, or to assume the posture of a perfect, divine mathematician whose operations seem, to others (including Pufendorf – see the 'Natural Law Positivism' section above), quite out of reach.[73]

The background of Rousseau's resort to the language of mathematics is unclear, but in the case of Pufendorf it is obvious. Though he does not mention Hobbes's notion of philosophy as 'cognition gained through right reasoning' (*per rectam ratiocinationem acquisita cognitio*), particularly his characterisation of reasoning as 'computation' (*De corpore* I.1.2),[74]

Pufendorf does note Hobbes's application of mathematical studies to moral philosophy.[75] Similarly, he frequently praises the precise 'mathematical demonstrations' of the Cartesians who, like Hobbes, rejected scholastic subtleties and *prejudicia*.[76] It was Erhard Weigel, however, whom Pufendorf knew already in Leipzig and Jena,[77] and with whom he remained in contact throughout his life, who most obviously provided him with the terminology that he wielded, in this regard, with so much greater effect. Weigel's *Arithmetische Beschreibung der Moral-Weißheit von Personen und Sachen*[78] did not appear until 1674, but Pufendorf indirectly acknowledged his influence already in April 1659, and it was evident in EJU and again admitted in DJN.[79]

Weigel's eclectic combination of metaphysics, mathematics and Platonic number mysticism briefly attracted Pufendorf, as EJU evinces, but that spell soon wore off. What remained was the unplatonic insight that mathematics does not require metaphysics or symbolism (and vice versa); that life necessarily involves an '*aestimative/quantitative* Erkenntnis', as Weigel put it; and that it is possible to regard ethics and politics as a sort of 'moralische Mathematik'[80] (with or without numbers) – as the discussion above has shown. Even a cursory glance at Weigel's table of contents shows both the debt and the difference, through section headings on 'Vom Unterscheid der Personen im Menschlichen Leben' (II), 'Von der Ehrenachtbarkeit insonderheit' (XV) and 'Von der Geltung und dem Werth' (XVIII).[81] The notion of *Achtbarkeit* (in the sense of notice or attention) is revealingly linked by Weigel to that of *commercium*,[82] understood as situatedness in social space – which coincides with notional and natural/physical space. Of course, Pufendorf left these latter associations behind, as well as Weigel's lifelong aspiration to a pansophic logical-ontological-mathematical-moral system, but he kept the concept and the language of calculability, comparison and relative distinction.

As with Rousseau, this move may seem at first like a betrayal of the mathematical ideal, and also opposed to Pufendorf's scattered comments on philosophical method, which seem to aspire to more.[83] For in such contexts he often defended Cartesianism against scholastic appeals to authority (both secular and theological) and criticised the Aristotelian relegation of ethics to the realm of the merely probable. Indeed, in the important post-EJU letters to Boineburg[84] he explicitly contrasted two ways (*viae*) of doing moral philosophy: one pursued especially (*potissimum*) by mathematicians, 'who love to bring forth [*elicere*] a large quantity [*vim*] of conclusions from a few principles', and the other by those 'who like to investigate natural things' so that 'from the observation and comparison of many singularities they may at last compose [*concluderent*] some general principle [*decretum*]'.[85] Of these he clearly chose the former. Still, caution is advised. For as the larger context evinces, what Pufendorf rejected in the latter 'slippery, unfocused, and indeed impassable [*lubrica, infinita, et vere invia*]' path is not reliance on observation and experience as such (i.e., so-called a posteriori beginnings, in later terms), but their use in inductive appeals to the authority of mere numbers (or the number of authorities). In turn, what he valued in the former path or way was not an abstract, a priori search for certainty through purification of or separation from experience, but rather its reliable starting points (hypotheses) and tight, deductive reasoning, as seen in the increasingly mathematicised (but nonetheless empirical) sciences of nature. Like these, Pufendorf rejected both the assertions of metaphysics and the presumptions (scholastic, religious) of authority, and sought instead to devise a moral science resting on the observation of human experience in which not objects ('natures', or essences), but the relations among them, were (re)calculable to various degrees.[86]

This reading is supported by another comment in the same Boineburg letter on method, where Pufendorf – after noting the important contributions of Grotius and Hobbes – acknowledges that '[m]uch has also been contributed by the industry of those men who have written about cases of conscience, and about justice and law [*iure*]'. This is a rather surprising (and backhanded) tribute to the moral casuistry of the Jesuits, whom Pufendorf castigated throughout his life. Why? In continuing, he mentions the pedantic bulk of such works, their inelegant (i.e., scholastic) style, and especially their frequent (*pleraque*) use to shore up the authority of the Catholic Church (*Staticam illam sacram*) while usurping individual freedom of judgement (*judicij libertatem*). That is, Pufendorf does not reject the approach as such. Instead, he says that among the others (*alij*) who have paid any attention to it, most (*plerique*) have been occupied only with specific matters (*circa particulam*), or have sought merely to weaken the method's traditional foundations (*eiusdem fundamenta quae hactenus credita sunt, subruere*) – in contrast to a few (*nonnullis*) who, like Pufendorf himself, are interested in 'hanc disciplinam stabilire'.[87] In short, Pufendorf's project appears in part as an attempt – through Weigelian moral mathematics – to salvage Jesuit casuistry!

One way in which he went about this was by adopting the Lipsian method of *exempla*, i.e., the use of contrastive examples (as in ancient 'parallel lives') to expose the difficulty of coming to terms with concrete decisions pulling in different directions. We find such an approach in many of the post-EJU dissertations, which abandon the former work's rigid mathematical form and methodologically anticipate the more discursive DJN. The new method (on display in DLS) did not reject the idea of morality as a rigorous science (as the Boineburg letters show) but redefined or refined it. Indeed, it remained 'mathematical' or calculative in a way, involving the use of 'hypotheses' *qua* well-founded principles that not only rested on but in turn deductively explained or guided observation and experience (in the case of human affairs: history, current events and particular examples or problematic 'cases'). Specifically, the study of *exempla* facilitated casuistry in two different senses: 1) by mediating between abstract principles and particulars – its traditional, systematising role; and 2) by articulating the conflicting and sometimes incommensurable demands of practice, which it had nonetheless to balance, bind and satisfy (i.e., justify) to the extent possible.[88]

In the latter form, casuistry or moral mathematics imposes moral entities, calculates quantities, fixes latitudes, and the like, thereby determining the value of persons, things and actions in relation to one another. As a concrete, (narrowly or widely) contextual activity occurring at different levels of association, it has a decisional (voluntaristic) aspect, albeit one guided by general, better established, and thus *de facto* less debatable principles. That is, as in the physical sciences, things are not all equally up for grabs, certainly not at the same time.[89] Also, as is to be expected, there are degrees of 'necessity', certitude or persuasiveness, as it were, made explicit whenever casuistry was termed 'probabilism'. As such, the approach was fiercely contested in the seventeenth century by those still committed to the certainty of scholastic syllogistic. However – and this is the point – it was not incompatible with Pufendorf's notion of a well-founded moral science. For what the latter mainly opposed in probabilism (like Pascal – whom Pufendorf quotes approvingly in this respect) was its appeal to authority (either of numbers or of individuals: i.e., *multior pars* and *sanior pars* alike),[90] and not (in this Pufendorf and Pascal differed) the recognition that moral matters may often not be sufficiently calculable or ultimately (finally) decideable.

Casuistry or probabilism in this sense differs from two other varieties: unconscious inference shaped by experience, as in Humean induction, and abstract mathematical reasoning as in statistics. In contrast to both of them, it involves ordinary reasoning about probabilities as in courts of law, scientific academies and laboratories, and at racetracks. The approach maps partially onto yet another distinction: between 'factual or stochastic or aleatory probability', which considers random sequences (as in dice or coin tossing, i.e. chance events); and 'logical or epistemic probability, or nondeductive logic', where propositions only partially support or confirm one another.[91] Both of these acknowledge or construct (in the sense of 'impose') contingency, and attempt predictively to control it. Both, moreover, thereby secularise it in different ways: the former by articulating laws about risk apart from (presumed) divine intervention, and the latter by leaving to humans themselves the constant re/calculation of their moral duties *in situ*.[92]

Abbreviations

DAS   S. Pufendorf, *Dissertationes academicae selectiores* (Lund: Haberegger, 1675).

DLS   S. Pufendorf, *Dissertatio academica de legibus sumtuariis* (Lund: Haberegger, 1672); also contained in DAS (1675), 513–43.

DJN   S. Pufendorf, *De jure naturae et gentium libri octo, editio secunda, auctior multo, et emendatior* (Frankfurt am Main: Knoch, 1684; first ed. 1672). See GW 4.1 and 4.2.

DO   S. Pufendorf, *De officio hominis et civis juxta legem naturalem libri duo* (Lund: Haberegger, 1673). See GW 2.

EJU   S. Pufendorf, *Two Books of the Elements of Universal Jurisprudence*, ed. T. Behme, trans. W. A. Oldfather (Indianapolis: Liberty Fund, 2009).

GW 1   S. Pufendorf, *Briefwechsel*, ed. D. Döring, *Samuel Pufendorf. Gesammelte Werke*, ed. W. Schmidt-Biggemann, Vol. 1 (Berlin: Akademie Verlag, 1996).

GW 2   S. Pufendorf, *De officio hominis et civis libri duo*, ed. G. Hartung, *Samuel Pufendorf. Gesammelte Werke*, ed. W. Schmidt-Biggemann, Vol. 2 (Berlin: Akademie Verlag, 1997).

GW 3   S. Pufendorf, *Elementa jurisprudentiae universalis*, ed. T. Behme, *Samuel Pufendorf. Gesammelte Werke*, ed. W. Schmidt-Biggemann, Vol. 3 (Berlin: Akademie Verlag, 1999).

GW 4.1   S. Pufendorf, *De jure naturae et gentium. Erster Teil: Text (Liber primus – Liber quartus)*, ed. F. Böhling, *Samuel Pufendorf. Gesammelte Werke*, ed. W. Schmidt-Biggemann, Vol. 4.1 (Berlin: Akademie Verlag, 1998).

GW 4.2   S. Pufendorf, *De jure naturae et gentium. Zweiter Teil: Text (Liber quintus – Liber octavus)*, ed. F. Böhling, *Samuel Pufendorf. Gesammelte Werke*, ed. W. Schmidt-Biggemann, Vol. 4.2 (Berlin: Akademie Verlag, 1998).

GW 5   S. Pufendorf, *Eris Scandica und andere polemische Schriften über das Naturrecht*, ed. F. Palladini, *Samuel Pufendorf. Gesammelte Werke*, ed. W. Schmidt-Biggemann, Vol. 5 (Berlin: Akademie Verlag, 2002).

Notes

1. J. T. Young, 'Law and Economics in the Protestant Natural Law Tradition: Samuel Pufendorf, Francis Hutcheson, and Adam Smith', *Journal of the History of Economic Thought*, 30:3 (2008), 283–4; J. T. Young and B. T. Gordon, 'Economic Justice in the Natural Law Tradition: Thomas Aquinas to Francis Hutcheson', *Journal of the History of Economic Thought*, 14:1 (1992), 1–17. Both articles cite additional literature.
2. Young, 'Law and Economics', 286.
3. W. Gaertner, 'De jure naturae et gentium: Samuel von Pufendorf's Contribution to Social Choice Theory and Economics', *Social Choice and Welfare*, 25:2–3 (2005), 239, 232, 238.
4. D. Brühlmeier, 'Natural Law and Early Economic Thought in Barbeyrac, Burlamaqui, and Vattel', in *Essays on the Political Thought of the Huguenots of the Refuge*, ed. J. C. Laursen (Dordrecht: Brill, 1995), 56.
5. Ibid., 59. Through Barbeyrac, Pufendorf's economic thought also influenced Burlamaqui and Vattel – in the same way, I would suggest, that it influenced his own natural law reasoning.
6. Ibid., 57, n. 13; DO I.9.2, in S. Pufendorf, *Les devoirs de l'homme et du citoyen*, 2 vols, trans. J. Barbeyrac (Caen: Centre de philosophie politique et juridique, Université de Caen, 1989), 236, 238. The term 'commerce' occurs repeatedly in different combinations, including 'commerce aves ses semblables' (I.3.3, 93) and 'commerce d'offices' (I.6.2, 195). Pufendorf's Latin, at GW 2, 38, reads: 'mutua inter homines officia, qui fructus est socialitatis'.
7. See R. Tuck, *Free Riding* (Cambridge, MA: Harvard University Press, 2008), 164ff., on Whewell's (et al.) critique of 'mathematical economics' for its 'neglect or perversion of facts, and . . . [its] trifling speculations, barren distinctions, and useless logomachies' – in short, its failure to calculate or take account of the larger social matrix in which it is embedded. Indeed, the upshot of Tuck's book is that the unsociable decision- or game-theoretical problem of 'free riding' seems insoluble precisely because of such narrowing of focus.
8. See R. Wokler, 'Rousseau's Pufendorf: Natural Law and the Foundations of Commercial Society', *History of Political Thought*, 15:3 (1994), 373–402; E. Hundert, 'Mandeville, Rousseau and the Political Economy of Fantasy', in *Luxury in the Eighteenth Century: Debates, Desires and Delectable Goods*, ed. M. Berg and E. Eger (New York: Palgrave Macmillan, 2003), 28–40; and G. Silvestrini, 'Rousseau, Pufendorf and the Eighteenth-Century Natural Law Tradition', *History of European Ideas*, 36:3 (2010), 280–301.
9. References are to J.-J. Rousseau, *The Social Contract and other later political writings*, ed. and trans. V. Gourevitch (New York: Cambridge University Press, 1997).
10. Rousseau, *Third Discourse*, §§24–5, 12–13; §§37–8, 21–2, §§74–6, 35–7; and *Social Contract* IV.8 (civil religion).

11. This term refers not to Pufendorf's anti-metaphysical approach but to his seamless application of natural law across different levels and types of action, individual as well as collective, in the private as well as the public sphere. His was not a serial 'ethics first' position that begins by building an ideal moral theory for individual persons, then extending this outward (more or less adequately) into the public or political domain. Rather, because of his social or interpersonal understanding of morality, the ethical and the politi- cal are connected from the start. See R. Geuss, *Philosophy and Real Politics* (Princeton: Princeton University Press, 2008), 6–11.

12. See K. Haakonssen, 'The Moral Conservatism of Natural Rights', in *Natural Law and Civil Sovereignty: Moral Rights and State Authority in Early Modern Political Thought*, ed. I. Hunter and D. Saunders (New York: Palgrave Mac- millan, 2002), 27–42; 'Protestant Natural Law Theory: A General Interpre- tation', in *New Essays on the History of Autonomy. A Collection Honoring J. B. Schneewind*, ed. N. Brender and L. Krasnoff (Cambridge and New York: Cambridge University Press, 2004), 92–109; 'Natural Law and Personhood: Samuel Pufendorf on Social Explanation' (2010), at http://cadmus.eui.eu/ handle/1814/14934.

13. Quotations from EJU, DJN and DO begin with the Oldfather versions, but are typically revised and always compared with and adjusted to the Latin text. (See the Abbreviations at the end.) Unattributed translations are my own. In the text above, note that moral imposition is collective rather than individual.

14. *Digest* I.5.1. See EJU I.D2.2, 25 [GW 3, 9], and Behme's note 3.

15. In his 1663 letter to Boineburg, at GW 1, §16, 26, Pufendorf says that 'many laws which we regard as having been derived from nature [*tanquam per naturam traditae*] are not so absolutely necessary for human society'.

16. S. Cremaschi, 'Two Views of Natural Law and the Shaping of Economic Science', *Croatian Journal of Philosophy*, 2:5 (2002), 181–96, esp. 187, notes the shift from classic categorial (noun/adjective) analysis to more fluid (mathematicised) Galilean descriptions of observed lawlike behaviors. See L. Daston and M. Stolleis, eds, *Natural Law and Laws of Nature in Early Modern Europe: Jurisprudence, Theology, Moral and Natural Philosophy* (Burlington, Ashgate, 2008), on the meanings of 'natural law' in early modern physical and social sciences. Also see the Epilogue to this chapter for Weigel's influence on Pufendorf's categories.

17. On this relationship, which should not be unnecessarily or anachronistically problematised, see P. Kitcher, *The Ethical Project* (Cambridge, MA: Harvard University Press, 2011), 253–82; and L. Daston, 'The Naturalistic Fallacy Is Modern', *Isis* 105:3 (2014), 579–87.

18. See S. Pufendorf, *Samuel Pufendorf's 'On the Natural State of Men'. The 1678 Latin Edition and English Translation*, ed. and trans. M. J. Seidler (Lewiston: Edwin Mellen, 1990), 26–42. For different conceptions of the 'natural state' in Pufendorf, see M. Seidler, 'Pufendorf's Moral and Political Philosophy',

Stanford Encyclopedia of Philosophy (2015), section 3.3, at http://plato.stan-ford.edu/archives/fall2010/entries/pufendorf-moral.

19. On an analysis of such states as intellectual 'deportment', 'grooming' or the fashioning of an intellectual persona, see I. Hunter, *Rival Enlightenments: Civil and Metaphysical Philosophy in Early Modern Germany* (Cambridge: Cambridge University Press, 2001), 1–29 and 364–76; 'Arguments over Obligation: Teaching Time and Place in Moral Philosophy', in *Teaching New Histories of Philosophy*, ed. J. B. Schneewind (Princeton: Princeton University Center for Human Values, 2004), 131–68; 'Hayden White's Philosophical History', *New Literary History*, 45:3 (2014), 331–58.

20. In the case of states, Pufendorf stresses the importance of studying not only the ideal or regular versions, but also the irregular or monstrous types, of which there are many. See *De republica irregulari* §1, at DAS, 381–2; DJN VII.5.2, and VII.5.14–15; also M. J. Seidler, '"Monstrous" Pufendorf: Sovereignty and System in the *Dissertations*', in *Monarchism and Absolutism in Early Modern Europe*, ed. C. Cuttica and G. Burgess (London: Pickering & Chatto, 2011), 159–75.

21. The unity is always relative and sometimes involves makeshift solutions. See Seidler, '"Monstrous" Pufendorf'.

22. For the last example, see S. Pufendorf, *An Introduction to the Principal Kingdoms and States of Europe*, ed. M. J. Seidler (Indianapolis: Liberty Fund, 2013), ch. 12, 500.

23. EJU I.Df.18 and Appendix. On Weigel's influence, see the Epilogue to this chapter.

24. The idea is similar to Kant's admission (at *Groundwork*, start of section II) that it is impossible for one to know (empirically) whether he or she has a 'good will', and whether their actions have 'moral worth'. Pufendorf acknowledges the point but makes nothing of it, moving on instead to more manageable moral calculations.

25. Note the conjunctions: *aut* expresses a strict opposition while *vel* adds a (consequentialist) articulation; i.e., Pufendorf is not asserting the in-seity of moral qualities but – as the DJN passage makes clear – challenging (by means of Horatian ridicule) Stoic claims about the equivalence of evils.

26. This is partly because people are not equally affected by the same punishments, nor equally deterred, and it is important to consider 'the condition of the individual [*personae*]' (DJN VIII.3.25: GW 4.2, 79).

27. In ethics as well as in politics, Pufendorf is averse to mixture and attentive to the qualitative impact of particular details.

28. See the end of the Conclusion to this chapter.

29. Here Pufendorf notes, as well, the distinction of real from imaginary goods, and the fact that goods and evils are often mixed together.

30. DJN VIII.3.7: e.g., acting socially (morally) in conditions where others do not (as in a pre-civil state of nature). Pufendorf tends generally to reason in a sort of 'tit-for-tat' manner, like the winning strategy in Axelrod's Prisoner's

Dilemma tournament. See R. Axelrod, *The Evolution of Cooperation* (New York: Basic Books, 1984).

31. For examples, see DJN VII.1.10, I.4.4, I.6.10, I.6.18, II.3.5, II.3.10–11, II.4.13; and Preface to Pufendorf, *An Introduction to the Principal Kingdoms and States of Europe*.

32. DJN II.3.16, II.5.3, VII.3.2, VIII.3.6, VIII.4.32.

33. Pufendorf also distinguishes here between needs and wants. On this problematic distinction, see R. Geuss, 'Economies: Good, Bad, Indifferent', *Inquiry*, 55:4 (2012), 331–60.

34. The second (1684) edition of DJN, at GW 4.1, 110, adds to this: 'superstition, concern for the future, [and] curiosity'.

35. Pufendorf also points out here, by reference to *Leviathan* I.11, that the human desire to outdo one another is exacerbated by a sort of escalator effect: one can never rest content at any point since others will raise the bar. Moreover, what might be seen as a mere 'leaky bucket' (i.e., quantity) problem in regard to goods is made worse by the fact that these are desired not only for their own sake but also for their role in emulating and outdoing others – which gives a somewhat different meaning to the idea of compulsory consumption. See on this Thorstein Veblen, 'Conspicuous Consumption', in *The Theory of the Leisure Class: An Economic Study of Institutions* (New York: Macmillan, 1899), ch. 4, 68–101.

36. As in the case of individuals, members of regular confederations or state systems typically demand (and sometimes receive) equal treatment and esteem, despite the significant differences that actually obtain; otherwise such cooperative schemes will not work, which is to everyone's detriment. See *De systematibus civitatum* §19, DAS, 320, and DJN VIII.4.15 ff., on various arrangements regarding equal and unequal intensive esteem among states.

37. DJN IV.4.2, and VIII.4.2. See Haakonssen, 'Natural Law and Personhood', esp. 7–8.

38. DJN I.7.13, II.2.3, III.4.2–3, and IV.4.5. See R. Geuss, *Public Goods, Private Goods* (Princeton: Princeton University Press, 2001), 131–52, on the difficulties facing rights language in general; and Haakonssen, 'The Moral Conservatism of Natural Rights', on why Pufendorf should not be read as a 'rights' theorist.

39. Humans resent being treated unequally (according to their own calculations) and such resentment undermines social living. See Haakonssen, 'Natural Law and Personhood', 6 and 9.

40. DJN III.2.2. See above, esp. the section 'Calculating Moral Quantities'.

41. VIII.4.3: GW 4.2, 803: Everyone has simple esteem 'so long as he does not destroy it through [his own] wickedness'; that is, so long as he remains capable of social interaction and of somehow benefiting others. Even though it is available to anyone and constitutes the necessary starting point for human relations, in practice it has degrees and may be whole, impaired or lost. By saying that every man is the enemy of every other, Hobbes limits himself to

the third possibility – a view that Pufendorf regards as a simplistic overstatement. Also, simple esteem may be regained by making reparations or showing a change of heart; it is not simply an intrinsic given over which humans have no control. These qualifications clearly distinguish Pufendorf's notion of dignity from views that attribute an intrinsic, inalienable quality to all humans no matter what.

42. See note 18 above.

43. The control of commerce is both limited and indirect; and, interestingly, it may be compared with the sovereign's control over religion. A concrete study of this complex process is provided by F. Palladini, *Die Berliner Hugenotten und der Fall Barbeyracs. Orthodoxie und 'Sozinianer' im Refuge (1685–1720)* (Boston: Brill, 2011), who examines the detailed workings of the Huguenot Refuge in Brandenburg at the end of the seventeenth century.

44. Similarly, DJN VIII.4.9: sovereigns cannot deprive citizens of simple natural esteem unless . . ., since such a power does not preserve or improve the state, and was thus 'not understood' to be part of the social pact.

45. On this notion, and the importance of economics to early modern statecraft, see M. Stolleis, *Pecunia Nervus Rerum. Zur Staatsfinanzierung in der frühen Neuzeit* (Frankfurt am Main: Vittorio Klostermann, 1983).

46. DJN VII.1.6: it is cities that relieve human want and generate luxury. This creates (security) problems that eventually require the formation of states (sovereignty). See N. Bulst, 'Zum Problem städtischer und territorialer Kleider-, Aufwands- und Luxusgesetzgebung in Deutschland (13. – Mitte 16. Jahrhundert)', in *Renaissance du pouvoir legislatif et genese de l'etat*, ed. A. Gouron and A. Rigaudiere (Montpellier: Socapress, 1988), 29–57, and A. Hunt, *Governance of the Consuming Passions: A History of Sumptuary Law* (New York: St. Martin's Press, 1996), on the growth of sumptuary laws in late medieval and early modern cities.

47. DAS (1675) was (re)published in Pufendorf (1675), 513–43. On early modern dissertations and their ongoing links to oral disputation, see K. Chang, 'From Oral Disputation to Written Text: The Transformation of the Dissertation in Early Modern Europe', *History of Universities*, 19:4 (2004), 129–87, and H. Marti, 'Von der Präses- zur Respondentendissertation. Die Autorschaftsfrage am Beispiel einer frühneuzeitlichen Literaturgattung', *Examen, Titel, Promotionen. Akademisches und staatliches Qualifikationswesen vom 13. bis zum 21. Jahrhundert*, ed. R. C. Schwinges (Basel: Schwabe Verlag, 2007), 251–74. In many cases, dissertations were claimed by both *praeses* and *respondens*, partly because even student-authored works were still tightly controlled by the professors.

48. On the other hand, parts of the dissertation are sophisticated enough to suggest more than student work; thus, the use of ancient sources is adept and well integrated into the discussion. It is interesting, too, that Pufendorf's friend at Leipzig, Adam Rechenberg, was *praeses* for a dissertation defended there (by Johann Friedrich von Bisenroth) in the same year: *Lex sumtuaria:*

discursu politico-historico declarata (Leipzig: Wittigau, 1672). Rechenberg's work pays closer attention to Roman sumptuary legislation (§3), describes luxury as a problem in contemporary Germany (§4), identifies France as a corrupting influence (§5), and mentions merchants as promoters of consumption (§6). As in Pufendorf, sumptuary laws are deemed necessary and appropriate to protect the state.

49. Obrecht, Besold, Conring and others had written on public finances before Pufendorf. See Stolleis, *Pecunia Nervus Rerum*, 81–96.

50. Germany had the most sumptuary legislation in Europe and was the last country to turn against it; we still find discussions of the question towards the end of the eighteenth century. See D. Klippel, 'Luxus und bürgerliche Gesellschaft. Samuel Simon Wittes Schrift "Über die Schicklichkeit der Aufwandsgesetze" (1782)', in *Staat, Kirche, Wissenschaft in einer pluralistischen Gesellschaft. Festschrift zum 65. Geburtstag von Paul Mikat*, ed. D. Schwab, D. Giesen, J. Listl and H.-W. Strätz (Berlin: Duncker & Humblot, 1989), 327–34, and M. G. Muzzarelli, 'Reconciling the Privilege of a Few with the Common Good: Sumptuary Laws in Medieval and Early Modern Europe', *Journal of Medieval and Early Modern Studies*, 39:3 (2009), 597–617. There was debate outside of Germany as well, stoked especially by Mandeville. See Hundert, 'Mandeville, Rousseau and the Political Economy of Fantasy'; I. Hont, 'The Early Enlightenment Debate on Commerce and Luxury', in *The Cambridge History of Eighteenth-Century Political Thought*, ed. M. Goldie and R. Wokler (New York: Cambridge University Press, 2006), 379–418; B. P. Turner, 'Mandeville Against Luxury', *Political Theory*, 44.1 (2015), published online 18 May 2015; and L. Broussois. 'Francis Hutcheson on Luxury and Intemperance: The Mandeville Threat', *History of European Ideas*, 14 (2015), published online 1 October 2015.

51. For instance: M. Prinz, ed., *Der lange Web in den Überflluss. Anfänge und Entwicklung der Konsumgesell-schaft seit der Vormoderne* (Paderborn: Ferdinand Schöningh, 2003); U. Wyrwa, 'Luxus und Konsum – begriffgeschichtliche Aspekte', in *'Luxus und Konsum' – eine historische Annäherung*, ed. R. Reith and T. Meyer (New York: Waxmann, 2003), 47–60; J. Jennings, 'The Debate about Luxury in 18th- and 19th-century French Political Thought', *Journal of the History of Ideas*, 68:1 (2007), 79–105; F. Trentmann, ed., *The Oxford Handbook of the History of Consumption* (New York: Oxford University Press, 2012); and K. Sennefelt, 'A Discerning Eye: Visual Culture and Social Distinction in Early Modern Stockholm', *Cultural and Social History*, 12:2 (2015), 179–95. Some studies, like U. Rublack's *Dressing Up: Cultural Identity in Renaissance Europe* (New York: Oxford University Press, 2010), emphasise the positive role played by consumption in the development of early modern societies.

52. Tacitus, *Annales* III.52; Tertullian, *De habitu muliebri*, ch. 2. On Roman sumptuary laws more generally, which often served as models for European counterparts, see D. P. Miles, *Forbidden Pleasures: Sumptuary Laws and the Ideology of Moral Decline in Ancient Rome*, PhD dissertation, University of

London, 1987; V. J. Rosivach, 'The *Lex Fannia Sumptuaria* of 161 BC', *The Classical Journal*, 102:1 (2006), 1–15; V. Arena, 'Roman Sumptuary Legislation: Three Concepts of Liberty', *European Journal of Political Theory*, 10:4 (2011), 463–89; and E. Zanda, *Fighting Hydra-like Luxury: Sumptuary Regulation in the Roman Republic* (London: Bristol Classical Press, 2011).

53. Here Pufendorf quotes a passage from Plutarch's *De vitando aere alieno* 7 (830D–E) comparing money lenders to Centaurs and Gorgons.

54. See DJN III.3.11, on the export of horses.

55. Versions of the Latin expression (*pecuniam esse nervum rerum gerendarum*) go back to antiquity, including Diogenes Laertius IV.48 (life of Bion); and Cicero, *De imperio Cn. Pompei* 7, and *Phil.* 5.2.

56. Plutarch, *Romanorum apophthegmata* ('Sayings of the Romans', section on Titus Quintius), 197D.

57. *Iliad* VI.241–5: the Lycian Glaucus, fighting for the Trojans, exchanged his golden armour for the bronze armour of the Greek Diomedes.

58. Val. Max., *Facta et Dicta Memorabilia* V.2.8 (*De censoria nota*).

59. Tac., *An.* III.53.

60. For examples of actual sumptuary legislation, see Stolleis, *Pecunia Nervus Rerum*; Rublack, *Dressing Up*; and Bulst, 'Zum Problem städtischer'.

61. The idea of using human vices against themselves, for opposite effect, is similar to 'unsocial sociability', except that it is a conscious strategy here and not an unintended process.

62. Pufendorf recommends a *sobria elegantia* (§19, 536) modeled by the sovereign. The term *arbiter elegantiae* is used by Tacitus (*An.* XVI.18) to describe Gaius Petronius, who served Nero in that capacity.

63. It is interesting to note here how the valuation of persons can affect the valuation of things – the inverse of Pufendorf's observation about the pursuit of luxury as a comparative, positional good. Influence goes in both directions as a so-called 'economy of esteem' interacts with the ordinary economy of (material) goods and services. The terminology derives from G. Brennan and P. Pettit, *The Economy of Esteem: An Essay on Civil and Political Society* (Oxford: Oxford University Press, 2004).

64. On the way that concepts and distinctions function at different levels in Pufendorf, see Seidler, '"Monstrous" Pufendorf'.

65. C. R. Sunstein, 'Incompletely Theorized Agreements', *Harvard Law Review*, 108:7 (1995), 1733–72.

66. Geuss, 'Economies: Good, Bad, Indifferent'.

67. They include: 'listen to reason' (*rationes audire*), 'cannot possibly' (*sane nequit*), 'depraved judgement' (*prava judicio*), 'it is idle to maintain' (*frustra jactatur*), 'cannot possibly be presumed' (*hautquaquam praesumi potest*), 'the force of necessity' (*vim necessitatis*), and rhetorical appeals like 'surely everyone realises' (*quis est, qui ignoret*) and 'who will deny' (*quis negabit*).

68. A special thanks to John Robertson, whose comments at the conference where this paper was first presented induced me to reflect more explicitly on the connections with casuistry and probabilism as such.

69. See L. S. Temkin, *Rethinking the Good: Moral Ideals and the Nature of Practical Reasoning* (New York: Oxford University Press, 2012), who speaks of 'aggregation' problems, 'impossibility' arguments and 'nontransitivity' – i.e., (logical) incoherence or incommensurability among different moral judgements.

70. J. Barnes, *The Sense of an Ending* (London: Vintage Books, 2011), 85–6.

71. Rousseau, *The Social Contract and other later political writings*, 85. This passage differs from that cited by R. Douglass (*Rousseau and Hobbes: Nature, Free Will, and the Passions* [Oxford: Oxford University Press, 2015], 139, and n.165), who associates Rousseau with Leibnizian calculation of 'eternal truths in accordance with certain rules of equality and proportion', and notes the former's statement (in *Lettre à Voltaire*, OC4: 1064–65 / CW3 = 112) that 'nature is subject to the precision of quantities and of forms'.

72. See Johannes Vermeer, *Woman Holding a Balance* (ca. 1662–5), at http://www.essentialvermeer.com/catalogue/woman_holding_a_balance.html#.VgRrKMtViko.

73. Cf. R. Campe, *The Game of Probability: Literature and Calculation from Pascal to Kleist* (Stanford: Stanford University Press, 2012), 107, about Arnauld: '"In order to decide the truth about an event and to determine whether or not to believe in it, we must not consider it nakedly and in itself," without its relation to other events. In pure isolation, Arnauld argues, we can determine the truth only in the case of things mathematical and metaphysical. In order to grasp the truth of a singular event, "we must pay attention to all the accompanying circumstances, both internal and external." This clearly brings the topoi into relevance: when we wish to achieve the effect of a true argument in the case of singular events, we cannot proceed by pure syllogistic reasoning, but must complement and fill the event in with additions that are linked by topical relations to the respective matters at hand. In the rhetorical and dialectical tradition, such supplements required for a logic of events would be called topoi, or, more specifically, the circumstances of an event (*circumstantiae*). *Circumstantiae*, the topoi of narration, make up the core of the production of a probability of events in Arnauld. From this inconspicuous moment on, the interpretation of gaming theory as probability theory is intimately related to the history of modern narration.' Campe (31–2) also notes that Pufendorf seems to make unacknowledged use of Arnauld's (and Nicole's) *Port Royal Logic* (1662) in his discussion of contracts involving chance (DJN V.9.5), and that chance is understood there as a construct consisting of certain 'framing conditions'. Indeed, one can view contract theory in general as a kind of contextual wagering. Note, too, the similarity of Arnauld's *topoi* and *circumstantiae* to Lipsius's *exempla* (below).

74. Hobbes, *De corpore*, I.1.2: 'By reasoning, I mean computation. Now to compute is either to collect the sum of many things that are added together, or to know what remains when one thing is taken away from another. Reasoning is therefore the same as adding and subtracting.' T. Hobbes, *Elementorum Philosophiae Sectio Prima De corpore* (London, 1655).

75. *Specimen controversiarum* IV.1.6, in GW 5, 126.

76. 'Unvorgreifflich Bedencken über der Deputierten requeste', in S. Pufendorf, *Kleine Vorträge und Schriften. Texte zur Geschichte, Pädagogik, Philosophie, Kirche und Völkerrecht*, ed. D. Döring (Frankfurt am Main: Vittorio Klostermann, 1995), 439. Also see *Commentatio*, GW 5, 271.

77. D. Döring, in *Pufendorf-Studien. Beiträge zur Biographie Samuel von Pufendorfs und zu seiner Entwicklung als Historiker und theologischer Schriftsteller* (Berlin: Duncker & Humblot, 1992), 44, notes that there is no evidence for the claim that it was Weigel, specifically, who introduced Pufendorf to Hobbes and Descartes.

78. E. Weigel, *Arithmetische Beschreibung der Moral-Weißheit von Personen und Sachen* (Stuttgart-Bad Canstatt: Fromman-Holzboog, 2004).

79. GW 1, §8, 17 April 1659, 14. Also see DJN I.2.3, I.8.1, and the start of the 'Calculating Moral Quantities' section above.

80. See Behme's editorial introduction to Weigel, *Arithmetische Beschreibung*, vii–xxvii, which quotes and summarises many of the key passages.

81. Weigel, *Arithmetische Beschreibung*, v–vi.

82. See Barbeyrac at note 6 above, and note 63 on the idea of an 'economy of esteem'.

83. W. Röd, *Geometrischer Geist und Naturrecht. Methodengeschichtliche Untersuchungen zur Staatsphilosophie im 17. und 18. Jahrhundert* (Munich: Bayerische Akademie der Wissenschaften, 1970), 10ff., and H. Denzer, *Moralphilosophie und Naturrecht bei Samuel Pufendorf: eine geistes- und wissenschaftsgeschichtliche Untersuchung* (Aalen: Scientia Verlag, 1972), 283, distinguish two senses of *mos geometricus* (or the mathematical ideal). The first (Weigel's) is a purely Euclidean approach that uses mathematics merely to clarify and exhibit shared structural relations; the second refers to the analytic-synthetic method of the natural sciences, which begin in experience and aim to establish defensible hypotheses that lead, in turn, back 'down' to (further) empirical conclusions which are deduced or derived therefrom. Pufendorf began with the first approach and moved quickly towards the second. This needs to be properly understood, however: Pufendorf's chosen method (the first Boineburg alternative – see hereafter) is actually the second *mos geometricus*.

84. GW 1, §§16–17, 24–32.

85. GW 1, §§16, 26; and DJN I.2.4. Also see Grotius, *De jure belli ac pacis* (1625), I.1.12.

86. On the hypothetical-deductive method, see – beside Röd and Denzer (n. 83) above – T. Behme, 'Die *Fictio contrarii* als methodisches Werkzeug in Pufendorfs Naturrechtslehre', in *Begriffe, Metaphern und Imaginationen in Philosophie und Wissenschaftsgeschichte*, ed. L. Danneberg, C. Spoerhase and D. Werle (Wiesbaden: Harrassowitz Verlag, 2009), 266–86, and especially Cremaschi, 'Two Views of Natural Law', 181–5. The latter notes that the new natural science was both empirical and scientifically certain, or reliable. It rejected essentialism, not deductive rigour. Of course, abandonment of the syllogistic (and in that sense 'analytic') deductions of the former left the merely 'synthetic' connections of the latter exposed to the charge of

being merely probable (as Hume would show), even if highly so. And this is what drove Kant to abandon empiricism once more through his so-called (and ironically, in a more basic sense, anti-) Copernican inversion.

87. GW 1, BW §16 (dated 13.1.1663), 25. On Jesuit casuistry in this period, see Stefania Tutino, *Uncertainty in Post-Reformation Catholicism. A History of Probabilism* (New York: Oxford University Press, 2018), which came too late to consider in this chapter.

88. M. Hörnqvist, 'Exempla, Prudence and Casuistry in Renaissance Political Discourse', in *(Un)masking the Realities of Power: Justus Lipsius and the Dynamics of Political Writing in Early Modern Europe*, ed. E. De Bom, M. Janssens, T. Van Houdt and J. Papy (Leiden: Brill, 2011), 25–41., esp. 37–40.

89. See Brühlmeier, 'Natural Law and Early Economic Thought', on Pufendorf's supposed rule-utilitarianism.

90. DJN I.3.5. On this distinction, see P. Urfalino, 'Deciding as Bringing Deliberation to a Close', *Social Science Information (Special Issue: Rules of Collective Decision)*, 49:1 (2010), 111–40, 132–3, and (in reference to Pufendorf) P. Pasquino, 'Samuel Pufendorf: Majority Rule (Logic, Justification and Limits) and Forms of Government', *Social Science Information*, 49:1 (2010), 99–109.

91. See J. Franklin, *The Science of Conjecture: Evidence and Probability Before Pascal* (Baltimore: Johns Hopkins University Press, 2001), esp. (for these distinctions) the Preface, ix–xiii.

92. See Palladini, *Die Berliner Hugenotten*, 401–6: Barbeyrac's last work in Berlin was *Traité du Jeu* (1709), a long treatise on gaming and chance that focused mainly on gambling problems in the Huguenot community there. Campe notes, however, that it also summarises the work of jurists on the theology of games of chance, including the theologically risky consideration of chance apart from divine intervention (*The Game of Probability*, 33–4). By thus turning mere happenstance, and divine intervention, into managed chance – a form of social construction also found in Pufendorf's treatment of pacts in general and economic contracts in particular – natural law contributed, says Campe (34), to 'the fabrication of serial contingency'.

11

The Legacy of Smith's Jurisprudence in Late Eighteenth-Century Edinburgh

John W. Cairns

Smith's failure to complete his intellectual ambitions by writing the 'sort of theory and History of Law and Government' that he promised has to some extent – one suspects – affected our understanding of the legacy of his jurisprudence.[1] The student notes of his *Lectures on Jurisprudence* allow us now to know what he thought, and to have an idea of what he intended to publish; but, until their rediscovery, the issue of the continuing influence of his jurisprudence understandably fell out of sight in the early nineteenth century and was largely ignored.[2] Recently, despite recovery of the *Lectures*, Charles Griswold has claimed that the reason Smith did not write his account of jurisprudence was because he simply could not, as he was attempting an intellectual impossibility. As Griswold put it: 'How can history yield general normative principles that are always the same?'[3] Haakonssen and Donald Winch, however, have commented that Griswold's criticism is applicable only if one is 'looking for universality in some absolute sense'.[4] Indeed, study of Smith's *Lectures* has made scholars aware that his historical and critical jurisprudence was cogently elaborated and expounded by his pupil John Millar, Regius Professor of Civil Law in Glasgow. And Millar was the most influential law teacher in the British Isles in the later eighteenth century.[5]

Smith's influence on Millar is clear and generally acknowledged; but what has not yet been properly investigated is the significant influence his jurisprudence exerted through the Law School in Edinburgh, where the teaching of the professors was to create a legacy that had two main offshoots, one in history, the other in law. Both of these were rooted in the type of historical analysis associated with individuals such as William Robertson, David Hume and Edward Gibbon.[6]

History, of course, provided one of the key means of understanding man and society and the development of civil society in the Scottish Enlightenment. Some history writing in this era still echoed older humanist concerns

with corruption, virtue and exemplary lives; some was detailed and anti-
quarian in its focus.[7] But what, rightly or wrongly, is generally considered
to be the mainstream or perhaps the most significant is the type of cosmopolitan writing that examined the great movements of history through
stages, focusing on material and social conditions.[8] Smith wrote no work
entitled a history; but he was very definitely a historian in this last sense, as
is evident not only from the *Wealth of Nations*, but also in particular from
his *Lectures on Jurisprudence* and those on *Rhetoric and Belles Lettres*.[9]

As part of a bigger project on the reform of legal education in Edinburgh in the second half of the eighteenth century, this chapter will examine the legacy of Smith in late-Enlightenment Edinburgh. What will here
be explored is an intellectual influence that resulted from institutional
and political developments in the University. At stake were four crucial
appointments to the chairs that were seen as constituting the Faculty of
Law; three of these were made in a very short period between 1779 and
1786, the other following slightly later in 1792. These appointments reori-
ented law teaching at Edinburgh, moving it from a humanist-inspired curriculum, which was seen as increasingly outdated, towards one founded
on an empirical and historically oriented attitude to law and government,
reflecting how Scots lawyers were increasingly coming to understand the
nature of their law. These were changes of tremendous importance. They
also point to the way in which we can understand how Enlightenment
thinking was perpetuated into the nineteenth century, while adapted and
transformed. There are implications for how we understand both nineteenth-century history writing and the evolution of the contemporary
approach to law and its teaching in Scotland.

The Faculties of Law in Edinburgh and Glasgow

The Scots bar, the Faculty of Advocates, followed policies on admission to
its ranks – and hence admission to practise at the bar of the Court – that
first privileged and then required a high level of competency in Roman
law (generally referred to in this period as the Civil Law, the *ius civile*).
It is unnecessary to explore the requirements in detail; but the Faculty
introduced examinations in Latin on Roman law that replicated standard
procedures for the award of a doctorate in law at a continental European
University.[10] One consequence of this – presumably an intended consequence – was to favour the admission of men who had studied law in a
university, where Civil Law was the main focus of scholarly work. By the
late seventeenth century, the universities of choice for Scots were those of
the Dutch Republic, where young men studied law in significant numbers

(though it is impossible to produce reliable statistics). The expense of such an education led to attempts to establish legal education in Scottish universities. This came early in the eighteenth century, first in Edinburgh, and then, in emulation, in Glasgow.[11]

The model followed for legal education in Scotland was that provided by the Dutch law schools, where, in the later seventeenth century, to courses on the *Digest* and *Institutes* of Justinian, were added ones on the laws of nature and nations (*ius naturale* and *ius gentium*) and on the *ius publicum*, as well as on the modern law (the *ius hodiernum*). Thus, the first chair in law in Edinburgh was that of Public Law and the Law of Nature and Nations, founded in 1707, quickly followed by that of Civil Law in 1710, which was the first active chair. In 1717 was established the Chair of Universal History (sometimes known as the Chair of Civil History), from which was also taught courses on antiquities aimed at law students, to be followed in 1722 by a chair in Scots law.[12] In Glasgow, a single chair in law – in Civil Law – was established late in 1712 and filled in 1713, the first professor offering classes in 1714.[13] By the middle years of the eighteenth century, it had been decided that the duties of the Glasgow chair were to teach a course on Justinian's *Institutes* (generally twice a year, which was also the practice in Edinburgh) and (once a year) one on Justinian's *Digest*.[14]

Given the significant interrelationship between the requirements of the Faculty of Advocates and the development of the Law Schools, it is important to note a number of developments that have a bearing here. In 1748, the newly appointed Lord President, Robert Dundas of Arniston, had recommended to the Faculty that those intending to join its membership should 'be careful to learn thoroughly the principles of the Roman Law and the Laws of Nature and Nations . . . and other Sciences and accomplishments becoming the Character of Gentlemen, [and] particularly not . . . neglect Academical learning, before they should apply themselves to study the municipal Laws of their Country'.[15] In 1750, the Faculty introduced a compulsory examination in Scots Law.[16] Six years later, the Faculty recommended that intending advocates (or intrants) should be examined by the Examinators in Civil Law on 'the History and Antiquities of the Roman Law', and decided that a copy of the Resolution should be sent to all the professors in Edinburgh so it could be intimated to the students, so they would attend the classes on 'Universal History and Roman Antiquities'.[17] On 8 January 1760, the Faculty, noting that 'regular Colleges upon the Law of Nature and Nations' were 'now given in the University of Edinburgh', recommended that prospective members should attend them, ordering that the resolution to this effect should be intimated to the students at the University.[18] In 1762, the Faculty established a small committee of the Dean and Council, the Senior Examinator in Civil Law and both Professors (of Universal History and Public law and the Law of Nature and Nations) to find a way to make these two recommendations effective.[19] The Faculty duly recommended that the Examinators in Scots Law and Civil Law should examine 'Candidates upon the Law of Nature & Nations in so far as it is connected with the Civil Law or with the law of this Country'. A copy of the Resolution was again to be sent to all the professors so they could intimate this to the students. This Resolution did not mention Universal History and Roman Antiquities, perhaps because the 1756 Resolution was thought still to be operative.[20] In 1768, the Faculty made a resolution to the same effect as regards the Class of Universal History and Greek and Roman Antiquities.[21]

It is possible that the aim of these Resolutions on the Law of Nature and Nations and Universal History and Antiquities was to boost the fee-income of the professors, who were all members of the Faculty of Advocates; but, if so, this does not diminish the nature and significance of their intended intellectual impact. The Resolutions certainly form part of the backdrop to John Millar's expansion of the curriculum at Glasgow during the 1760s.

Millar made two crucial, linked innovations. First, he turned one of the two courses on Justinian's *Institutes* into a course on Smithian Jurisprudence, while, by 1770, he had added new courses on Scots Law and Government, and eventually, in the 1790s, he introduced one on English law. Secondly, he structured the content of his courses to reflect his Smithian philosophy of law. Thus, he taught the Scots, Civil and English law according to an analysis of law into rights and actions. For Millar rights concerned persons and things. The rights of persons concerned husband and wife, parent and child, master and servant, and guardian and ward; those of things were split into real and personal. The former dealt with property, servitude and exclusive privilege; the latter with rights arising from contract, delinquency or crime. Millar's lectures on government covered: the origin and progress of government in society; illustrations from history of such origin and progress; and the contemporary government of Great Britain. Millar was probably also taking the opportunity to build up his classes in the face of contemporary deficiencies in law teaching in Edinburgh.[22] His new structure necessarily affected his use of textbooks, which became less important in shaping his classes.

This means that by the 1770s, both universities – at least in theory – had the capacity to teach jurisprudence, public law, history and Scots law, as well as Roman law.

The Professors of Law in Edinburgh

Millar moved to teaching Roman law entirely in English instead of in Latin, thereby drawing criticism from the Faculty of Advocates.[23] But, in general, members of the Faculty showed themselves rather more concerned with the teaching of law in the University of Edinburgh rather than in that of Glasgow. This no doubt reflected the fact that the Faculty had come to hold the patronage of three of the four chairs – Civil Law, Scots Law and Universal History – and could exert considerable influence over the royal appointments made to the fourth – Public Law and the Law of Nature and Nations. They therefore ensured that men who were members always held these chairs.[24] The Faculty's regulations on the education of intrants and the structure of its examinations were also geared to practice in Edinburgh.[25]

Both as an institution and as a collection of individuals, the Faculty of Advocates was deeply entrenched in the political system of patronage under which Scotland was governed after the union of 1707, and which helped assimilate the Scots into the new British state. Members of the Faculty were typically drawn from the prosperous mercantile and minor landed classes. They themselves competed for judicial and legal offices, such as Senator of the College of Justice, Commissioner of Justiciary, (after 1747) Sheriff Depute, and Baron of Exchequer, as well for clerkships of Session, all under the patronage of the Crown, and hence controlled by government ministers. They themselves were also patrons, and not just of the University's chairs in law. Those members who were landowners might hold the distinctly valuable bargaining chip of a vote in the Westminster elections, or be closely linked to those who did. They might also be related to powerful landowners and great noblemen or be able to influence them.[26] For example, Henry Dundas was close to Adam Smith's pupil, the Duke of Buccleuch, and was allowed to manage the Duke's political interest.[27]

It is tempting to see the making of appointments through this complex system of patronage as a classic example of what radicals, such as William Cobbett, were later to call 'Old Corruption'.[28] Of course, university chairs were lucrative offices, and politicians wished them to go to supporters and sought to use them for rewards and as inducements. This, however, does not mean that those who were appointed were not qualified. Modern research has suggested that we need to understand the system of patronage in a nuanced way. Roger Emerson has argued this particularly strongly for academic patronage.[29] If this was an eighteenth-century version of machine politics, the machine had a complex and responsive structure and operated in a sophisticated way. In the long run, it was not to the advantage of a patron to force an incompetent into a position in a university. To do so would be to squander his political capital.

For a variety of reasons, those who held the chairs of law in Edinburgh in the later 1760s and the 1770s were less successful in attracting classes than Millar in Glasgow, who was vigorously developing the curriculum drawing on Smith's theories of justice and government.[30] There were a number of factors at work. Not only may they have been uninspiring as teachers, but, in so far as they taught, and some of them did not, their teaching – at least from the perspective of the developing Scottish Enlightenment – was becoming increasingly old-fashioned, rooted in an approach derived from a late Dutch humanism.[31] Thus, in 1777, Lord Kames attacked the current teaching of Roman law in Scotland because of its emphasis on authority and neglect of reasoning; the only professor whose teaching he exempted from his criticism was Millar.[32] The criticism must therefore have been aimed at Edinburgh.

Between 1779 and 1786, three of the law chairs were filled with candidates in whose choice Henry Dundas played a major role; six years later, the fourth chair was filled with a candidate in whose appointment Dundas, at the very least, acquiesced.[33] Thus, in 1779, Allan Maconochie purchased the reversion of the Chair of Public Law and the Law of Nature and Nations from James Balfour of Pilrig. As a regius chair it was necessary to procure a royal warrant. This likely came through Dundas, then Lord Advocate as well as Dean of the Faculty of Advocates, and already well advanced on his rise to power.[34] A few months later, the Professor of Universal History, John Pringle, had Alexander Fraser Tytler joined with him in the chair. The aim being that, while Pringle lived, he would take the salary and Tytler the fees. Again, Dundas will have been involved in this appointment; Tytler was very clearly one of his protégés.[35] On the death of William Wallace, Professor of Scots Law, in late 1786, Dundas acted decisively to ensure that his candidate, David Hume, was appointed, even, though he was now no longer Dean, soliciting the votes of all members of the Faculty in Hume's favour.[36] Finally, in 1792, the aged Robert Dick, Professor of Civil Law, had John Wilde appointed jointly with him in the Chair, on the usual arrangement of Dick taking the salary and Wilde the fees, until the chair reverted entirely to the latter on Dick's death. Dundas was in Edinburgh during the later stages of the working of this appointment; no doubt he acquiesced in the choice of Wilde, whose appointment clearly owed much to Ilay Campbell of Succoth, the Lord President and friend of Dundas.[37]

Fewer than ten years later, Dundas wrote that he had 'too great an interest in the prosperity of this country to admit any consideration whatever to enter into my mind in recommending professors to any university except what is truly best for the education of our youth in the sound principles not only of science but also of the constitution'. He claimed that every professor appointed in Edinburgh and St Andrews for the past twenty years had been appointed either by himself or on his recommendation.[38] Even allowing for some exaggeration, this reinforces the assumption that Dundas played a major role in these four appointments. On the principle of know-ing them by their fruits, one may conclude that Dundas was concerned with the quality of legal education, and was deliberately choosing energetic men who could and would compete with John Millar in Glasgow, and hopefully exceed him. It can be no coincidence that the work of all these professors supported by Dundas was influenced by the legacy of Adam Smith, which they each perpetuated in new ways.

Jurisprudence, History and Government

The tenure of Maconochie and Tytler has been generally ignored. As regards the first, this is probably because Bower, in his *History of the University*, incorrectly stated that he only taught for two sessions.[39] Grant, in his account of the University, remarked that Maconochie did not suc-ceed 'in attracting a class'.[40] These opinions were reinforced and propa-gated by the *Report* of 1830 of the Royal Commissions of 1826 and 1830 that investigated the Scottish universities, which Francis Jeffrey, in typi-cally robust style, had informed that the chair had 'proved in practice a complete failure'.[41] Grant wrote:

> In fact, the Class of Public Law, etc., seems to have held a position similar to that of Civil History. It was regarded as a *dilettante* class . . . [T]he Chair was held by a succession of Advocates who were engaged in successfully pushing their way to the Scottish Bench, and who naturally treated their Academical position and duties as of minor importance. It is no wonder, then, that the Class was a failure.[42]

But this is incorrect.[43] It is also doubtful if either professor would have appreciated their classes being described as '*dilettante*'.

Maconochie's classes were advertised continuously through to his resignation of the chair in 1796.[44] In addition to an entry in the general annual advertisement of classes entered in newspapers by the University, he sometimes inserted a special advertisement of his own.[45] His classes initially began in the winter session sometime after 20 November, like the rest of those in law;[46] but in 1786, he advertised lectures beginning on 10 March in which the 'Course will treat of the Origin of Government – Of the Rise and Characters of the different Forms it has assumed – and, par-ticularly, of the Modern European Governments, the Revolutions which they have undergone, and the various causes to which they owe their pres-ent Form'.[47] Thereafter he seems always to have taught in the summer rather than the winter session.[48]

Within a year of Maconochie's admission as Professor, his friend Alexander Fraser Tytler took up his office as Professor of Civil History and Greek and Roman Antiquities. He advertised his classes as beginning in November 1781;[49] and, virtually without exception, each year thereafter they can be found advertised in the newspapers until he became seriously ill in November 1795, so that no classes were advertised as starting that month.[50] By November 1796, he had recovered sufficiently to resume teaching, once more advertising his classes.[51] He taught thereafter until his resignation from the chair in 1801.[52] The only course he ever advertised was that on Universal History.

It may be that Maconochie started to teach in the summer session to make it easier for students to attend both his and Tytler's classes in the same year. The two men obviously cooperated. In February 1781, they jointly petitioned the Lord Provost, Magistrates and Town Council as patrons of the University asking that a room in the University buildings be fitted up for their specific use. They had consulted James Craig, the architect, and had sent a plan and estimates to the College Bailie. They stressed that without their own classroom, they had to teach at inconvenient times, discouraging for students; they also wanted their own classroom because of the need they both had to use maps in their teaching; these, both ancient and modern, had already been 'constructed and delineated for the illustration of their courses of lectures', and had, of necessity, to remain behind fixed in the classroom. They added that one room would suit them both, as their 'departments in science have a natural connection with each other, and require the same apparatus'. They proposed that the vacant room under the museum, formerly used as a printing house by Balfour and Neil, would be suitable.[53]

Two accounts of Maconochie's classes survive. This first, by Hugo Arnot, who discussed all the classes taught in the University, is as follows:

He traces the rise of political institutions from the natural characters and situation of the human species; follows their progress through the rude periods of society; and treats of their history and merits, as exhibited in the principal nations of ancient and modern times, which he examines separately, classing them according to those general causes to which he attributes the principal varieties in the forms, genius, and revolutions of governments. In this manner he endeavours to construct the science of the spirit of laws on a connected view of what may be called the natural history of man as a political agent; and he accordingly concludes his course with treating of the general principles of municipal law, political economy, and the law of nations.[54]

The second is by Henry Brougham, who had access to Maconochie's lecture notes. He outlined the content of the classes in some detail:

> They are arranged under two great divisions – the State of Nature, and the Political State. Under the first, by which is meant the earlier state, are treated, the savage state; the origin of political union; the first structure of government; language, and the origin of its grammatical structure; the agricultural and pastoral state; the rise of religion and mythology; women and their domestic relations in uncultivated society. The other principal branch begins with the gradual changes and transitions from the rude to the polished state. It then treats of the pastoral nations with movable habitations; the Nomadic tribes; the origin and nature of the Tartar and Arabic governments; the Nomadic conquests, and the governments thus formed – those of the Israelites, of Persia, of Hindostan [sic], of Turkey. He then treats of pastoral nations with fixed habitations. This leads to a consideration of the rise and progress of European society, the Celto-German governments, and the Gothic governments on the conquered provinces of the Roman Empire. Then comes the progress of government, where the ancient confederacies of pastoral nations have been dissolved. Under this head we have the governments of Greece, especially of Lacedæmon and Athens, and of Italy. Next we have the progress of government where those pastoral confederacies have been consolidated. Those that have been consolidated by the neighbourhood of Nomadic tribes, are Egypt, Assyria, China, Russia, all of which are fully treated. Those which have been consolidated by other causes, as form of the country, superstition, wants of cultivated nations, are Macedon, the monarchies of Western Asia, Thibet [sic], India. The head follows of nations not fully within any of the foregoing descriptions – and, first, nations that have never been pastoral, yet have made progress in civilisation; Mexico, Peru, Japan, and all nations that have made no such progress, and yet have formed a political union; the African tribes, those nations which have acquired knowledge of property, with little or no political union; the Laplanders and Siberians. Next comes a general view of the revolutions in political society; and out of this arises a treatise on the principles of the different forms of government. We are thus, by slow degrees, but from a most comprehensive view of the world and its history, led to the origin, predominancy, and decline of the feudal institution; and then comes the present state of the European governments.[55]

These accounts chime with the accessible surviving, if somewhat scrappy, manuscript notes of the lectures.[56] These types of ideas are also clearly reflected in Maconochie's 'Essay on the Origin and Structure of the European Legislators', which he delivered before the Royal Society of Edinburgh on 15 December 1783 and 19 July 1784.[57] The latter may have arisen out of his classes; but the same type of historical approach can even be identified in the introduction to the theses he prepared for admission as an advocate. He was allocated the title D. 37.14, *De iure patronatus*, which concerned the rights of one who has freed a slave. He reflected on the reasons for the rise of slavery and its place in the law of nature and nations, and even discussed the significance of geography.[58]

If we turn now to consider Tytler's classes, we can once more quote a description by Arnot:

> This very useful branch of education, which teaches the knowledge of men and manners, had been for several years neglected in this University. . . . The present Professor, who has revived this necessary branch of education, considered the science of History in a more enlarged point of view [than earlier teachers], as the school both of politics and of morality. In the course of lectures, he describes the condition of society, and the progressive state of mankind from the earliest ages of which we have any authentic accounts, to the beginning of the present age. Departing from the order of a chronicle, which of necessity must present a confused and uninstructive picture, he delineates separately the origin of the different states and empires, the great outlines of their history, the revolutions which they have undergone, the causes which have contributed to their rise and grandeur, and operated to their decline and extinction. He bestows attention, particularly, on the manners of nations, their laws, the nature of their government, their religion, their intellectual improvements, and their progress in the arts and sciences; and he takes care to inculcate to his pupils those important lessons of morality which the pages of history furnish.[59]

In 1782, Tytler published a very detailed analytical breakdown of his lectures for the use of his students.[60] He followed this with *A Short Comparative View of Ancient and Modern Geography*, which was intended to supplement the analysis.[61] In 1801, the year he gave up teaching, he published an expanded, two-volume, version of his synopsis.[62] By 1818, it had reached a seventh edition. The eighth contained a continuation of the history in a third volume by Edward Nares.[63] This in turn went through many further editions in the United Kingdom. There were also several editions of both versions in North America. In 1834, his actual lectures were published in six volumes, edited by his son, William.[64] These again went through many editions both in the United Kingdom and North America. Comparison of these publications with each other, and with surviving student notes, confirms the general accuracy of Arnot's description of Tytler's class, though all deserve further study.

Tytler told his class that teaching by 'a series of disquisitions on the various heads or titles of public law, and the doctrines of politics, illustrated by examples drawn from ancient and modern history', was insufficient. This was because 'for the most important purposes of history, the tracing events to their causes, the detection of the springs of human action, the display of the progress of society, and the rise and fall of states and empires' was necessary. Moreover, 'by confining history to the exemplification of the doctrines of politics, we lose its effect as a school of morals'.[65] Indeed, he stressed that '[t]he value of any science is to be estimated according to its tendency to furnish improvement, either in private virtue, or in those talents which render man useful in society'.[66] His general attitude is revealed by a paragraph:

> The superior efficacy of example to precept is universally acknowledged. All the laws of morality and rules of conduct are verified by experience, and are constantly submitted to its test and examination. History, which adds to our own experience an immense treasure of the experience of others, furnishes innumerable proofs by which we may verify all the precepts of morality and of prudence.[67]

The emphasis on experience 'verifying' rules of morality is reminiscent of the thinking of Smith on moral sentiments.

Tytler's jurisprudence reflected the same intellectual approach. Thus, he explained the development of laws in this way:

> Laws arise necessarily and imperceptibly from the condition of society; and each particular law may be traced from the state of the manners, or the political emergency which gave it birth. Hence we perceive the intimate connection between history and jurisprudence, and the light which they must necessarily throw upon each other. The laws of a country are best interpreted from its history; and its uncertain history is best elucidated by its ancient laws.[68]

He had commented:

> Laws, and good policy, essential to the stability of kingdoms, are the fruit of intellectual refinement, and arise only in a state of society considerably advanced in civilization.

The progress from barbarism to civilization is slow; because every step in the progress is the result of necessity, after the experience of an error, or the strong feeling of a want.[69]

This said, he was not a slavish follower of what he would have called 'system'. He realised the complexities of history and the contingencies involved in the complex interactions of economy and politics. He accordingly admitted that:

It is in general a very just opinion that political establishments and forms of government have owed their origin not so much to the genius of any lawgiver or politician, as to a natural progress in the condition of men, and the state of society in which they arose; but this observation, in general true, is not universally so.[70]

Both Maconochie and Tytler were propounding from their professorial chairs a type of global history, thereby producing a complex narrative that explained the rise of the modern world; this account is evidently rooted in the thought of earlier Scottish and other scholars on 'conjectural' history (to use Dugald Stewart's familiar term), with a focus on the interrelated material and cultural conditions of life to flesh out the schematic structures. It is close in approach to Smith and, indeed, to Millar;[71] furthermore, it reflects the ideas of the introductory essay, 'A View of the Progress of Society in Europe, from the Subversion of the Roman Empire, to the Beginning of the Sixteenth Century', to which Robertson had devoted the first volume of his *History of Charles V.*[72] While there is no reason to deny Maconochie and Tytler their own originality, the foundation of their thinking is obvious. The continuing success of Tytler's publications preserved these Smithian approaches well into the middle years of the nineteenth century.[73]

Tytler's approach to law is particularly telling in this respect. He applied it to Scotland. In the Preface to the first his two volumes of *Decisions of the Court of Session*, he commented that Scotland had few statute laws, but this was not 'at all to be considered as a misfortune'. Written law was always imperfect, so it was better that a court should have 'ample and extensive' powers to supply 'the defects of the statute-law', which allowed 'daily scope for the exertion of the reasoning talents of its judges', rather than that 'these should supinely repose themselves under the shadow of a code of statutes, which, establishing general rules, would, in their application to particular cases, often sanctify the greatest injustice'. He added that the 'indolence of the human mind' preferred the 'guidance of authorities'. He

therefore concluded that '[i]t is no paradox, therefore, to assert, that a system of law which is gradually formed from the rules and practice of a court
the judges of which are little fettered by authorities, must in time be much
more perfect, than such as is founded on the most voluminous collection of
statutes'.[74] This emphasis on reasoning over authority may reflect the views
of Tytler's mentor Kames;[75] but it is also very Smithian, and very revealing
of how Scots lawyers were thinking in the final quarter of the eighteenth
century.[76]

Scots Law and Civil Law

David Hume looms large in the history of Scots law and remains a powerful presence in the collective memory of contemporary Scots lawyers;[77] in
contrast, John Wilde is basically forgotten, except by scholars of Benjamin
Constant, who remain interested in him because the two men were friends
at university.[78] But Hume and Wilde were major innovators in the approach
they took to their disciplines, and both drew on a distinctly Smithian heri-
tage to develop their classes.

Hume's appointment to the chair of Scots Law in 1786 marked a major
change in the way the topic was taught. He had been admitted to the bar in
1779, having studied law in Glasgow with Millar as well as in Edinburgh.[79]
Because of Hume's differing politics, he is often, as a Tory, contrasted with
his teacher in Glasgow; but there can be no doubt of Millar's profound
effect on Hume's approach to law. This was not particularly because of the
detailed content of Millar's classes but rather because of the analytical and
evolutionary approaches to law that he had adopted from his own teacher,
Adam Smith. But this is an issue that could be explored further.

Hitherto, classes in Scots law had lasted for from fifty to sixty lectures;[80]
but Hume now elaborated the class into a lengthy course in which cover-
age of the syllabus could still take more than one academic session, despite
his moving from lecturing thrice to five times a week.[81] While Hume did
refer to Erskine's *Principles of the Law of Scotland*, the standard teaching
work on Scots law, his lectures were quite independent of any textbook,
covering the whole of private law in a structure closely derived from that
used by his teacher Millar, except that he did not deal with criminal law in
the discussion of personal rights, while reversing Millar's treatment of real
and personal rights over things.[82]

In 1793, Hume advertised that he would 'deliver a Course of Lectures
on the Law Respecting Crimes', during the summer session of the University, starting in May.[83] His own notes for these lectures cannot be located,
but student sets indicate that these lectures were, as Hume himself stated,
the direct foundation of his treatise on criminal law.[84] He delivered them

five days a week. Hume was still giving these lectures in 1795;[85] the Introduction to his *Commentaries* could be read as suggesting he was still delivering them in 1797.[86]

Hume's lectures on Scots law were not just simply quantitatively greater than those of his predecessors; they were qualitatively different, even if the difference was facilitated by their greater length. Within the structure derived from Millar, and ultimately from Adam Smith's *Lectures on Jurisprudence*, he set out an account of Scots law that is detailed and thorough and, in appearance, thoroughly modern in approach. Hume, of course, essentially accepted the analytical constructs of Smithian jurisprudence as a given; but he used this foundation of constitutionalism and individual rights to shape an account of the law out of a detailed reading of decided cases. His synthesis of these materials also relied on a reading of history to make sense of the cases and statutes. He presents a nuanced and subtle picture of the law of Scotland, with rich and complex description, avoiding too much deduction from first principles in an abstract fashion.

Hume himself described his classes as providing (borrowing the term from Blackstone) a 'general map of the law'; but he further stressed the need to provide the history of the law 'tracing its progress to its present state, through the successive changes it has undergone, and pointing out the causes and motives of these alterations'. He added:

> This sort of learning is on many occasions useful, even in business. Nay, it is necessary for enabling us to estimate, with any accuracy, the weight we should allow the older decisions to have, in questions relative to the same subjects, when they occur in our own days. It facilitates also to the hearer the means of gaining clear and distinct conceptions of the law, because the minute features of the present doctrine become more remarkable and more prominent when contrasted with those it bore at a former period. Besides, to such as have any love of knowledge, those inquiries are for their own sake of some value, which connect the study of the Law with the history of past times, and of manners and morals of our forefathers.[87]

Though Hume's lectures were focused on a description of the current law, one can sense in these sentiments the influence of Millar and Smith, and perhaps even of Kames. This is reinforced by remarks such as this:

> The basis of this part of our practice [the common law] lies, of course, in those feelings of natural justice by which, as men, our forefathers were instructed in the rudiments of this Science; and in their sense of what was suitable and convenient for them in their state of society and the circumstances in which they lived.[88]

The development of the law, however, was then affected by influence from other laws, such as feudal law as well as that of England and the civil law of Rome.[89] But the crucial point is that Hume's lectures were not as devoid of a theoretical underpinning as might initially be imagined.

To the superficial observer, however, Hume's lectures could seem simply to be a discussion of cases. Thus, James Brougham, younger brother of Henry, wrote to his friend James Loch: 'The excellency of Hume's course is acknowledged by everybody, but this excellency consists chiefly, I may say only, in his arrangement of the decisions. This you may have from the notes of his lectures as well as from the lectures themselves.'[90] Hume himself seems to emphasise that his lectures are not 'speculative' in the fashion of those of his teacher, Millar. Instead, he commented on criminal law, for example, that he did not think it 'any part of my duty, to enlarge at this time in observations on the due measure, proportion, or application of punishments, or on the style, the objects, and proper qualities of penal laws, which are rather the business of the political philosopher than of the lawyer', commenting that on these much had been 'rashly written, in a loose and general way, by authors but moderately skilled in the business of life, and very unequal to the arduous task of improving the science of legislation'.[91] He told his class in Scots Law:

> We may find in the laws of different nations many points of analogy, which may be collected into a treatise of universal jurisprudence, a noble department of science, and fit to employ an ingenious mind, but which it is not the proper business of this class to teach. You are here to be made acquainted with the special laws of your own country, as they actually stand; and must not expect to find everywhere, the beauty and harmony of a Philosophical System.[92]

But this should not be taken as meaning anything more than that his lectures stood on their own as an account of Scots law 'forming themselves a kind of Institute of the Law', as Arnot put it;[93] they had a theoretical foundation and analytical structure founded in the work of Millar and Smith. He was not criticising such an approach. But in Edinburgh, in contrast to Glasgow, other law professors – Maconochie and Tytler – taught 'universal jurisprudence' and 'universal history'. As Hume put it, discussion of these topics was not part of his 'duty'.

In 1792, John Wilde entered on the joint Professorship of Civil Law with Robert Dick on the arrangement already explained.[94] Wilde had been admitted as an advocate in 1785;[95] a learned and talented man, his appointment was meant to revive and renew the teaching of Civil Law and increase enrolment – this it initially did.[96]

The approach he took was rather different from that already taken by Millar. The latter had turned one of his courses on the *Institutes* into a course on Jurisprudence. Wilde did not need to do so, because of the teaching of the other professors: Tytler and Maconochie covered this type of material. Thus, Wilde noted in his *Preliminary Lecture* that:

> It has frequently been esteemed (and it has unquestionably, and in some instances, been executed with great success) a necessary part of lectures on the civil law, to give an account of what is called the progress of law; or, in other words, a view of the beginnings and progression of society; or, in other language still, an history of man; or sometimes also an history of government.[97]

After some criticism, probably of the private teacher of Civil Law in Edinburgh, John Wright – the reference to execution 'with great success' is probably to be understood as an allusion to Millar – Wilde stressed that this subject 'does not belong to the duty of a professor of civil law'.[98] He explained:

> Where a law college is employed as a sort of general institution, in science, history, and philosophy; delivered under the general name of LAW; which is a term most wide and comprehensive; of most universal and unlimited range; and to which (so far as regards the moral part of man's nature, whether considered as an individual or as the member of a policied community) no bounds whatever can be set; where a system of education, such as this, is expected or designed, the teacher is, in that case, not only warranted, but of necessity must, and merely in doing his duty, endeavour to give those, who put themselves under his charge, that broad and general instruction, for the attainment of which they resort to him. But this is not the case with me. There are other institutions in this university, where that knowledge may be amply acquired. My duty is to instruct you only . . . in the principles of the Roman law.[99]

But the nature of Wilde's course was more than just the product of a recognition that others taught jurisprudence and government. Kames had queried the need for teaching topics of Civil Law that had no equivalent in Scots law, '[w]hat use, for example, to our students is the chapter *De lege Fufia cani[n]ia tollenda*[?]', as he rhetorically put it.[100] Wilde responded directly: '[I]t would indeed be a strange thing if the professor of Civil law, whose office it is to explain the legal institutions of the Roman people, should pass over so very remarkable and conspicuous a part of their law as that which regards the establishment and regulations, and progress and decline, of domestic slavery.'[101] Wilde emphasised the need to understand Civil Law on its own terms.

When first admitted to the chair, for the convenience of the students already preparing for the examination in Civil Law for admission as an advocate, Wilde had initially continued the traditional practice of delivering the same course of lectures on the *Institutes* twice in the year.[102] But he then substituted for these two classes a single, year-long course on the *Institutes* that started with a lengthy account of the history of Roman law, covering both its development in the ancient world and its second life. He thus reinvented the class on Civil Law as one focused on the history and development of the Roman law.[103]

Wilde explained that, though he would not enter 'into any minute detail of the antiquities of Rome', he would 'give a comprehensive view of every thing relating to the government and laws of that people'. He further explained that there were two advantages to this way of proceeding: first, 'as they relate to the communication and continuance of a classical spirit of study'; and, secondly, 'as such accounts of the government, and legal institutions of a renowned people, form by far the best and surest means of studying and imbibing the real principles (delivered in their proper length and science elsewhere) of *even* public law and government'.[104]

In a sense, Wilde was arguing for something akin to a renewal of the humanist and elegant approach to Roman law. He greatly praised the work of Cujas, 'the greatest lawier [sic] of modern times'.[105] He emphasised the era of the Antonines as the most significant. He told his class that with the death of Modestinus 'the living system of the Roman jurisprudence expired'.[106] But he stressed that without knowledge of the history he expounded, it would be impossible for his class to understand how Roman law had developed, a development ultimately leading to the compilation of the *Corpus iuris civilis* under the Emperor Justinian.[107] This approach also made the law easy to comprehend. History was the key to understanding and even enjoying the study of the Roman law.[108]

The lectures on the substance of the *Institutes* are very detailed. Wilde expected the students to use Heineccius's *Elementa juris civilis secundum ordinem Institutionum Justiniani*; but his classes were not founded on the work.[109] Indeed, he criticised Heineccius's definitions of marriage as anachronistic, being based on modern philosophy.[110] Similarly, in his discussion of *patria potestas*, he commented that it 'has been little the practice of modern times to look at antient [sic] institutions in an antient [sic] view'.[111]

But Wilde was making a point beyond the need to return *ad fontes*. He was sceptical of some modern approaches to natural law, which, he stated, could be 'made to signify, just whatever any body wishes it should signify'.[112] Given his attack on Heineccius's natural law, he emphasised to his class that 'no institutions or Laws exist among Mankind, at least certainly do not exist for their benefit, which are not relative to Situation, and Circumstances, and which do not mutually influence these, and are influenced by them'. He added the very Smithian remark 'that to pretend to form any universal Code of Laws, applying to Men in every situation thro' the world, is a chimerical attempt in those who mean well, and is a very powerful engine of evil in those, whose designs are of another cast'.[113]

Both Hume and Wilde were each conscious that they were only one of four law teachers in the University of Edinburgh, and that they accordingly should not trespass into the others' provinces. What is notable about both, however, is the very strong empirical and historical approach that each had to the study of law. For Hume, this meant building up the modern law from the cases; for Wilde it meant understanding the Roman law against the particularities of Roman government, society and history.

Conclusion

Tytler, Maconochie and Hume were trying to ensure that legal education embodied a particular intellectual approach, one that focused on a science of legislation understood in a Smithian way. They aspired to provide a legal education that was historical and empirical, recognising the significance of government, economy and society in shaping the development of the law. Wilde's ambition was to create a proper historical approach to Roman law, cleansing it from the philosophical accretions of the eighteenth century and focusing on Roman law as the Romans understood it. This was why he emphasised that Roman law had to be understood contextually; that is, its rules had to be seen as the product of specific situations and historical contingencies. At a more abstract level, this was much the same lesson about law as that found in the work of the other three professors. Law was not to be based on 'authority' in the sense used by Kames. It was to be reasoned out by lawyers, who eventually would reach the best rule of practice through constant testing of the principles on which earlier judgements were made. Common law in this sense, not codes, was the best law, as precedents gradually matured the law into a system.[114] Law was an empirically founded, historical product.

It seems an inescapable conclusion that the appointment of these men was intended to introduce a reformation in the nature of the teaching offered from the professorial chairs of the Faculty of Law in Edinburgh.

Of course, Tytler, Maconochie and Hume were political supporters of Henry Dundas, a fact which may have assisted him in making decisions about their appointments, or at least sweetened the choice; the selection of Wilde, however, though the political circumstances were different, supports the idea that good political placemen were not what was being sought. The intellectual quality of the individuals was significant in influencing Dundas to seek their appointment.

The consequences of these appointments were far-reaching. First, university studies in history, politics, government and legal doctrine were now designed to assist Scots lawyers in developing their law through the decision-making of courts informed by enlightened lawyers. A version of Smith's science of legislation had thus come to dominate university education in law in Scotland. The increasing orientation of Scots law towards a system of precedent was thereby given an intellectual foundation and justification. Secondly, historical writing was developing in a new way.

This second strand of Smithian influence deserves further study; but it also links with the first. The only scholar hitherto who, in the past hundred years, has paid any real or considerable attention to Tytler's history writing is the late Marinell Ash. She emphasised his careful way with sources: 'Evidence was to be studied, considered and then either accepted or rejected. It was never to be modified or changed to fit preconceptions.' Ash attributed this to his training as a lawyer.[115] She remarked of Tytler's approach more generally that '[g]eneral principles only helped to explain history not make it, just as the general principles of Scots law gave a framework of reference within which the law and society which produced it could operate'.[116] Ash discussed Tytler in the context of the writing of his pupil, Walter Scott.[117] It is hardly a novelty to note that Smithian thought influenced Scott; this has long been recognised by literary critics.[118] But it should be recalled that Scott attended the classes of Professor Hume, and praised them in a way some might have deemed extravagant.[119] The Smithian-type influences on Scott may have had varied origins, as Peter Garside has pointed out.[120]

Given the number of literary (in the broadest sense) figures who joined the Faculty of Advocates, and the intellectual significance of men such as Henry Brougham, Francis Jeffrey and Henry Cockburn, with their varied politics, the significance of this education in history, government and law cannot be denied.[121] Michael Michie's brilliant study of Archibald Alison – to give but one example – demonstrates the latter's appropriation of Smithian views to present a 'High Tory' vision of politics and economics.[122] A significant legacy was being passed on through these crucial teachers in the Faculty of Law. Thus, these four influential law professors in Edinburgh, like Millar in Glasgow, gave classes that collectively focused on the 'general principles of law and government, and of the different revolutions which they have undergone in the different ages and periods of society'.[123] This attempt to fulfil a version of Smith's intended project permeated Scottish history writing.

Of course, all this leaves many questions unanswered. As the links with Dundas show, these four law teachers had – and were recognised as having – different political affiliations and views from those of their Glasgow rival Millar. Did such affiliations affect their teaching and scholarship in a way that clearly differentiated their thought from that of Millar? What are the differing nuances in their approach to Smith's thinking? What tensions are to be identified in their thought? Should it indeed be separated from the thought of Smith as simply analogous? Has the historical empiricism of Wilde and Tytler, if building on a Smithian philosophical or conjectural history, gone beyond it, and hence beyond Millar's thought? I rather think it has. How has this influenced later historians such as Macaulay as well as later novelists, given the significance of Scott?[124] Some current orthodoxies about nineteenth-century Scottish historiography may need to be rethought.[125] Much more work needs to be done. In pursuing the further work, a dialogue with Knud Haakonssen's work on Smith and other major Scottish figures will continue to be necessary.

Acknowledgements

Permission to cite and quote from MS and archival material in their care is courtesy of the National Library of Scotland, the Keeper of the Records of Scotland, the Centre for Research Collections of Edinburgh University Library, the Keeper of the Advocates' Library, the Society of Writers to Her Majesty's Signet, Glasgow University Library, Glasgow City Archives and Edinburgh City Archives.

Notes

1. Adam Smith to Duc de la Rochefoucauld, 1 Nov. 1785, in *The Correspondence of Adam Smith*, ed. E. C. Mossner and A. S. Ross; Glasgow Edition of the Works of Adam Smith VI (Oxford: Clarendon Press, 1977), 286–7. See, e.g., Knud Haakonssen and Donald Winch, 'The Legacy of Adam Smith', in *The Cambridge Companion to Adam Smith*, ed. Knud Haakonssen (Cambridge: Cambridge University Press, 2006), 366–96, at 372–88.
2. Adam Smith, *Lectures on Jurisprudence*, ed. R. L. Meek, D. D. Raphael and P. G. Stein; Glasgow Edition of the Works of Adam Smith V (Oxford: Clarendon Press, 1978).

3. C. L. Griswold, *Adam Smith and the Virtues of Enlightenment* (Cambridge: Cambridge University Press, 1998), 256–8, found quoted in Haakonssen and Winch, 'Legacy of Adam Smith', 388.

4. Haakonssen and Winch, 'Legacy of Adam Smith', 389.

5. Ibid., 388–90; J. W. Cairns, '"Famous as a School for Law, as Edinburgh . . . for Medicine": Legal Education in Glasgow, 1761–1801', in J. W. Cairns, *Enlightenment, Legal Education, and Critique: Selected Essays on the History of Scots Law, Volume 2* (Edinburgh: Edinburgh University Press, 2015), 192–218. Millar had influence outside the British Isles: J. W. Cairns, 'John Millar, Ivan Andreyevich Tret'yakov, and Semyon Efimovich Desnitsky: A Legal Education in Scotland, 1761–1767', in *Enlightenment, Legal Education, and Critique*, 219–37.

6. J. G. A. Pocock, 'Adam Smith and History', in *Cambridge Companion to Adam Smith*, 270–87.

7. See László Kontler, 'Historical Discourses and the Science of Man in the Late Eighteenth Century: Separate Scottish and German Paths?', in *The Enlightenment in Scotland: National and International Perspectives*, ed. Jean-François Dunyach and Ann Thomson (Oxford: Voltaire Foundation, 2015), 107–37, at 108–17; David Allan, *Virtue, Learning and the Scottish Enlightenment: Ideas of Scholarship In Early Modern History* (Edinburgh: Edinburgh University Press, 1993); David Allan, 'Scottish Historical Writing of the Enlightenment', in *The Oxford History of Historical Writing. Volume 3: 1400–1800*, ed. José Rabasa, Masayuki Sato, Edoardo Tortarolo and Daniel Woolf (Oxford: Oxford University Press, 2012), 497–517.

8. See Karen O'Brien, *Narratives of Enlightenment: Cosmopolitan History from Voltaire to Gibbon* (Cambridge: Cambridge University Press, 1997). From a different perspective, see M. S. Phillips, *Society and Sentiment: Genres of Historical Writing in Britain, 1740–1820* (Princeton: Princeton University Press, 2000).

9. See, e.g., Pocock, 'Adam Smith and History', 270–5; J. W. Cairns, 'Adam Smith and the Role of the Courts in Securing Justice and Liberty', in *Adam Smith and the Philosophy of Law and Economics*, ed. R. P. Malloy and Jerry Evensky (Dordrecht: Kluwer Academic Publishers, 1994), 31–61, showing how Smith's historical analysis led to a particular view on the structure of courts.

10. J. W. Cairns, 'Advocates' Hats, Roman Law, and Admission to the Scots Bar, 1580–1812', in J. W. Cairns, *Law, Lawyers, and Humanism: Selected Essays on the History of Scots Law, Volume 1* (Edinburgh: Edinburgh University Press, 2015), 330–70.

11. See, e.g., J. W. Cairns, '"Importing our Lawyers from Holland": Netherlands Influences on Scots Law and Lawyers in the Eighteenth Century', in Cairns, *Law, Lawyers, and Humanism*, 223–41. The favoured Dutch university was probably Utrecht: Kees van Strien and Margreet Ahsmann, 'Scottish Law Students in Leiden at the End of the Seventeenth Century: The Correspondence of John Clerk, 1694–1697', *Lias*, 19 (1992), 271–330, at 279–82.

For detailed discussion of Scots experiences there see K. G. Baston and J. W. Cairns, 'An Elegant Legal Education: The Studies of Charles Binning, A Scottish Pupil of Cornelis van Eck', *Tijdschrift voor Rechtsgeschiedenis*, 83 (2015), 179–201; J. W. Cairns, 'Legal Study in Utrecht in the Late 1740s: The Education of Sir David Dalrymple, Lord Hailes', in Cairns, *Law, Lawyers, and Humanism*, 253–99.

12. Cairns, '"Importing our Lawyers from Holland"'; J. W. Cairns, 'The Origins of the Edinburgh Law School: The Union of 1707 and the Regius Chair', *Edinburgh Law Review*, 11 (2007), 300–48.

13. J. W. Cairns, 'The Origins of the Glasgow Law School: The Professors of Civil Law, 1714–1761', in Cairns, *Enlightenment, Legal Education, and Critique*, 113–60, at 115–48.

14. J. W. Cairns, 'William Crosse, Regius Professor of Civil Law in the University of Glasgow, 1746–1749: A Failure of Enlightened Patronage', in Cairns, *Enlightenment, Legal Education, and Critique*, 161–91, at 184–5.

15. *The Minute Book of the Faculty of Advocates, Volume 2: 1713–1750*, ed. J. M. Pinkerton (Edinburgh: The Stair Society, 1980), 225 (3 Nov. 1748).

16. Ibid., 231–2 (3 Jan. 1749), 239 (2 Jan. 1750), 241 (16 Jan. 1750), 241–2 (2 Feb. 1750).

17. *The Minute Book of the Faculty of Advocates, Volume 3: 1751–1783*, ed. Angus Stewart (Edinburgh: The Stair Society, 1999), 62 (30 Nov. 1756).

18. Ibid., 94 (8 Jan. 1760).

19. Ibid., 112 (5 Jan. 1762).

20. Ibid., 119 (24 Nov. 1762).

21. Ibid., 186–7 (19 Nov. 1768).

22. Cairns, '"Famous as a School for Law, as Edinburgh . . . for Medicine"', 194–201, 203, 205, 211–13.

23. *Advocates Minutes, Volume 3*, 184 (5 Mar. 1768). On the background, see J. W. Cairns, 'Rhetoric, Language, and Roman Law: Legal Education and Improvement in Eighteenth-Century Scotland', in Cairns, *Enlightenment, Legal Education, and Critique*, 37–63.

24. R. L. Emerson, *Academic Patronage in the Scottish Enlightenment: Glasgow, Edinburgh and St Andrews Universities* (Edinburgh: Edinburgh University Press, 2008), 255–72.

25. J. W. Cairns, 'The Formation of the Legal Mind in the Eighteenth Century: Themes of Humanism and Enlightenment in the Admission of Advocates', in Cairns, *Law, Lawyers, and Humanism*, 303–29, at 315–16.

26. There are many studies: see, e.g., Alexander Murdoch, *'The People Above': Politics and Administration in Mid-Eighteenth-Century Scotland* (Edinburgh: John Donald, 1980); J. S. Shaw, *The Management of Scottish Society, 1707–1764: Power, Nobles, Lawyers, Edinburgh Agents and English Influences* (Edinburgh: John Donald, 1983); R. M. Sunter, *Patronage and Politics in Scotland, 1707–1832* (Edinburgh: John Donald, 1986).

27. Brian Bonnyman, *The Third Duke of Buccleuch and Adam Smith: Estate Management and Improvement in Enlightenment Scotland* (Edinburgh: Edinburgh University Press, 2014), 156–62.

28. Philip Harling, 'Rethinking "Old Corruption"', *Past and Present*, 147 (1995), 127–58; Philip Harling, *The Waning of 'Old Corruption': The Politics of Economical Reform in Britain, 1779–1846* (Oxford: Clarendon Press, 1996).

29. Emerson, *Academic Patronage*, 523–54; R. L. Emerson, *Professors, Patronage and Politics: The Aberdeen Universities in the Eighteenth Century* (Aberdeen: Aberdeen University Press, 1992), 1–17.

30. Cairns, '"Famous as a School for Law, as Edinburgh . . . for Medicine"', 214–15.

31. See J. W. Cairns, 'Late-Humanist Legal Education in Edinburgh: A Preliminary View' (provisional title) (forthcoming).

32. [Henry Home, Lord Kames], *Elucidations Respecting the Common and Statute Law of Scotland* (Edinburgh: Printed for William Creech, 1777), viii–ix.

33. J. W. Cairns, 'Politics and Knowledge: Henry Dundas and the Reform of the Edinburgh Law School' (forthcoming). See D. J. Brown, 'The Government of Scotland under Henry Dundas and William Pitt', *History*, 83 (1998), 265–79.

34. See J. W. Cairns, 'The First Edinburgh Chair in Law: Grotius and the Scottish Enlightenment', in Cairns, *Enlightenment, Legal Education, and Critique*, 82–109, at 99.

35. Emerson, *Academic Patronage*, 258.

36. Ibid., 266.

37. Ibid., 264; John Wilde to Ilay Campbell of Succoth, 23 Nov. 1792, Glasgow City Archives, Campbell of Succoth, TD219/214. I am grateful to John Finlay for bringing this letter to my attention.

38. Michael Fry, *The Dundas Despotism* (Edinburgh: Edinburgh University Press, 1992), 184.

39. Alexander Bower, *The History of the University of Edinburgh* (Edinburgh: Printed by Alex Smellie, [imprint varies] 1817–1830), Vol. 3, 215.

40. Alexander Grant, *The Story of the University of Edinburgh During Its First Three Hundred Years* (London: Longmans, Green, & Co., 1884), Vol. 2, 316.

41. Cairns, 'The First Edinburgh Chair in Law', 106.

42. Grant, *Story of the University of Edinburgh*, Vol. 2, 316.

43. See Cairns, 'The First Edinburgh Chair in Law', *passim*.

44. Ibid., 100.

45. See, e.g., *Edinburgh Evening Courant*, 28 Oct. 1780; *Caledonian Mercury*, 20 Oct. 1781.

46. See, e.g., *Edinburgh Evening Courant*, 1 Oct. 1785.

47. *Caledonian Mercury*, 25 Feb. 1786.

48. *Edinburgh Evening Courant*, 9 Sept. 1786 (starting 12 Mar. 1787); 20 Sept. 1787 (starting 11 Mar. 1788); 20 Sept. 1788 (starting 9 Mar. 1789); 7 Sept. 1789 (starting 8 Mar. 1790); 13 Sept. 1790 (starting 9 Mar. 1791). Later advertisements leave the date of the start of his class blank, presumably because of uncertainty as to the precise date.

49. *Caledonian Mercury*, 1 Oct. 1781.

50. Notebook of Alexander Fraser Tytler, N[ational] L[ibrary of] S[cotland], Acc. 11737/5, fos. 130f–131f (bis) (the modern foliation of the Notebook is inaccurate).

51. *Edinburgh Evening Courant*, 12 Nov. 1796; Notebook of Alexander Fraser Tytler, NLS, Acc. 11737/5, fo. 136r.

52. See the surviving set of student notes dated 1800: E[dinburgh] U[niversity] L[ibrary], C[entre for] R[esearch] C[ollections], MS Dc.6.115.

53. A. F. Tytler to Lord Provost, 13 Feb. 1781; Petition of Allan Maconochie and Alexander Tytler to the Lord Provost, Magistrates, and Town Council of Edinburgh, both in Edinburgh City Archives, MacLeod's Bundle 11, Shelf 36, Bay C.

54. Hugo Arnot, *The History of Edinburgh from the Earliest Accounts to the Present Time* (Edinburgh: Printed for William Creech, 1788), 398.

55. [Henry Brougham], *Memoir of the Late Hon. Allan Maconochie of Meadowbank, One of the Senators of the College of Justice etc. etc. etc. in Scotland* (Edinburgh: [Printed for T. Constable], 1845), 10–12.

56. EUL, CRC, Coll-1137; EUL, CRC, Mic M 1070.

57. Allan Maconochie, 'Essay on the Origin and Structure of the European Legislators', *Transactions of the Royal Society of Edinburgh*, 1 (II.II. Papers of the Literary Class) (1788), [3]–42, [135]–180; 'History of the Society', in ibid., (Part I), 17, 26.

58. Allan Maconochie, *Disputatio juridica, ad tit. xiv. Lib. XXXVII. Digest. De jure patronatus* (Edinburgh: William Gibb, 1770), [3]–7.

59. Arnot, *History of Edinburgh*, 399–400.

60. Alexander Tytler, *Plan and Outlines of a Course of Lectures on Universal History, Ancient and Modern, Delivered in the University of Edinburgh. Illustrated with Maps of Ancient and Modern Geography, and a Chronological Table* (Edinburgh: Printed for William Creech, 1782).

61. [Alexander Tytler], *A Short Comparative View of Ancient and of Modern Geography* ([Edinburgh?]: [W. Creech?], [1783?]); see Notebook of Alexander Fraser Tytler, NLS, Acc. 11737/5, fo. 35v.

62. Alexander Fraser Tytler, *Elements of General History, Ancient and Modern. To Which Are Added, a Table of Chronology, and a Comparative View of Ancient and Modern Geography. Illustrated by Maps* (Edinburgh: William Creech, 1801).

63. Alexander Fraser Tytler, *Elements of General History, Ancient and Modern. To Which Are Added, a Table of Chronology, and a Comparative View of Ancient and Modern Geography* (London: T. Cadell, 1821–1822).

64. Alexander Fraser Tytler, *Universal History from the Creation of the World to the Beginning of the Eighteenth Century* (London: John Murray, 1834).

65. Tytler, *Plan and Outlines*, 4–5.

66. Ibid., 1.

67. Tytler, *Elements of General History*, Vol. 1, 2. Cf. Tytler, *Plan and Outlines*, 2

68. Tytler, *Elements of General History*, Vol. 1, 22.

69. Ibid., Vol. 1, 21.

70. Alexander Fraser Tytler, *Universal History from the Creation of the World to the Beginning of the Eighteenth Century*, 2nd edition (London: John Murray, 1835). Vol. 1, 157. See the comments of Marinell Ash, *The Strange Death of Scottish History* (Edinburgh: Ramsay Head Press, 1980), 23–4.

71. As I have pointed out elsewhere, the son of the Edinburgh-educated Maconochie at one time owned one of the surviving sets of Smith's *Lectures on Jurisprudence*: had his father acquired them to help prepare his classes? See J. W. Cairns, 'The Influence of Smith's Jurisprudence on Legal Education in Scotland', *Enlightenment, Legal Education, and Critique*, 64–81, at 81.

72. William Robertson, *The History of The Reign of the Emperor Charles V. With A View of the Progress of Society in Europe, from the Subversion of the Roman Empire, to the Beginning of the Sixteenth Century. In Three Volumes* (London: Printed . . . for W. Strahan, etc., 1769), Vol. 1.

73. The continuing use of his works on history as standard textbooks is revealed by: *Questions on Select Sections of Tytler's Elements of History, Ancient and Modern; for the Use of the Junior Department of the Royal Military College* (London: Whittaker, Treacher & Co., 1832); William Horner, *Questions, for the Examination of Pupils, on Tytler's Elements of General History* (Bath: E. Collings, Saville Row, 1843); Christian Lenny, *Questions for Examination on Tytler's Elements of General History and Dr Nares' Continuation* (London: Edwards and Hughes, 1843).

74. *The Decisions of the Court of Session, From Its First Institution to the Present Time, Abridged, and Digested under Proper Heads, in Form of a Dictionary. Collected from the Printed Decisions, Session-Papers, and Manuscripts. Vol. III* (Edinburgh: W. Creech, 1797), [iii]–iv.

75. See [Kames], *Elucidations*, [vii]–viii.

76. Tytler first published this volume of *Decisions* in 1778: Notebook of Alexander Fraser Tytler, NLS, Acc. 11737/5, fo. 32. It was, as he noted, a continuation of Kames's *Decisions*. On the general point, see J. W. Cairns, 'Attitudes to Codification, and the Scottish Science of Legislation, 1600–1830', in Cairns, *Law, Lawyers and Humanism*, 144–220, at 189–208.

77. J. W. Cairns, 'Hume, David (*bap.* 1757, *d.* 1838)', *Oxford Dictionary of National Biography* (Oxford: Oxford University Press, 2004); online edition, May 2007, at http://www.oxforddnb.com/view/article/14142.

78. See, e.g., Dennis Wood, 'Constant's *Cahier Rouge*: New Findings', *French Studies*, 38 (1984), 13–29, at 13–16; but see Cairns, 'Rhetoric, Language, and Roman Law', 55–60.

79. *Advocates Minutes, Volume 3*, 302–3 (10 July 1779); Cairns, 'Hume, David'; G. Campbell H. Paton, 'A Biography of Baron Hume', in *Baron David Hume's Lectures, 1786–1822. Volume VI*, ed. G. Campbell H. Paton (Edinburgh: Stair Society, 1958), 327–410, at 332–4.

80. See, e.g., NLS, MS 19324 (sixty-one lectures); Cairns, '"Famous as a School for Law . . . as Edinburgh for Medicine"', 206 (around fifty lectures).

81. Paton, 'Biography of Baron Hume', 403 and 407. For his initial three hours, see *Caledonian Mercury*, 3 Nov. 1787: '[f]or some time, only three Lectures will be given weekly'.

82. J. W. Cairns, 'John Millar's Lectures on Scots Criminal Law', in Cairns, *Enlightenment, Legal Education, and Critique*, 271–310, at 305–6; J. W. Cairns, 'From "Speculative" to "Practical" Legal Education: The Decline of the Glasgow Law School, 1801–1830', in *Enlightenment, Legal Education, and Critique*, 238–68, at 263–7 (Appendix A contains an analytical comparison). The textbook referred to is John Erskine, *Principles of the Law of Scotland: In the Order of Sir George Mackenzie's Institutions of that Law*, 2 vols (Edinburgh: Hamilton, Balfour and Neill, 1754). There were numerous subsequent editions.

83. *Caledonian Mercury*, 30 Mar. 1793, 27 Apr. 1793; *Edinburgh Evening Courant*, 30 Mar. 1793.

84. Signet Library, MS 67 (1–3) (these are the lectures, once mislaid, but now identified with a new MS number; they are student notes: see Cairns, 'Millar's Lectures on Scots Criminal Law', 305 n. 165); G[lasgow] U[niversity] L[ibrary], MS Murray 135–9; David Hume, *Commentaries on the Law of Scotland, Respecting the Description and Punishment of Crimes* (Edinburgh: Bell and Bradfute, 1797), Vol. 1, [xxxvii].

85. See GUL, MS Murray 135–9.

86. Hume, *Commentaries*, Vol. 1, [xxxvii].

87. *Baron David Hume's Lectures, 1786–1822. Volume I*, ed. G. Campbell H. Paton (Edinburgh: Stair Society, 1939), 8.

88. Ibid., 12.

89. Ibid., 12–13.

90. James Brougham to James Loch, 25 Apr. 1802, in *Brougham and his Early Friends: Letters to James Loch 1798–1809*, ed. R. H. H. Buddle Atkinson and G. A. Jackson (London: Privately Printed, 1908), Vol. 1, 325–30, at 328.

91. Hume, *Commentaries*, Vol. 1, 2–3. This is different, at least in nuance, from what I wrote in Cairns, 'Millar's Lectures on Scots Criminal Law', 395–400.

92. *Hume's Lectures, Volume I*, 6–7.

93. Arnot, *History of Edinburgh*, 399.

94. Grant, *Story of the University of Edinburgh*, Vol. 2, 365.

95. Books of Sederunt of the Lords of Council and Session, 2 Aug. 1785, National Records of Scotland, CS1/17, fo. 17.

96. J. W. Cairns, 'The Face that did not Fit: Race, Appearance, and Exclusion from the Bar in Eighteenth-Century Scotland', *Fundamina: A Journal of Legal History*, 9 (2003), 11–41, at 21.

97. John Wilde, *Preliminary Lecture to the Course of Lectures on the Institutions of Justinian. Together with an Introductory Discourse* (Edinburgh: Bell and Bradfute, 1794), 59.

98. Ibid., 60: 'Yet men very little qualified for the task, and in no degree worthy to assume the name, have had the temerity to put their hands to it. I do not say (because I do not know it to be the fact) that his has been done (I mean by such men as these) in the chairs of universities. The matter has certainly been introduced here; and by men (as I have already said) not unworthy to introduce it. It is not of them that I speak this language of condemnation.' On Wright, see Cairns, 'The Face that did not Fit', 21–33.

99. Wilde, *Preliminary Lecture*, 61–2.

100. [Kames], *Elucidations*, viii.

101. NLS, Adv[ocates] MS 81.8.7, fos. 229–30.

102. Adv. MS 81.8.3, fos. 80–1.

103. On his reforms of the class on the *Digest*, see Cairns, 'Rhetoric, Language, and Roman Law', 57–9. I hope to discuss this more fully elsewhere.

104. Wilde, *Preliminary Lecture*, 68–9.

105. Adv. MS 81.8.5, fo. 76

106. Adv. MS 81.8.5, fo. 84.

107. Adv. MS 81.8.5, fo. 185.

108. Adv. MS 81.8.5, fo. 194.

109. J. G. Heineccius, *Elementa juris civilis secundum ordinem institutionum, commoda auditoribus methodo adornata* (Edinburgh: Printed by Gordon and Murray, 1780). There were numerous editions.

110. Adv. MS 81.8.8, fos. 86–93.

111. Adv. MS 81.8.8, fo. 68.

112. Adv. MS 81.8.8, fos. 167–70.

113. Adv. MS 81.8.8, fos. 29–30.

114. Tytler, Preface, *Decisions of the Court of Session. . . Vol. III*, iv–v.

115. Ash, *The Strange Death of Scottish History*, 26.

116. Ibid., 24.

117. Ibid., 22–30. The other scholar who has paid recent attention to Tytler is Claire Lamont in a series of illuminating literary historical studies starting with 'William Tytler, his son Alexander Fraser Tytler (Lord Woodhouselee) and the Encouragement of Literature in late Eighteenth- Century Edinburgh' (University of Oxford: unpublished B.Litt, 1968).

118. To pick but one: Kathryn Sutherland, 'Fictional Economies: Adam Smith, Walter Scott and the Nineteenth-Century Novel', *English Literary History*, 54 (1987), 97–127. Andrew Lincoln, *Walter Scott and Modernity* (Edinburgh: Edinburgh University Press, 2007), includes interesting relevant discussion. Particularly perceptive are Catherine Jones, *Literary Memory: Scott's Waverley Novels and the Psychology of Narrative* (Lewisburg: Bucknell University Press, 2003), 77–81, 108–10; and Catherine Jones, 'History and Historiography', in *The Edinburgh Companion to Walter Scott*, ed. Fiona Robertson (Edinburgh: Edinburgh University Press, 2012), 59–69.

119. Walter Scott, 'Memoirs', in *Scott on Himself*, ed. David Hewitt (Edinburgh: Scottish Academic Press, 1981), 1–44, at 42–3.

120. P. D. Garside, 'Scott and the "Philosophical" Historians', *Journal of the History of Ideas*, 36 (1975), 497–512.

121. See, e.g., the remarks in R. B. Sher, *Church and University in the Scottish Enlightenment: The Moderate Literati of Scotland* (Edinburgh: Edinburgh University Press, 1985), 315–16.

122. Michael Michie, *An Enlightenment Tory in Victorian Scotland: The Career of Sir Archibald Alison* (East Linton: Tuckwell Press, 1997).

123. Adam Smith, *The Theory of Moral Sentiments*, ed. Knud Haakonssen (Cambridge: Cambridge University Press, 2002), 404 (VII.iv.37).

124. Mark Phillips, 'Macaulay, Scott, and the Literary Challenge to Historiography', *Journal of the History of Ideas*, 50 (1989), 117–33.

125. As others also recognise from different perspectives: see R. A. Marsden, *Cosmo Innes and the Defence of Scotland's Past c. 1825–1875* (Farnham: Ashgate Press, 2014); C. M. M. Macdonald, 'Andrew Lang and Scottish Historiography: Taking on Tradition', *Scottish Historical Review*, 94 (2015), 207–36, at 208–16.

12

Declaring Rights: Bentham and the Rights of Man

David Lieberman

Bentham's critique of the idea of natural rights forms one of the best-known features of his jurisprudence; and one, as he correctly perceived, of direct relevance to his broader political theory. In his own lifetime, Bentham's hostility to rights-based arguments for political and legal change isolated him from more popular reform advocacy, particularly in the setting of his own embrace of democratic radicalism. His critique of natural rights continues to attract scholarly notice among jurists and philosophers. In the teaching of political theory, he is yoked together with Edmund Burke and Karl Marx as a trio of rights critics, whose arguments against the doctrines of the French Revolution usefully map a range of issues which modern theorists of liberal or human rights cannot afford to avoid.[1]

My aim in this chapter is to revisit Bentham's treatment of rights theory. This will inevitably involve some consideration of his most famous discussion of rights theory: the remorseless savaging of the French Declaration of the Rights of Man and Citizen he composed in 1795 under the title, 'Nonsense Upon Stilts'. But much of the attention will be directed at other writings, neglected in previous discussions, where he managed a distinct and often more appreciative response to the constitutional practice of declaring rights. As we shall see, he appropriated selected elements of this practice in his own writings in support of radical political reform. To add to the discussion in this way is not to challenge the importance Bentham ascribed to the critique of natural rights, nor to call into question his insistence on the deep intellectual confusions and grave political dangers presented in natural rights claims. His most famous statement against the French Declaration – 'Natural rights is simple nonsense: natural and imprescriptible rights, rhetorical nonsense, nonsense upon stilts'[2] – is notable for its vehemence, but not for the sentiment expressed. The advancement of the general happiness, he consistently maintained, was not to be served by the perpetuation of such 'nonsense'.

Law and Liberty

Well before he turned to the example of the French Declaration of the Rights of Man and Citizen, Bentham had developed at length the materials of his critique. In the years 1774–76, he interrupted work on his own developing codification programme to compose two critiques of William Blackstone's *Commentaries on the Laws of England*. The effort produced his first major publication, *A Fragment on Government*, which appeared anonymously in 1776, as well as the longer and unpublished *A Comment on the Commentaries* from which *A Fragment* had been extracted. Both compositions involved careful discussion of the relationship between law and liberty. Blackstone celebrated English law for its unrivaled protection of individual liberty, and his introductory treatment of law and political society deployed conventional arguments concerning natural rights and the contractual origins of political authority. Bentham first embarked on the critiques of Blackstone in collaboration with his older friend, John Lind. Months after the April publication of *A Fragment*, Lind prepared for the English government *An Answer* to the 'Declaration of Independence' issued in July by the American Congress. Bentham (who, in later years, would link together the French and American revolutionary appeals to natural rights) collaborated with Lind on the publication and produced his own 'Short Review of the Declaration' which appeared as the concluding section of Lind's *An Answer to the Declaration of the American Congress*. Bentham focused on the 'theory of government' set out in the opening two paragraphs of the Declaration. Rather than the articulation of 'self-evident' truths, the theory, Bentham maintained, 'was subversive of every actual or imaginable kind of Government'. Government did not operate by preserving the 'inalienable' rights to life, liberty and the pursuit of happiness. Instead, government secured the purposes for which it existed by limiting such rights: 'in as many instances as government is ever exercised, some one or other of these rights, pretended to be unalienable, is actually alienated'.[3]

In reaching this conclusion, Bentham drew on an interpretation of law and liberty that he arrived at in his first jurisprudential explorations. The centerpiece of the interpretation was to view individual liberty as the product of human law, created through the imposition of legal duties and restraints on others. 'The Definition of Liberty', he reported to Lind, 'is one of the corner stones of my system.' His early 'discovery' was 'that the idea of liberty, imported nothing in it that was positive: that it was merely a negative one . . . *"the absence of restraint"'* and of *'"constraint"'*.[4] In the series of works on jurisprudence and legislation he composed in the following years, which culminated with the belated publication in 1789 of

An Introduction to the Principles of Morals and Legislation, Bentham greatly refined this early discovery. He began with organised political society (and not pre-political nature) and defined law in terms of the commands issued by those endowed with sovereign power. Rather than aiming to preserve pre-political natural freedom, law and government's correct moral goal was to promote the greatest happiness of the community. Law accomplished this by providing a publicly announced and maintained structure of security which enabled the members of the community to realise their own plans for happiness. Law's most typical operation was to prohibit lines of conduct that harmed the community's happiness by imposing duties through the sanction of threatened punishment. Law in its basic functioning simultaneously established legal offences, created legal duties and imposed punishment. The legal rights that the members of the community enjoyed and relied upon were the products of this structure. Individuals thus acquired rights because others acquired duties; to have rights and duties was to operate under a system of legal constraint. 'A law by which nobody is bound, a law by which nobody is coerced, a law by which nobody's liberty is curtailed, all these phrases would be so many contradictions in terms.'[5]

On this account, the natural rights theorist confused the foundational logic of legal ordering. Rather than preserve natural freedom, law created security by restricting liberty. Legal rights were among the most important features of this structure of legal security. But the relevant moral standard was happiness, not freedom; liberty and rights were valuable for their contribution to happiness. In addition to these foundational errors, rights theorists stood convicted of a range of sins that Bentham frequently rehearsed in connection with his criticisms of rival forms of moral argument 'adverse' to the principle of utility.[6] Appeals to rights introduced fatal ambiguities and imprecision into the difficult work of determining which duties and rights the law should in fact maintain. In the case of legal rights, one could identify a structure of commands, duties and sanctions in terms of which the exercise of individual freedom was established and shaped. In the case of alleged natural rights, this positive structure was absent, making it possible to assert any number of individual attributes as part of the universe of moral entitlement and making it impossible to know how such rights in practice were to be instantiated and coordinated. If taken and applied literally, the asserted rights of nature rendered illegitimate the legal prohibitions that were basic to the successful ordering of collective life. As Bentham curtly explained to the defenders of American independence, their divinely sanctioned 'inalienable' natural rights meant 'that thieves are not to be restrained from theft, murderers from murder, rebels from rebellion'.[7] Bentham returned to the same point in his 1789 Concluding Note to *An Introduction to the Principles of Morals and Legislation*, where he considered several of the constitutional declarations of rights adopted by the state governments in North America following Independence. The North Carolina Declaration identified among the 'natural rights' of which men 'cannot deprive or divest their posterity' the rights 'of acquiring, possessing and protecting property'. Bentham impatiently countered that the alleged natural right rendered void any coercive regulation 'to pay money on the score of taxation, or of debt from individual to individual'.[8]

If not taken literally, the appeal to natural rights typically (and often purposefully) confused a statement of moral preference for a statement of fact. What was generally offered by such theorists was advocacy concerning which rights and securities law and government should protect. But by presenting the case in terms of 'natural rights', the theorist freed himself from the hard work of providing reasons to support the advocated freedoms or of undertaking the critical task of showing how these rights were to be legally shaped for the purposes of individual and collective happiness. The specific content of natural right was thus indeterminate and arbitrary. In his critique of Blackstone, Bentham insisted that Blackstone's conventional appeals to the moral standards of 'nature' or 'reason' as grounds of law might best be translated as an appeal 'to what I like'.[9] In 1789, Bentham deployed the term 'principle of *caprice*' to refer generically to the kind of moral principle that took the individual's given dispositions or preferences as the standard for moral assessment. In sharp contrast to the principle of utility, which specified the calculation of anticipated pleasures and pains as the grounds for morals and legislation, the 'principle of *caprice*' failed to provide any external framework in terms of which laws and institutions could be evaluated and determined.[10]

To the extent that natural rights theorists did suggest such a rival framework, their constructions obscured moral evaluation by introducing terms and devices that avoided a direct appeal to considerations of utility and happiness. Blackstone's *Commentaries* furnished Bentham with a classic example of this kind of error in the form of Blackstone's reliance on the idea of an 'original contract' to explain the foundations of political society. Blackstone's treatment was largely conventional. The idea of an 'original contract' captured the relationship between government authority and political obedience, whereby the individual members of a political community wisely abandoned natural freedom for the benefits of collective life. Bentham devoted the first chapter of *A Fragment on Government* to this discussion, much of it covering the loose and inconsistent language Blackstone used to contrast natural and political 'society'.[11] In addition,

Bentham focused on the use of the idea of an 'original contract' to treat the limits of political obligation, as in the case of a supposed compact 'made by the King and People', in which the community promised 'general obedience' and the king promised to govern in 'a particular manner'. Failures to govern according to the terms of the supposed 'compact', in turn, dissolved the bonds of authority and obedience.[12] For Bentham, the related ideas of an 'original contract' or political 'compact' were unnecessary 'fictions' that unhelpfully deflected analysis away from the proper foundational question of general happiness. 'It is manifest, on very little consideration', Bentham insisted, 'that nothing was gained by this maneuver after all: no difficulty removed by it.' The fiction turned the question of political obligation into a question of contractual obligation, without settling the nature or limits of either form of obligation. The situation in which members of a political community needed to determine whether or not it was appropriate to continue to obey existing authority was ill-served by examining the terms of a non-existent original contract. Instead, the direct calculation of anticipated pleasures and pains, benefits and costs, determined both forms of obligation. In the case of political obligation, 'subjects should obey . . . *so long as the probable mischiefs of obedience are less than the probable mischiefs of resistance*'.[13] Having so established the principle of utility as the proper framework for treating these questions, the confused and confusing language of rights, contracts and compacts could be confidently discarded. Such fictional devices, he reported, might once have 'had their use', but 'the season of Fiction is now over' – 'the indestructible prerogatives of mankind have no need to be supported upon the sandy foundation of a fiction'.[14]

Finally, for Bentham, natural rights presented a volatile and potentially explosive standard for public life. The appeal to rights had anarchic potential. 'The obvious effect of the word *right*', he maintained, 'is to make people suppose themselves justified in disobeying or even opposing any Laws they happen not to like'. Existing law contained many unnecessary and harmful restrictions on liberty which demanded reform for the sake of the advancement of the community's happiness. The invocation of natural rights did not aid such discussions and came with clear costs. The phrase served 'to confound men's understandings and inflame their passions'. The argument was thus politically 'pernicious' as well as conceptually incoherent. 'Nothing is gained to Liberty by such language, and much is lost to common sense.'[15]

Bentham's early engagement with Blackstone also provided the setting for his consideration of an alternative version of rights theory, especially influential in the treatment of England's law and constitution. In this version too the protection of individual rights served as the organising goal for the assessment and understanding of the institutions of law. But the emphasis was not on those universal rights of nature invoked at the opening of the American Declaration of Independence or later in the French Declaration of the Rights of Man and Citizen. Instead, the rights in question – alternatively styled customary, historical or immemorial – were identified with a specifically English practice of law and governance. Blackstone placed the experience of English liberty at the centre of his celebration of the kingdom's law. 'The idea and practice of this political or civil liberty', he intoned, 'flourish in their highest vigour in these kingdoms, where it falls little short of perfection.'[16] This achievement rested on the successful preservation of those natural and 'absolute rights of man' which formed the 'principal aim of society'.[17] Nevertheless, the vast majority of English law did not relate directly to the foundational 'absolute rights' established by the law of nature, but instead to what Blackstone referred to as 'relative' rights created by 'states and societies'. These covered the vast apparatus of rules governing estates and titles, exchange and succession, crimes and sanctions, social conditions and labor. In the case of England, the protection of historical liberties had been the heroic theme of legal development: a centuries-long process by which ancient Anglo-Saxon freedoms had been preserved against the threat of royal absolutism and arbitrary rule. At the constitutional level, the perfecting of liberty had been marked by a series of famous enactments – the thirteenth-century Magna Carta and Charter of Forests (and their subsequent re-enactments), the 1628 Petition of Right, the 1679 Habeas Corpus Act, the 1689 Bill of Rights – that preserved rights through a system of legal procedures and political guarantees. Historically, such declarations of rights had frequently involved acknowledgement by monarchs of specific privileges and liberties, forged in moments of political crisis and necessity. The indictment of the government of James II that introduced the 1689 English Bill of Rights, like the detailed charges against George III's government in North America in the 1776 Declaration of Independence, focused on alleged abuses concerning such historical rights and procedural protections.

Once more, for Bentham, the appeal to rights in the case of historical liberties involved fundamental confusions concerning the relations between law and liberty and the moral assessment of established law. One such error derived from an established juristic treatment of the idea of legal custom. Blackstone, following established conventions, treated England's unwritten common law as a body of legal custom; and drawing on classical Roman law sources, he maintained that this kind of law was inherently favorable to rights and liberty. 'It is one of the characteristic marks of English liberty', he explained, 'that our common law depends upon custom; which carries this internal evidence of freedom along with it, that it probably was introduced by the voluntary consent of the people.'[18] The claim, Bentham countered, simply mistook the institutional processes of law. Legal custom was law in England because the relevant institutional authority – here the courts of common law – imposed punishment upon certain lines of conduct. Custom only became law as a result of the practices of the courts and not the practices of the community. In England 'what is called Unwritten law', or common law, was 'not made by the people but by Judges: the substance of it by Judges solely: the expression of it, either by Judges, or by Lawyers who hope to be so'.[19] By extension, the individual rights preserved by England's historic customary law existed, as in the case of all legal rights, as a product of the threatened punishments and legal duties imposed by judges on the community. As such, customary rights had no better claim to manifesting 'the internal evidence of freedom' or of resting on the 'voluntary consent of the people' than any other species of legal right. All these rights ultimately rested on restrictions of freedom and imposed legal duties.

The appeal to customary and historical rights, like the invocation of natural rights, typically also confounded the moral assessment of the law's legitimacy. Bentham's general impatience with arguments drawn from the presumed wisdom of the past is well documented. He later described his published attack on Blackstone as the 'very first publication by which men at large were invited to break loose from the trammels of authority and ancestor-wisdom on the field of law'.[20] With regard to the historical record of English law, Bentham found little difficulty in countering Blackstone's language of immemorial rights and ancient liberties with the judgements of more critical historical scholarship, demonstrating the novelty and modernity of English freedoms.[21] But he devoted much less time to the interpretation of the historical record than to the manner in which the appeal to history and custom easily confused the exposition of the law with its moral assessment. The *Commentaries* systematically perpetrated this confusion. Blackstone stood guilty of confounding the task of the 'expositor' of the law ('to explain to us what . . . the Law *is*') with the task of the 'censor' ('to observe to us what he thinks it ought to be').[22] Blackstone's elegant summary of the law came freighted with flabby apologetics, earning him Bentham's dismissive caricature of 'every thing as it should be' Blackstone.[23]

Once the popular and historical pretensions of English liberties were discarded, the critical assessment of existing legal practices could properly proceed. As always for Bentham, this assessment was to be directly governed by considerations of utility: calculations of anticipated pleasures and pains, designed to achieve the greatest happiness of the community. The existing distribution of legal rights was highly relevant to this calculation because any departure from that distribution necessarily disrupted standing expectations. Bentham placed great weight on the pains associated with disappointed expectations and on the need for law to maintain sufficient stability to ensure its functioning as a reliable guide to social conduct. Accordingly, in explaining the reasons why common law judges properly deferred to the authority of established precedents, Bentham repudiated Blackstone's language concerning fitting 'deference to former times'. Judges maintained established rules 'not in compliment to dead men's vanity, but in concern for the welfare of the living'. Departures from established practices, no matter how meritorious in themselves, necessarily disrupted expectations. Judges adhered to the precedents of the past so that 'men may be enabled to predict the legal consequences of an act before they do it: that public expectation may know what course it has to take: that he who has property may trust to have it still'.[24] Legal rights, no less than legal duties, mattered greatly in any system of utilitarian jurisprudence, but not for the reasons typically assigned by the defenders of natural rights or historical liberties.

French Experiments

Bentham thus came to his most famous writing on the subject of natural rights theory, the 1795 'Nonsense Upon Stilts', equipped with a well-developed understanding of the relationship between law and liberty and an already-rehearsed critique of alternative rights-based approaches.[25] By this time, he had also acquired some expertise over several of the leading projects of reform debated in France in the years following the first calls in 1788 for a meeting of the Estates-General. 'For these five or six months past', he reported in March 1789, 'my head and heart have been altogether in France.'[26] Bentham was first drawn to Revolutionary France as an opportunity for the circulation and adoption of his own reform programme. But the situation soon became less one-sided, as the response to developments in France had a shaping impact on Bentham's own political ideas. This was most strikingly the case in those settings – such as his writings on the organisation of legislative assemblies or on the plan for a reformed judicial establishment, or his critique of France's imperial projects – where Bentham tackled for the first time topics that later become major elements in his mature constitutional programme.[27] Bentham displayed great sympathy for many of the projects of the Revolution, and he made no effort to enter the vociferous Burke-Paine debate which dominated so much of the initial discussion in Britain on the merits of the French Revolution.[28] Yet even during the period of constructive engagement with French developments, Bentham remained firmly opposed to the 1789 decision of the National Constituent Assembly (as the National Assembly had become) to issue a declaration of rights preliminary to the composition and adoption of a new constitution. Whatever the political pressures behind the 1789 decision, he explained in correspondence, he was certain that the resulting Declaration would contain material that was alternatively 'unintelligible' or 'false' or 'a mixture of both'. 'The best thing that can happen to the Declaration of Rights, will be, that it should become a dead letter; and that is the best wish I can breathe for it.'[29]

Bentham's engagement with French materials enabled him to clarify two separate dimensions in terms of which his critique of rights declarations proceeded. One dimension (explored thus far) concerned the dangers and confusions that attended any account of law that failed to recognise that law secured rights by imposing sanctions and constraining freedom. The other dimension concerned the attempt to place legal limits on the exercise of political authority; in this case, by identifying those foundational rights which no law might legitimately violate or curtail. Bentham understood the decision to adopt a Declaration of the Rights of Man and Citizen as one of several expedients pursued by the National Assembly to limit the future exercise of political power in France or, as he tendentiously put it, 'to chain down the legislator'.[30] In an unfinished set of 1789 'Observations' on the submitted drafts of the Declaration, Bentham linked this effort to a range of other, like-minded constitutional expedients. 'The doctrine of fundamental unreviewable laws, the contrivance of graduated majorities, and that of the division of assemblies in such a way as to convey to the minority the power of the majority', he explained, 'are all grounded upon the same weakness in the same regular affection.'[31] In 1791, Bentham returned to the topic in a critical examination of the new constitution's several provisions that postponed and hindered the adoption of future constitutional amendments. For Bentham, all of these devices were ill-advised; all violated his preferred alternative approach that 'there should be some one authority competent to do everything that may require to be done by government, and that that authority should extend to every case whatsoever'.[32]

Significantly, this was not a judgement dictated by Bentham's theory of law. Bentham explicitly repudiated the position adopted by other jurists, including Blackstone and John Austin (Bentham's best-known successor in what Austin termed 'the philosophy of positive law'), that political sovereignty by its very nature entailed an unlimited capacity to make and alter law. In Austin's classic formulation, 'Supreme power limited by positive law is a flat contradiction in terms.'[33] Bentham, in contrast, recognised several ways in which 'supreme power' was and could be limited. He explored the phenomenon in the same body of early writings in which he developed his first legislative programme and set out his understanding of the relationship between law and liberty. Bentham identified political society in terms of settled social experience: political society existed in those settings where stable patterns or 'habits of obedience' operated in relation to a given authority.[34] Given variation across communities, habitual obedience could differ in degree (how stable the obedience was) and in extent (the range of practices for which the obedience held). As a result, the operation of sovereign power would vary across political communities according to these variations in obedience. 'The power of the governor', he explained in a characteristic passage, 'is constituted by the obedience of the governed: but the obedience of the governed is susceptible of every modification of which human conduct is susceptible: and the rules which mark it out, of every diversity which can be clearly described by words.'[35] Against Blackstone's ornate claim that sovereignty inherently entailed a 'supreme, irresistible, absolute, uncontrolled authority', Bentham countered with a string of historical and contemporary examples where settled limits on government power plainly obtained. These included many federal systems, where the same ruler might be sovereign with respect to some areas of rule, but subservient to another authority with respect to other areas; or settings in which specific areas of social conduct – such as religious observance – might fall outside the routines of settled obedience. In addition, there were political societies in which an actual 'instrument of convention' was adopted which publicly specified boundaries to the operation of supreme political power.[36] In other settings, sovereigns unilaterally imposed limits on the exercise of their law-making power, which effectively bound themselves and their successors. Bentham termed these kinds of self-imposed restriction 'leges in principem' and attributed their efficacy to extra-legal forces. Whereas most laws relied on legal punishment (or, for Bentham, the political sanction) for enforcement, leges in principem typically relied on religious or moral sanctions operating against the sovereign.[37] (As we shall see, such extra-legal dynamics, in particular the moral sanction operating through the instrument of critical public opinion, assumed central importance in Bentham's mature democratic programme.)

The political reality of limited government needed to be distinguished from the question of its merits. From the start, as in his critical response to the American Declaration, Bentham believed it detrimental for the criticism of unwise or unpopular laws to take the form of declaring such laws 'void'. Likewise, he believed it unwise to assign to specific institutions, such as the courts, the negative authority to declare legislation void.[38] Political freedom, he explained in A *Fragment on Government*, was not secured through limitations to supreme power, but on quite different arrangements, such as '*liberty of the press*' and '*liberty of public association*', and 'the frequent and easy *changes* of condition between govern*ors* and govern*ed*'.[39]

Bentham's response to the constitutional experiments in France conformed to this framework. There was nothing about the logic of sovereignty that precluded the effort to create constitutional limitations on law-making power. These were practical questions of political design that turned on considerations of anticipated costs and benefits in service to public happiness. Bentham rejected the French embrace of constitutional limitations because they were ill-equipped to secure their intended benefits and because they introduced problems that it was important to avoid. In the language of his later political theory, such constitutional restraints failed as 'securities against misrule'.

Bentham's critical reaction to the 1791 French Constitution's several provisions to inhibit constitutional change provided the opportunity to explore these arguments at length. The constitution established a ten-year moratorium of constitutional amendments, restricted the source of proposed amendments to a special Assembly of Revision, and required for enactment the endorsement of three successive legislatures. In his response, Bentham raised the familiar objection to moments of constitutional rupture concerning the contradictory posture by which a particular group of revolutionary innovators assumed the authority to restrict the capacity of future generations. In the case in question, the members of the French National Constituent Assembly (who, for Bentham, enjoyed clear popular warrant for undertaking their sweeping innovations) designed a constitution which explicitly acknowledged the defects of the political system that first brought them to power, but which at the same time denied corresponding authority to future legislators chosen under a correct scheme of representation. As he challenged, 'Who are they who thus pretend to tie the hands of authority for ever? – the spurious representatives of the nation. – Who are they whose hands are thus attempted to be tied? – the genuine and legitimate representatives of the same nation for evermore.' For the most part, however, Bentham declined 'to plunge into the ocean of metaphysics' attending revolutionary authority, and instead focused on the deep folly of these measures.[40] Rather than advance the stability and survival of the new constitutional order, such measures actually undermined such goals.

The new constitution, like the 'habits of obedience' supporting all political societies, ultimately depended upon 'the approbation of the people'. In situations of extreme or impassioned opposition to the political order, the community was unlikely to be dissuaded from its political goals on account of formal constitutional hurdles placed upon the legislature. In situations of more stable political life, the difficulty of constitutional change would itself become a rallying-cry for political complaint and thus serve to undermine the larger constitutional system.[41] No less damaging, constitution limitations on law-making power introduced what Bentham regarded as a deep pathology by which contests over legal validity crowded out proper focus on the substantive question of advancing the community's happiness. Questions of legal interpretation would corrupt political argument. As the experience of statutory interpretation in England lavishly demonstrated, lawyers would be quick to offer exotic and obscuring interpretations of the written text in order to evade ill-designed constitutional provisions, and these ploys would subvert direct steps to political improvement. Rival court opinions would ensue concerning whether any particular law or practice was 'conformable to the constitutional code', and similar conflicts could be anticipated between the legislature and highest court. Opponents of any particular government measure or, more likely, those seeking to subvert the regime, would seize on the 'pretext' of constitutional legitimacy to advance partisan goals. 'Petition for redress', Bentham maintained, 'will be accompanied or rather superseded by protestation of invalidity: instead of complaint will come resistance.'[42]

Placing restraints on legislative capacity only made sense for Bentham on the basis of three false assumptions: that bad changes were more likely to be made than good ones; that political change itself could be prevented; and that measures designed to prevent constitutional change did not produce their own inconvenience. None of these suppositions could be sustained. The stability of any political rule was best maintained by the felicific goals and conduct of those who exercised government power. If a proposed change was meritorious, damage was done by delaying its implementation. If a proposed change lacked merit, its rejection was best served by a critical discussion and demonstration of its defects. The same process of reason and experience that lifted 'the body of laws from a less good state to a better' could be expected 'to operate with equal force against a bad change' that might degrade the laws 'from that good state . . . into a worse'.[43]

Bentham prepared this case for the 'Necessity of an Omnipotent Legislature' during the period he remained a sympathetic, if critical observer of French politics. In contrast, his critique of the Declaration of the Rights of Man and Citizen, 'Nonsense on Stilts', was composed at the time of his fierce reaction against the Revolution, which began with the increasing violence and extremism after 1791. The issuing in 1795 of a new constitution, along with a revised version of the Declaration, stimulated Bentham's writing. The several titles canvassed for the work – 'Nonsense Upon Stilts', 'Pandora's Box Opened', 'Pestilential Nonsense Unmasked' – revealed the distinctive emphasis he now brought to the critique of rights.[44] Having in the mid-1770s already noted the anarchic potential of natural rights to undermine political authority, this theme acquired central prominence. Among its many mischiefs, in France claims of natural rights were to be directly identified as a cause of revolutionary terror. As he later explained in correspondence with his brother, Samuel, 'I . . . wrote most strenuously against their Declaration of Rights, shewing it to be a compleat Code of Anarchy, article by article.'[45]

As an 'article by article' discussion, 'Nonsense on Stilts' covered more ground and in far more detail than any other of Bentham's critical comments on rights theory. Nonetheless, much of the discussion was orientated around a limited number of organising themes. As before, Bentham insisted on the foundational errors of any account of rights which failed to recognise that rights only existed because of law and because of restrictions on liberty. 'Rights are made at the expense of liberty', he maintained, 'no liberty can be given to one man but in proportion as it is taken from another'.[46] Accordingly, 'there are no such things as natural rights – no such thing as rights anterior to the establishment of government'. The expression proved 'merely figurative', and to give it a literal meaning was to deny law precisely those institutional resources through which security, rights and happiness were advanced.[47]

In this setting, though, the intellectual confusion that received more attention was the dangerous ambiguity and inconsistency by which the Declaration articulated those 'natural and imprescriptible rights of man' whose preservation comprised 'the end in view of every political association'. Bentham acknowledged much of his discussion was 'verbal' precisely because of the pervasive obscurity and imprecision of the document under review. The French Declaration was literally 'nonsense' because its language conveyed no clear meaning: 'words without meaning – or with the meaning too flatly false to be maintained by anybody, are the stuff it's made of'.[48] Hence, much of the resulting task was to give the Declaration a fixed meaning and then show how so much of its content contradicted the social and legal experience of organised political life. Unfortunately and fatally, the Declaration's 'nonsense' was hardly innocent. The confusion over the

relationship between law and liberty and the vacuous language of the Declaration's content were critical to its destructive and anarchic impacts.
The citizens of France were instructed they enjoyed rights that did not in
fact exist and which therefore could not be delineated. But, at the same
time, they were equipped with a destructive rallying-cry to invoke on any
occasion when a citizen disliked a particular law or government action.
'The avowed object of this clause', Bentham charged in response to Article
5, 'is to preach constant insurrection, to raise up everyman in arms against
every law which he happens not to approve of'.[49] Or, as he insisted of the
Declaration's articles as a whole: 'they plant and cultivate a propensity
to perpetual insurrection in time future. They sow the seeds of anarchy
broadcast.'[50]

Scarcely less emphasised was the denunciation of the French Declaration as a constitutional measure to limit government power. The Declaration was essentially an anti-legal document, designed to frustrate the law's
capacity to realise those benefits it was institutionally equipped to provide.
The idea received repeated rehearsal as Bentham worked methodically
through the Declaration's individual articles. 'It is for the hands of the
legislator and all legislators and none but legislators that the shackles it
provides are intended: it is against the apprehended encroachments of legislators that the rights in question . . . are intended to be made secure.'
The 'endeavour' is 'to tie the hand of the legislator and his subordinates
by the fear of nullity, and the remote apprehension of general resistance
and insurrection'. 'The professed object of the whole composition is to tie
the hands of the law, by declaring pretended rights over which the law is
never to have any power.'[51] The specific provisions of the Declaration may
have signally lacked meaning and thus comprised 'nonsense', but the anti-
legislative purposes of the document were clear.

Bentham's reading of the French Declaration of the Rights as above
all a device to establish limitations on the exercise of legislative authority
conforms to much in the modern experience of constitutional rights provisions. Rights are declared in order to entrench protections of individuals
against potential violations by majoritarian legislatures or other political
officials. This was in no sense an idiosyncratic reading. Indeed, Bentham
shared this interpretation with those advocates of the Rights of Man, such
as Thomas Paine, who likewise treated the rights in question as setting
absolute standards for the legitimacy of any structure of political authority. Still, the familiarity of this picture, and the tendency to treat the 1789
French Declaration as the key ancestor-document to modern statements
of human rights, poses some risk of rendering much too settled and mono-
lithic the historical developments to which Bentham and Paine responded.

For both, the interpretation was developed in the context of fierce political controversy and competed with other understandings. In the case of France, the absence of agreement over the meaning and political implications of the original Declaration of the Rights of Man and Citizen was evident well before the document was formally adopted, and these continued beyond the ratification of the 1791 Constitution. The 1795 Declaration modified the extreme language of its 1789 precursor, so much so that Bentham thought it left unclear whether the authors still intended that 'all laws that should at any time presume to strike' against the rights of man 'would become *ipso facto* void'.[52] The 1795 version also introduced a new Declaration of the Duties of Man to supplement its statement of rights; a measure that had been urged and narrowly defeated in 1788.[53]

In the case of the Declarations of Rights enacted by the newly-independent states of North America, to which Bentham drew attention in the 1789 *Introduction to the Principles of Morals and Legislation*, the content and status of the enactments were equally unsettled. As in the French case, these Declarations served as preliminaries to new constitutions and typically included a familiar canon of individual rights, such as liberty of the press or prohibitions on arbitrary imprisonment or *ex post facto* laws. Bentham, as we have seen, treated these constitutional declarations as designed to 'void' laws that were, in fact, basic to the maintenance of government and law. But this was a very selective review of the enactments. The American States' Declarations of Rights varied in length and were heterogeneous in content. Many included materials addressing structural features of the new governments, such as provisions concerning office holding or the organisation of elections.[54] Some provisions were cast in clearly aspirational terms, rather than as inviolable requirements for political legitimacy. The Virginia Bill of Rights reported that in private suits, 'the ancient trial by jury is preferable' and ought to be held 'sacred'. The North Carolina Declaration maintained that General Warrants 'ought not to be granted' and that elections 'ought to be free'. The Pennsylvania Declaration broadly observed that state leaders should adhere to 'justice, moderation, temperance, industry and frugality'.[55]

Nor did the approaches of the American and French revolutionaries eclipse the alternative tradition by which foundational rights appeared as concessions granted by those in authority in conformity with established historical practice. When Bentham returned to questions of constitutional reform in the final decades of his career, French liberty no longer depended on the claims of nature and the imprescriptible Rights of Man. Instead, according to the terms of the Constitutional Charter issued in 1814 by the restored monarchy of Louis XVIII, the declared 'Public Rights of the French' were granted 'by the free exercise of our royal authority' in conformity with 'the French character and in the venerable monuments of past centuries'. And it was on such terms that the rights to life, liberty and property were to be enjoyed and understood.[56]

This more varied practice of rights declarations is especially valuable in turning next to those settings in which Bentham found it advantageous to treat such devices in different terms. By 1809 Bentham became committed to radical Parliamentary reform in Britain, or what he termed 'democratic ascendency'. During the 1820s through to his death in 1832, he devoted himself to preparing an elaborate *Constitutional Code* for representative government and to related efforts for 'bettering this wicked world by covering it over with Republics'.[57] Throughout this period, Bentham's jurisprudence concerning the relationship between law and liberty remained unchanged and his repudiation of rights theory as an approach to law and government remained unqualified. Still, his rejection of natural rights denied him the resources which formed a leading argument for political democracy in his own era. Likewise, the rejection of the language of historical and customary rights denied him materials that continued to orientate debates in Britain over constitutional reform. His constructive arguments for democratic government did not depend on such appeals. But his radical programme came to embody features that purposefully selected and adapted these materials in important and novel ways.

'Acknowledgement of Rights'

Given the vehemence of Bentham's treatment of the confused and destructive features of rights declarations, a comment of 1820 addressed to Spanish legislators was quite striking. The American Declaration of Independence, he reported, 'stands at the head of their constitutional code' and 'plainly and openly avowed' the doctrine of popular resistance. 'The logic of that document' deserved no endorsement. Nonetheless, 'there is *thus much* in it of *good politics*'. The 1689 English Bill of Rights, Bentham continued, displayed even more disgraceful logic, since its justification for resistance to James II relied on the falsehood that 'the king had entered into a contract with the people: whereas, to the perfect knowledge of all who said he had, he had never done any such thing'. (The falsehood, Bentham could not resist noting, was the handiwork 'of lawyers: for without a lie in his mouth, an English lawyer knows not how to open it'.) But here too, 'the consequent' of the Bill of Rights 'was in itself good'.[58]

Bentham's selective praise for the two rights declarations is unexpected, and also requires some care. By repudiating the 'logic' of the two documents, he clearly returned to well-rehearsed arguments concerning the incoherence and indeterminacy he associated with arguments based on fundamental rights. Nonetheless, the distinction between 'the logic' and 'the politics' of the two documents seems strained, given the earlier emphasis on the direct political damage caused by the appeal to natural or foundational rights. By the beneficial 'politics' of the measures Bentham may have referred generally to the gains to human happiness secured by the acts of political resistance in question; a judgement he advanced with little qualification in the case of beneficial effects of American democracy. But the setting of the passage provides the best clue to the meaning of the 'good politics' in question. The statement appeared in a series of public letters *On the Liberty of the Press and Public Discussion* Bentham prepared in the failed effort to dissuade Spain's political leaders from proposed measures that he believed threatened both freedoms. As we have seen, as early as 1776 Bentham identified freedom of the press and public assembly as key devices for the maintenance of political liberty. In the various writings in support of radical political reform he began publishing in 1817, the importance of these freedoms featured even more critically. Bentham's understanding of democracy placed ultimate responsibility for successful self-government upon the processes of public discussion and critical public opinion, and these processes could not succeed in the absence of a free and uncensored political press. The institutional supports for effective public opinion emerged as a vital part of the design of democratic structures. Measures such as the American Declaration of Independence or the English Bill of Rights contributed positively to these political dynamics. The theory of law and government they publicly declared was erroneous. The fact that they were public and widely circulated mattered deeply.

A political tract of 1822, which again emphasised the role of public opinion and the political press, is particularly revealing in this context. The work in question, 'Securities Against Misrule', comprises one of the most unusual contributions to Bentham's mature political theory. He drafted the material at a time when his own plan for representative government occupied his chief attention. The work formed part of a brief collaboration with Hussana D'Ghies, then stationed in London as ambassador from Tripoli, to reform the government of Tripoli. 'Securities Against Misrule' presumed the continuation of monarchic government in Tripoli under the current Pasha, which stimulated Bentham to consider the available resources to prevent the abuse of power (or 'misrule') in the absence of the instrument of democratic election. Much of the discussion turned on a plan for the introduction of a political press in Tripoli, by which means the growth of critical public opinion could be nurtured and advanced. In his own programme for representative government, Bentham gave institutional expression to critical public opinion in what he termed the 'Public Opinion Tribunal'. 'Securities Against Misrule' developed strategies for the operation of the Public Opinion Tribunal under conditions of autocratic rule.

Among such measures, Bentham proposed that the Pasha issue the kind of public charter other monarchs granted to specify the terms by which they ruled. For the ruler, the charter offered a way to control those charged with the execution of his government. Bentham produced a draft charter, 'Constitutional Securities of the Tripolitan Nation', which contained as its centerpiece an 'Acknowledgement of Rights'. Bentham began his discussion by referencing the rights declarations of the American government, the French Declaration of the Rights of Man and Citizen, and the English 1628 Petition of Right and 1689 Bill of Rights. Like these more famous enactments, Bentham's 'Acknowledgement of Rights' was designed to protect individuals against the abuse of political power. Bentham's charter, of course, contained no appeal to 'nature' or to the idea of pre-legal rights. He explained the gains to conceptual clarity provided by his own terminology of 'securities' rather than 'rights'.[59] The rights that were acknowledged expressly existed on account of the security provided by the law. Thus, for each of its proposed protections, Bentham's 'Acknowledgement of Rights' specified that the security operated 'in the manner determined and declared by law'.[60]

Bentham always insisted that his notion of 'security' captured all that was worth capturing in the conventional treatments of political liberty. Modern commentators, such as H. L. A. Hart and Jeremy Waldron, have noted that Bentham had the conceptual resources to advance more robust accounts of individual rights than he sought to offer, including the idea of pre-legal moral rights.[61] The draft 'Acknowledgement of Rights' is the one text that came closest to embodying a Benthamic rights declaration. The great freedoms covered by the French Declaration's invocation of 'liberty, property, security, and resistance to oppression' found protection in his draft charter. Thus, Bentham protected freedom of religion, freedom of speech and public discussion, and freedom of publication. Given his concern in other writings with the security of property and the benefits of market exchange, it is notable that 'property' did not receive particular emphasis. On the other hand, given his emphasis on the beneficial impacts of critical public opinion, there was ample provision to secure the individual from censorship and intimidation which went well beyond the better-known rights declarations of his era. Bentham included provisions against the seizure or destruction of private papers; securities against 'national gagging'; and securities against banishment and arbitrary imprisonment. Protections that in other contexts would be linked to rights of privacy or the integrity of the person were here oriented to the mechanisms of effective public opinion.[62]

Beyond the overlap with the canon of eighteenth-century liberties, the proposed 'Acknowledgement of Rights' was a strikingly Anglophone composition. Bentham followed what he took to be an English practice in ranging beyond matters concerning the constitutional design of government to consider measures concerning criminal justice and judicial procedure. The proposed securities expressly sustained and went beyond the protections provided by the institutions of habeas corpus and the coroner's inquest.[63] Bentham also included in his canon of securities the 'right to keep arms'.[64] The inclusion of the right reflected Bentham's concern with the practice of political resistance. But it also aligned him with a native tradition in rights claims. The right to arms appeared in the English Bill of Rights of 1689 and in the Bill of Rights that amended the US Federal Constitution, as well as in many of the US state constitutions.[65] It was, however, absent in the French Declaration of the Rights of Man and Citizen and its many successors.

'Securities Against Misrule' was an exotic composition and there was much that was fanciful in Bentham's strategy to win the Tripoli Pasha's support for his reforming recommendations. But there was a good deal of pragmatic realism in his thoughts concerning the likely impacts of the publication of a rights charter in this political context. In the case of English examples of Magna Carta or the Bill of Rights, for example, these measures represented concessions forced on otherwise unwilling monarchs at moments of political weakness. Their political status amounted to little more than promises of future conduct; and in practice, kings were as adept at evading and disregarding such promises as they were in issuing them. 'Abundant and flagrant', Bentham reported, had been 'the violations of both' Magna Carta and the Bill of Rights. Nevertheless and no less significantly, these concessions were critical to 'every security against misrule' that had become such a valuable part of the English political experience.[66] As public documents, these declarations 'afforded a determinate denomination and standard of reference' for judging acts of government and 'a rallying point for sufferers with their complaints'.[67] The efficacy of such measures did not depend on the generosity or integrity of those who ruled, but on the capacity of public opinion to judge political practice in light of declared and well-known standards.

In his own advocacy in support of radical political reform in England, Bentham can be seen to have practised the kind of political activism he sought to nurture in Tripoli. A publication of this same period, again devoted to the liberty of the press and the power of critical public opinion, offers an illuminating example. The tract in question, *The Elements of the Art of Packing*, was published in 1821, though Bentham had first drafted the material well before, stimulated by a February 1809 newspaper report on current government prosecutions of twenty-six printers for violations of the law of libel. The composition dealt at length with the practice in London and Westminster of empanelling 'special juries' in libel cases. Such juries, Bentham maintained, comprised a captured instrument of regularly serving jurors, who readily supported judicial efforts to suppress political dissent through the application of libel law. The process of jury 'packing' kept in place the outward forms of the law, but the reality involved a 'puppet-show' in the service of political repression and the violation of judicial office.[68] While much of the discussion necessarily covered technical matters of legal procedure, the point of the exercise concerned those structures Bentham credited for the survival of political liberty. The 'alarming political grievance' that prompted the tract was 'the utter destruction impending over the palladium of the English constitution, the liberty of the press'.[69]

Bentham's posture in the polemic was quite complicated. His guiding assessment was that the boasted liberty of the press in England was the product of the non-enforcement of the law. The law itself was sufficiently unclear in its content and arbitrary in its execution to provide any direct security for free publication and discussion. Instead, it was the failure to implement this illiberal law that provided as much of the security for political debate as England actually enjoyed. The suppression of political protest during the period of the French Wars and through to the post-war agitation for political reform rendered the situation all the more precarious, as the senior judges of Westminster Hall worked in alliance with political elites to stifle the voices of reform and protect the powerful. According to established wisdom, common law juries provided one important resource against the abuse of judicial office, by operating 'as a check upon the power of the learned and experienced judge or judges'.[70] The condemned technique of 'jury packing' undermined this institutional function, by creating a group of compliant jurors unable and unwilling to challenge the suppression of free speech. Under ideal conditions, freedom of the press and public discussion would be secured through the express provisions of a legislative code and preserved through a simple and transparent legal procedure. But under the existing conditions of entrenched political and legal abuse, 'the

intelligence and fortitude of a jury' supplied 'a momentary palliative'.[71]
A key task was to mobilise critical public opinion by making plain the
nature and extent of the present danger.

As was typical of his style as a radical polemicist, Bentham avoided
any risk of inappropriate brevity. His denunciation of jury packing covered wide ground and included a key indictment of England's judges and
elite lawyers – to which he returned in other polemics – for aggrandising
power in a manner that violated the authority of parliament. According
to Bentham, 'Judge and Co.' operated as an extra-legal force in manipu-
lating common law process for its institutional benefit and power. 'If the
authority of parliament had not been set at naught by judges, the package
of juries could not have been established, much less, as we have seen it,
openly defended.'[72] In seeking to rescue press freedom, Bentham also took
advantage of a settled stock of famous milestones that figured standardly
in the celebrations of English liberties. He invoked the 1689 Bill of Rights
and those of its provisions addressed to the strength and integrity of jury
process.[73] He reviewed the infamous efforts of the seventeenth-century
Stuart kings to manipulate the institutions of law, undermine trial by jury
and establish arbitrary rule.[74] He compared the practices of the current
judges to the notorious historical examples of judicial disregard for common law rights and protections, claiming that the contemporary bench
operated in the spirit of 'the most sanguine hopes of the Scroggses and
the Jefferies'.[75] He cited a string of famous libel cases from the eighteenth
and early nineteenth centuries to remind readers of the settled connection
between England's political liberty and the fate of freedom of publication.[76]
'Am I indeed awake?', he tendentiously charged, 'is not this a dream? –
What century is this? – can it be the 19th? – is it not the 17th? – Who
reigns now? – can it be a Brunswick? – is it not a Stuart king . . .?'[77] The
upshot of these charges was to make evident the gravity of the danger
posed by jury packing. 'The subject which alone belongs to the present
purpose', he explained, 'is the subversion of the constitutional order.' 'The
constitution, in short, is already at an end, and the government a mere
tyranny in the hands of the judges.'[78]

Bentham's readiness to utilise the conventional language of English
liberty was a frequent feature of his arguments in support of radical political reform at home. The 1817 *Plan of Parliamentary Reform*, which like
Elements of the Art of Packing had been composed years earlier, set out a
radical programme for 'democratic ascendency' through the introduction
of near universal manhood suffrage, annual parliamentary elections and
the secret ballot.[79] Bentham emphasised how his own plan differed from

more moderate versions of parliamentary reform and defended the radical position with a characteristic analysis of the manner in which 'the state of interests' aligned specific groups for and against genuine political reform.[80]

But the lengthy polemic also included more traditional elements. Bentham again invoked the 1689 Bill of Rights to show how current parliamentary practice violated the constitutional norms specified in the declaration. He carefully reviewed earlier efforts to combat political corruption and previous unsuccessful calls for sweeping parliamentary reform. These, he acknowledged, on occasion had treated the democratic franchise in terms of '*unalienable rights*'; a formula that lacked much 'in point of reasoning', but 'not in point of power of persuasion'.[81] He examined at length the record of parliamentary history, drawn from 'grave and universally respected authors', to show that the practice of frequent elections and annual parliaments was the norm for over two hundred years, only ending in the late fifteenth century.[82] Bentham appreciated the oddity of a political programme that embraced '*utility*' as its 'sole arbiter' and which at the same time devoted so much attention to matters of precedents and usage. But, he explained, while relying on 'reason and utility', he saw no reason to repudiate '*imagination*, with its favourite instrument, the word *right*, used in a figurative and *moral* sense, that insensibly it may be taken and employed in a *legal* sense'. By the same process of imaginative extension, he continued, 'why should not *usage* . . . be regarded as creative of *right?*' In these situations, 'to the ground of *utility* is *superadded* the ground of *right*'.[83]

Bentham's appeal to constitutional norms and historical liberties in these settings easily contrasts with sharper and more disparaging sentiments he expressed in other writings and, indeed, in these same tracts. For example, the appeal in *Elements in the Art of Packing* to 'the intelligence and fortitude of a jury' to combat the 'subversion of the constitutional order' was thoroughly an argument of time and context. Liberty of the press and publication ultimately required a more '*radical* cure' to prevent the abuses of 'Judge and Co.' If not for the abuses of the present system, there would be no need for the 'momentary *palliative*' of the common law jury.[84] Again, the appeal to 'usage' and 'figurative' constitutional rights in the *Plan of Parliamentary Reform* contained no element of prescriptive title or 'ancestor-wisdom'. For Bentham, the democratic features of England's constitutional order had been created historically only because of the monarchy's need for tax revenue from the House of Commons, and these democratic elements had been all but destroyed by entrenched practices of political corruption and the sectional interests of the 'ruling few'. In practice, England's constitutional system comprised 'monarchy and aristocracy above: sham democracy beneath – a slave crouching under both'. Bentham would leave the conventional pieties concerning England's constitutional mixture and balance 'to Mother Goose and Mother Blackstone'.[85]

There was thus a strong measure of opportunism in Bentham's dramatisation in these writings of the perilous state of English liberty. His readiness to make use of such documents as the 1689 Bill of Rights or the record of historic English liberties represented a forward-looking enterprise directed at the tribunal of critical public opinion. Like the 'Acknowledgement of Rights' Bentham urged on the Pasha of Tripoli, these materials were embraced because they provided an express public standard in terms of which the abuses of power could be judged and condemned. In making the case for radical political reform, 'reason and utility' properly ruled. But in seeking to mobilise critical public opinion, the resources of 'imagination' and 'right' offered welcome supplementary support.

Constitutional Declarations Redux

The contributions to radical politics considered thus far offered constrained opportunities for reform, in which Bentham adapted his proposals to established institutions and practices. From 1822 onwards, he devoted himself to the composition of a three-volume *Constitutional Code* directed at 'all nations professing liberal opinions'. Still unfinished at the time of his death in 1832, this detailed plan for representative government contained his most ambitious contribution to political theory and effort at codification.[86] In this setting, his designs were unencumbered by the kind of existing political structures that shaped his advocacy in otherwise substantial writings, such as *Elements in the Art of Packing* and the *Plan of Parliamentary Reform*.

Key features of the *Constitutional Code* conformed to the doctrines Bentham had elaborated decades earlier in his critical reaction to the constitutional efforts of the French Revolution. Unsurprisingly, the code contained no foundational declaration of the Rights of Man. Nor were there any other provisions 'to chain down the legislator' through such measures as the entrenchment of constitutional provisions, supermajority requirements, or special procedures for constitutional revision. Bentham's design located 'sovereignty in *the people*'. A major power exercised by the people's sovereign 'constitutive authority' was the election of legislative representatives who made law, chose the prime minister and justice minister, and comprehensively monitored the performance of the government. Although the legislature was placed in a condition of 'absolute and all-comprehensive' dependence on the sovereign people, as a law-making body it enjoyed 'omnicompetent' authority. No limits were placed on its power to make and alter law, including its capacity to revise the constitution itself. If the legislature enacted any law 'which to some shall appear repugnant to the principles of this Constitution', the law itself remained legally valid and was not to be 'treated or spoken of' by any judge 'as being null and void'. This held even in situations where the suspect law appeared 'to diminish the mass of power hereby reserved' to the sovereign people.[87]

Bentham's reasons in support of legislative 'omnicompetence' again largely conformed to the arguments he advanced to the French legislators. Constitutional limitations on law-making created more problems than they could solve, and different kinds of 'checks' were needed to prevent the abuse of political power. The adoption of this position was not the result of Bentham's failure to perceive the political challenges which typically prompted the adoption of those kinds of constitutional restraints he repudiated. The *Constitutional Code*'s elaborate programme for courts and judicial procedure expressly denied the judiciary any power to nullify legislation and any capacity to create a body of judge-made law. But the same scheme made plain his recognition of the fragility of basic legal rights in the face of inequalities of economic wealth and political power.[88] The *Code* identified spheres of individual conduct which were to be protected from public notice. The state could not require disclosure of religious opinions; government health officials could not release the identity of persons 'who have been labouring under any disease to which disrepute is attached'; and aspirants for public appointment were not be questioned regarding 'any irregularities of the sexual appetite'.[89] Complete freedom of religion and religious expression was emphasised, and any state-supported religious establishment was emphatically rejected.[90] Yet, none of these protections was legally shielded from legislative alteration.

For Bentham, the maintenance of the constitutional order, the prevention of 'misrule', the creation and preservation of a government that systematically advanced the greatest happiness of the community, all required quite different and varied instruments. The general challenge was to fashion a political form in which the 'ruling few' (those limited numbers exercising legislative, administrative or judicial power) did not operate as a 'sinister interest' separate from and contrary to the interests of the entire community. To achieve this, Bentham relied on a dense range of institutional structures and routines; representative democracy, to flourish, needed an array of arrangements to secure utilitarian goals. Among them, of course, was the process of democratic election by which legislative representatives were chosen and removed from office when they abused their trust. Bentham's radical plan was especially notorious for its electoral provisions: virtual manhood suffrage; equality of the suffrage; annual elections; a secret ballot.[91] Yet, the feature he singled out as the most important for the realisation of democratic government was, once more, critical public opinion. 'Public opinion', Bentham maintained, 'may be considered as a system of law emanating from the body of the people.' The Public Opinion Tribunal ensured the community's rulers were held accountable for their policies and decisions, vigorously accused public officials who were suspected of misconduct, and brought to bear the power of moral censure against those found guilty. This moral sanction, Bentham believed, constituted the most potent instrument of popular sovereignty. 'Of the aggregate mass of securities against the abuse of power . . . the greatest part . . . unavoidably depends upon the power of the Public Opinion Tribunal.'[92] Much of his design of government was shaped by the overriding concern to insure the kind of transparency, accountability and information on the basis of which the Public Opinion Tribunal could effectively combat political abuse.[93]

One of the most neglected elements of Bentham's mature political programme was the systematic reliance on public 'Declarations' by those endowed with political power. Bentham scripted a series of Declarations into the fabric of *Constitutional Code* and carefully specified the settings in which these statements would be publicly and prominently avowed. Democratic electors acquiring the franchise publicly offered a Declaration 'to [their] fellow-countrymen', assuring the integrity and confidentiality with which they exercised their vote. Those assuming judicial responsibility publicly pronounced an 'Inaugural Declaration' that contained twenty-one separate articles, specifying at length the qualities and goals they brought to their assigned tasks. Local government officials and local record-keepers publicly repeated the same declaration in first assuming office.[94] In his private correspondence, Bentham reported the pains he took in composing and revising these declarations, along with the political importance he ascribed to them.[95]

Of all these constitutional declarations, the most substantial and consequential was the fourteen-part Legislator's Inaugural Declaration which comprised an entire chapter of the *Constitutional Code*. The Inaugural Declaration was to be 'read aloud' before 'the assembled multitude' by each successful legislative candidate immediately following his election. In fact, the Legislator's Declaration reached such length and detail that even Bentham worried that it might not fulfil its purpose as a publicly delivered statement absorbed by a democratic multitude.[96] In content and format, the document differed considerably from the 'Acknowledgement of Rights' Bentham drafted in 'Securities Against Misrule' and from the 1689 Bill of Rights he invoked in *Elements of the Art of Packing* and *Plan of Parliamentary Reform*. The protection of individual rights was principally covered in a substantial article in which the legislator promised 'Justice Accessible to All'. Here the citizenry was assured the full execution of the law and 'security or redress . . . against injury in any shape'. Such promised justice especially served the security of the poor, who were most vulnerable to the costs, delays and vexation that disgraced legal process under existing political systems. The opening article of the Legislator's Inaugural Declaration presented the 'ends aimed at' by the government, which included '*security*' and '*equality*' as among the component parts of the general goal: '*Greatest happiness of the greatest number maximized.*'[97]

The bulk of the Declaration, however, did not deal directly with matters of the individual's legal security and equality. Instead, the emphasis was on those moral qualities and commitments with which the elected legislator promised to exercise his 'omnicompetent' constitutional powers. The Declaration served as a primer on the manner in which public power in a utilitarian democracy would reverse the norms of monarchy and aristocracy. The legislator systematically pledged to renounce those vices Bentham most associated with the corrupt politics of sinister interest: insincerity, mendacity, partiality, arrogance, secrecy, abuse of office, self-enrichment and non-performance.

Bentham additionally specified the constitutional status and purpose of the Legislator's Inaugural Declaration. The Declaration did not qualify as law, since the *Constitutional Code* contained no provision of legal punishment for its violation. Bentham believed that 'the force of the legal sanction' could not be brought to bear in this situation. Instead, the Declaration was to be received 'as a sort of *Moral Code*, adapted to the situation of legislators; and as containing a sort of map of the field of legislation'. As in the case of the famous historical declarations issued by monarchs in moments of political weakness, the Legislator's Declaration produced its benefits by providing an express public standard for the conduct of political power in the community. It was according to these certain and acknowledged terms that legislators would be held to account by critical public opinion. Its 'chief use', Bentham explained at the outset, 'is to keep the Legislature and other constituted authorities in the more effectual subjection to the Constitution'. It did so 'by means of the power of the moral sanction, as exercised by the Public Opinion Tribunal'.[98]

Ironically, in adopting this feature of constitutional politics, Bentham largely echoed the position adopted by the authors of the 1789 Declaration of the Rights of Man and Citizen in the brief preamble to the famous enactment. There the 'representatives of the French people' presented 'the natural, unalienable, and sacred rights of man' not in order to nullify future legislation or to 'tie the hands of the law'. The purpose of the Declaration, as explained in its introductory paragraph, was rather to provide a clear public statement – which 'being constantly before all the members of the Social body' – reminded the citizens 'of their rights and duties' and rulers of 'the objects and purposes of all political institutions'. In this way, the operation of a 'solemn declaration' of 'simple and incontestable principles' would 'tend to the maintenance of the constitution and redound to the happiness of all'.[99] For all the critical attention Bentham directed at the work of the French National Assembly, this was a section of the Rights of Man and Citizen upon which he chose not to comment. His own radical constitutional programme was striking for the way in which it embraced and extended this specific function of declaring the rights of man.

Acknowledgements

I have benefitted from questions and comments received at several workshop presentations of earlier versions of this paper. I am particularly indebted to Michael Quinn for his detailed written review and many suggestions for improvement.

Notes

1. A distinguished example of this approach in political theory is provided by Jeremy Waldron in 'Nonsense Upon Stilts': Bentham, Burke and Marx on the Rights of Man (London: Routledge, 1987). Philip Schofield identifies the large body of scholarship on Bentham's critique of rights in his recent, 'A Defence of Jeremy Bentham's Critique of Natural Rights', in Bentham's Theory of Law and Public Opinion, ed. Xiaobo Zhai and Michael Quinn (Cambridge: Cambridge University Press, 2014), 213n. In addition to the discussions by Waldron and Schofield, I also have benefited from the study by Emmanuelle de Champs, Enlightenment and Utility: Bentham in France/Bentham in French (Cambridge: Cambridge University Press, 2017).
2. Jeremy Bentham, Rights, Representation, and Reform. Nonsense upon Stilts and Other Writings on the French Revolution, ed. Philip Schofield, Catherine Pease-Watkin and Cyprian Blamires (Collected Works of Jeremy Bentham; Oxford: Oxford University Press, 2002), 330.

3. Jeremy Bentham, 'Short Review of the Declaration', in [John Lind and Jeremy Bentham], *An Answer to the Declaration of the American Congress* (London, 1776), 119–20.

4. *Correspondence of Jeremy Bentham: Volume 1*, ed. Timothy L. S. Sprigge (*Collected Works of Jeremy Bentham*; London: Athlone Press, 1968), 310–11. For an important account of this early discussion, see Douglas G. Long, *Bentham on Liberty* (Toronto: University of Toronto Press, 1977).

5. Jeremy Bentham, *Of the Limits of the Penal Branch of Jurisprudence*, ed. Philip Schofield (*Collected Works of Jeremy Bentham*; Oxford: Oxford University Press, 2010), 75–6.

6. Jeremy Bentham, *Introduction to the Principles of Morals and Legislation*, ed. J. H. Burns and H. L. A. Hart (*Collected Works of Jeremy Bentham*; London: Athlone Press, 1970), chapter 2.

7. Jeremy Bentham, 'Short Review of the Declaration', in [John Lind and Jeremy Bentham,] *An Answer to the Declaration of the American Congress* (London: T. Cadell, 1776), 4th edition, 122.

8. Bentham, *Introduction to the Principles of Morals and Legislation*, 309–10.

9. Jeremy Bentham, *A Comment on the Commentaries and A Fragment on Government*, ed. J. H. Burns and H. L. A. Hart (*Collected Works of Jeremy Bentham*; London: Athlone Press, 1977), 198.

10. Bentham, *Introduction to the Principles of Morals and Legislation*, 21–2n.

11. *Fragment on Government*, 425–31.

12. Ibid., 442–3.

13. Ibid., 444.

14. Ibid., 441. Bentham credited Hume as the intellectual inspiration for his critique of the original contract, see the lengthy note at 439–41n.

15. *Comment on the Commentaries*, 54, 56.

16. William Blackstone, *Commentaries on the Laws of England* (1765–69), 11th edition, 4 vols (Dublin, 1788), 1: 126–7.

17. Blackstone, *Commentaries*, 1: 123–4.

18. Ibid., 1: 74.

19. *Comment on the Commentaries*, 223.

20. *Fragment on Government*, 424n.

21. Bentham relied heavily on the historical studies of Daines Barrington and Henry Home, Lord Kames, to counter Blackstone's legal history; see, for example, *Comment on the Commentaries*, 165–70, 175–80.

22. *Fragment on Government*, 397.

23. Ibid., 407.

24. *Comment on the Commentaries*, 202, 196.

25. The issuing of a new constitution and revised version of the Declaration of the Rights of Man and Citizen in August 1795 prompted Bentham's writing. Most of the tract is devoted to the 1789 version, though Bentham also discussed the version of 1795, as well as the 'Observations' on the draft Declaration presented by Sieyès in 1789.

26. *Correspondence of Jeremy Bentham: Volume 4 (1788–93)*, ed. Alexander Taylor Milne (*Collected Works of Jeremy Bentham*; London: Athlone Press, 1981), 33.

27. This critical phase of Bentham's development is treated in the important discussions by J. H. Burns, 'Bentham and the French Revolution', *Transactions of the Royal Historical Society*, Fifth Series, XVI (1966), 95–114, and most recently by de Champs, *Enlightenment and Utility*.

28. Bentham remained hostile to Burke's critique of the French Jacobins even during the period of his own conservative reaction against the Revolution; see *Rights, Representation, and Reform*, lix. 'The system of the Democrats is absurd and dangerous: for is subjugates the well-informed to the ill-informed *classes* of mankind. Mr. Burke's system, though diametrically opposite, is absurd and mischievous for a similar reason, it subjugates the well-informed to the ill-informed *ages*.'

29. *Correspondence: Volume 4*, 84–5 (Bentham writing to Jacques Pierre Brissot. He continued with the thought: 'It would be some remedy if any declaration were made provisional, or temporary').

30. *Rights, Representation, and Reform*, 186 and 186n; and see 263–88 (on the 'Necessity of an Omnipotent Legislature').

31. Ibid., 186n.

32. Ibid., 265.

33. John Austin, *Lectures on Jurisprudence*, 5th edition, ed. Robert Campbell, 2 vols (London, 1885), 1: 263.

34. Bentham's critique of Blackstone furnished the occasion for his first published discussion of sovereignty and political society, see *Fragment on Government*, chapter 1. Among modern scholars, H. L. A. Hart deserves credit for drawing attention to the significance of Bentham on sovereignty; see my discussion in 'Bentham's Jurisprudence and Democratic Theory: An Alternative to Hart's Approach', in *Bentham's Theory of Law and Public Opinion*, ed. Zhai and Quinn, 119–42.

35. *Limits of the Penal Branch*, 92n.

36. *Fragment on Government*, 428–34, 485–90.

37. See *Limits of the Penal Branch*, 86–93. See also *Introduction to the Principles of Morals and Legislation*, 34–7 (on sanctions).

38. *Fragment on Government*, 485–8.

39. Ibid., 485.

40. *Rights, Representation, and Reform*, 271, 270.

41. Ibid., 272–8.

42. Ibid., 267, and 266–70.

43. Ibid., 283–4.

44. The several titles considered for the work are discussed in *Rights, Representation, and Reform*, i–liii. See also Burns, 'Bentham and the French Revolution', 111; and *Correspondence: Volume 4*, 409.

45. *Correspondence of Jeremy Bentham: Volume 7*, ed. J. R. Dinwiddy (Oxford: Oxford University Press, 1988), 285.

46. *Rights, Representation, and Reform*, 334.
47. Ibid., 329.
48. Ibid., 322.
49. Ibid., 341.
50. Ibid., 320.
51. Ibid., 333, 336, 350; see also 400, where natural rights were expressly styled 'anti-legal rights'.
52. Ibid., 376.
53. The contested understandings and purposes attributed to the French Declaration are carefully surveyed in Stéphane Rials, *La declaration des droits de l'homme et du citoyen de 1789* (Paris: Hachette, 1989), and Keith Michael Baker, 'The Idea of a Declaration of Rights', in *The French Idea of Freedom*, ed. Dale Van Kley (Stanford: Stanford University Press, 1994), 154–96.
54. *Constitution of Maryland* (November 1776), 'Declaration of Rights', Articles XXX–XXXII; *Constitution of Pennsylvania* (September 1776), 'Declaration of the Rights of the Inhabitants', Article VI; *Constitution of North Carolina* (December 1776), 'Declaration of Rights', Article XX
55. *Constitution of Virginia* (June 1776), 'Bill of Rights', Section 11; *Constitution of North Carolina*, 'Declaration of Rights', Articles XI, V; *Constitution of Pennsylvania*, 'Declaration of the Rights of the Inhabitants', Article XIV. The starkly changing meanings of constitutional rights in the US context are well developed in Richard A. Primus, *The American Language of Rights* (Cambridge: Cambridge University Press, 2004).
56. *Constitutional Charter of France* (1814), Preamble and Articles 1–12.
57. *Memoirs of Bentham*, in *Works of Jeremy Bentham, published under the Superintendence of his Executor, John Bowring*, 11 vols (Edinburgh, 1838–43), 10: 542.
58. Jeremy Bentham, *On the Liberty of the Press, and Public Discussion and other Legal and Political Writings for Spain and Portugal*, ed. Catherine Pease-Watkin and Philip Schofield (*Collected Works of Jeremy Bentham*; Oxford: Oxford University Press, 2012), 31–2.
59. Jeremy Bentham, *Securities Against Misrule and Other Constitutional Writings for Tripoli and Greece* (1822–3), ed. Philip Schofield (*Collected Works of Jeremy Bentham*; Oxford: Oxford University Press, 1990), 23–4n, and see *Liberty of the Press*, 169.
60. *Securities Against Misrule*, 84–5.
61. See Waldron, *'Nonsense Upon Stilts'*, 37–8, and H. L. A. Hart, *Essays on Bentham: Jurisprudence and Political Theory* (Oxford: Oxford University Press, 1982), 83–6.
62. See *Securities Against Misrule*, 74–102. The same focus on the political value of freedom of the press as a check on the abuse of power was sustained in Bentham's more extensive discussion of the topic; see *On the Liberty of the Press*, 4–17, 131–2.
63. Ibid., 132–4.

64. Ibid., 83.
65. The liberty, for Protestant subjects, to 'have arms for their defence' was identified as one of the 'ancient rights and liberty' in the 1689 Bill of Rights (item #7). In the US case, the 'right of the people to keep and bear arms' appeared in the Second Amendment to the federal Constitution. Bentham's concern in *Securities Against Misrule* with the possibility of armed resistance in Tripoli may have prompted the emphasis on arms in his 'Acknowledgement of Rights'.
66. *Securities Against Misrule*, 140.
67. Ibid., 25. For Bentham, the publicity enjoyed by the document was the key to its efficacy.
68. Jeremy Bentham, *The Elements of the Art of Packing, as Applied to Special Juries, particularly in Cases of Libel Law* (1821) in *Bowring*, 5: 61–186, 104.
69. Ibid., 171.
70. Ibid., 67. Although this was an orthodox view, Bentham expressed scepticism over the capacity of the jury in practice to control the judge.
71. Ibid., 66.
72. Ibid., 176.
73. See ibid., 176–8.
74. See ibid., 66–7, 176–8.
75. Ibid., 177.
76. See ibid., 80n, 102–5n, 106.
77. Ibid., 66–7.
78. Ibid., 180, 183.
79. Jeremy Bentham, *Plan of Parliamentary Reform in the Form of a Catechism . . .* (1817) in *Bowring*, 3: 433–552. Bentham summarised leading features of the Plan at 518–21. The reasoning from 'interests' came to be treated as a leading feature of the political theory of the Benthamite radicals in the polemics over parliamentary reform in the 1820s.
80. See ibid., 438–41, 526–33.
81. Ibid., 446. Bentham here referred to the 1780 proposal for manhood suffrage presented by Charles Lennox, 3rd Duke of Richmond.
82. See ibid., 513–16.
83. Ibid., 515.
84. See *Art of Packing*, 66, 88–9.
85. *Plan of Parliamentary Reform*, 478n and 450.
86. My account of the *Constitutional Code* is heavily indebted to the work of other scholars, in particular Frederick Rosen, *Jeremy Bentham and Representative Democracy* (Oxford: Oxford University Press, 1983), and Philip Schofield, *Utility and Democracy: The Political Thought of Jeremy Bentham* (Oxford: Oxford University Press, 2006). For a brief overview, see also my 'Bentham's Democracy', *Oxford Journal of Legal Studies*, 28:3 (2008), 605–26.
87. Jeremy Bentham, *Constitutional Code: Volume 1*, eds. F. Rosen and J. H. Burns (*Collected Works of Jeremy Bentham*; Oxford: Oxford University Press, 1983), 41–2, 45.

88. See *Constitutional Code: Volume 3*, in *Bowring*, 9: chapters 12 and 20. The nineteenth-century edition of Bentham's *Works* contains the only available published version of these chapters of the *Constitutional Code*.

89. See *Constitutional Code: Volume 1*, 292, 164, 322.

90. *Constitutional Code: Volume 3*, in *Bowring*, 9: 452–3.

91. The electoral law Bentham drafted for the purposes of parliamentary reform (eventually published as *Radical Reform Bill, with Extracts from the Reasons*) was incorporated into the Electoral Code of the *Constitutional Code*; see *Constitutional Code: Volume 1*, xxv–xxvi, 48.

92. *Constitutional Code: Volume 1*, 36, 125.

93. I develop this theme in an unpublished paper, 'Jeremy Bentham's Constitutional Code and the Politics of Information' (an early version is available at http://www.scribd.com/doc/62684279/Jeremy-Bentham-s-Constitutional-Code).

94. See Jeremy Bentham, *Radical Reform Bill, with Extracts from the Reasons*, in *Bowring*, 3: 565–6; *Constitutional Code: Volume 3*, in *Bowring*, 9: 532–5, 625, 636.

95. *Correspondence of Jeremy Bentham: Volume 11*, ed. Catherine Fuller (*Collected Works of Jeremy Bentham*; Oxford: Oxford University Press, 2000), 397 (letter of 1824 to Leicester Stanhope).

96. See *Constitutional Code: Volume 1*, xxix.

97. Ibid., 141–2, 136–7.

98. Ibid., 133–4n. To clarify further: under the provisions of the *Constitutional Code*, public officials were eligible for punishment for legal offences they committed. For failings that concerned the wisdom and merit of their conduct, Bentham believed the moral sanction of the Public Opinion Tribunal provided the appropriate remedy.

99. 'Declaration of the Rights of Man and Citizen' (1789), Preamble (paragraph 1).

13

Rights After the Revolutions

Richard Whatmore

I

There was no logic to the discussion of rights in France and Britain in the 1790s. As the decade progressed the assertion of rights became pervasive, but could be found on every side in politics and was used to justify every political action. The conclusion for contemporaries was that by the turn of the century a major consequence of the French Revolution was the failure of rights-based politics. For those involved, rights had failed in the same way that republicanism had failed during the English Civil War and once more during the French Revolution, making any plea for the creation of a republic an exceptionally difficult argument for the following generations. Similarly for early nineteenth-century authors, it began to be difficult to enunciate rights-based arguments in politics in such circumstances, when overwhelming evidence indicted them. Those who did feel that rights could be the basis of a transformed political world felt that they were starting again, and had to prove that rights would not lead to the kinds of politics that rights had failed to outlaw, terror and domestic and international war. The claim by historians and social commentators that the French Revolution was a model that determined nineteenth-century political argument has caused these facts to be set aside. Numerous teleological historical narratives have been composed in which a radical reformist baton is passed from revolutionary to revolutionary, sometimes from the late eighteenth century to the present. In actuality, all reformers, of whatever stamp, had to begin by accepting that the experiment with republicanism and rights had met with disaster.

Political languages advocating the transformation of communities through rights had to be employed carefully by early nineteenth-century reformers because they tended to obfuscate the precise set of actions necessary to change the world from a state of corruption to a state of virtue.

When rights-based arguments failed in their coupling with republicanism in the 1790s, their advocates began to combine them with other political languages, and we have to pay attention to what these were rather than lumping authors together because they advocated the implementation of certain rights. With reference to a more capacious period, Knud Haakonssen has made exactly this point, underlining the changing moral content and political import of rights doctrines.[1] In regard to the eighteenth century Haakonssen has differentiated between the advocacy of rights, from Locke to Madison, derived from Calvinist perceptions of the divine voice in an individual, in which the exercise of the conscience became a duty and a right; rights derived from duties among Christian natural law theorists such as Leibniz or Wolff; rights as the act of a moral sense or morally perceptive conscience such as in Francis Hutcheson and Thomas Reid; rights as acts contributing to the providential happiness of creation, as in the case of Hutcheson (again) and William Paley; and rights as acts of free agents as in Kant. In all of these doctrines the idea of rights was determined by substantial normative moralities. An illustration of Haakonssen's approach to the history of rights will be provided in this chapter, which considers the breakdown of rights-based politics at the end of the eighteenth century and the repercussions for their exponents. More particularly, the chapter reveals the responses to a situation in which projects for reform, erected either partially or in their entirety on the universal rights that define personhood, were held responsible for social and political catastrophe.

II

By 1795 claims about the benefits of universal rights, and the transformation of the world that would follow their adoption by governments, had become ubiquitous.[2] Mary Wollstonecraft had vindicated 'the rights of men and the liberty of reason' in addition to the rights of woman.[3] James Mackintosh had stated the existence of the rights of man to have been 'proved', declaring that the French had 'wisely and auspiciously' commenced their 'regenerating labours' with a 'solemn declaration of these sacred, imprescriptible and inalienable rights'.[4] In 1795 Charles Pigott defined rights as 'those claims which belong to us by nature and justice'. He went on to claim that rights were 'quite obsolete and unknown' in Britain and that 'learned political antiquarians' had doubted 'whether such things ever existed on this island'.[5] Pigott was an enthusiast for the French Revolution. Educated at Eton and at Trinity College, Cambridge, his father was a baronet. He turned against his class in revealing the scandalous private lives of the English aristocracy, especially when gathering at Newmarket to gamble on the horses, in successive editions of *The Jockey Club: or, A Sketch of the Manners of the Age* from 1792.[6] In his *Political Dictionary* of 1795 he defined 'monarch' as 'a word which in a few years is likely to be obsolete' and 'aristocrat' as 'a fool, or scoundrel, generally both; a monster of rapacity, and an enemy to mankind'. Rights and republicanism went hand in hand for Pigott, as for increasing numbers of his contemporaries. So did social metamorphosis. People were on the verge of living different lives without ranks or prejudices that limited their liberty. As one patriotic ballad declared: 'For kings and lords the rights of man were first of all intended/ And since the reign of kings began the rights of man are ended.'[7]

It is significant that the advocacy of universal rights was always described as the product of philosophy. Statesmen and legislators were said to be finally learning from history, in the form of the philosophers whose insights into the human condition could be translated into a new politics. Sometimes the sketched lineage was recognisably republican. Pigott's publisher, Daniel Isaac Eaton, recommended the study of More, Buchanan, Milton, Algernon Sydney, Harrington, Locke, Rousseau, Price, Burgh, Paine and Godwin, whose writings he published as *Political Classics*, to reveal 'the beauties of a just and equitable form of government, in comparison with those profuse, venal, and corrupt systems which now almost universally obtain through the globe'.[8] Compendia justifying rights always included numerous quotations from Edmund Burke defending the American Revolution, with a nod to the presumed hypocrisy of the great enemy of the French Revolution. Lists of supporters of rights could be remarkably extensive, from Cicero to Godwin.[9] Most observers, however, described the obsession with rights as of more recent origin, and especially the eighteenth-century assault upon social, religious and political life undertaken by the *philosophes* and philosophers who today are associated with 'The Enlightenment' or the various enlightenments of the long eighteenth century.[10] As the Alsatian jurist Pierre-Louis Roederer put it on the eve of the French Revolution, 'for forty years, a hundred thousand Frenchmen have been conversing with Locke, Rousseau, and Montesquieu; each day they received great lessons from them on the rights and duties of men in society'.[11] For Burke himself it was Rousseau, Voltaire and Helvétius who had done the damage, in stuffing the French with 'blurred shreds of paper about the rights of man'; they had 'subtilized [themselves] into savages'.[12]

Many historians continue to see the age of revolutions, and the French Revolution more particularly, as a time when human rights were properly invented.[13] Rights are too often associated with processes, sometimes called 'a political logic', expressive of the view that once released from Pandora's box rights are sooner or later realised, and remain valuable in any reformist tool-kit seeking a better world.[14] In such histories the progress of the rights of man is either straightforwardly a story of discovery and gradual implementation, or a tale of the 'two steps forward, one step back' kind, when initial discernment is impeded by various forms of backwardness, only to be re-established by the next generation.[15] None of this would have been obvious to those who lived through the time when rights began to dominate political argument. Inherited ideas about rights were at least as diffuse and as complicated as ours today, centring on the uncertain relationship between individual rights, nation states, forms of property, religious communities and humanity as a whole. Jean-Baptiste Cloots, calling himself Anacharsis Cloots, wrote in 1793 that rights could only be said to exist if they extended to all of humanity, whatever their condition, and wherever they resided; the mission of the French Revolution was to establish equality on earth and between the propertied and property-less by initiating the journey towards universal rights.[16] The problem was that rather than having the effect anticipated by their vocal champions, the avowal of universal rights seemed to be having the opposite effect. Optimism about the future was harder to find as the 1790s progressed. Civil war in France and international war across Europe, the outbreak of terror, and the collapse of states and empires by domestic impulse or revolutionary arms, gave critics of revolutions in the name of universal rights ever more ammunition. Attacks on universal rights appeared in increasingly vitriolic registers, holding that their advocates were 'rebels, rioters and incendiaries', and dangerously heterodox in violating the Holy Writ of 'fear God and honour the King'.[17] As William Cobbett put it, the advocacy of universal rights could not be separated from the bloodshed and violence of events in France, the 'multitude of acts of horrid barbarity'.[18] It was not necessarily the case that rights did not exist, but when they were associated with social reorganisation, democracy and cosmopolitan improvement, disaster was bound to be the result. As an opponent of republicans and levellers declared in 1793, 'Let us no longer then be imposed upon by these savage theories about natural liberty and the rights of man; let us consider our rights as swallowed up in our interests, and let us disclaim all those boasted rights which are incompatible with our real happiness.'[19] From Ireland the point was made that the country had been assailed by French principles, 'their spurious liberty, and mock equality, the rights of man, republican fanaticism, the rage of political innovation, and the monstrous union of atheism and superstition'; this was why the people rebelled in 1798, considering the constitution and the government 'a foreign usurpation'.[20]

Against universal rights narrower conceptions of traditional rights, sometimes termed the rights of Britons or associated with a particular nation or community, and expressive of the existing constitution, were attested to. As one poem had it, 'For tho' the Rights of Man bold faction sings/ Supremacy's the privilege of Kings!'[21] For another commentator, 'the lowest of the people, especially the industrious poor, have a right, not to govern, but to be well governed'.[22] In the French case, 'murder and plunder are constituted freedom and anarchy and confusion established as law'.[23] Revolutionaries were accused of being 'men without religion', who 'under the pretence of natural rights would erect a universal tyranny'.[24] Radicals were also ignorant of the fact that 'where power is, it is ridiculous to talk of rights'.[25]

III

Advocates of a transformative politics founded on ideas about rights tended to be animated by either Thomas Paine or Emmanuel Joseph Sieyès, or both men wrongly lumped together as republican revolutionaries. Sieyès was widely acknowledged to be the architect of the events of 1789. As one commentator put it, 'Most of the new principles which prevail in France are contained in the Declaration of the Rights of Man. This Declaration, which is evidently intended to comprehend all the elementary principles of a free government, is said to have been framed by the Abbe Sieyès.'[26] In Sieyès' *Vues sur les moyens d'exécution dont les Représentants de la France pourront disposer en 1789* and *Essai sur les privilèges*, both of which appeared at the end of 1788, and above all in his *Qu'est-ce que le Tiers Etat?*, following in January 1789, Sieyès provided a script for revolution. Sieyès convinced the Estates General at Paris to declare itself a National Assembly, on the grounds that every member represented the national union of productive labourers, informing those present that 'you are today just what you were yesterday'. In drafting the Declaration of Rights, Sieyès affirmed the equality of rights and national sovereignty against the authority of the church, nobility, locality and king.[27] The purpose of society was 'to maintain and develop' natural and civil rights. Sieyès asserted that 'every social union, and consequently every political constitution, can have no other object but to manifest, extend and secure the rights of men and citizens'.[28] This was the only means to avoid the civil war that existed in every society where the overwhelmingly privileged faced those without rights.[29] Due to such remarks, Sieyès was forever associated with the Declaration of the Rights of Man and the Citizen. This was a mistake in the sense of his contribution to the actual declaration, because he wrote only a fraction of the final text.[30] One of the most significant facts about Sieyès is that he saw himself as being misinterpreted in his own time, and saw a gap between what he was seen to have done and what he had intended to do. Sieyès always used rights as an element of a broader reform programme, variously entitled the 'social art', 'science of politics', 'social science' or 'science of the social order', and never envisaged the implementation of rights outside of such a framework. He rejected those, such as Paine, who had faith in a rights-inspired transformation of society.[31]

Paine's canvass was grander than that of Sieyès' in foreseeing sister republics bringing peace to the entire globe. His vision of a rights-based republican revolution proved singularly popular. Paine's writings outsold every book except the Bible between 1792 and 1802. As Paine put it, although the British government had 'honoured me with a thousand martyrdoms, by burning me in effigy in every town in that country', the *Rights of Man*, published in two parts in 1791–2, 'had the greatest run of any work ever published in the English language. The number of copies circulated in England, Scotland and Ireland, besides translations into foreign languages, were between four and five hundred thousand.'[32] Although their view of the form of government most suited to rights differed, both Sieyès and Paine went through the same process in response to the reception of their ideas.[33] Initially they were seen as seers and prophets and envisaged the rapid alteration of the world. This was followed, when their projects were equivocally endorsed, with the formulation of transmission mechanisms to bring their proposals to fruition. When the transmission mechanism failed, both Paine and Sieyès turned to what they perceived to be the principal reason for their failure, the corrupted manners of the general population, and sought to rebuild and rehabilitate the mores of the general populace. When this too foundered, their responses were divergent.

Having been lauded as someone who 'led the leaders' and whose boldness knew no example in history, Sieyès believed that the National Assembly betrayed him, in the autumn of 1789, by nationalising the property of the church, and by giving the king a suspensive veto over acts of law.[34] Yet he was widely seen as the author of the first constitution of 1791. This was the view of Etienne Dumont, the Genevan pastor and speechwriter for Mirabeau, who saw Sieyès at first hand for a year from March 1789. When Dumont met Sieyès at Paris he knew that he was encountering genius. Dumont was, however, apprehensive about the future. Sieyès was an enemy of the British constitution and Dumont felt this to be a mistake. Some form of the separation of powers had to be instituted; that made the British constitution relevant to any political thinker since it had operated successfully since 1688.[35] Sieyès' timidity in debate and lack of clarity about his vision of a new politics caused Dumont to blame him for the first revolutionary constitution, calling it 'a genuine monster, being too much of a republic for a monarchy, and too much of a monarchy for a republic. The King was an *hors-d'oeuvre*; he appeared everywhere, but had no real power.'[36]

Dumont also blamed Sieyès for the Terror, although Sieyès had gone into hiding in 1793 and did not emerge until July 1794. Others were of the same opinion. For the royalist Jean Peltier, Sieyès dreamed of 'the rights of man, the sovereignty of the people, royal democracy, the philosophical mania for a written constitution, universal levelling, and the general will in the place of right reason'; the result was the collapse of the social order, and the translation of power to those who 'lived in the darkness of Plato's cave', leading in turn to 'anarchy and famine'.[37] For other contemporaries Sieyès had a 'career of crime and blood which characterized the reign of terror' and his rights of man had caused '*the loss of an entire generation in the midst of the most awful torments*'.[38] To Edmund Burke, Sieyès had 'whole nests of pigeon-holes full of constitutions ready made, ticketed, sorted, and numbered; suited to every season and every fancy'. Repeated attempts to create a perfect constitution were both farcical and deadly, because there was no defence against political extremism and judicial assassination: 'no constitution-fancier may go unsuited from his shop, provided he loves a pattern of pillage, oppression, arbitrary imprisonment, confiscation, exile, revolutionary judgment, and legalised premeditated murder, in any shapes into which they can be put'.[39]

In the aftermath of the rejection of his script for revolution, Sieyès began to argue that what had gone wrong was that society in its entirety had been reconstituted, at the expense of public order, whereas what he had envisaged was a new constitution, which would have taken time to influence and to direct national culture. In other words, revolutionary extremists had opted for what Sieyès called a 'ré-totale', reorganising society and redefining the included and the excluded on the basis of a presumed shared consensus, while Sieyès had planned only a 'ré-publique', being a government expressive of the common good, and bringing the diverse interests of society together, but founded on the adherence to civil liberties alone.[40] As such, Sieyès' proposals had been hijacked, reinterpreted, and put into practice by mad fools. In such circumstances, Sieyès acknowledged that it was necessary to rework the transition mechanism to the creation of a true republic. Sieyès had begun to do precisely this with Jean-Antoine-Nicolas de Caritat, Marquis de Condorcet, and Jules-Michel Duhamel in their *Journal d'instruction sociale* of 1793, which was intended to counter

Jacobinism by reshaping French political culture. It appeared, fortuitously, just after the *journées* of 31 May to 2 June, which saw the people of Paris turn against the Convention and destroy the Gironde deputies as a political force. The central objective of the *Journal d'instruction sociale* was to understand rights properly. As the three authors explained in their prospectus, guiding the people entailed the development of a social science with three branches, natural right (*droit naturel*), political right (*droit politique*) and public economy (*économie publique*). The subject of each branch was the rights, duties and interests of men in society. Morals or the art of good conduct derived from natural right, the social art of how to behave well in society from political rights, and the art of administering society properly from the science of public economy. Equality was described as the key value in politics, to be placed before even justice and liberty. Equality had to be won, however, through the development of forms of public instruction that would prevent the populace from being fooled by Caesars and by Cromwells.[41]

In the *Journal d'instruction sociale* liberty was defined as the satisfaction of human needs in accordance with reason, to be extended through labour as social progress took place. The substance of morality was whatever promoted such liberty, identified as the power to enjoy happiness in the sense of being able to satisfy basic needs. A Stoic morality emerged, demanding the control of the passions by individuals. Sieyès repeatedly praised himself for his hard work and simple manners and considered emigration to the United States to pursue a more natural and happy life.[42] Such private virtues were not, however, deemed sufficient for the public at large. The primary task of legislators was to intervene in public and private life to shape the character of all political and economic agents in society. The goal was to 'recall men to simple and natural needs' with 'habits and passions lightly worn'.[43] Citizens needed to be supplied with the moral and political information necessary to republican life. Sieyès' plan, presented to the Convention's Committee of Public Instruction on 26 June 1793, included Condorcet's proposal for national schools that developed the mind and the body of every child, supplying an education 'literary, intellectual, physical, moral and industrial'.[44] The centrepiece of Sieyès' strategy was, however, a system of local, district, provincial and national fêtes, to commemorate 'the work of nature, of human society, and of the French Revolution'. For example, each locality, called by Sieyès a 'canton', would celebrate on fifteen distinct occasions the beginning of work in the countryside, enclosure and fencing, domestic animals, youth, marriage, maternity, old age, the perfection of language, the invention of writing, the origins of commerce and the arts, the art of navigation and fishing, the first political union, the sovereignty of the people, popular elections and a selected subject of local pride. Each district would commemorate the return of spring, the harvest, the gathering in of grapes or some other local crop, ancestors, equality, liberty, justice and benevolence. Every *departement* would celebrate the four seasons at the time of the equinox or solstice; the arts and sciences, printing, peace and just war, the destruction of social orders and the recognition of the unity of the people on 17 June 1789; and the abolition of particular privileges on 4 August 1789. The entire republic would come together to recall 'visible nature' on 1 May, fraternity on 1 January, the French Revolution on 14 July, the abolition of the monarchy on 10 August, and 'the republic one and indivisible' on the day the new constitution was to be accepted.[45] A system of prizes was intended to maximise competition among citizens and cantons in carrying out each fête. These institutions were to be seconded by national theatres with the identical aim of guiding popular manners away from violence and towards virtue, by means of constant practice and reward. None of these projects came to anything as the turmoil of the summer of 1793 turned into the Terror from September until July 1794.

Having survived, Sieyès blamed the Terror on the ignorant masses, who had fallen prey to demagogues and allowed their violent passions free reign. The solution was to limit the involvement of the people in politics, and discipline politicians who showed any signs of extremism. Avoiding democracy through representation became ever more important to Sieyès.[46] This allowed Sieyès' critics to present him as the arch-hypocrite of the Revolution, someone who increasingly enjoyed the company of aristocrats and kings, because they alone could be trusted not to turn terrorist. Acting as special envoy to the court of Berlin, where he remained for almost a year from May 1798, it was said that the renowned regicide 'apes the majesty of Bourbon princes at the Luxembourg'.[47]

When Sieyès returned to the political stage in 1799, acting first as Executive Director and subsequently as president of the Directory from 18 June 1799, he was accused of renewing the Terror. The transition mechanism to a society founded on rights was now the destruction of internal enemies, being the Jacobins who did not share Sieyès' politics.[48] Ultimately acknowledging that the Directory could not maintain order, and that a leading military figure alone could unite the nation, Sieyès agreed to work with Bonaparte in planning what became the coup d'état of 9–10 November 1799. Having become the second of three consuls, he was outmanoeuvred in the exercise of power by the more populist Bonaparte, despite being heralded, once more, as the great author of a new constitution that would bring a regime of rights and liberty to the French people.[49] Bonaparte reputedly said that 'this hypocritical priest has the physiognomy of a Jesuit'.[50] For others Sieyès was a latter-day Satan, being one of the leaders of the cosmopolitan masonic plot to destroy religion.[51] Sieyès was made first president of the Senate, maintained his senatorial status throughout the Empire, and became a count in 1808, enjoying the life of a country nobleman with extensive lands at Crosne, north of Paris, granted to him by Bonaparte. Having seen all of his constitutional experiments fail, Sieyès ceased to write about politics. He was continuously vilified and had to flee from France, for Belgium, in 1815 because he was about to be arrested as a regicide. Although he lived until 1836, Sieyès refused to defend himself, his constitutionalism, or his political creed.[52] Silence appeared to be his response to the problem of creating a society based on rights without descending into terror. This was in fact only partially the case because he did address the issue of, and to an extent set the terms for, post-revolutionary argument.

IV

The case of Thomas Paine parallels that of Sieyès in many respects. Like Sieyès, Paine had a vision of a new world of peace, prosperity and equality. Like Sieyès, he was directly involved in politics, enjoyed a good deal of power and much greater influence. Like Sieyès too Paine was not short of confidence, declaring in *The American Crisis* of 1777, 'what I write is pure nature'.[53] The lessons of nature were so clear that Paine insisted that he did not read any books at all except his own and would gladly burn libraries as repositories of ignorance.[54] Paine, like Sieyès, was blamed for the extremism of the revolutionary era. He was described as a leveller, quack doctor, fantasist, utopian, anarchist, iconoclast and infidel, a solvent to government and religion, and hiding a cloven hoof.[55] John Adams summarised the view of many in calling Paine a 'disastrous meteor' and his writings 'profligate and impious'.[56] Writing in 1805, Adams stated that Paine's influence over thirty years had been enormous, the consequence being that rather than there being an 'age of reason', the 'age of Paine' was characterised by 'folly, vice, frenzy [and] brutality'.[57] Both Sieyès and Paine were attacked by the Jacobins and narrowly avoided death during the Terror; Paine escaped the guillotine by accident, and spent over a year imprisoned in the Luxembourg. One difference between them was that Paine had far more faith in democratic politics than Sieyès, and in the transformative effect of living under republican government. Another was Paine's response to the failure of the French Revolution.

None of the attacks on Paine hit home, as he continued to reiterate his faith in the implementation of a rights-based politics derived from the certain truths of nature. Indeed, Paine was among the most confident revolutionaries of the 1790s. He was certain that the old world he hated was passing away. Events were momentous and apocalyptic. There was no going back. As Gouverneur Morris recalled, in 1791 Paine was 'inflated to the eyes and big with a litter of revolutions'.[58] The Declaration of Rights in France, Paine wrote, 'is of more value to the world, and will do more good than all the Laws and Statutes that have yet been promulgated'. Republican government was natural to man, and the American and French revolutions 'a renovation of the natural order of things, a system of principles as universal as truth and the existence of man, and combining moral with political happiness and national prosperity'.[59] Human nature itself was changing. Paine anticipated the end of war, poverty, corruption and inequality.[60] A new era for humanity was dawning that would be characterised by greater wealth and an end to strife. Paine blamed wars on the forms of government that had an interest in maintaining them. Europe in recent decades had been characterised by 'a perpetual system of war and expense . . . [which] drains the country and defeats the general felicity of which civilization is capable'. Paine stated that 'All the monarchical governments are military. War is their trade, plunder and revenue their objects.'[61] In future, as in North America, there would be 'no riots, tumults, and disorders'.[62] Furthermore, conditions would improve for all to the extent that an end would be seen to the poor and wretched people who are 'far below the condition of an Indian'.[63] Paine expected the creation of a republican constitution to bring stability and calm to politics, and the benefits of republican life to be both obvious and self-sustaining, as a culture of republican virtue permeated the populace. The people, Paine was sure, had a passionate interest in maintaining a republican constitution, because it protected their interests as no alternative could, and accordingly it was the people as a body who would defend the republic against domestic and external enemies.

The transition mechanism to the new world was the institution of the 'equality of Rights . . . the true and only basis of representative government'.[64] Neither the rule of monarchs, priests nor aristocrats was compatible with the equality of rights. The source of all the evils of humanity was 'distortedly exalting some men, so that others are debased, till the whole is out of nature'.[65] In future there would be no courtiers and no patronage. The term 'commons' Paine damned as degrading, being 'unknown in free Countries'.[66] It was vital to 'exterminate the monster Aristocracy, root and branch'.[67] Paine had high hopes initially that the success of the French

Revolution would mean that his doctrines would gradually permeate every country. When this did not happen he argued that the new republican philosophy had not been instituted with sufficient speed. He wrote in 1795 that 'All the disorders that have arisen in France during the progress of the Revolution have had their origin, not in the *principle of equal rights*, but in the violation of that principle.'[68] Above all, however, he blamed the monarchical and aristocratic powers of Europe, and William Pitt and the government of Britain more especially. Paine did not lose faith in the ongoing French republican experiments. His pamphlet *Agrarian Justice* (1797) was dedicated to the French Directory and noted that 'the present constitution [1795] of the French Republic [is] the best organised system the human mind has yet produced'.[69] Writing in 1804 from America, Paine condemned William Pitt for violating the Peace of Amiens and for causing all of the instabilities of the French Revolution. Still anticipating a popular uprising, he advised Britons to look to America, because 'the new world is now the preceptor of the old'.[70]

While Sieyès considered it vital to arrest would-be Jacobin terrorists in order to save the Revolution in the later 1790s, and ultimately advocated a coup d'état, the transition mechanism Paine envisaged to a better world was the destruction of Britain. Paine had supported the war since 1793. In the *Rights of Man, Part the Second* he ridiculed William Pitt as the chief supporter of a mercantile system of corrupt trade, which ransacked Europe and America for the malign commercial interests that dominated British politics.[71] Paine's presumption was that Britain was becoming weaker and weaker. Either domestic revolution would occur, or a national bankruptcy would cause the end of Britain as a military power, and the dismemberment of the existing political structure. This was the message of Paine's *Decline and Fall of the English System of Finance*, appearing in April 1796, which declared Britain to be on the brink of ruin and 'in the gulf of bankruptcy', being defeated by the French Republic in war and unable to fund the European powers to continue to be enemies to the French.[72] When Britain did not end the war, Paine was heavily involved in the Directory's plans for the invasion of England, and continued to advocate invasion after he returned to North America.[73] In 1801 he was still writing attacking Britain as the mammoth monopolist, fighting the innocent French to engorge their commerce. His tone had changed because he accepted that French naval power had been annihilated. The hope for the world was a union of powers, including France, Russia and North America, to combat Britain's piratical Jacobinism at sea.[74] By this time, however, he was also acknowledging that the French revolutionary project was itself foundering. Advising Thomas Jefferson to purchase Louisiana in 1802, Paine wrote that the 'French Treasury is not only empty, but the Government has consumed by anticipation a great part of the next year's revenue.'[75] He was as gloomy about the future of the North American Republic. Where in France he blamed Robespierre and the Jacobins for tarnishing the republicanism experiment, in America the transgressors or would-be tyrants were deemed to be George Washington and John Adams. Their faction had perverted the political mores of the country by reintroducing ideas from the old world, including aristocracy, a standing army, irregular elections, luxury and controls over trade, and even the aspiration to empire.[76] Like Sieyès, Paine died despondent. Rights-based politics had suffered an endless series of blows, had failed to remodel the world, were tarnished in North America and dead in a France governed by an emperor.

V

What was to be done when rights failed? The solution to the problem was clear to most revolutionaries. As Jacques-Pierre Brissot put it, the solution could be found by imagining what Montesquieu would do if he could be restored to life in the present. He would, accordingly to Brissot, 'blush to have spent twenty years making epigrams about laws and [would instead] write for the people'. A latter-day Montesquieu would recognise immediately that 'the revolution cannot maintain itself except by means of the [actions of the] people, and the people have to be instructed'.[77] How then to instruct the people in the duties necessary to sustain a republic, leading them in turn to respect each other's rights? Condorcet, who died in prison at the end of March 1794, had frantically addressed precisely this question when in hiding for six months from 3 October 1793, after he had been accused of being a traitor to the Revolution. Condorcet stated that he had always sought to 'hasten the perfection of the human species' by establishing a regime in which 'all laws would be based on natural right'.[78] Proof that this was possible lay, Condorcet stated in the *Esquisse d'un tableau historique des progrès de l'esprit humain*, in the experience of the North American republics, founded 'on the solemn recognition of the natural rights of man'. Although imperfect in Condorcet's view, the American experiment had been successful because the constitutions had incorporated a means of reforming themselves without violence, entirely separate from the power of making law; there was no need to call the people to arms in consequence when they felt their rights were not being respected. Creating a rights-based society was then attempted in France, a place 'the most enlightened and among the least free', with the best of philosophers living under a government of the ignorant.

The task of realising rights was much harder in France. North America was fortunate in not having 'to reform an unfair tax system, and not having to destroy feudal tyrannies, hereditary distinctions, rich or powerful privileged corporations, or an intolerant religious establishment'. In France, society as a whole had to be remade in order to establish a true equality of rights.[79] Despite the bloodshed that had accompanied the reconstitution of social relationships, Condorcet was optimistic about the future on the grounds that 'every error in politics or in morality derived from a philosophical mistake'; this error in turn could be traced to 'ignorance of the laws of nature'. Condorcet was certain that reason had increased and was forever becoming more influential in social organisations. As the development of reason tended to be accompanied by peace and social harmony, in time the inequalities between nations would be reduced, equality within every community would increase, and human nature would gradually be perfected.[80] In the case of revolutionary France, the fundamental mistake was that by dividing power between the monarch and the people, in 1791, a civil war had been instituted. It was the case that the people were ill educated in the peaceful enjoyment of their rights, but the root cause of revolutionary violence lay elsewhere; the first revolutionary constitution had not been sufficiently republican, and had not been established by means of a national convention. The people had to become violent in order to assert their rights because they had not been able to exercise their sovereignty through their representatives united in a national constitutional convention.[81]

In the hope that Condorcet's republican constitution might finally be put into practice, alongside his schemes for a moral and political education in rights, his friends Dominique-Joseph Garat and Pierre-Jean-George Cabanis continued to publish his writings into the new century, with a new edition of Condorcet's works. Condorcet inspired disciples during the Directory and the Consulate, and his *Esquisse* was continuously reprinted during these years, described as a Stoic and Socratic defence of scientifically justified rights.[82] Malthus's notorious comment was that the *Esquisse* was a utopian fantasy, inapplicable to reality and riven by contradiction, being 'a singular instance of the attachment of a man to principles, which every day's experience was so fatally for himself contradicting'. The human mind in France was 'debased by a fermentation of disgusting passions, of fear, cruelty, malice, revenge, ambition, madness, and folly, as would have disgraced the most savage nation in the most barbarous age'.[83] What Malthus did not notice was that Condorcet's perspective on societies in which rights could be said to be flourishing had altered. Whereas for Paine and for Sieyès the point of putting rights into practice was to move the world beyond Britain, the pariah state characterised by corruption and doomed to collapse, Condorcet ended his life asserting that the American Revolution was more peaceful because civil rights had been inherited from Britain.[84]

A major consequence of the failure of rights-based politics in France was praise for the operation of rights in Britain. Sieyès' close friend Roederer was another survivor of the Terror who altered his perspective on this front. Although he continued to attack Britain's economy as a mercantile system, and was critical of the excessive political influence of the landed interest, Roederer argued that France needed to learn from Britain, as early as the lectures he gave in the spring of 1793 before going into hiding.[85] In Britain, life and property were secure, and the failure to respect such natural rights explained the French descent into chaos. For Condorcet and for Roederer, the difference in the violence of the French Revolution as compared with the American Revolution derived from the peaceful manners of the British, in turn founded upon a respect for civil liberty, which was passed on to the North Americans. This point became commonplace in political argument, and was employed by John Adams, Friederich Gentz and other critics of the French Revolution to berate the Paineites.[86] That Britain rather than France was the country of rights gained ever more currency as the Directory failed to establish a stable republic, and became still more prevalent as Bonaparte inaugurated the First French Empire. It is significant that James Mackintosh, the author of *Vindiciae Gallicae*, paid particular attention, in his defence of the royalist Jean Peltier against the accusation that he had libelled Bonaparte, to a poem that stated '[In Britain] man's free spirit, unconstrain'd/ Exults, in man's best rights maintained/ Rights, which by ancient valour gain'd/ From age to age descend.'[87] Mackintosh's successful strategy in the Peltier case was to present Britain as the state where the rights of man, carefully defined over time, characterised domestic law; the rights of nations equally defined international policy.[88]

A second consequence of the failure of rights was to fall back upon the old republican argument that the people had to be made ready for liberty before they could ever enjoy it in peace.[89] Prior to 1789 many reformers, including Condorcet and Jacques-Pierre Brissot, had taken it for granted that the immediate introduction of liberty would be foolish, because the people had to be made ready, potentially over a generation. The initial step might be a constitutional convention, as Condorcet demanded, to be followed by a revising convention two decades later. Such claims were reiterated after 1794 on the grounds that the Terror could be traced to the corrupt manners of the Old Regime.[90] In order to re-found the republic, schemes for republican education abounded during the Directory, envisaging the exercise of duties that would ensure that rights did not lead to violence and to war. The aspiration behind the 'Daunou law' of 25–26 October 1795 was the teaching of 'republican morality' to boys and girls in *écoles primaires* and the creation of an *Institut National des Sciences et des Arts*, under whose auspices republican manners were discussed and propagated.[91] The *Institut* was divided into three classes, 'Physical and Mathematical Sciences', 'Moral and Political Sciences' and 'Literature and the Fine Arts'. The goal of the *Institut* was to bring together the best minds in a variety of disciplines for the furtherance of truth and the interests of the French Republic. The second class, of Moral and Political Sciences, was unlike any other educational establishment in Europe, with sections for 'The Analysis of Sensations and Ideas', 'Morals', 'Social Science and Legislation', 'Political Economy', 'History' and 'Geography and Statistics'. The five volumes of papers published by the class between 1798 and 1802, and the innumerable newspaper articles they inspired, reveal an extensive debate about the relationship between manners and rights.[92] Partly this was conducted by means of prize essay competitions. The question set by the Morals Section in 1798 was *Quels sont les moyens les plus propre à fonder la Morale chez un peuple?*[93] Roederer later announced that this question had been mistakenly issued, and was considered too broad by the leaders of the *Institut*. The revised question asked *Quelles sont les institutions les plus propres à fonder la morale d'un peuple?*[94]

For Roederer, at the centre of many of these projects as Professor of Political Economy at the *Institut*, if the French republican experiment was to be salvaged, a new culture had to be instilled in the general population, founded on a respect for civil liberties. Roederer held that if productive labour became the basis of civic identity, any society would flourish. This was the product of his view that manners had to come before laws and rights:

> there is only one moral code, and therefore there is only one good species of manners; morals being anterior to governments, governments must order themselves in accordance with moral precepts, and not subject morals to the base interests of governments; since manners determine the life of governments, the first care with which we must be occupied is the institution of good manners, and we must next ensure that the government adheres to them.[95]

Creating a society based on rights and labour, in the midst of a violent revolution, Roederer acknowledged to be difficult. He sought help from Scottish authors, and especially Adam Smith. Creating institutions in harmony with 'the moral and physiological nature of man', Roederer argued, had to rest upon the insights of Smith's *Theory of Moral Sentiments*, being 'the first book to reconstruct the true foundations of morals, by analysing the phenomena of the heart in its entirety in order to discover the principles which direct it'.[96] The *Theory of Moral Sentiments* was 'the most excellent collection of observations through which the science of morals has ever been enriched'.[97] At this time too, Sophie Grouchy, Condorcet's widow, produced a translation of Smith's book, which appeared with her six letters on sympathy in 1798. During these years Smith's *Wealth of Nations* was being recommended as a 'system of social economy', embracing every aspect of the 'government of large empires', and Smith's major works and essays were being translated into French.[98]

VI

Why did the French turn to the Scots? Part of the reason was the failure of revolution to take hold in Britain, and more especially in Scotland, where the populace had remained loyal, at least in the eyes of the French, despite the temptations presented by rebellion against London politicians. Another was that Scotland was recognised to have thrived economically, and indeed undergone a commercial revolution, since the time of the union. The fact that the Scots had undergone social transformation and managed to avoid more than minor explosions of violence – this was the perception of Scots Jacobitism by the 1790s – suddenly became of enormous significance to the generation who lived through the Terror. The genius of Scottish authors, and the prominence of Scottish universities, had to be related to the politics, morals and wealth of the inhabitants. Accordingly, the turn to Smith was part of an aspiration to persuade French citizens to follow the Scots, who were perceived to have successfully made the practice of certain duties habitual, making the exercise of rights compatible with civil peace. Smith was of course only one of a number of Scottish writers being studied. As the indefatigable translator Pierre Prévost put it, there was a Scottish school of authors 'so ingenious and so profound' that their writings were being venerated 'across all of Europe'.[99] Scottish authors were seen to have specifically addressed many of the problems faced by France in the 1790s.[100] With increasing French interest in the kinds of natural jurisprudence then thriving in the Scottish universities, ideas about rights very different to those associated with Paine, Sieyès or Condorcet began to emerge.

Correlating rights with the duties necessary to articulate the range of human behaviour compatible with the proper exercise of particular rights began to dominate the discussion of rights both in Britain and in France. One of the key figures was Thomas Reid, the great advocate of common-sense philosophy at the universities of Aberdeen and Glasgow, for whom 'right' and 'duty' 'cannot even be conceived without the other'.[101] Reid had initially been a supporter of events in France, but his extensive work on the importance of the exercise of duty in public office and private life fitted a time when politics was accepted to be the consequence 'of the state of the people'.[102] Reid developed a following in Britain, France and America that was especially marked in the new century, as the revolutionary upheavals ceased but while the trauma they had generated continued to be evident.[103]

The transmission of the ideas of Scottish philosophers was accompanied by dispute about their true meaning. Dugald Stewart, the Professor of Moral Philosophy at Edinburgh, suffered after making positive remarks about Condorcet's educational projects in Elements of the Philosophy of the Human Mind, published in 1792. Although he tempered such comments in subsequent editions, a major point he reiterated in all of his writings was that rights could not be sustained except in a polite and civilised culture immune to enthusiasm and fanaticism. Stewart's role as biographer of Reid, Smith and William Robertson, in addition to his Europe-wide epistolary connections, made him a highly significant figure in the movement for a duty-based civic philosophy.[104] Henry Cockburn's later memoir, on the influence of the moral philosophy curriculum at Edinburgh over a generation of Scottish writers, made the point that Stewart, 'With Hume, Robertson, Millar, Montesquieu, Ferguson and De Lolme . . . supplied [the liberal young] with most of their mental food.'[105] They were doing the same for a French generation.

Part of this process entailed attacks upon authors who had got rights wrong. Identifying French writers whose philosophies had contributed to revolutionary excess and the abuse of rights became something of a literary parlour game. William Playfair provided a characteristic summary in stating that in France:

The philosopher aimed at overturning religion, in order to destroy an order of society that hurt their pride; they had formed a most absurd theory that all distinction among mankind should consist in genius and talents; they considered themselves then as entitled to the first rank, and looked down from their philosophic thrones with contempt on kings and princes.[106]

The focus of Playfair's ire was the physiocrats or *économistes*, because 'The leaders of the revolution were all oeconomists', from Sieyès and Condorcet to Mirabeau and Necker, 'though [Necker's] pride and vanity hindered him from subscribing implicitly to their faith.'[107] By contrast, Scottish political economists such as Smith were immune to the revolutionary contagion because their work was 'founded on facts', while the French, reducing everything to a system, turned into 'enthusiasts'.[108] The turn towards duty-based philosophies helps to explain one of the conundrums in the history of the reception of Smith's ideas in France. Smith, as Roederer anticipated, was lauded as a brilliant mind whose works were full of ideas of practical relevance. Smith had sought to combat projectors and fanatics, and any philosophy imparting lessons about avoiding such forces was invaluable. Perceiving Smith to have done this led a new generation of interpreters to focus on a distinction between the science of government and the science of political economy. While politics remained the arena of passion and potential excess, the hope was that political economy, teaching specific duties that lead to the stable increase of wealth and national well-being, could be placed on a more objective footing. This was an idea that attracted Dugald Stewart, naturally concerned with accusations of revolutionary excess.[109] In France it had far more adherents. Jean-Baptiste Say, one of the major advocates of this position, wrote in 1803 that:

> Until Smith's work, the study of politics, properly speaking the science of government, had been confounded with political economy, which shows how wealth is created, distributed and consumed. This confusion stems perhaps solely from the unfortunate title given to researches of this kind ... [in consequence] the demand has been made that political economy concern itself with all of the laws that regulate the domestic life of the political family.[110]

Say remained a republican supporter of revolution, an atheist and a critic of what he saw as Britain's corrupt economy and political system. His revelation, as he saw it, was that republicans and revolutionaries could not advocate the transformation of the world without first changing the behaviour of the people. An economy founded on virtue had to be established, by which Say meant a society characterised by frugality and industry, respect for the liberties of others, and adherence to a moral code that eschewed luxury and was dedicated to the public good. The science of political economy was intended to persuade individuals to take seriously their duties, in the knowledge that by so doing they would be helping to make an entirely different politics possible. What had gone wrong with rights could be traced to the kinds of religious dispute that had characterised the era of the Reformation. If religion could be replaced by dedication to industry, and the duties that accompanied the practice of labour, everything would be different.[111]

Notes

1. Knud Haakonssen, 'From Natural Law to the Rights of Man: A European Perspective on an American Debate', in A Culture of Rights: The Bill of Rights in Philosophy, Politics and Law, 1791 and 1991, ed. Michael J. Lacey and Knud Haakonssen (Cambridge: Cambridge University Press, 1993), 19–61; 'The Moral Conservatism of Natural Rights', in Natural Law and Civil Sovereignty: Moral Right and State Authority in Early Modern Political Thought, ed. David Saunders and Ian Hunter (Basingstoke and New York: Palgrave, 2002), 27–42; 'Natural Rights or Political Prudence? Toleration in Francis Hutcheson', in Natural Law and Toleration in the Early Enlightenment, ed. John Parkin and Tim Stanton (Oxford: Proceedings of the British Academy/ Oxford University Press, 2012), 261–89; 'Natural Jurisprudence and the Identity of the Scottish Enlightenment', in Religion and Philosophy in Enlightenment Britain, ed. Ruth Savage (Oxford: Oxford University Press, 2012), 258–77.

2. Albert Goodwin, The Friends of Liberty: The English Democratic Movement in the Age of the French Revolution (Cambridge, MA: Harvard University Press, 1979); Florence Gautier, Triomphe et mort du droit naturel en Revolution, 1789–1795–1802 (Paris: PUF, 1992); Dan Edelstein, The Terror of Natural Right: Republicanism, the Cult of Nature, and the French Revolution (Chicago: Chicago University Press, 2009); Marc Belissa, Yannick Bosc and Florence Gautier, eds, Républicanismes et droits naturels à l'époque moderne. Des humanistes aux révolutions des droits de l'homme et du citoyen (Paris: Kimé, 2009); Jonathan Israel, Democratic Enlightenment: Philosophy, Revolution, and Human Rights (Oxford: Oxford University Press, 2013) and Revolutionary Ideas: An Intellectual History of the French Revolution from The Rights of Man to Robespierre (Princeton: Princeton University Press, 2014).

3. Mary Wollstonecraft, A Vindication of the Rights of Men, in a Letter to the Right Honourable Edmund Burke; Occasioned by His Reflections on the Revolution in France (London: J. Johnson, 1790), 2; A Vindication of the Rights of Woman with Strictures on Political and Moral Subjects (London: J. Johnson, 1792), 256.

4. James Mackintosh, Vindiciae Gallicae and Other Writings on the French Revolution, edited and with an Introduction by Donald Winch (Indianapolis: Liberty Fund, 2006), 98.

5. Charles Pigott, A Political Dictionary Explaining the True Meaning of Words (London: D. I. Eaton, 1795), 3, 80, 118.

6. Robert Rix, ed., 'A *Political Dictionary Explaining the True Meaning of Words*' by *Charles Pigott. A Facsimile of the 1795 Edition*' (Aldershot: Ashgate, 2004), xiii–xxi.

7. R. Thomson, A *Tribute to Liberty. Or, New Collection of Patriotic Songs; Entirely Original, to Which Are Added the Most Select Songs Which Have Lately Appeared* (London, 1793), 43.

8. Eaton was later tried for libel for publishing the second part of Paine's *Rights of Man*: D. I. Eaton, *The proceedings on the trial of Daniel Isaac Eaton upon an indictment, for selling a supposed libel, 'The second part of the Rights of man, Combining principle and practice' by Thomas Paine: At Justice Hall, in the Old Bailey, before the recorder of London, on Monday the third day June, 1793* (London: Daniel Isaac Eaton, 1793).

9. Anon., *The Manual of Liberty: or, Testimonies in behalf of the rights of mankind; selected from the best authorities* (London: H. D. Symonds, 1795), 36–58.

10. John G. A. Pocock, *Barbarism and Religion, Vol. 1: The Enlightenments of Edward Gibbon* (Cambridge: Cambridge University Press, 1999); John Robertson, *The Case for the Enlightenment: Scotland and Naples, 1680–1760* (Cambridge: Cambridge University Press, 2005) and The *Enlightenment: A Very Short Introduction* (Oxford: Oxford University Press, 2015).

11. Pierre Louis Roederer, De la Députation aux États Généraux . . . 8 Novembre 1788, in Œuvres de Rœderer (Paris: Firmin-Didot, 1859), 8 vols, VII, 539–74.

12. Edmund Burke, *Reflections on the Revolution in France, and on the proceedings in certain societies in London relative to that event* (London: J. Dodsley, 1790), 2nd edition, 127–8.

13. Marcel Gauchet, *La Révolution des droits de l'homme* (Paris: Gallimard, 1989); Stéphane Rials, *La Déclaration des droits de l'homme et du citoyen* (Paris: Hachette, 1988); Kate E. Tunstall, ed., *Self-evident Truths? Human Rights and the Enlightenment* (New York: Bloomsbury, 2012); David A. Bell, 'Global Conceptual Legacies', in David Andress, ed., *The Oxford Handbook of the French Revolution* (Oxford: Oxford University Press, 2015).

14. Lynn Hunt, *Inventing Human Rights: A History* (New York: W. W. Norton and Company, 2008).

15. Israel, *Democratic Enlightenment*, 897–932.

16. Jean Baptiste de Cloots, *Bases constitutionnelles de la République du genre humain* (Paris: L'Imprimerie Nationale, 1793). See further Florence Gauthier, 'Universal Rights and National Interest in the French Revolution', in Otto Dann and John Dinwiddy, eds, *Nationalism in the Age of the French Revolution* (Gloucester: Hambledon Press, 1988), 27–38; István Hont, 'The Permanent Crisis of a Divided Mankind: "Nation-State" and "Nationalism" in Historical Perspective', in *Jealousy of Trade: International Competition and the Nation-State in Historical Perspective* (Cambridge, MA: Harvard University Press, 2005), 447–528.

17. William Hawkins, *Regal Rights Consistent with National Liberties. A Sermon Preached at St. Mary's, Oxford, on Sunday, June 21, 1795* (London: J. Cooke, 1795), 2.

18. William Cobbett, *The Bloody Buoy, Abridged. Thrown Out as a Warning to Britons . . . Containing a Faithful Relation of a Multitude of Acts of Horrid Barbarity, Such as the Eye Never Witnessed . . . until the Commencement of the French Revolution* (London: J. Wright, 1798).

19. Alexander Chalmers, ed., *The British Essayists: The Looker-On* (London: J. Johnson et al., 1808), No. 35, Saturday, 5 January 1793, 93.

20. Anon. ['An Orangeman'], *A Letter to Theobald McKenna, Esq., The Catholic Advocate; In Reply to the Calumnies against the Orange Institution* (Dublin: J. Milliken, 1799), 9.

21. Anon. – *The Rights of Monarchy, a Poem; On the Late Unanimous Celebration of His Majesty's Birth Day, on the Fourth of June, 1792, at the Hotel, in Birmingham* ([Birmingham]: Sold by all the booksellers, 1792), 14.

22. Hawkins, *Regal Rights Consistent with National Liberties*, 9.

23. Anon., *The True Briton's Catechism; on the principles of government, the rights of man, and the liberties of Englishmen; interspersed with occasional strictures on seditious and democratic writers* (London: W. Richardson, 1793), 17.

24. Rev. Robert Nares, *Man's Best Right; a Solemn Appeal in the Name of Religion* (London: J. Stockdale, 1793), 9, 46.

25. John Charnock, *Rights of a Free People. An essay on the origin, progress, and perfection of the British constitution, with an historical account of the various modifications of monarchy from the Norman invasion to the Revolution* (London: J. Sewell, 1792), 6. See also Anon., The Interests of Man in *Opposition to the Rights of Man: or, an inquiry into the consequences of certain political doctrines lately disseminated* (Edinburgh: J. Watson, 1793).

26. James Thomson, *The Rise, Progress, and Consequences, of the New Opinions and Principles Lately Introduced Into France; With Observations* (Edinburgh: Bell, Bradfute et al., 1799), 7.

27. Jean-Paul Rabaut Saint-Étienne, *Précis de l'histoire de la Révolution françoise* (Paris, 1792) 139, 200.

28. Konrad Engelbert Oelsner, *Notice sur la vie de Sieyes, membre de première Assemblée nationale et la Convention* (Switzerland, 1795), 90–8.

29. Emmanuel Joseph Sieyès, *Qu'est-ce que le Tiers-état? Troisième édition* (Paris, 1789), 93; *Préliminaire de la Constitution françoise: reconnoissance et exposition raisonnée des droits de l'homme & du citoyen* (Paris: Badouin, 1789).

30. Christine Fauré, *Les Déclarations des droits de l'Homme de 1789, textes réunis et presents* (Paris: Payot, 1988).

31. István Hont, 'The Permanent Crisis of a Divided Mankind: Contemporary Crisis of the Nation State in Historical Perspective', *Political Studies*, 42 (1994), 166–231; Michael Sonenscher, *Before the Deluge: Public Debt, Inequality, & the Intellectual Origins of the French Revolution* (Princeton: Princeton University Press, 2007); *Sans-Culottes: An Eighteenth-Century Emblem in the French Revolution* (Princeton: Princeton University Press, 2008).

32. Thomas Paine, *Letters to the Citizens of the United States* (New York, 1802), Letter 1, printed in William Cobbett, *Political Register, Volume 3* (London: Cox and Bayliss, 1803), 5.

33. Michael Sonenscher, ed., *Sieyès: Political Writings: Including the Debate Between Sièyes and Tom Paine in 1791* (Indianapolis: Hackett Publishing, 2003).

34. Dumont to Samuel Romilly, 1 June 1789, J.-M. Paris, 'Lettre inédite d'Étienne Dumont sur quelques séances du Tiers État (May 1789)', *Mémoires de la Société d'Histoire et d'Archéologie de Genève*, XIX (1877), 16.

35. Henry Frederick Groenvelt [Etienne Dumont, Samuel Romilly, John Scarlett], *Letters containing an account of the late Revolution in France, and Observations on the Constitution, Laws, Manners, and Institutions of the English* (London: J. Johnson, 1792), 52, 69–72.

36. Etienne Dumont, *Souvenirs sur Mirabeau et sur les deux premières assemblées legislatives*, ed. J. L. Duval (Paris: Charles Gosselin, 1832), 340. See further Richard Whatmore, 'Etienne Dumont, the British Constitution, and the French Revolution', *Historical Journal*, 50:1 (2007), 23–47.

37. Jean-Gabriel Peltier, *Histoire de la révolution du 10 aoust 1792, des causes qui l'ont produite, des événemens qui l'ont précédée, et des crimes qui l'ont suivie* (London, 1795), 8–11, 48–52, 253.

38. Irving Brock, *The Patriots and the Whigs, the most dangerous enemies of the state* (London: J. M. Richardson, 1810), 20–1; Anon., L'Accusateur public, Volume 1, No. IV ([Paris], [1797]), 18.

39. Edmund Burke, *A Letter from the Right Honourable Edmund Burke to a Noble Lord: on the attacks made upon him and his pension, in the House of Lords, by the Duke of Bedford, and the Earl of Lauderdale, Early in the present Sessions of Parliament* (London: J. Owen, 1796), 8th edition, 63–4.

40. Sieyès, 'Opinion de Sieyes, sur plusieurs articles des titres IV et V du projet de constitution, prononcé a la Convention le 9 thermidor de l'an troisieme de la République', in *Œuvres de Sieyès*, ed. Marcel Dorigny (Paris: EDHIS, 1989), 3 vols, III, nr. 40.

41. Sieyès, Condorcet and Duhamel, 'Prospectus', *Journal d'instruction sociale* [1793], in Condorcet, *Œuvres de Condorcet*, ed. Arthur O'Connor and François Arago (Paris: Firmin Didot frères, 1847–49), 12 vols, XII, 605–13.

42. Sieyès, *Notice sur la vie de Sieyes, membre de la première Assemblée Nationale et de la Convention* (Paris, l'an III), 8, 55.

43. Sieyès, 'Des intérêts de la Liberté dans l'état social & dans le système représantatif', *Journal d'instruction sociale; par les Citoyens Condorcet, Sieyes et Duhamel*, no. 2, 8 June 1793, 34–48.

44. Sieyès, Condorcet and Duhamel, 'Du nouvel Etablissement publique de l'instruction en France', *Journal d'instruction sociale*, no. 3, 22 June, 1793, 81–96.

45. Sieyès, Condorcet and Duhamel, 'Des Fêtes Républicaines particulières et communales', *Journal d'instruction sociale*, no. 4, 29 June 1793, 98–118.

46. Sieyès, *Des manuscrits de Sieyès, 1773–1799*, ed. Christine Fauré (Paris: Honoré Champion, 1999), 457–9, 462–4, 470–1, 505–15.

47. Letter to Sylvanus Urban [Edward Cave], *The Gentleman's Magazine, And Historical Chronicle*, Volume 69, Part 2 (London: John Nicols, 1799), 843; Anon., 'Representative of the Government of Regicides at the Court of

Berlin', *The Antigallican Monitor and Anti-Corsican Chronicle*, Volume 142, 10 October 1813.

48. Sieyès, *Découverte d'un nouveau rassemblement de Jacobins, arrestation de cinquante des principaux chefs*. . . (Paris, [13 August] 1799); *Conspiration infâme découverte par le Directoire, tendante à allumer la guerre civile et livrer la France aux ennemis, Liste générale et noms des conspirateurs arrêtés par ordre du Directoire, et qui vont être jugés par le tribunal criminal* (Paris: Lachave, n.d. [September 1799]).

49. Pierre-Louis Lacretelle l'aîné, *Sur le dix-huit brumaire: à Sieyès et à Bonaparte* (Paris: Marchants des Nouveautés, 1800).

50. Louis Marie Prudhomme, *L'Europe tourmentée par la révolution en France: ébranlée par dix-huit années de promenades meurtriéres de Napoléon Buonaparte* (Paris: Palais-Royal, 1815), 2 vols, I, 109.

51. John Robison, *Proofs of a Conspiracy Against all the Religions and Governments of Europe. Carried on in the Secret Meetings of Free Masons, Illuminati and Reading Societies*, 4th edition (New York: George Forman, 1798), 290–310; Konrad Engelbert Oelsner, Ernst Ludwig Posselt, Emmanuel Joseph Sieyès, *Sieyès's Geist aus seinen Schriften* (n.p., n.d.), 45.

52. Paul Bastid, *Sieyès et sa pensée* (Paris: Hachette, 1939); Sonenscher, *Sans-Culottes: An Eighteenth-Century Emblem in the French Revolution*.

53. Thomas Paine, 'The American Crisis', 13 January 1777, *The Works of Thomas Paine* (Philadelphia: W. Carey, 1797), 2 vols, I, 74.

54. Dumont, *Souvenirs sur Mirabeau*, 331–2.

55. Arthur Young, The Example of France, a Warning to Britain (London: W. Richardson, 1794), 4th edition., 62; Anon., *The Last Dying Words of Tom Paine, executed at the gullotine [sic] in France on the 1st of Sept. 1794, With a description of the genuine water for converting Jacobines* (London, 1794); Anon., *Remarks on Revelation & Infidelity, Speeches Delivered in a Literary Society in Edinburgh* (Edinburgh: John Moir, 1797), 135; Jeremiah Whitaker Newman, *The Lounger's Common-Place Book. Or Miscellaneous Anecdotes, A Biographic, Political, Literary, and Satirical Compilation*, Vol. 3 (London: Newman, 1798), 230; Patrick Kennedy, *An Answer to Mr. Paine's Letter to Gen. Washington: or Mad Tom convicted of the blackest Ingratitude* (London: Kennedy, 1797), 25.

56. John Adams autobiography, part 1, 'John Adams', through 1776, sheets 9 and 23 of 53 [electronic edition], *Adams Family Papers: An Electronic Archive*, Massachusetts Historical Society, http://www.masshist.org/digitaladams.

57. John Adams to Benjamin Waterhouse, 29 October 1805, in *Statesman and Friend. Correspondence of John Adams with Benjamin Waterhouse, 1784–1822*, ed. Worthington Chauncey Ford (Boston: Little, Brown and Co., 1927), 31.

58. Gouverneur Morris, *The Diary and Letters, Minister of the United States to France, Member of the Constitutional Convention*, ed. Anne Cary Morris (London: Kegan Paul, Trench & Co., 1889), 2 vols, I, 429.

59. Thomas Paine, *Rights of Man: Being an Answer to Mr. Burke's Attack on the French Revolution* (London: J. S. Jordan, 1791), 167.

60. Thomas Paine, *A Letter Addressed to the Abbé Raynal, on the Affairs of North America, in Which the Mistakes in the Abbe's Account of the Revolution in America are corrected and cleared up*, 3rd edition (London: J. Stockdale, 1783).

61. Thomas Paine, *Rights of Man. Part the Second. Combining Principle with Practice*, 3rd edition (London: J. S. Jordan, 1792), 4, 79.

62. Thomas Paine, *Two Letters to Lord Onslow: Lord Lieutenant of the County of Surry: and one to Mr. Henry Dundas, Secretary of State, on the subject of the late excellent proclamation* (London: James Ridgway, 1792), 13.

63. Paine, *Rights of Man. Part the Second*, 79. See further Gareth Stedman Jones, *An End to Poverty? A Historical Debate* (New York: Columbia University Press, 2005).

64. Thomas Paine, *Dissertation on First Principles of Government* (London: R. Carlile, 1819), 11.

65. Paine, *Rights of Man: Part One*, 37.

66. Thomas Paine, *Letter Addressed to the Addressers on the Late Proclamation* (London: H. D. Symonds, 1792), 16.

67. Paine, *Rights of Man: Part One*, 73.

68. Paine, *Dissertation on First Principles of Government*, 19.

69. Thomas Paine, *La justice agraire opposée à la loi et monopole agraire, ou, Plan d'amélioration du sort des hommes: Fondé sur l'établissement d'un fonds national dans chaque pays* (Paris: Chez les marchands de nouveautés, 1797).

70. Thomas Paine, *A Letter to the English People, on the invasion of England* (London: W. T. Sherwin, 1817), 7–10.

71. Paine, *Rights of Man. Part the Second*, 156–8.

72. Thomas Paine, *The Decline and Fall of the English System of Finance* (London: D. I. Eaton, 1796).

73. Paine, *A letter to the English People, on the invasion of England*, 7–10.

74. Thomas Paine, *Compact Maritime: Under the following heads: I. Dissertation on the law of nations: II. On the Jacobinism of the English at sea: III. Compact maritime for the protection of neutral commerce, and securing the liberty of the seas: IV. Observations on some passages in the discourse of the judge of the English admiralty* (Washington: Samuel Harrison Smith, 1801), 10–15.

75. Paine to Thomas Jefferson, 25 December 1802, in Moncure Daniel Conway, *The Life of Thomas Paine* (London: G. P. Putnam and Sons, 1892), 2 vols, II, 313.

76. Thomas Paine, *A Letter to George Washington: On the subject of the late treaty concluded between Great-Britain and the United States of America, including other matters* (London: T. Williams, 1796).

77. Jacques-Pierre Brissot, *Nouveau voyage dans les états-unis de l'Amérique septrionale, fait en 1788* (Paris, 1791), xxxii–iii.

78. Condorcet, 'Fragment de justification', July 1793, in Œuvres de Condorcet, V, 574–5.

79. Condorcet, Esquisse d'un tableau historique des progrès de l'esprit humain (Genoa: Yves Gravier, 1798), 255–9.

80. Ibid., 287–8, 304–6.

81. Condorcet, 'Fragment de justification', in Œuvres de Condorcet, V, 576–606.

82. Pierre Louis Roederer, 'Review of Condorcet's Esquisse d'un tableau historique des progrès de l'esprit humain, Journal de Paris, 21 Germinal, year III, 10 April 1795', in Œuvres de Rœderer, IV, 465; Antoinne Diannyère, Notice sur la vie et les ouvrages de Condorcet (Paris: Institut National, 1796); Anon., 'Avertissement', in Condorcet, Esquisse d'un tableau historique des progrès de l'esprit humain (Paris: Agasse, 1797), 3rd edition, v–viii.

83. Thomas Robert Malthus, An Essay on the Principle of Population, as it Affects the Future Improvement of Society with Remarks on the Speculations of Mr. Godwin, M. Condorcet, and Other Writers (London: J. Johnson, 1798), 144–5.

84. Condorcet, Esquisse d'un tableau historique des progrès de l'esprit humain, 258.

85. Pierre Louis Roederer, 'Cours d'organisation social fait au Lycée en 1793', in Œuvres de Roederer, VIII, 129–305; Notice de ma vie pour mes enfants, in Œuvres de Roederer, III, 287.

86. Richard Whatmore, 'The French and American Revolutions in Comparative Perspective', in Manuela Albertone and Antonio De Francesco, eds, Rethinking the Atlantic World: Europe and America in the Age of Democratic Revolutions (London: Palgrave, 2009), 219–38.

87. James Mackintosh, The Trial of John Peltier, esq for a Libel Against Napoleon Buonoparte (London: Peltier, 1803), 127.

88. Ibid., 154–80.

89. J. G. A. Pocock, 'Virtues, Rights and Manners: A Model for Historians of Political Thought', in Virtue, Commerce and History: Essays on Political Thought and History, Chiefly in the Eighteenth Century (Cambridge: Cambridge University Press, 1985), 37–50.

90. Condorcet, 'De l'influence d'un monarque et d'une cour sur les mœurs d'un peuple libre', Œuvres complètes de Condorcet (Brunswick and Paris: Henrichs, Fuchs et al., 1804), 21 vols, XVII, 3–8; Discours sur les conventions nationales: prononcé à l'Assemblée des Amis de la constitution, séante aux Jacobins, le 7 août 1791.

91. Andrew Jainchill, Reimagining Politics after the Terror: The Republican Origins of French Liberalism (Ithaca: Cornell University Press, 2008), 75–88.

92. Martin Staum, 'The Class of Moral and Political Sciences, 1795–1803', French Historical Studies, 11 (1978), 371–97; and 'Individual Rights and Social Control: Political Science in the French Institute', Journal of the History of Ideas (1987), 411–30.

93. Anon., Nouvelles littéraires, faits remarquables, *etc.*, *La Décade philosophique, littéraire et politique / par une société de républicains*, no. 29, 20 Messidor, an V, 104–6.

94. Anon., Nouvelles littéraires, faits remarquables, etc., *La Décade Philosophique*, no. 2, 20 Vendémiaire, an VI, 107–10.

95. Pierre Louis Roederer, 'Cours d'Organisation Sociale', in *Œuvres de Rœderer*, VII, 265, 297. See further Ruth Scurr, 'Social Equality in Pierre-Louis Roederer's interpretation of the modern republic, 1793', *History of European Ideas*, 26:2 (2000), 105–26.

96. Review of Prévost, ed., *Ouvrages posthumes d'Adam Smith*, in *Œuvres de Rœderer*, IV, 494–5, originally in *Journal de Paris*, 20 Thermidor, an V.

97. Roederer, 'Cours de l'organisation sociale', 11 March 1793, *Œuvres de Rœderer*, VIII, 131, 188–200; review of Grouchy-Condorcet, *Lettres sur la sympathie*, *Œuvres de Rœderer*, IV, 499, *Journal de Paris*, 26 Messidor, an VI.

98. Le Breton, review of Roucher's translation, *La Décade philosophique*, V, 401–9; Pierre-Louis Ginguené, review of Blavet's translation, *La Décade*, xxviii, 363–9; Gilbert Faccarello and Philippe Steiner, 'The Diffusion of the Work of Adam Smith in the French Language: An Outline History', in Keith Tribe, ed., *A Critical Bibliography of Adam Smith* (London: Pickering and Chatto, 2002), 61–119.

99. Pierre Prévost, *Cours de rhétorique et de belles-lettres, par Hugues Blair, . . . traduit de l'anglais par M. Pierre Prévost* (Manget and Cherbuliez: Geneva, 1808), 4 vols, I, xvi.

100. Anna Plassart, *The Scottish Enlightenment and the French Revolution* (Cambridge: Cambridge University Press, 2015).

101. Thomas Reid, *Essays on the Active Powers of Man* (Edinburgh: John Bell, 1787), 387–94.

102. Francis Jeffrey, review of 'Short Remarks on the State of Parties at the Close of the Year 1809', *The Edinburgh Review*, January 1810, Article XV, 504.

103. Benjamin W. Redekop, 'Reid's Influence in Britain, Germany, France, and America', in Terence Cuneo and Rene van Woudenberg, eds, *The Cambridge Companion to Thomas Reid* (Cambridge: Cambridge University Press, 2004), 313–40.

104. Claire Etchegaray, Knud Haakonssen, Daniel Schulthess, David Stauffer and Paul Wood, 'The Correspondence of Dugald Stewart, Pierre Prevost and their Circle, 1794–1829', *History of European Ideas*, 38:1 (2012), 1–73.

105. Henry Cockburn, *Memorials of His Time* (Edinburgh: Adam and Charles Black, 1854), 46.

106. William Playfair, 'The Life of Dr. Adam Smith', in Adam Smith, *An Inquiry into the Nature and Causes of the Wealth of Nations*, ed. William Playfair (London: T. Cadell and W. Davies, 1805), 3 vols, Vol. I, xviii–xix.

107. Ibid., Vol. III, 514–15.

108. 'Preface' to ibid., Vol. I, vii.

109. Stefan Collini, Donald Winch and John Burrow, 'The System of the North: Dugald Stewart and his Pupils', in *That Noble Science of Politics: A Study in Nineteenth-Century Intellectual History* (Cambridge: Cambridge University Press, 1983), 25–61.

110. J.-B. Say, 'Discours préliminaire', in *Traité d'économie politique* (Paris, 1803), 2 vols, Vol. I, ii–iii.

111. J.-B. Say, 'Obituary of Gibbon', *La Décade Philosophique*, no. 54, 30 Vendémaire, an IV, 147–52; *Traité*, Vol. I (1803), 81–2n, 262–4; Richard Whatmore, *Republicanism and the French Revolution: An Intellectual History of Jean-Baptiste Say's Political Economy* (Oxford: Oxford University Press, 2000).

Index